D1147719

Explorer
Cyprus

George McDonald

 Publishing

Front cover (a): *Greek woman*
(b): *Panagia tou Kykkou*
(c): *Petra tou Romiou, birthplace of Aphrodite*
Spine: *Shepherd*
Back cover: *Machairas Monastery*
Page 3: *Nun working in the garden at Agios Irakleidios monastery*
Page 4: *Enjoying a day's cruise off the coast of Agia Napa*
Page 5 (top): *Sunset over the Troodos Mountains*
Pages 6–7: *Moutoullas, Marathasa Valley, Troodos*
Page 8: *Episkopi*
Page 9: *Lefkara village, southwest Cyprus*
Page 25: *Votive statue from Golgoi (c 600 BC)*
Page 251: *Road sign*
Page 269: *Ledra Hotel, Greek Nicosia*

Written by George McDonald
Original photography by Alex Kouprianoff
Revision verified by George McDonald
Reprinted 2002
Reprinted 2001
Reprinted 1999, 2000 (twice); revised third edition 2000
First published 1995
© Automobile Association Developments Ltd 1995,1997, 2000.
Maps © Automobile Association Developments Ltd 1995, 1997, 2000
Mountain High Maps Image © copyright © 1993 Digital Wisdom, Inc.

Distributed in the United Kingdom by AA Publishing, Millstream, Maidenhead Road, Windsor, Berkshire SL4 5GD.

The contents of this publication are believed correct at the time of printing. Nevertheless, the publishers cannot be held responsible for any errors or omissions or for changes in the details given in this guide or for the consequences of any reliance on the information provided by the same. Assessments of attractions, hotels, restaurants and so forth are based upon the author's own personal experience and, therefore, descriptions given in this guide necessarily contain an element of subjective opinion which may not reflect the publishers' opinion or dictate a reader's own experiences on another occasion. Every effort has been made to ensure accuracy in this guide, but things do change, and we would be grateful if readers would advise us of any inaccuracies they may encounter.

A CIP catalogue record for this book is available from the British Library.
ISBN 0 7495 2356 5

Published by AA Publishing (a trading name of Automobile Association Developments Limited, whose registered office is Millstream, Maidenhead Road, Windsor, Berkshire SL4 5GD. Registered number 1878835).

Colour separation by Fotographics Ltd
Printed by Printers Trento srl, Italy

Titles in the Explorer series...
Australia • Boston & New England • Britain • Brittany
California • Canada • Caribbean • China • Costa Rica • Crete
Cuba • Cyprus • Egypt • Florence & Tuscany • Florida • France
Germany • Greek Islands • Hawaii • India • Ireland • Israel
Italy • Japan • London • Mallorca • Mexico • New York
New Zealand • Paris • Portugal • Provence • Rome
San Francisco • Scotland • South Africa • Spain • Tenerife
Thailand • Tunisia • Turkey • Turkish Coast • Venice • Vietnam

AA World Travel Guides publish nearly 300 guidebooks to a full range of cities, countries and regions across the world. Find out more about AA Publishing and the wide range of services the AA provides by visiting our Web site at www.theAA.com

How to use this book

ORGANISATION

Cyprus Is, Cyprus Was
Discusses aspects of life and culture in contemporary Cyprus and places the island in its historical context, exploring those past events whose influences are felt to this day.

A-Z
Breaks down the island into regional chapters, and covers places to visit, including walks and drives. Within this section fall the Focus On articles, which consider a variety of subjects in greater detail.

Travel Facts
Contains the strictly practical information vital for a successful trip.

Hotels & Restaurants
Lists recommended establishments throughout Cyprus, giving a brief summary of what each one has to offer.

ABOUT THE RATINGS
Most places described in this book have been given a separate rating. These are as follows:

▶▶▶   **Do not miss**

▶▶   **Highly recommended**

▶   **Worth seeing**

MAP REFERENCES
To make each location easier to find, every main entry in this book has a map reference to the right of its name. This comprises a number, followed by a letter, followed by another number, such as 176B3. The first number (176) refers to the page on which the map can be found, the letter (B) and the second number (3) pinpoint the square in which the main entry is located. The maps on the inside front cover and inside back cover are referred to as IFC and IBC respectively.

Contents

Feeding the pelicans, Limassol

Agios Nikolaos

The coastline of Akamas

George McDonald dates his love of travel from a career move that saw him switch from editing local newspaper stories to, a few weeks later, being paddled down the River Ganges in Bangladesh. He has rarely taken a backward glance since then. He has written articles for magazines in Europe, North America and Asia. He has written or contributed to 15 guidebooks, among them AA guides to *Amsterdam*, *Belgium* **and** *China*.

My Cyprus

From my house in a village near Pafos I look downhill, past citrus orchards, olive groves and banana plantations to the sparkling blue of the Mediterranean. The sea is generally empty but every now and then a black dot appears on the horizon. It usually resolves itself into the car ferry from Piraeus or a rustbucket freighter heading for Limassol, though not before I have indulged my pastime of imagining a bronze-tipped trireme cutting through the water, bringing the latest word – and, of course, ideas – from ancient Greece.

It is easy to get carried away by Cyprus. This, after all, is Aphrodite's Island, where the goddess of love drifted ashore on a sea shell. I have scented her perfume all over the island in the white anemones that are said to be her tears over the death of her lover, Adonis. At the Baths of Aphrodite, a fresh-water pool where she bathed, I have dipped my hands in crystal-clear water, hoping a little of the eternal youth it promises might seep in.

Cyprus has abundance and romance, and I experienced much of both while researching this guidebook. These are mixed, however, with rather too much concrete in resorts where 'development' has overwhelmed the natural beauty. But even this fades to insignificance compared with the unresolved conflict between the island's Greek Cypriot and Turkish Cypriot communities, that led to the 1974 Turkish invasion and division of the island.

I remember standing beside the sea at the beautiful Apostolos Andreas Monastery in the Turkish zone, gazing thoughtfully across the water towards Turkey and Syria. Beside me, the monastery's elderly Greek Cypriot caretaker wept as he told me that 'not many pilgrims' come any longer to the shrine where Saint Andrew called forth a sacred spring.

Thinking of present-day Cyprus induces in me a sadness that never quite goes away. Yet life, as always, goes on and Cyprus specialises in idyllic days. When Minoans, Phoenicians, Mycenaeans, Egyptians, Persians, Romans, Arabs, Byzantines, Crusaders, Venetians, Turks and British all crossed Cyprus's shores, only to be seduced by her soft Levantine ways and absorbed by the landscape, you have every reason to expect that the same experience lies in store for you.

George McDonald

Cyprus Is

Cyprus is a Mediterranean holiday island whose landscape, people, climate and history offer visitors unsurpassed interest and charm, but it must guard against the overdevelopment that threatens some of its most scenic places. It must also work out a solution to the division between its Greek and Turkish communities.

Gazing back through the mists of time, all nations like to think their birth was attended by some portent of greatness, by heroes who left future generations an indelible legacy of virtue or by a mystic sign of heaven's special favour. But only Cyprus can claim to be the birthplace of the goddess of love, for this is indeed Aphrodite's island. Here the favoured child of Olympus, gold-crowned and beautiful, made her abode after being wafted ashore from the wine-dark sea, and here she loved and bathed and rested. Cyprus is Aphrodite's garden, a mosaic of mountains, woodland and plains charmed by the spell of an enchantress.

That enchantment is evident in many ways. The peaks of two mountain ranges, the Troodos in the west and the Kyrenia (Beşparmak) in the north, grasp at the sky, while between them stretches the Mesaoria (Mesarya) Plain, fraying into rugged foothills at the edge of the mountains. Broad bays sweep the coastline, sharpening to points on peninsulas whose layout led ancient writers to compare the shape of Cyprus to that of a spread-out sheepskin. Nowadays, a frying-pan is a more favoured – and, in view of the long, hot

10

> ❏ Cyprus is the third largest island in the Mediterranean, after Sicily and Sardinia. It lies in the eastern Mediterranean, 65km from Turkey, 105km from Syria, 340km from Egypt and 385km from the nearest Greek territory on the island of Rhodes. ❏

The beach is the big attraction

summers, perhaps more appropriate – image, with the Karpas (Karpaz) Peninsula forming its handle.

THE OTHER FACE Veterans of past tourist campaigns will not be surprised to find that this Mediterranean holiday destination also has attributes less amenable to legendary treatment: rush-hour traffic jams, for example, and cheek-by-jowl holiday hotels that no amount of tourist-board doctoring can re-create as traditional dwellings set in groves of lemon trees. Similarly, beaches

> ❑ The permanent population of Cyprus is estimated at 720,000, of whom 560,000 are Greek Cypriots, 130,000 are Turkish Cypriots and 30,000 are from various minorities, the most important of these being Maronites and Armenians. ❑

exist on which it may scarcely be possible to find a few grains of sand to call your own, and not all the local cuisine has been approved by rhapsodic gourmets before appearing on your plate. There are even Cypriots who look upon visitors as cash-dispensers on the hoof – herds to be shepherded, milked and fleeced.

In most aspects, however, the downside is the exception rather than the rule. The island's ethnic Greek and Turkish populations, who have caused each other so much grief, extend a welcome to their foreign visitors that is all the more refreshing for being genuine. 'Friendly natives' is such a patronising cliché that the phrase is best avoided, but Cypriots come close

enough to the ideal. Their island (Kypros in Greek; Kıbrıs in Turkish) boasts a wild beauty that does not submit easily to the dictates of 'development', and even if large tracts along the coast have by now submitted, there remains much that is fresh and untamed.

POISONED ATMOSPHERE Yet a serpent is loose in Aphrodite's garden. The island of love is divided by 40 years of hatred and conflict between its Greek and Turkish communities, split across the middle by the great unnatural barrier of a United Nations buffer zone separating the two feuding parties. As Abraham Lincoln once said, 'A house divided against itself cannot stand,' and even if Cyprus's line of division is marked more by boredom than by gunfire, it is a threat to peace and a sign of its people's inability to live in harmony,

A place of escape in the Troodos

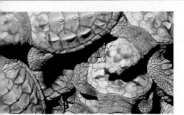

The reward for turning your back on the beach is a glimpse of another Cyprus, one far removed in spirit from the heavily developed resorts that crowd sections of the coast. With scarcely a backward glance at the turquoise shimmer of the warm Mediterranean, the adventurous spirit heads for the hills.

When Lawrence Durrell first set eyes on Cyprus 40 years ago, his ship berthed in 'a gloomy and featureless roadstead, before a town whose desolate silhouette suggested that of a tin-mining village in the Andes' (*Bitter Lemons*, 1957). Resort hotels and real-estate developments have replaced this bedraggled scene and, although the coastal strip can still beguile, the real Cyprus lies elsewhere. You could do worse than leave the toasting bodies behind occasionally to follow the road into the Troodos or Kyrenia (Beşparmak) Mountains.

Dusty trails lead into the wild interior and to sections of coast where the development bandwagon has never rolled. There is nature aplenty, although this is not to say the natural world remains intact. Prehistoric flora and fauna have been drastically modified by agriculture, logging, mining and other interference. Even in the high mountains, terraces have been carved to provide a level platform for orchards.

SCENIC HIGHS There are only a few good roads to the Troodos Mountains, and once there the going can get tough. The Troodos draw their attraction from cool mountain air, pretty villages, Byzantine churches and the chance to get close to nature. On the western slopes is the Pafos Forest, where the wild mountain sheep of Cyprus, the moufflon, roams. If the Kyrenia peaks are less dominant, they are no less scenic, nor are their crusader castles less noteworthy than the churches of the

Top: loggerhead turtles. Below: the Akamas Peninsula wilderness area

☐ Nature has been a victim of the Cyprus conflict. The Greek Cypriot economy was virtually ruined by the 1974 war and subsequent refugee influx. Development, particularly tourism development, on a massive and uncontrolled scale revived it, but only at the expense of the natural world. ☐

Foxes breed all over the island

a solo performer. Foxes, hedgehogs and shrews can be found all over the island, while wild donkeys roam the Karpas Peninsula. Bird-watching is a popular activity, thanks to the many species that stop over in Cyprus during their migration – and despite the fact that millions of songbirds continue to be slaughtered on the island in the name of sport. The Salt Lakes at Akrotiri and Larnaka (see pages 116 and 96) are prime observation sites in winter and spring, when pink flamingos and a host of ducks, waders and other water-oriented species fly in. Indigenous birds like the Cyprus warbler can also be seen.

Of flowers and butterflies – many unique to Cyprus – there is an abundance, and this is also true of trees, plants and shrubs. Add freshwater fish species in reservoirs, marine life that can be seen on scuba-diving expeditions and the rare loggerhead turtles that lay their eggs on the island's beaches, and it may be seen that the natural world still has much to offer in Cyprus.

Troodos. The Kyrenia (also known as the Pentadaktylos) Mountains run parallel to the north coast before petering out in the Karpas (Karpaz) Peninsula. This mountain chain is less frequented by tourists than the Troodos, improving the chances of a peaceful escape.

COASTAL DELIGHTS The coast also has its wild places, with more open coastline overall than developed; the Turkish Cypriot zone is better off in this respect. Peninsulas are favoured areas for wilderness and wildlife protection, both the Akamas Peninsula (see page 159) and the Karpas Peninsula (see page 241) being potential locations for national parks dedicated to preserving their unique character. The Akrotiri Peninsula (see page 102) is a semi-wilderness, partially protected by the presence of a British military base.

LIVING WORLD The moufflon, which is now thriving after only just avoiding extinction, is the star of Cyprus's wildlife show, but it is far from being

☐ Extinction of indigenous species began at about the same time as the first evidence of human occupation is noted on the island, some 10,000 years ago. Fossils of pygmy hippopotamuses and elephants have been found at various locations (see page 203). ☐

No country as strategically positioned as Cyprus, at the historic crossroads of the world's great civilisations, could avoid attracting so many different ethnic communities. The irony today is that community spirit has proved to be both a blessing and a curse.

Cypriot veins course with the blood of Phoenicians, Persians, Greeks, Romans, Arabs, French, Italians, Turks and Britons, to name just the more prominent sources. Heritage is not necessarily community, however, and at its worst the Cypriot concept of community has come down to armed individuals glaring at each other across a gulf of fear and hatred. At its best, on the other hand, community spirit is one of the island's greatest delights.

The two main communities are of Greek and Turkish origin. Whether or not Cyprus is Greek is a question that has taxed experts in international law, as well as historians peering back through the dimly lit corridors of time. All that can be said with confidence is that most Cypriots feel themselves to be either Greek or Turkish – with the historical bonds that that implies – and yet, as Cypriots, not exactly identical to either, so that the visitor must speak of Greek Cypriots and Turkish Cypriots and never confuse the two.

An elderly Greek Cypriot

14

NEW THINKING Cypriots are cosmopolitan, belonging to a widely travelled community of emigrants, and there are large Cypriot communities – both Greek and Turkish – in Britain, the United States, Australia and western Europe. Many young Cypriots go to university in Athens or Istanbul, although locally established universities have reduced this traffic. That said, a lack of career opportunities, even allowing for the island's virtually full employment, still persuades young people to leave.

The Cypriot concept of community shows most strongly at the village level, and one of the sadder aspects of the changes wrought by economic growth is the slow death of villages as young people leave for a more prosperous life in the towns and resorts. The Greek Cypriot government is almost obsessive about the health of its villages, supporting projects to keep them going concerns. However, such well-meaning plans often lead to an artificial state which is arguably worse than extinction; wealthy newcomers buying quaint village houses are no substitute for the living communities that have left them.

COMMUNITY CHEST Beyond its two main ethnic groups, Cyprus is a melting-pot of minorities. Maronites (Syrian or Lebanese Christians), Armenians and Latins (Roman Catholics, mainly Italian in origin) are the main minorities, with the Maronite component having been reinforced by Lebanon's descent into chaos. Lebanese Muslims also came over, and Cyprus took on Beirut's old mantle as the main entrepôt of the Middle East.

The British have long considered Cyprus to be the Mediterranean jewel of their lost empire, and today British communities can be found virtually all over the island, particularly around Limassol and Pafos, and at Kyrenia (Girne) in the Turkish Cypriot sector. They are being joined by other expatriates, most notably Germans.

In Turkish Cyprus, the new arrivals have mostly been Turkish. Immigrants from Anatolia, and more recently from Bulgaria's persecuted Turkish minority, have boosted the Turkish Cypriot population. Greek Cypriots complain that these people are part of a demographic offensive, and that they are occupying land and houses that belong to Greek Cypriots. In Cyprus, sadly, community can be a source of conflict as well as a badge of distinction.

> ❏ After Nicosia and Limassol, the largest Greek Cypriot city is London, with some 100,000 residents. The in-flight magazine of Cyprus Airways features London's Cypriot community regularly, just as if it were on the island. ❏

In old Nicosia, two Turkish Cypriot boys find fun in a tyre

15

Such is the mystical lure of Cypriot religious foundations, that people who at home rarely or never set foot inside places of worship can be seen marvelling at murals, following in the footsteps of monks or standing barefoot before a mosque mihrab (prayer niche). Religious tourism, it seems, is sanctioned on high.

Cypriot Christians happily venerate their icons and seek assistance from the saints in time of need, yet low attendance at religious services (except those on festival days) can hardly be encouraging to the priests. Cypriot Muslims, in the main, have a laid-back approach to the mosque which would be anathema to a fundamentalist. It seems that if each group's attitude to the other had been infused with such tolerance, there would be no Cyprus problem.

Two millennia of Christian tradition have filled Cyprus with churches and monasteries, the finest of which have won the United Nations' badge of approval as key elements in the cultural patrimony of mankind. Some of the finest mosques are basically churches with a minaret or two tacked on.

16

❏ The schism between Roman Catholicism and the Orthodox tradition has lasted a long time, encapsulated in the capture and sacking of Constantinople in 1204 by the Fourth Crusade. As recently as 1965, Pope Paul VI and the Orthodox Patriarch Athenagoras lifted excommunication orders on each other that dated from 1054. ❏

PAST GLORIES The ruins of colossal early Christian basilicas are to be found at various archaeological sites around the island – most notably at Pafos, Kourion and Salamis (see pages 172, 110 and 247). They symbolise the new religion's power and wealth soon after it had stepped into paganism's shoes as the state religion of the Roman, and later Byzantine, Empire. Yet with their classical colonnades and multi-coloured marble floors, the remains sometimes look little different from the ruined gymnasia, palaces and villas that surround them.

More evocative of the Christian empire of Byzantium is the constellation of little frescoed churches that glitters in the Troodos Mountains and a few other places. Externally, none of them is worth much more than a passing glance, being based, it would appear, on the same architectural principles as the barn. Inside, however, the Byzantine tradition's true impact may be seen in wonderful murals that cover the walls and vaulted roofs with scenes from the Bible, the lives of the Holy Family

A Greek Orthodox monk at the Royal Chapel of Agia Ekaterina

❏ The Orthodox Church in Cyprus has six dioceses: Kyrenia, Larnaka, Limassol, Morfou, Nicosia and Pafos. Kyrenia lies wholly, Nicosia and Morfou partly, in the Turkish zone, where the Church's writ does not run. ❏

and saints, and the primary images of Christ crucified, risen from the dead and as 'Ruler of the World'.

LIVING LEGENDS The proudest institutions in Cyprus are the great hilltop monasteries of Panagia tou Kykkou, Stavrovouni and Machairas (see pages 142, 96 and 190), stout vessels which have borne the ideals of Orthodox Christendom and Hellenism safely down the stream of time. These monasteries have been the source of a determination that Byzantium should not die in spirit, although no longer counted among the powers of the earth. This timeless quality is impressive, with perspectives spanning a thousand years and more, yet ultimately such rigour passes the casual visitor by, leaving only a vague impression of bearded monks and glowing icons. More easily absorbed are the convents where nuns maintain a simpler spirituality, softened by flowers and spiced with sales of honey and souvenirs.

It could be that Cyprus's deepest spirituality is to be found away from the monasteries, churches and mosques, whose zealots, after all, have been at least partially responsible for the island's troubles. Alone, in the high mountains or by some wild deserted shore, the earth's own sanctity can be experienced.

17

Top: detail, Lala Mustafa Paşa Mosque, Famagusta. Below: modern frescos, Panagia tou Kykkou

Religious, folkloric and modern festivals are scattered conveniently through the calendar, ensuring that there is nearly always a colourful celebration taking place somewhere in Cyprus. Not all are major events, as the tradition of local village festivals remains strong.

Considering the island's religious legacy, it is no surprise that most Cypriot festivals are based on some holy day or event, while feast days, or 'name days', of the saints provide an eternal excuse for a party. Villages are the traditional venues for festivals, and the venues for traditional festivals. Nowadays, however, more people live in towns and cities, so the celebrations have either been adapted or celebrants return to their home village for the occasion.

Easter, culminating in the celebration of Christ's resurrection from the dead, is the principal festival. Palm Sunday, the Sunday before Easter, is the start of Holy Week. On Maundy Thursday, icons are shrouded in black, and on the next day, Good Friday, processions carry Christ's flower-bedecked image through the streets. On Easter Saturday, the black shrouds are removed from the icons and in the evening bonfires are lit, onto which are thrown effigies of Judas. Easter Sunday itself is marked by much feasting.

❏ The Curium Drama Festival takes place on various days during July and August, using the 2,000-year-old theatre at Kourion (see page 110) for performances of ancient Greek plays, as well as works by Shakespeare and other dramatists ❏

CARNIVAL CAPERS Easter begins, in a sense, with the pre-Lenten Carnival – ten days of fun, games, masquerades and feasting, ending on Green Monday, 50 days before Easter Sunday. Limassol is the centre of Carnival and the Carnival king's entry by float into the city kicks off the proceedings, culminating in a massive float parade through Limassol on the final Sunday. Vegetarian picnics on Green Monday 'cleanse' the body in preparation for the coming fast.

Fun and games at Limassol's pre-Lenten Carnival

Christmas is the other important Christian festival. Olive twigs and branches, symbols of purity, are placed over doorways and inside houses as decoration, with a Christmas tree symbolising life and prosperity. In the villages, fattened pigs are slaughtered for a feast, although turkey is also popular. Gifts are often exchanged on New Year's Day rather than at Christmas. Those not going to a village festival or special restaurant party stay at home and play simple games before cutting the *vasilopitta*, or New Year cake.

HIGH TIMES Other important events include the Anthestiria flower festivals at Limassol, Pafos and

several other towns in May, recalling the floral festivals of pagan times. The International State Fair held in May at the State Fair Ground outside Nicosia showcases Cypriot products and services.

At Kataklysmos (the Festival of the Flood), in June, three days of seafront fairs and mutual-soaking contests celebrate Noah's sojourn on the Ark during the 40 days and nights of the Great Flood. In the same month, the Carlsberg Beer Festival concentrates on liquid refreshment based on hops and water.

Another important religious event takes place on 15 August – the Assumption of Our Lady. Perhaps most eagerly awaited of all, however, is the Limassol Wine Festival in September, when the city's Municipal Gardens become an open-air venue for contemporary Dionysiac revelry.

In the Turkish zone, most festivals are related to Islam or to political events associated with the Turkish Cypriots' struggle against Enosis (union with Greece) and finally for independence. Islamic festivals include Kurban Bayrami, which commemorates Abraham's willingness to sacrifice his son Isaac at God's command, and the three-day Seker Bayrami festival at the end of Ramadan's 40 days of fasting.

For a calendar of public holidays and festivals, see pages 254–5.

19

❏ A ten-day International Arts Festival takes place in Limassol during June and July. The city's Municipal Gardens are the open-air venue for a programme of music, song and dance by both local and international artists. ❏

In the Republic of Cyprus, religion is the source of a strong festival tradition

As in other countries where mass production has overwhelmed demand for traditional products, Cyprus has struggled to retain a foothold on the artisanal ladder. Government support, assisted by burgeoning demand from visitors and collectors, has helped to bring about a renaissance in the old skills.

A case could be argued that Cypriot arts and crafts began with young women's need for a dowry. The men crafted objects from copper, gourds and wood, but the finest products emerged – and still do – from the fingers of home-working embroiderers. A self-respecting bride had to have a hundred sheets and pillowcases and towels, as well as heaps of table linen and other furniture- and floor-coverings. As families were large and girls many, both mother and daughters had to start laying in the linen early.

Hand-embroidered lace from Pano Lefkara and Kato Lefkara represents the stellar end of the spectrum, but the products from other areas – including different forms of embroidery – also have merit. Pafos, for example, is noted for *pafitika*, white material woven with bright, geometric designs. The cloth is then made up into table-mats, cloths, runners, cushion-covers, bedspreads and curtains. Handloom weaving has all but disappeared, particularly as its finest

Selling lace in the village of Lefkara

exponents, from Lefkonikon (Geçitkale), abandoned their village ahead of the Turkish army in 1974. Re-established around Pafos, Lefkonikon work – brightly coloured and striped – is making a comeback.

MANLY VIRTUES In ancient times, the copper mines of Cyprus were famous and their metal formed a primary component of the Bronze Age. Even in the Iron Age the armies

The unique pattern of Lefkara lace

❏ Lefkara's superb hand-made lace is generally thought to have originated when local women observed the lace-work of vacationing Venetian noblewomen and adapted it to their own embroidery forms. Turkish Cypriots trace *lefkaritika* to the traditional patterns of Turkey's Antep region, and equally fine work of this kind is on sale in Turkish Cyprus. In both cases, the products are sold locally for one-third or less of the price in Europe and America. ❏

of Alexander the Great were said to have worn armour of Cypriot copper. Copper cauldrons coated with tin have lost their place in the kitchen to aluminium pots, but can still be found, along with copper ornaments, in handicraft shops.

Other metalworking crafts have retained their popularity, especially gold- and silverware, with demand existing for ecclesiastical vessels as well as elaborate jewellery worked in these materials.

Pottery-makers have had to lower their sights from the days when demand was insatiable for hand-thrown *pitharia*, pots of a size and shape that look ideal for boiling missionaries, although they were actually used for storing olive oil and wine. The curvaceous forms of these pots can still be seen in gardens, monasteries and along roadsides, although they are now more likely to be filled with flowers than wine.

Their main centre of production is Kornos (see page 109). Pottery cats were a speciality of Lapithos. (Lepta – see panel on page 216).

❑ No craft tradition would be complete without the dull but worthy art of basket-weaving. In Cyprus, baskets for carrying potatoes are made in the Kokkinochoria region and for grapes in the Pafos area, and, less reputably, around Larnaka for trapping small songbirds. ❑

21

SKILLS SHORTAGE Nicosia's Cyprus Handicraft Service (see page 48) is a vital element in the drive to retain the island's heritage of traditional arts and crafts. Fewer people learn these skills now, as the practice of handing them down from parent to child gets broken. The centre, an ultramodern institute at the city's edge, provides teaching and practical experience in the old ways. It is questionable whether such an organised place can also preserve the spirit of the original crafts, but it at least offers the possibility of doing so.

Handicrafts are popular souvenirs

Economic growth differs on either side of the demarcation line, for while a similar base sustains each part, the Greek Cypriot sector generates three times its neighbour's wealth. Both utilise their geographical situation to provide offshore centres for banking.

The location of Cyprus, which has brought unwelcome visitors in the past, has had compensations in the economic sphere. Tourism is the most obvious of these, with Greek Cyprus welcoming around 2 million and Turkish Cyprus 350,000 visitors each year – and the number is growing. Tourism forms the principal source of foreign exchange, and, in addition, is a major provider of jobs, both directly and indirectly.

HARVEST THE PROFIT Agriculture remains the biggest economic sector, comprising several subsectors, of which citrus fruit (including products such as processed juices) is the most important in terms of exports, followed by potatoes, grapes and wine. The light-industrial sector is large and growing, with exports of clothing and footwear combined outweighing the revenue generated by the island's agricultural exports. Greek Cyprus's principal trading partner is the European Union, which supplies just over half the island's imports and takes just under half its exports.

❑ Despite Cyprus's ancient reputation for mining, this is now a declining industry. Iron pyrites is the principal product at around 50,000 tonnes, with copper reaching barely one-twentieth of this amount. ❑

The Turkish Cypriot sector's main partner is Turkey, followed by the European Union.

BANKER'S DRAFT Banking is an important growth area, as Greek Cyprus develops as an offshore centre, but is one which has credibility problems to overcome before achieving wide-spread acceptance. The government has been cautious in granting licences, preferring to build slowly on a base of reputable banks. Recent years have seen a huge influx of dollars and marks from Russia – the origins of some of this money can really only be described as 'suspect'.

Women picking shallots in a field near Polis

Cyprus's misfortune is to be so located that no power of any consequence in the eastern Mediterranean could accept a competing power controlling it. The military forces swarming over the island are proof that little has changed in this respect.

PRIME LOCATION Geography is often the main determinant of history, and Cypriots could be forgiven for wishing they could attach sails to their island and slip away to a less desirable but more tranquil location. With its mines, forests and ports, there have always been reasons enough for wanting the island, but even more important was to deny its use to a potential or actual enemy.

A vital consideration in Turkey's 1974 invasion of the island, in addition to protecting Turkish Cypriots, was to prevent the coup against Archbishop Makarios leading to Greek possession of a base off Turkey's southern shore. Ironically, Greece and Turkey were, and are, NATO allies, but the Atlantic Alliance often had better grounds for fearing a shooting match breaking out between them than a Soviet offensive into the Mediterranean.

AREA DEFENCE Britain's bases at Akrotiri and Dhekelia undoubtedly have different *raisons d'être* than those highlighted in public relations briefings. The provision of good-weather exercise areas for air force and army units, and logistics support to United Nations peacekeeping forces, scarcely justifies such a commitment by the British government. Rather, it seems the bases are being retained for such events as the 1990 Gulf War and for possible 'out of area' operations by NATO in the Middle East.

Tides of strategic thinking have ebbed and flowed over Cyprus for 3,000 years. Swords have been beaten into missile-armed jets, but the troops and the hardware are still there—and will probably remain so for quite some time yet.

This view of the known world, dating from 450 BC, places Cyprus at its centre. The island has remained important right up to the present day, a consequence of this strategic location at the crossroads between East and West

23

❏ 'A race advancing on the East must start with Cyprus. Alexander, Augustus, Richard and Saint Louis took that line. A race advancing on the West must start with Cyprus. Sargon, Ptolemy, Cyrus, Haroun al-Rashid took this line.'
– W Hepworth Dixon, *British Cyprus*, 1887. ❏

The island's division without war is preferable to war without division, yet it remains an unstable situation which leaves a very uneasy peace. The international community can help, but only Greek and Turkish Cypriots can choose to live together in harmony.

When Cyprus first became a problem in the eyes of the world in the 1950s, Dag Hammerskjöld was Secretary-General of the United Nations. Since then his successors have employed their 'good offices' in the search for a solution, but there is still no end in sight to the island's division.

The problem has evolved from liberation struggle to intercommunal conflict, to military coup, to invasion, to partition and finally to the back-burner of world attention as the international community has become preoccupied with hotter conflicts. Resolutions of the UN Security Council and General Assembly are clear, however: a solution must involve an end to partition, the withdrawal of foreign military forces (meaning the Turkish army) and an agreement that recognises both communities' rights.

War of the flags: Greek and Republic of Cyprus flags...

...confronting Turkish and Turkish Cypriot flags across the way

CASE-HARDENED Greek Cypriots believe that the problem began with Turkey's invasion and that the 180,000 refugees who fled from their homes in northern Cyprus had little choice, faced with a 'Peace Operation' whose instruments were tanks, rockets and napalm. Few Turkish Cypriots have any desire to live again within rifle range of their Greek Cypriot neighbours without copper-bottomed guarantees for their security. To them, Turkey's intervention in 1974 was a 'Peace Operation' that saved them from the murderous attentions of terrorists bent on their annihilation.

As Cyprus moves towards European Union membership, there is growing international pressure for a solution to the Cyprus problem.

❏ 'Cyprus is the common home of the Greek Cypriot community and the Turkish Cypriot community. Their relationship is not one of majority and minority, but one of two communities in the state of Cyprus.'
– From a statement by former UN Secretary-General Javier Pérez de Cuéllar, February 1990. ❏

Cyprus Was

Civilisation in Cyprus developed slowly as the result of colonisation from the Asian and European land masses, and trade with the more developed cultures of ancient Mesopotamia, Egypt and Greece. Already, at this early stage in its history, Cyprus had become a crossroads between east and west.

Some 90 million years ago, Cyprus lay under an ocean called Tethys that stretched from northern Europe to Asia. The majestic rhythms of geological time witnessed the formation of limestone and sandstone layers which were forced upwards by the slow collision of Africa with Eurasia. Mountains and volcanoes formed two chains of islands, today's Troodos and Kyrenia (Beşparmak) ranges, while erosion gradually laid down the Mesaoria (Mesarya) Plain and the coastal flatlands. Water from melting Ice Age glaciers then poured into the Mediterranean basin and isolated Cyprus from Asia. Thus the scene was set for the arrival of humankind.

Palaeolithic man must have stood on the shores of present-day Turkey and Syria, gazing thoughtfully at the green haze of Cyprus, some 65km distant over the water. It was an immense voyage to undertake, but the lure of a new land outweighed the risks. Dug-out canoes were prepared, and Stone Age migrants set out across the sea. The first traces of human habitation date to the mesolithic period, around the 7th

Embossed gold plaque (top) and (above) sculpture of a warrior, both in the Cyprus Museum, Nicosia

and 6th millennia BC, at Kastros in the Karpas (Karpaz) Peninsula and at Khirokitia (modern Choirokoitia) between Limassol and Larnaka.

RISING CIVILISATION By the Bronze Age, from 3000 BC, Cyprus was at the forefront of the new metal technology, thanks to its copper mines. Contacts and trade with the ancient Middle East brought Babylonians, Assyrians and Egyptians, thereby opening the island to their influence. Tablets from the 18th century BC onwards found at Tel el-Amarna in Egypt refer to the copper-making centre of 'Alasia', which may mean the city of Enkomi (modern Egkomi) alone, or possibly the whole of Cyprus.

The Phoenicians, seafarers from Lebanon and Palestine, set up

> ❏ The origins of the name 'Cyprus' are uncertain. In the *Iliad*, Homer calls it 'Kypros', which may come from the Greek word for the henna plant that flourished on the island. Its association with copper offers a more likely explanation – the Latin name for copper is *aes cyprium*. However, the question remains: did Cyprus take its name from copper, or copper take its name from Cyprus? ❏

26

❏ Aphrodite, the goddess of love, like the first Cypriots and many since, was an immigrant. Despite Homer's colourful tale of her birth in the sea, Aphrodite originated with the Assyro-Babylonian earth goddess Ishtar and the Phoenician Astarte. ❏

absolute monarchs, often referred to as 'tyrants' – although their rule was not necessarily cruel or arbitrary.

Cyprus was on the periphery of the great civilisations of the period, never at the centre of trade or culture, but one of the first places that any expanding imperialistic powers reached as they moved out across the Mediterranean from east to west, or west to east. Colonised, courted, conquered: the pattern of Cyprus's history was set.

trading cities around Cyprus, at Kition, Amathus and Lapithos (Lapta). The Minoans of Crete also came to trade and settle, and they introduced the Cypro-Minoan script (based on Cretan Linear A) which remains undeciphered. The cities were prosperous, a sign of progress that brought its own problems, as may be seen by the walls raised to ward off pirates and invaders.

Earthquakes, born of the unstable geology in an area of colliding land masses, struck the newly established centres of civilised life.

ENTER THE GREEKS From about 1400 BC, Mycenaean Greeks traded with Cyprus, as seen in the many examples of their pottery and other implements found by archaeologists. Later, they came to colonise as their homeland was invaded by Dorian tribes from the north who were equipped with superior iron weapons. The Greeks founded new cities and took over existing ones, although Cyprus remained under intermittent Egyptian, Assyrian and possibly Hittite control. The city-states, which included Enkomi, Salamis, Soloi, Marion, Kition, Palaia Pafos and Kourion, were kingdoms ruled by

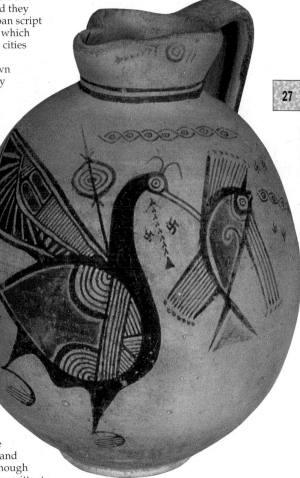

The different styles of pottery found in Cyprus indicate a range of cultural influences. This jug dates from between 750 and 600 BC

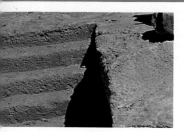

The tug-of-war between Persia and Greece over Cyprus had profound implications for the island. It was too vital to Persia's security to be relinquished except in the face of over-whelming force, but too far from Greece for that force to be applied, and so Cyprus remained under Persian control throughout the great age of classical Greece.

Egyptian hegemony over Cyprus ended in 540 BC, when the Cypriot kings threw in their lot with the Persian Empire under Darius I, who was on the rampage throughout the Middle East, swallowing up rivals before breakfast and taking Egypt in his stride. Little Cyprus would have been unwise to do anything other than bow the knee – as it was later to discover in brave but foolhardy bouts of rebellion. In the meantime, the island became part of the Persian Empire's Fifth Satrapy, which

❑ The first known biography of a living person was the eulogy written by the Athenian teacher Isocrates on the Cypriot hero, King Evagoras I of Salamis, who expelled the Persians and united the whole of the island between 411 and 374 BC. ❑

Palaia Pafos and Soloi, were taken under siege and eventually succumbed to the Persians.

WRONG SIDE Persia went on to invade mainland Greece twice, in 490 BC and 480 BC. So thoroughly cowed was Cyprus that when Greece was fighting for its life in the great battles at Marathon, Thermopylae, Salamis and Plataea, Cypriot naval forces served under the banner of the invader. At Salamis no fewer than 150 Cypriot galleys fought in Xerxes' fleet – but they performed so badly that perhaps their real allegiance should have been clear.

The Kyrenia Ship (c300 BC), in the Shipwreck Museum, Kyrenia Castle

included territory covering present-day Israel, Lebanon and Syria.

The quality of Persian rule can be judged by the fact that all the Cypriot cities, save Phoenician Amathus, raised the standard of revolt in support of the Ionian Greeks of Asia Minor, when they launched their great rebellion against Persia in 499 BC. The Persians reacted swiftly, landing an army at Salamis. The city was soon recaptured after Stasenor, king of Kourion, deserted the rebel cause, and then Salamis itself deserted. Other cities, including

The golden age of classical Greece passed Cyprus by, running its course far beyond a horizon circumscribed by the island's role as a Persian naval base. One man, King Evagoras I of Salamis, a brilliant political and military leader, succeeded in uniting Cyprus by force and kicking out the Persians – not without resistance, however, from Cypriots of Phoenician origin and others who supported Persia. With Evagoras' death in 374 BC, the old forces reasserted themselves.

CULTURAL QUESTION Cyprus had absorbed much of Greek culture, even if such developments as

28

democracy never reached it, but it was never truly Greek, nor had it ever been allowed to become truly Greek. Its population make-up and geographical location inevitably determined that it looked east as well as west. The question of whether or not Cyprus has been Greek since the dawn of history is now an intensely political question. The historical record does not support those Hellenist partisans who say that no other indigenous cultural tradition ever flourished in Cyprus.

Ironically, by the time the island came under the undisputed control of Hellenism, Greece itself had been defeated by Macedon. The young Macedonian king, Alexander the Great, was off on the trail of conquest that would swamp Persia and extend the Hellenistic world to the borders

❏ The last independent king of Cyprus was Nicocreon, who ruled over Salamis. In 310 BC he was killed, and he and his family are thought to have been commemorated by, but not buried in, the so-called Cenotaph of Nicocreon, a tumulus at the village of Egkomi (Tuzla) near Famagusta (Gazimağusa). ❏

of India. In such a vast scheme, Cyprus was a mere morsel. By 325 BC, the island was swallowed up into Alexander's empire; one of its great ages was about to begin.

Top: Hellenistic rock-cut tombs, Makronisos. Below: the forces of King Evagoras sack Persian Tyre

The might of Rome tore Cyprus away from the enfeebled grasp of Hellenistic Egypt and incorporated it into the Roman province of Cilicia. Centuries of peace and prosperity followed, disturbed only by the occasional disastrous earthquake. During this time, Christianity took a firm hold on Cypriot hearts and minds.

Alexander the Great's approach to his succession was simple: let the strongest rule. His three top generals carved up his empire, leaving Cyprus a bone of contention between them. The island was finally won by Ptolemy, whose power-base was Egypt. In the Hellenistic Age that followed, Greek art, literature, language and philosophy were diffused throughout the three Hellenistic kingdoms. As a province of Ptolemaic Egypt, Cyprus was administered by a governor based at Salamis, and later at Pafos. The strongly eastern-influenced culture of the island became indelibly tinged with that of Greece.

For 250 years Cyprus developed in peace, with fine market-places and temples being constructed in the cities. Outstanding monuments, such as the Tombs of the Kings at Pafos, date from this period. In the 4th century BC Cyprus produced one of the brilliant minds of antiquity: Zeno of Kition, a Cypriot who founded the Stoic philosophy. A modified version of Zeno's ideas became the guiding philosophy of the Roman nobility.

Right: Emperor Septimius Severus. Top: mosaic at Soloi

❏ In AD 115, the Jews of Cyprus joined the revolt of their compatriots in Judaea. Some 200,000 non-Jews were said to have been massacred – a figure that is probably greatly exaggerated. The Roman general Lucius Quietus savagely suppressed the rebellion in AD 117, and all Jews were expelled from the island. ❏

ROMAN RULE In 58 BC, the Roman general Marcus Portius Cato annexed Cyprus to Rome, the new power from the west which had brought the entire area of the Mediterranean under its rule. Rome was in a state of transition at the time, from the old republican oligarchy in which the senate had predominated, to the triumvirate, led by the powerful generals Caesar, Crassus and Pompey, and later by Octavian (Augustus), Mark Antony and Lepidus. Although Cyprus was at one time governed by the renowned orator Cicero, it gained a better indication of its position in the new order when Mark Antony, temporarily triumphant, gave the island to Queen Cleopatra of Egypt as a lover's gift.

From the Emperor Augustus onwards, Cyprus was a tranquil backwater of the Roman Empire. For more than two centuries the island was a major beneficiary of the *Pax*

Greco-Roman theatre overlooking the sea at Kourion, west of Limassol

Romana. The Mediterranean was freed of pirates and hostile fleets, and trade flourished.

Pafos became the seat of Roman government, a city of villas, theatres and gymnasia – archaeologists have uncovered some of the magnificent mosaic floors that graced the governor's palace and adjacent villas (see page 170). The coastline of Cyprus was dotted with other wealthy cities, a string of pearls connected by a Roman road that encircled the island.

CHRISTIAN VIRTUES Cyprus can – and does – claim to be the first Christian country. St Paul converted the Roman governor, Sergius Paulus, in AD 45, a remarkable 'catch' for a religion just off the theological drawing-board. Periods of persecution followed, but by AD 313, when the Emperor Constantine issued the Edict of Milan permitting religious freedom throughout the empire, Christianity was the dominant force in Cyprus. The ancient sanctuaries of Aphrodite and Apollo Hylates (see pages 165 and 116 respectively) remained in business until 391, when Emperor Theodosius abolished the pagan cults.

By then, Salamis had replaced Pafos as the island's capital. Demolished by an earthquake in 342, Salamis was rebuilt by the Emperor Constantius and renamed Constantia. Rome's empire subsequently split into a Greek east and a Latin west; when the western empire collapsed in the 5th century, Cyprus remained a province of the eastern empire, ruled from Constantinople.

❏ Roman tastes in performance art were less refined than those of the Greeks. Theatres like the one at Kourion (see page 110), more familiar with plays by Sophocles and Aristophanes, were converted to arenas for bloody spectacles between gladiators and wild animals. ❏

Column capital from the archaeological site at Kourion

No period of Cyprus's history left such an undying legacy as the Byzantine. This era began as the swansong of classical civilisation, was swept away when Islam's armies scorched the land, and then returned even stronger as the majestic empire whose twin fountainheads were Orthodox Christianity and Hellenism.

No citizen of 'Byzantium' would have recognised this modern term. Byzantium was an insignificant town occupying a strategically vital position on the Bosporus. When the Roman Emperor Constantine transferred the imperial capital from Rome to Byzantium, he built a magnificent new city which was named Constantinople in his honour. From the start, it was a Christian city. When the Roman Empire in the west collapsed, Constantinople continued for nearly another thousand years as capital of the east. In their own eyes, the Byzantines were Romans.

❏ The 6th-century Emperor Justinian, who is often considered to be the first important Byzantine emperor, was well aware of his own august heritage. He had a commemorative medallion struck at Constantinople, preening himself as 'the Glory of the Romans'. ❏

While the empire's land frontiers were threatened on all sides, Cyprus continued to live the same peaceful existence it had known for centuries under Roman rule. Christian basilicas adorned its cities in place of pagan temples, but these new foundations lacked nothing of the wealth and elegance of their religious predecessors.

It was, in a sense, a golden age, but just as gold is the colour of a late after-noon in summer, so the drowsy centuries of the imperial peace were coming to an end for Cyprus. From the depths of Arabia, a storm was springing up to shake the Byzantine world to its foundations.

SWORD VERSUS SCIMITAR In 622, Islam bloomed in the desert like a rain-blessed flower and the armies of the Prophet erupted from the sands, tearing across Syria, Palestine and Egypt to stand within a few years on

Brilliantly coloured Byzantine frescos adorn the church of Panagia tou Asinou

32

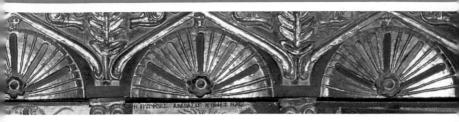

the Mediterranean shore opposite Cyprus. The hard-pressed Byzantine armies could not defend the island. In 632, an initial raid destroyed Kition, and a more determined follow-up attack in 647 did the same to Constantia (Salamis). Pafos fell the following year. The Cypriots began scrambling inland, away from the coastal cities which were little more than sitting ducks to the new religion's rampaging warriors.

The island returned once more to its role as a frontier outpost, fought over and ravished by the forces of two great, irreconcilable powers. By 650 it was split between the Byzantines and Arabs, and gradually depopulated as its inhabitants fled to safer parts of the empire. In 688, those who remained were forced to pay tribute to both the Byzantine emperor and the Muslim caliph.

The disasters of the 7th century were fatal to civilised life, and the roster of cities whose millennia-old histories reached an end at this time makes for a grim chapter in the archaeological record.

THE EMPIRE STRIKES BACK In 965, Byzantium – which at one stage had been on its knees, with hostile armies at the walls of Constantinople itself – made a dramatic comeback in Cyprus under the Emperor Nicephoros Phocas, who expelled the Arabs. For the next two centuries Christian arts and architecture flourished once more in what had again become a relatively peaceful backwater. Nicosia (Lefkoşa) grew on the foundations of ancient Ledra, the castles in the Kyrenia (Beşparmak) Mountains were established, and monasteries and frescoed churches sprang up in the Troodos Mountains.

❑ In 1959, when Archbishop Makarios signed the London Accord in red ink, he was exercising a right to use that imperial colour granted by the Byzantine Emperor Zeno to the head (ethnarch) of the Cypriot Church in 478. Zeno also permitted the ethnarch to wear a cloak of Tyrian purple and to carry an imperial sceptre. ❑

33

Top and below: Panagia Angeloktistos church, Kition

Cyprus remained unaffected by the blood and violence of the First and Second Crusades, but its luck ran out by the Third. The Cypriots had been invaded, repressed and auctioned like so many goods and chattels in the past, but now they were to see their island handed over to a dynasty of failed crusaders who would rule it for 300 years.

34

The fires of religious fundamentalism swept once more across the Levant. This time, Islam was the victim. In 1095, Pope Urban II launched the First Crusade to recover the Holy Land from the infidels. The flower of European chivalry carried the crusader banner to the walls of Jerusalem and, in 1099, took the city by storm. A massacre of its Muslim population ensued. The Holy Land had been delivered, but the new Christian kingdom immediately came under intense pressure from Saracen armies bent on its destruction. Cyprus, dangerously close to the flames, had so far escaped unscorched...but not for long. In 1184, Isaac Komnenos, a

Below: England's King Richard, who first bought, then sold Cyprus. Top: Isaac Komnenos pleads with him for his daughter's return

member of Byzantium's imperial family, seized Cyprus and declared it independent. He ruled tyranically for seven years until fate caught up with him in a drama worthy of Hollywood. Komnenos had promised the Saracen ruler Saladin, who had recaptured Jerusalem, that he would not help the Third Crusade to re-recapture the city. When the fleet of England's King Richard the Lionheart was scattered by a storm, the king's fiancée, Princess Berengaria, landed on Cyprus where Komnenos treated her badly. Richard promptly invaded, routed Komnenos's army and had the usurper hauled before him.

MUSICAL CHAIRS King Richard soon alienated the Cypriots by scooping up their wealth and forcing the Latin (Roman Catholic) Church on them. They revolted. As his mission was to fight for the Holy Land, not for Cyprus, Richard sold the island to the Knights Templar, an élite order of crusader monks. No strangers to repressing subject peoples, the Templars went to work on the rebels with a will, but even they could make no headway and they unloaded the island back on Richard. He then handed the Cyprus hot potato to his ally, Guy de Lusignan, the then out-of-work French king of Jerusalem. Guy de Lusignan was an able ruler

❏ King Richard the Lionheart of England married Princess Berengaria of Navarre at Limassol in 1191. It was 800 years before another reigning British monarch dropped in – Queen Elizabeth II in 1993. ❏

Famagusta's 14th-century Citadel

35

who began the process of restoring Cyprus's wealth and stability. The island's Byzantine character was pushed into second place, however, and the Orthodox Church was likewise relegated as the Lusignans introduced a feudal system and granted Catholicism the privileges it enjoyed in France. Short of bluebloods for the upper crust of his new realm, Guy issued an invitation to the French nobility of the Holy Land to join him. Comparing their current lot – hot, dusty and beset on all sides by Saracens – with an offer of land, servants and peace, many packed their bags and sailed for Cyprus.

BALANCE SHEET From 1192 until 1489, the Lusignans guided their ship of state through the treacherous currents of the Levant, although at times the hand on the tiller was a shaky one. Famagusta (Gazimağusa) became a source of awe to visitors from backward Europe as its merchants grew rich on profits from the crusaders and, after the Holy Land was finally lost, from trade with the Saracens.

Monuments of Lusignan rule remain throughout Cyprus, including the Cathedral of St Nicholas in

Famagusta (now the Lala Mustafa Paşa Mosque, page 236), the Cathedral of St Sophia in Nicosia (now the Selimiye Mosque, see page 64) and the Abbey of Bellapaix at Bellapais (Beylerbeyi, see page 207).

> ❏ Thomas Aquinas dedicated his *De Regimine Principium* to the 13th-century Lusignan King Hugh III, a mild ruler who was both soldier and scholar. ❏

Geoffroy de Lusignan, of the French dynasty that ruled Cyprus for three centuries (1192–1489)

> ❏ In 1260, Pope Alexander IV issued a papal decree, the Bulla Cypria, establishing the Latin Church's sovereignty over the Orthodox. However, most Cypriots retained their allegiance to the Orthodox Church. ❏

The Ottoman Turks were the nemesis of the thousand-year-old Byzantine Empire. With Constantinople captured and the entire Levant in their hands, Cyprus was clearly next on the menu. Venice had replaced the Lusignans and taken over the island just in time to find the Turks heading their way.

The decline and fall of the Lusignans had a touch of comic opera, yet was preceded by the reign of a dashing soldier-king, Peter I, who thrashed the Turks and Egyptian Mamelukes before being assassinated by his own barons. Meanwhile, Genoa and Venice had been muscling in on the eastern Mediterranean trade routes and seizing bases to protect their investments. In 1372, the coronation of Peter's successor at Famagusta (Gazimağusa) was disrupted by clashes between the Genoese and Venetian representatives. To avenge their slighted honour, the Genoese invaded Cyprus and captured Famagusta. In 1426, the Mamelukes invaded and devastated the island, and were only bought off with a huge indemnity.

Anyone knowing Cyprus's history would have recognised the signs: things were heading downhill. Venice, the Most Serene Republic, serenely bided its time. It helped

❑ The Venetians cared little for Lusignan art and architecture. Faced with an imminent Ottoman invasion, they drastically reduced the circuit of Nicosia's walls and demolished everything outside them to provide clear fields of fire for artillery. The Lusignan royal palace, as well as many Gothic churches and mansions, were destroyed in the process. ❑

King James II kick the Genoese out, then generously provided him with a Venetian wife, Caterina Cornaro. Such selfless benevolence was uncharacteristic, to put it mildly, and King James no doubt spent a lot of time watching his back – though not well enough, apparently. He died in

Map of Cyprus (1601) by the great Flemish cartographer, Ortelius

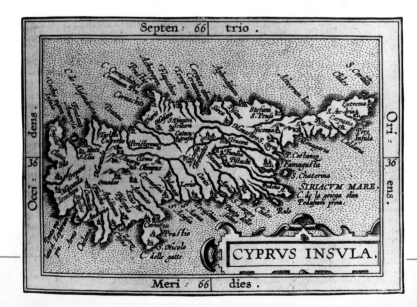

suspicious circumstances in 1473, as did his son James III, the last of the Lusignans, in the following year. Caterina Cornaro was 'persuaded' to turn Cyprus over to Venice, an act made official in 1489.

VICTOR'S SPOILS In one of Cypriot history's many ironies, Venice, which had schemed assiduously to annex Cyprus, now found that its new possession lay squarely in the sights of the Ottoman Turks. The Turks had captured Constantinople in 1453, an event that shook the Mediterranean world as no other had since the fall of Rome a thousand years earlier. While the Ottomans pushed ahead with their conquest of the adjacent mainland, Venice fortified the island, and in 1546 they suppressed a revolt of Cypriots embittered by brutal military rule and punitive taxation.

The long-awaited invasion, ordered by Sultan Selim II and commanded by Lala Mustafa Paşa, was launched in 1570. Venice concentrated its defence at Famagusta, Nicosia and Kyrenia (Girne), whose walls had been enormously strengthened to withstand artillery. Lala Mustafa drew up his vastly superior army before Nicosia and, after a six-week siege, stormed the defences and slaughtered 20,000 inhabitants. Kyrenia quickly surrendered. Famagusta's commander, Marco Antonio Bragadino, and his 8,000-man garrison kept Lala Mustafa's supposed 200,000-strong force at bay

Nicosia's Venetian walls, raised in vain against the Ottoman threat

for ten months before the survivors finally surrendered in August 1571.

TURKISH TAKE-OVER Despite their harsh measures in wartime, the Turks were welcomed by most Cypriots. They eliminated the oppressive Latin (Roman Catholic) Church and restored Orthodoxy, not as a sign of goodwill but because the Orthodox Church was less threatening to their interests than Western-oriented Catholicism. Feudalism was abolished and freed serfs given the right to own land, although Turkish immigrants tended to take the best of it and taxation remained heavy

Apart from these measures, and converting a few Latin churches to mosques, the Turks allowed Cyprus to slide into that state of bureaucracy-infested indolence which is arguably among the Ottomans' principal bequests.

> ❏ Heavy taxation and greedy officials, along with poor harvests, led to famine, high mortality rates and emigration during Ottoman rule. In 1641, this deadly combination reduced the island's population to 25,000, down from 150,000 two years earlier. ❏

Britain first became involved in Cyprus as a by-product of shoring up Turkey against the might of Russia. When the island was ceded to Britain in 1878, however, its attractions became more appealing to the empire, and the British settled down for an indefinite stay.

One of the charges laid by Cyprus's Hellenist partisans against the Ottomans is that they left little of worth behind them. Maybe the Turks' cultural bent lay in other directions, and their state of graceful indolence may have been preferable to one where poor peasants footed the bill for palaces, cathedrals and villas that would one day be gawped at by tourists in air-conditioned coaches. Unfortunately, the poor peasants still paid, but their money went to venal officials in Cyprus and to the Sublime Porte in Istanbul, who no doubt made good use of it.

Seen from history's vantage-point, every empire's glorious trail of conquest fades ultimately to weakness and oblivion. So it was with the Ottomans, as it had been with the Persians, Greeks, Romans, Byzantines and Venetians. By the 19th century, the 'terrible Turk', whose name once struck fear across Europe, had become 'poor little Turkey', a toothless tiger beset on all sides. Greece rebelled in 1821 and won its independence 11 years later, aided, if not achieved single-handedly as romantics imagine, by the British poet Lord Byron.

WAVING THE RULES Britannia had arrived. As the century progressed and the Suez Canal opened, Britain sought to protect its lifeline to India by bolstering Turkey against the Russian bear, which seemed set on washing its dirty feet in the Mediterranean. British naval power was deployed to hold the bear in its northern lair. At first, Cyprus's only role in this drama was as a victim of Turkish paranoia, when several hundred leading Greeks were executed in 1821 to prevent the island joining Greece in rebellion. Turkey then only just managed to hang on to Cyprus, as Egypt broke free of Ottoman rule.

By 1878, Britain was in the driving-seat. The Union Jack fluttered aloft after the Ottoman Empire ceded Cyprus to Britain by a treaty that sanctioned British subsidies to Istanbul and other assistance against Russia, while retaining Ottoman sovereignty and allowing for the island's possible return to Ottoman rule. The British legal and

British troops take over Cyprus in July 1878, under an agreement with the Ottoman government

❏ Luigi di Cesnola, the American consul-general, began excavating ancient monuments in Cyprus in 1873. He was thought to be a scientific investigator, but was in fact a con-man who plundered the sites and looted thousands of objects of great historical and monetary value. ❏

administrative systems were introduced, as well as other political reforms. A road- and bridge-building programme was begun, and reafforestation started in the Troodos and Kyrenia (Beşparmak) Mountains.

GREEK GIFT Greek Cypriots had high hopes that Britain would support their desire for Enosis (union with Greece), but strategic considerations ensured that the time for this was somehow never appropriate. In 1914, Turkey sided with Germany in World War I and Britain annexed the island. During the course of the war, however, the British offered Cyprus to Greece on condition that Greece declare war on Germany and Turkey. Greece declined, a decision that would later be the cause of some embarrassment in its claim to be the Cypriots' motherland.

In 1925, Cyprus became a British Crown Colony and a governor replaced the previous high commissioner – a development which the average Cypriot probably did not even notice. As far as the British were concerned, Cyprus could look forward to no future other than as part of the empire on which the sun never set. Within a few years they would learn that not all Cypriots held the same views as His Britannic Majesty's government.

❏ Cyprus's historical record is well represented in Claude Delaval Cobham's *Excerpta Cypria*, published in 1908 (republished 1969) and incorporating material from some 80 writers, ranging from AD 23 to 1849. ❏

Archbishop Makarios inspects British troops in 1961

The road to independence was a hard and rocky one, and the outcome was only accepted by Greek Cypriots as a second-best to their goal of union with Greece (Enosis). The machinations of international power politics had sown the seeds of future conflict in Cyprus.

By 1920 the population of Cyprus was around 300,000. Greek Cypriots outnumbered Turkish Cypriots by five to one, so that in any vote on the island's future the Greek Cypriot viewpoint would prevail – and that viewpoint, it became increasingly clear, was in favour of Enosis. Britain permitted no such vote, and in 1931 serious rioting, which resulted in Government House being burned down, broke out in Nicosia. British troops were brought in from Egypt to put down the rebellion, whose leaders were captured, tried and exiled.

Little more was heard of Enosis until after World War II. Some 36,000 Cypriots, both Greek and Turkish, served in the British Commonwealth armed forces during the war. The consciousness of having earned their right to self-determination revitalised the demand for Enosis among Greek Cypriots, and the slogan 'Enosis and only Enosis' began to appear on buildings. A referendum organised by the Orthodox Church, which had always seen itself as the guardian of Hellenism, resulted in a 96 per cent vote in favour of Enosis. Greece took the Greek Cypriot case to the UN.

BLIND RESPONSE The writing was, literally, on the wall, but Britain ignored it. Rioting broke out. Britain

> ❏ The 1960 constitution allowed for a Greek Cypriot president and a Turkish Cypriot vice-president, each of whom had veto powers over government decisions. The House of Representatives had 35 Greek Cypriot members and 15 Turkish Cypriot members. ❏

invited Greece and Turkey to a conference on the island's future, which ended without positive result yet confirmed these three countries as arbiters of Cyprus's destiny. However, the Greek Cypriots determined to take a hand in that destiny. A Cyprus-born Greek army colonel, George Grivas, landed secretly in 1955 on the coast near Pafos and formed EOKA (Ethniki Organosis Kyprion Agoniston, or the National Organisation of Cypriot Fighters) to wage a guerrilla war against the British in order to achieve Enosis.

Bombs in crowded streets; bullets in the back of the head: EOKA's war lacked glamour, but it made its way. The British declared a state of emergency and drafted in troops to

Greek Cypriot girls welcome EOKA fighters to Nicosia in 1959

40

combat the guerrillas. Turkey and the Turkish Cypriots watched these developments with alarm and a determination that Cyprus must not be handed to Greece. In 1957, the United Nations adopted a resolution to establish an independent Republic of Cyprus. Two years later the Greek Cypriot political leader, Archbishop Makarios, signed treaties at Zürich and London, and in 1960 the Republic of Cyprus took its place among the nations.

UNCERTAIN FUTURE Under the treaties establishing the state, Britain, Greece and Turkey were 'guarantor powers', able to intervene militarily if Cyprus's independence was threatened. Britain retained two military bases which were (and still are) British sovereign territory. The real difficulty shifted to relations between the two communities, with the Greek Cypriots eager to move, albeit stealthily, towards Enosis, and the minority Turkish Cypriots unwilling to accept this. Calls within the Turkish population for Taksim (partition) grew

Turkish troops celebrate their 1974 invasion of Cyprus

as the power-sharing constitution broke down and Turkish communities came under attack, provoking the threat of Turkish intervention.

Bad as the situation became through the 1960s, with a UN peace-keeping force being deployed to keep the communities apart, the real disaster to Cyprus as a unitary state came in 1974. Greece's military junta launched a pro-Enosis coup against President Makarios. Turkey promptly invaded and Cyprus has been divided ever since.

❏ Both Greece and Turkey had the right to station military forces in 'independent' Cyprus. Each side accused the other of exceeding the permitted number and of using them to train local forces. As the intercommunal conflict spread, these units took part in the fighting. ❏

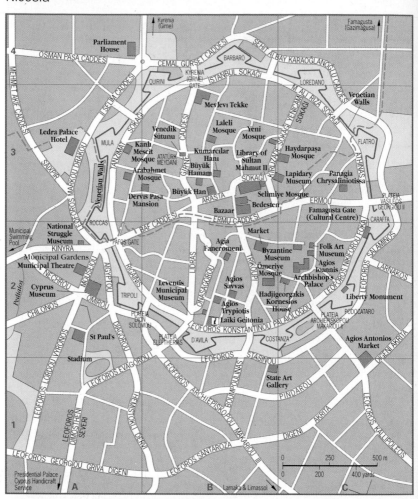

*Left: Ömeriye Mosque,
originally St Mary's
Church
Far left: all in a day's
work at an atelier near the
Green Line*

NICOSIA Cyprus's capital is a place apart. No sea breeze or mountain tang reaches here, only the heat-shimmered air of the Mesaoria (Mesarya) Plain at the island's heart. To a Greek Cypriot the city's name is Lefkosia; to a Turkish Cypriot it is Lefkoşa (not much difference one might think); to the world at large it is Nicosia. It remains locked in a 40-year time-warp, its Greek and Turkish halves interfacing in what has become the traditional Cypriot manner: with barbed wire, oil-drum barricades and sandbagged sentry posts.

The Green Line is the United Nations-patrolled buffer zone, separating the two communities so completely that they might as well be living on different planets. Across the divide, each side taunts the other with prominently displayed flags. The barrier is as much psychological as physical: Cypriots trying to imagine what life is like 'on the other side' come up with a picture of grim-faced men ready to storm across at a moment's notice. Tourists and others who have visited both sides – as most Cypriots cannot – know better.

CAPITAL NAMES
The city's name, Lefkosia (Lefkoşa in Turkish) comes from Lefkos, the son of Ptolemy Soter, a 3rd-century BC ruler of Hellenistic Egypt, of which Cyprus was then a province. Nicosia owes its international name to the French-speaking Lusignan kings of Cyprus, who named it Nicosie some 15 centuries later.

NAME GAMES I
In Greek Cyprus, place-name spellings have changed in favour of a new method of transliterating Greek into Roman letters. Paphos became Pafos, Larnaca changed to Larnaka and Ayios became Agios. More disconcertingly, Yermasoyia becomes Germasogeia and Khirokitia changed to Choirokoitia. You can find yourself staying at the Paphos Beach Hotel in Pafos or the Ayia Napa Hotel in Agia Napa. Confused? Many road-signs certainly are. But what the heck, the sun shines as brightly on Latsi as it ever did on Latchi, and Panagia Chrysorrogiatissa is no more of a tongue-twister than was Panayia Khrysoroyiatissa. If it's any consolation, few Cypriots understand what's going on either.

GROWING FAST Thankfully, Nicosia and its 210,000 inhabitants add up to more than an object lesson in human folly. The Greek Cypriot sector is a vibrant hemi-city, half-surrounding the old Ottoman core. Propelled by the impetus of a booming economy, this half of the capital has been expanding rapidly, swallowing up hapless villages in its path and making shapeless suburbs of them. Housing, industrial and business developments, and the road links they require, have combined to make the outskirts a giant construction site.

By contrast, the old city within the Venetian walls is a colourful collage of narrow streets lined with houses, workshops, cafés and shops, interrupted occasionally by an upmarket shopping or dining area. The workshops are concentrated along the Green Line, forming an enclave of dens lit by flaring oxyacetylene torches or echoing to the carpenter's hammer. The workshops and Green Line together form an unlikely yet popular tourist attraction.

Some sections of the inner city are falling down, some are getting ready to, others are being refurbished. In the case of the Laïki Geitonia (or Gitonia, as it is often spelt) district (the Greek name means 'Popular District'), an attractive if somewhat twee and over-touristy taverna-and-gift-shop centre has been the result.

BRIDGING THE GULF Tourists in the Turkish Cypriot sector in the north cannot cross to the Greek Cypriot sector. The Turkish sector can be reached by tourists from the south via the Ledra Palace Hotel checkpoint, but only for a daytime visit.

Everything moves a little slower on the Turkish side. Traffic is less intense, office and apartment blocks fewer, the pace of redevelopment more lackadaisical. Some things don't change on this side of the great divide, however: the summer heat strikes equally hard; hospitality carries the same weight; and the workshops beside the Green Line churn out the same abundance of baffling gadgets on the Turkish side.

Sheer necessity in the area of vital public services, as well as a flickering awareness that the two communities share a common city, has led to some official contact across the gulf of mistrust and hatred. Sliced in two as it is by the 'Cyprus problem', Nicosia has its own underlying unity which may yet outlast the guns and the barbed wire fortifications. Seen from the air, the old city is a perfect circle delineated by the defensive perimeter of the Venetian walls. Defensive mentalities still reign supreme, but there is some hope that the circle of reconciliation can be squared.

NAME GAMES II
At the time of independence, it was agreed that places should have two names: Greek and Turkish. Paphos (now Pafos) was Baf in Turkish, and Episkopi was Piskobu. Since the partition of 1974, only Turkish names have been used in the Turkish Cypriot zone, except in cases like Kyrenia and Famagusta, which many Turkish Cypriots still call by their Greek name, although road signs refer to Girne and Gazimağusa. In addition, some of the existing Turkish names were changed. Greek Cypriots complain, and their complaint is upheld by the UN, that such changes are illegal. The reality on the ground and on maps, however, is that Greek names are never used.

45

Murals fill the interior of Agios Ioannis (Cathedral of St John) in the monumental heart of Nicosia

NAME GAMES III
The Greek Cypriot authorities, and to a lesser extent the Turkish Cypriot, have adopted a policy of latinising street names wherever possible. This often simply means transliterating the Greek or Turkish letters to Roman ones. In many, but not all cases where a word also has a familiar English translation, such as a historical character or city name, this or the nearest equivalent English word may be used instead. In all this, problems are caused by a lack of consistency and patchy implementation of the system.

SCHOOL DAYS

Across the road from Agios Ioannis and the Archbishop's Palace is the Pancyprian Gymnasium, where Lawrence Durrell taught English in the 1950s. Here Aphrodite, of the Girls' Sixth, once asked him slyly why English had only one word for 'love' while Greek had several, and here he received a petition from his class asking politely that Cyprus should be free. 'They were admirable children,' wrote Durrell in Bitter Lemons, 'each wrapped in the bright silken cocoon of a dream'.

Richly decorated Agios Ioannis is Nicosia's most important Greek Orthodox church

Greek Cypriot Nicosia

▶ Agia Faneromeni
(Church of St Faneromeni)   42B2

Faneromenis Street
Open: irregularly. Admission free

In 1821, the Ottoman governor of Cyprus instituted a series of executions on the off-chance that the victims might be contemplating rebellion. Among those who paid the ultimate penalty in this pre-emptive strike were the ethnarch of the Cypriot Church, Archbishop Kyprianos, and several bishops, who lie buried under this otherwise dull 19th-century church close to the Green Line. The diminutive Arablar Mosque stands near by.

▶▶▶ Agios Ioannis (St John's Cathedral)   42C2

Archiepiskopou Kyprianou Square
Open: Mon–Fri 8–12 and 2–4, Sat 8–12. Admission free

Compared with the great European cathedrals, Nicosia's Orthodox cathedral is a dinky little place. Completed in 1662 on the ruins of the Lusignan-era Benedictine abbey church of St John the Evangelist, which had been sacked by invading Mamelukes in 1426, it is much too small to accommodate the tour groups that descend upon it for a snatch of tour-guide exposition amidst a multilingual babble. It was not built with tour groups in mind, of course, and its size reflects its abbey origins rather than any assessment of its worth. For Agios Ioannis is splendid and justifies the superlatives the tourist guides lavish upon it (even if it is best visited early, before the guides start their rounds).

Situated beside the Archbishop's Palace, Agios Ioannis has become the state church, with an ornate throne for His Beatitude and special places for Their Excellencies, the

president of the republic and the Greek ambassador. The abundant murals on its ceiling and walls, mostly dating from the early 18th century, depict scenes from the Christian history of Cyprus, such as the evangelising mission of St Paul and St Barnabas in AD 45. Icons, gilt decoration and multicoloured lamps sparkle in the otherwise gloomy interior. The pulpit is graced with a magnificent but sinister-looking double-headed eagle, the emblem of Byzantium.

▶ Agios Trypiotis (Church of St Michael Trypiotis) 42B2

Solonos Street
Open: irregularly. Admission free
Evidence for its former status as the top people's church in Nicosia may be seen in the silver-chased icons and other offerings donated by the well-heeled faithful. The church's solid 17th-century bulk is lightened by some earlier Byzantine touches, such as the carved lintels on some doorways. Otherwise, the most notable point about the Trypiotis may be the difficulty of actually getting inside, since it is invariably locked.

▶▶ Archbishop's Palace 42C2

Archiepiskopou Kyprianou Square
Officially described as neo-Byzantine, the palace looks suspiciously neo-Venetian but in any case dates to 1960 and seems oddly uninspired. The modest private apartments of its first occupant, Archbishop Makarios, the late ethnarch of the Cypriot Orthodox Church and first president of the Republic of Cyprus, are occasionally open to the public for organised visits. A gargantuan bronze sculpture of the archbishop obstructs the otherwise light and delicate lines of the palace's façade.

▶ Bayraktar Mosque 56C1

Costanza bastion of the Venetian walls
Generally closed
The Standard Bearer's Mosque is in the Constanza bastion at the point where a Turkish soldier planted the Ottoman colours on the Venetian walls during the final assault of the 1570 siege. He was shot down immediately and his remains lie in the mosque which was raised in his honour. Gardens that once surrounded the mosque were truncated in favour of a bus station.

▶▶▶ Byzantine Museum 42C2

Archiepiskopou Kyprianou Square (tel: 02-430008)
Open: Mon–Fri 9–4.30, Sat 9–1
Admission charge
Part of the monumental complex beside the Archbishop's Palace, this museum and art gallery features the largest and most impressive icon collection on the island, although there are individual pieces of greater worth in other locations. One part of the collection, which spans a thousand years, is given over to items looted from the Turkish area after 1974 and bought back at great expense by the Greek Cypriot government when they turned up on the international black market and even at legitimate art sales. Other floors of the museum house paintings, most of which are seriously undistinguished.

Controversial and colossal, the statue of Archbishop Makarios stands outside the Archbishop's Palace

47

BUILDING ON MUD
In the area around the Archbishop's Palace are many old Ottoman-style houses built using traditional mud-brick construction methods. These have been literally crumbling to the ground and some are past saving. Others, however, are being restored in a campaign to preserve the city's original appearance as far as possible.

Elegant street lamps in Archbishop Kyprianou Square

Terracotta figures in the Cyprus Museum

48

The Aphrodite of Soloi takes pride of place in the museum

►► Cyprus Handicraft Service 42A1
186 Athalassis Avenue (tel: 02-305024)
Open: Mon–Fri 7.30–2.30, Thu also 3–6 (except Jul–Aug)
Admission free

The pristinely modern centre on the edge of Nicosia seems a strange place for preserving the endangered folk arts and artisanal skills of simpler times – a bit like making flint tools aboard a space station. Yet there is no question that such a venture is needed, as modern technologies and changing social habits sweep away the knowledge of generations. Each traditional Cypriot village handicraft has its place here: basket-making, pottery, weaving, iron-working, lace-making, wood-carving. Visitors can watch the craftsfolk at work and the finished products are on sale in an unobtrusive way.

►►► Cyprus Museum 42A2
Mouseiou Avenue (tel: 02-865864)
Open: Mon–Sat 9–5, Sun 10–1. Admission charge

The modest dimensions of this museum will please those more familiar with the blister-inducing museums of countries which like to think they not only invented culture but retain a monopoly on it still. This unassuming style begins with the almost perfunctory neo-classical portico. The real surprise is inside, however, where the cultural harvest of 10,000 years seems comparatively thin until it is realised that much of Cyprus's heritage has been siphoned off (the word 'stolen' also springs to mind) to various museums and private collections all over the world.

Nevertheless, the museum contains much that is downright surprising as well as merely interesting. Following the progression of displays is to make a journey forward in time.

The first faint traces of human occupation appear in the neolithic period, with the aceramic (literally, 'without pottery') settlements at Khirokitia and Kastros, represented by stone figurines and simple implements of bone and flint. A great array of Bronze Age exhibits includes some 2,000 votive terracotta figurines that were uncovered at the sanctuary of Agia Eirini (Akdeniz) in the Turkish Cypriot zone.

Even minus her arms and legs, the superb Aphrodite of Soloi (Soli) still charms visitors, who gather around the marble sculpture as though awaiting some words of ineffable wisdom. The goddess is also represented by a conical stone, an archaic symbol of her worship. Keeping Aphrodite company is a superb, larger-than-lifesize bronze nude statue of the Roman emperor Septimius Severus.

The 12th-century BC 'horned god', found at Engomi (Enkomi) near Famagusta (Gazimağusa), and an ornamented bronze cauldron uncovered at Salamis are equally memorable.

▶▶ Famagusta Gate   42C2

Caraffa bastion of the Venetian walls, Athinon Avenue
(tel: 02-430877)
Open: Mon–Fri 10–1 and 4–7 (Jun–Aug 5–8). Admission free
The coming and going of art exhibitions has replaced the
to and fro of people and goods through this robust,
tunnel-like gateway in the city walls, one of three built by
the Venetians when they established the walls between
1567 and 1570. The structure had fallen into disrepair
until it was restored and reopened as the Nicosia
Municipal Cultural Centre.

The Famagusta Gate is not only popular in its own right,
but it also helps to support a nearby enclave of upmarket
cafés. Its restored passages and side-chambers are usually
in use for exhibitions, conferences, lectures and performance art.

▶▶ Folk Art Museum   42C2

Archiepiskopou Kyprianou Square (tel: 02-432578)
Open: Mon–Fri 9–5, Sat 10–1. Admission charge
Housed in the Old Archbishopric, the Folk Art Museum
reopened in the summer of 1996 after rebuilding. Its
collection includes 19th-century costumes, tapestry,
embroidery, pottery and wood-carvings.

▶ Freedom Square (Plateia Eleftherias)   42B2

Between Lidras Street and Evagorou I Avenue
Greatly oversold as Nicosia's principal square, Plateia
Eleftherias consists of little more than a bridge over the
moat around the Venetian walls, with some office blocks
and cafés at either end. Not even the adjacent D'Avila
bastion and the Town Hall add greatly to the attraction.
The square is a popular meeting-point, however.

▶▶ Green Line   42B2

A line of artisans' workshops follows this man-made scar
that runs east-west across the middle of old Nicosia. Here
Greek Cypriot troops face their Turkish opposite numbers across a band of destruction while United Nations
peacekeepers man the thin blue line in the middle. In
some places the opposing forces are only a few metres
apart and incidents occasionally take place, ranging from
insults to fatal shootings. The more usual profile along the
Green Line, however, is one of suffocating boredom.

ART OF PEACE
Art often has a resonance
that transcends the petty
calculations of politicians
and others interested in
preserving the status quo,
however demeaning. One
show at the Famagusta
Gate cultural centre
caused controversy and
hope in equal amounts
through featuring contem-
porary works by both
Greek Cypriots and
Turkish Cypriots.

49

GREEN EXCURSION
For an interesting stroll in
Greek Cypriot Nicosia,
start at either the Pafos
Gate or the Municipal
Gardens and walk beside
the Venetian walls on
Markou Drakou avenue.
Continue towards the UN
headquarters at the Ledra
Palace Hotel and the
Green Line crossing point
that is situated there.

A glimpse of the other
side, through a hole in the
Green Line barricade

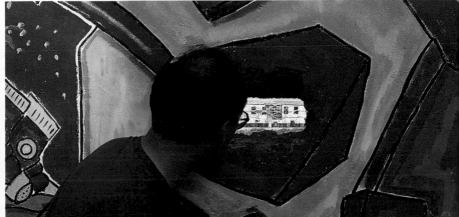

The career of Archbishop Makarios encompassed a dramatic period in the history of Cyprus. For the first time in a thousand years the island had a government of its own choosing. Yet by the time of his death it was a divided island wrestling with a bitter legacy of bloodshed and hatred.

50

DEAR COLONELS...

Makarios despised the military junta that seized power in Greece, the fountainhead of democracy, in 1968. In turn, the Greek colonels hated Makarios and tried to eliminate him. In July 1974, Makarios wrote to them in protest at such unneighbourly behaviour: 'I have more than once so far felt, and in some cases I have almost touched, a hand invisibly extending from Athens and seeking to liquidate my human existence.' Two weeks later the junta launched the *coup* aimed at the archbishop's overthrow and assassination.

Memorials to the archbishop-president are ubiquitous

ΜΑΚΑΡΙΟΣ Γ
ΕΘΝΑΡΧΗΣ ΚΑΙ

Rites of passage High in the Troodos Mountains, on a hill above the great monastery of Panagia tou Kykkou, Greek Cypriot soldiers form a guard of honour standing watch over the tomb of Archbishop Makarios III: sometime novice at Kykkou; priest, bishop and head of the Cypriot Church; revolutionary and first president of the Republic of Cyprus. His black-robed figure became a familiar public presence from the 1950s to the 1970s, not only on the strife-torn stage of his own country but to a worldwide audience as a leading light in the Movement of Non-Aligned States.

For one whose love of his homeland was all-consuming, the view from his last resting-place could scarcely be bettered. The island is laid out around the memorial like some vast exercise in geography, all its savage beauty encompassed in a single sweep, and none of its pain. For good or ill, almost everything that may be said of modern Cyprus can be placed at the portals of that tomb on Throni hill.

Ideals in action Makarios Mouskos was born in 1913 into a poor farming family in the village of Pano Panagia in the western Troodos foothills. He was educated within the proud cloisters of Kykkou, where the fires of Hellenism and the memory of the Christian empire of Byzantium were kept alive during centuries of foreign oppression. It was a potent cocktail, this mix of religion and nationalism, and when its ingredients were thrown together during the fading years of Britain's empire they combined with explosive force.

While Colonel Grivas led EOKA in a terror campaign against the British and those Cypriots who opposed Enosis (union with Greece), Makarios provided the spiritual staying power. 'Cyprus is Greek,' the ethnarch later proclaimed. 'Cyprus has been Greek since the dawn of history and it will remain Greek. Greek and undivided we have taken it over, Greek and undivided we shall preserve it. Greek and undivided we shall deliver it to Greece.' With his charisma and the mystical nature of his call, he united the Greek Cypriots behind his ideal. In 1960 Cyprus achieved independence from Britain – but not union with Greece. Makarios was elected president.

On the way If Makarios had been content with independence, Cyprus might now be a model of intercommunal calm, a flourishing and united island. But that is to mistake the forces that were at work. Makarios himself saw independence as only a half-way house, a forward position from which new advances could be made towards the eventual goal of Enosis. With the British out of the way, the main obstacle to achieving Cyprus's destiny was the island's Turkish community.

It has been said that Greek Cypriot policy during the Makarios years was made purely on the basis of his intuition or whim. The outcome was that the Turkish Cypriots withdrew into enclaves – whether in fear of their lives or as a deliberate effort to sabotage the new republic is a fiercely contested issue of recent Cypriot history.

Final recognition After the Greek-inspired *coup* of 1974 that almost killed Makarios (see panel) and led to the Turkish army's occupation of northern Cyprus, the ethnarch appeared to regret the harsher aspects of the pro-Enosis drive and to reach out to the Turkish Cypriots for a solution that recognised their rights. Too late. He then focused his efforts on dealing with the post-partition humanitarian crisis among his own people and in pressing for an end to occupation and division.

Makarios died in 1977. The Greek Cypriots who pay their respects at his tomb on Throni hill come to honour his achievements even as they must live with the consequences of his failings.

COLOSSAL MISTAKE
A 10m-high, 20-tonne statue of Archbishop Makarios has been a source of controversy among Greek Cypriots ever since it was placed in the grounds of the Archbishop's Palace in Nicosia (see page 47). General opinion seems to be that it is a monstrosity, though few go so far as to suggest that the archbishop should be melted down and sold for scrap.

Independence secured: Archbishop Makarios announces the good news

Inside the house of Hadjigeorgakis Kornesios, who was executed by the Turks in 1809

►►► Hadjigeorgakis Kornesios House   42C2

Patriarchou Grigoriou Street (tel: 02-305316)
Open: Mon–Fri 8–2, Sat 9–1. Admission charge
Georgakis Kornesios was a *dragoman*, a Greek official appointed by the Sublime Porte in Istanbul to be the 'interpreter' between the Ottoman court and its Greek Cypriot subjects. Kornesios's job combined opportunity and danger in equal measure. The former is seen in the elegant wealth of his mansion, while the latter is confirmed by his execution in 1809 for failing in the delicate balancing act between his own people and the ruthlessly suspicious Turkish authorities.

The restored 18th-century mansion, which houses the Ethnological Museum, encloses a courtyard containing a Turkish hamam, or bath. Its upper level features rooms decorated in the style appropriate to a wealthy Ottoman official, including a divan-lined reception room, a living room and bedroom. Downstairs are the servants' quarters and storage rooms. Colonnades and fine Ottoman-style woodwork add to the mansion's graceful aspect.

►► Laïki Geitonia   42B2

Adjacent to Lidras Street and the D'Avila bastion
An area just inside the city walls near Plateia Eleftherias, Laïki Geitonia is a model of urban restoration and renewal in old Nicosia. An attractive but crumbling quarter of traditional houses and shops has been totally refurbished and lined with trees. Boutiques, artisanal workshops, tavernas and souvenir shops have opened, and the area teems with life throughout the day and into the small hours. A small **Jewellery Museum** is worth a quick inspection.

► Ledra Palace Hotel   42A3

Markou Drakou Avenue
Formerly Nicosia's most elegant hotel, the Ledra Palace was damaged in the intercommunal fighting of the 1960s and 1970s and now stands in UN territory inside the buffer zone as UNFICYP headquarters. The hotel itself cannot be visited except on official business, but outside it is Nicosia's 'Checkpoint Charlie', the crossing-point between the two sectors for UN personnel, diplomats, those few Cypriots living on the 'wrong side' of the demarcation line, pre-1974 foreign residents and tourists passing from the Greek to the Turkish zone on a one-day pass. These categories exclude almost all Cypriots, who cannot move freely between the two zones.

GREEN SOLUTION
The term Green Line was coined in 1964, when a British officer of the pre-United Nations peacekeeping force in the capital, negotiating the separation of the city's battling Greek and Turkish communities, used a green chinagraph pencil to draw a line across his map of Nicosia, thereby establishing the dividing line between their two sectors.

► Leventis Municipal Museum   42B2

17 Ippokratou Street, Laïki Geitonia (tel: 02-451475)
Open: Tue–Sun 10–4.30. Admission charge
Situated within the renovated Laïki Geitonia district, the museum is a moderately interesting evocation of Nicosia in days gone by. Its most notable exhibits are those which refer to those distant days when Greek and Turkish Nicosians lived side by side in apparent harmony.

►► Liberty Monument   42C2

Podocataro bastion of the Venetian walls
Cypriot civilians emerge rejoicing from the dark dungeon of British oppression into the bright sunshine of freedom,

as gallant EOKA fighters raise the bars on their prison cell. This marble and bronze memorial to Cyprus's struggle against colonial rule has a symbolism that may be standard government-issue patriotism, but its execution raises the quality of the Liberty Monument's sculpture group beyond this predictable mould.

▶ Lidras Street   42B2

This popular pedestrian-only shopping street runs north from Plateia Eleftherias up to the Green Line, where it ends abruptly in concrete barriers and Greek Cypriot sentry posts. The incongruity of Nicosia's (and indeed Cyprus's) division seems encapsulated here, in an otherwise ordinary shopping street that ends in what is virtually a war zone.

▶▶ Municipal Gardens   42A2

Between Mouseiou Avenue, Kinyra Street and Nechrou Avenue

Although not the only patch of green in Nicosia, the Municipal Gardens, located just outside the city walls near the Pafos Gate, are by far the most attractive and accessible of the city's parks. Filled with well-tended flowers and shaded by trees, the gardens provide a blessing not to be underestimated in the savage heat of summer-time Nicosia.

An open-air café, the Garden Café Restaurant, stands on the edge of the park, beside the neo-classical **Municipal Theatre,** opened in 1967, which presents productions of classical and modern plays.

FINEST COMPLIMENT

Laïki Geitonia's success, both in restoration and commercial terms, has spawned imitators, not only in Greek Cypriot towns such as Limassol, Larnaka and Polis, but also to a certain extent across the great divide, in Turkish Cypriot Nicosia, Kyrenia (Girne) and Famagusta (Gazimağusa).

The Liberty Monument honours the struggle for independence

53

COOL CHARACTER
Nature, which has arranged for Nicosia to be baked thoroughly during the long summer days, has been gracious enough to allow for some relief. In the evenings, a cool breeze rises in the Kyrenia (Beşparmak) Mountains, wafts across the Mesaoria (Mesarya) Plain and sweeps through the city like a benediction. It is an old friend and a welcome is prepared for it in every Nicosian home, where open doors and windows ease its passage.

54

The minaret of the Ömeriye Mosque soars above the divided capital

▶▶ Municipal Swimming Pool   42A2
Louki Akrita Avenue (tel: 02-781155)
Open: Jun–Aug daily 10–8; Sep–May daily 10–7. Admission charge

An unpromising name disguises one of Nicosia's most useful places: an open-air complex of wonderfully cool water in extravagant quantity. Its pools mimic the azure blue of the sea and its sunbathing areas are the stuff of which dreams are made after a sticky expedition along Nicosia's cultural trail.

▶ National Struggle Museum   42C2
7 Kiniras Street (tel: 02-304550)
Open: Mon–Fri 8–2 and 3–5. Admission charge

This museum records the more favourable aspects (from a Greek Cypriot point of view) of the conflict between 1955 and 1959 to free Cyprus from British rule and attain union with Greece. For this cause EOKA (the National Organisation of Cypriot Fighters) waged a terror campaign, and the museum's exhibits are grim – educational but scarcely entertaining.

Pride of place goes to a reproduction of an execution cell complete with rope and trapdoor, the mechanisms of martyrdom for young EOKA fighters convicted of murder.

▶▶ Nicosia Municipal Arts Centre   56C2
19 Apostolou Varnava Street (tel: 02-432577)
Open: Tue–Sat 10–3 and 5–11, Sun 10–4. Admission free

This important cultural centre (also called the 'Power House' as it is housed within the old power station) stages art exhibitions on different themes and is home to an art reference library.

▶▶ Ömeriye Mosque   42B2
Trikoupi Street
Open: daylight hours. Admission free

Greek Nicosia's Muslim population is small, consisting of diplomats, businessmen and tourists, but the Ömeriye Mosque remains open to serve them and is, in addition, a point of general tourist interest, which the mosque's authorities are quite happy to go along with. It was formerly the Latin Church of St Mary, dating from the 14th century, until the victorious commander of the 1570 Ottoman invasion, Lala Mustafa Paşa, ordered its conversion to a mosque. Its tree-shaded entrance leads to a cool interior and, on payment of a fee, to a superb view of Nicosia from the top of the minaret.

▶ Pafos Gate   42A2
North end of Mouseiou Avenue

One of the three historic openings in the Venetian walls, the Pafos Gate is the one most affected by the division of the city, as the Green Line runs

*A proud priest (above)
watches over his church,
the superb Panagia
Chrysaliniotissa (left)*

55

within a few metres of it, and the Roccas bastion, which
overlooks it, is flag-festooned Turkish Cypriot territory.
The gate itself is unaffected, but traffic moving into the
old city has to swing hard right immediately to avoid the
barricades.

▶▶ Panagia Chrysaliniotissa
(Our Lady of the Golden Flax)   *42C3*

Odysseos Street
Open: irregularly. Admission free
Although slightly off the beaten track, this 15th-century
church is worth the extra distance, being perhaps unique
in its calm, age-worn evocation of the religious sentiment
described as 'sacred' or 'holy'. The church stands amidst a
part of old Nicosia that seems to be emerging slowly from
the neglect of recent decades.

▶ State Art Gallery   *42B1*

Stasinou Avenue (tel: 02-302951)
Open: Mon–Fri 10–5, Sat 10–1. Admission charge
The collection comprises sculptures and paintings by
Cypriot artists, dating from about 1930 onwards.
Inevitably, the quality of the work shown is variable, but
at least the items represent a change from the often
unvarying diet of religious art in other Cypriot collections.

▶▶▶ Venetian Walls   *42A3*

In the years preceding the 1570 Ottoman invasion, the
Venetians knew it was only a matter of time before the
Turks attacked. The Lusignan walls were too extensive
and puny to be defended, so the Venetians demolished
them, along with churches, palaces and houses, to build a
powerful, tighter defensive system around the old city.
All their work was in vain, as the overwhelming Ottoman
army stormed the walls and subjected Nicosia to an orgy
of looting, burning, rape and murder (an estimated 20,000
inhabitants were killed).

EQUAL SHARES
The British officers who
established the Green
Line in 1964 were scrupu-
lous in sharing out the
'Venetian walls' 11 bas-
tions, spaced equally
around the circuit. So that
neither side could
complain of a 'bastion
gap', the strongpoints
were shared out 50:50.
Caraffa, Podocataro,
Costanza, D'Avila and
Tripoli are entirely in the
Greek sector; Roccas,
Mula, Quirini, Barbaro and
Loredano in the Turkish;
and Flatro is divided
between the two in the
UN buffer zone.

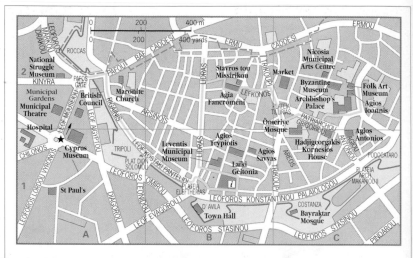

Walk

Greek Cypriot Nicosia

This walk through Greek Cypriot Nicosia includes part of the Venetian walls and the Green Line. It could take four hours if you visit the various sights mentioned, or one hour if you choose to do it quickly. The sights on the walk are covered in more detail on pages 46–55.

The Garden Café Restaurant in the **Municipal Gardens**►► is a good place for a coffee or soft drink before starting out. Cross Mouseiou Avenue to the excellent **Cyprus Museum**►►►.

Note the United Nations and Cyprus National Guard military positions near the **Venetian Walls**►►► at the **Pafos Gate**►. Although spectacular as an ensemble, some sections of the walls have lost much

of their former glory – the Tripoli bastion, for example, is now a car park.

From Plateia Eleftherias you can make a detour to **Laïki Geitonia**►► before turning into **Lidras Street**►, which ends abruptly at a roadblock just short of the Green Line. Nikokleous Street and Faneromenis Street lead, via the courtyard of **Agia Faneromeni Church**►, to Lefkonos Street. Turn right into Trikoupi Street, where the **Ömeriye Mosque**►► is open to the public. Climbing the minaret is a popular option, although soldiers on roof-mounted UN observation posts near by may forbid photography.

A short walk via Tillirias, Patriarchou Grigoriou and Isokratous streets brings you to the monumental heart of Nicosia, Plateia Archiepiskopou Kyprianou, with the **Archbishop's Palace**►► and **Agios Ioannis**►►►, as well as the **Byzantine Museum**►►►, **National Struggle Museum**► and **Folk Art Museum**►►.

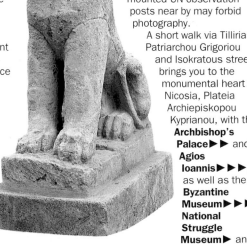

The Lion of Venice stands guard at the Cyprus Museum

Turkish Cypriot Nicosia

▶ Arabahmet Mosque 42A3

Salahi Şevket Sokağı
Open: irregularly. Admission free
Built in 1845 and named after an Ottoman governor, the
mosque stands amidst a grove of cypress trees. In the surrounding graveyard are the white marble tombstones of
various notables, including the four-times grand vizier to
the Ottoman sultans, Kamil Paşa. The mosque contains a
relic: a hair said to have come from the beard of the
Prophet Muhammad.

▶▶ Atatürk Meydanı (Atatürk Square) 42B3

Southern end of Girne Caddesi
In British times, this elegant little square was bordered by
government offices and was a centre of the island's
administration. Now it is more of a commercial hub. At its
heart stands a Venetian column, which was once topped
by a sculpted lion of St Mark. The Turks made short work
of the lion, as was only fair, seeing that they had made
equally short work of the Venetians. The British placed a
burnished copper globe atop the marble shaft, and
although the sun has long since set on the empire that it
symbolised, the globe sits there still, presumably in
default of inspiration for some other uplifting emblem.

▶ Bazaar (Belediye Pazarı) 42B3

Opposite the eastern end of Arasta Sokağı
Open: Mon–Fri 6–3, Sat 6–1
This big bazaar stands opposite the Bedesten and
Selimiye Mosque. The covered shopping area, although
more Westernised than its counterparts in Turkey, offers
the kind of bargain buys that are the unique selling point
of any bazaar.

▶ Bedesten 42B3

Opposite the eastern end of Arasta Sokağı
Generally closed
Ruined walls and arches are the most obvious attributes
of this former Orthodox cathedral of Venetian times
which to the conquering Ottomans in 1570 was well
suited to be a grain store and later a covered market
(hence the name 'Bedesten'). It
stands next to the Selimiye
Mosque, a fact that apparently
precluded its continuation as a
Christian religious foundation.
This building is a hybrid, featuring Byzantine, Gothic and
Renaissance elements from the
remains of two side-by-side
churches dating from the 12th
to the 16th centuries, and incorporating some later Ottoman
elements. Scrambling around in
the rubble is not as rewarding
as it ought to be, although there
are some interesting gargoyles
and other carved pieces still
to be seen.

*Arabahmet Mosque: its
lofty minaret rises above
a large dome*

57

DOWNHILL SLIDE
The Venetians were far
less kind to Nicosia than
the Lusignans, viewing it
primarily as a fortified
base. Even so, at the time
of the Ottoman conquest
in 1570 it was still a cosmopolitan city of 50,000
people. Three centuries
later, when the British
took over, Nicosia was all
but derelict, with fewer
than 12,000 inhabitants.

*Fruit and vegetables in
the bazaar*

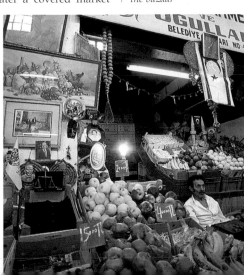

58

The tiny mosque in the courtyard of the late 16th-century Büyük Han

►► Büyük Hamam (Great Bath) 42B3

Mousa Irfan Sokağı
Open: daily 7.30am–10pm. Admission charge

There are some doubts about the origins of this building, but they don't seem important inside the marvellously evocative, steam-suffused Turkish bath. A nail hammered into the wall shows the height the Pediaios (Kanlı) River reached in 1330, when 3,000 people drowned.

If the photographs on the wall are anything to go by, the attendants are particularly adept at massaging visitors to the baths – 'Try and you feel well,' writes one satisfied client. These bone-cracking massages, a touch of the old camel-hair-glove treatment and even self-service are all available for a modest fee. Fridays are reserved exclusively for women.

►►► Büyük Han (Great Inn) 42B3

Arasta Sokağı
Closed for restoration, but you can usually stroll into the courtyard

A long-term process of restoration has been under way at this caravanserai. It was built by the Turks in 1572, just one year after they completed their conquest of Cyprus – an indication of how important such places were in the Ottoman scheme of things. The main entrance is big enough to take a loaded camel and rider; a smaller door in the wall – the 'eye of the needle' – was used either by vertically disadvantaged camels or by people only.

A caravanserai was more than a place of accommodation with parking for camels. It was a social centre, trading-place, warehouse and business services centre for merchants on the move. Inside the slab-sided edifice there is a courtyard surrounded by 68 rooms on two levels, with lodgings on the upper floor and storage space below.

Every room of the inn had a fireplace, and their hexagonal chimneys can still be seen in a line around the roof. The fort-like set-up was admirable for defensive purposes. In the middle of the court-yard stands a small octagonal mosque reached by a stairway.

Hexagonal chimneys line the Büyük Han's roof

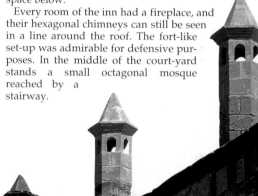

▶▶▶ Dervış Paşa Mansion

42B3

Belig Paşa Sokağı
Open: daily 9–1 and 2–5. Admission charge

Once the residence of a wealthy Turkish publisher, this mansion near the Green Line was in a disastrously dilapidated state before restoration began in 1979. Today, the mansion, dating from 1807, has had all its Ottoman grace restored and functions as the Ethnographic Museum. It can be compared in some respects to the Hadjigeorgakis Kornesios House in the Greek Cypriot sector (see page 52). Dervış Paşa was the publisher and editor of the first Turkish newspaper in Cyprus, *Zaman* (Time), which hit the streets in 1891.

Journalism could clearly be a lucrative profession in those days, and Dervış Paşa lived in style. The museum re-creates that style room by room, beginning with the servants' quarters on the arcaded ground floor and continuing upstairs to the wood-panelled luxury of his family's living quarters. Divan-lined rooms combine with display-cases featuring a myriad items, such as inkpots and pens, jewellery, ornamental scimitars, lamps, 17th-century ceramics, embroidery, clothes, a beautifully ornamented hookah and rugs.

▶▶ Green Line

42B2

Nicosia's self-inflicted wound seems little different when seen from this side of the west–east line than from the Greek Cypriot side, except that the Turkish army keeps people further away.

Otherwise there is little to choose between the two in terms of their devoted attention to barbed wire, booby traps and rifles. The workshops along the line are perhaps more interesting on this side, even if the noises and smells emanating from some make them seem like the anterooms of hell.

The **Mula bastion** of the Venetian walls overlooking the buffer zone and the UN-occupied Ledra Palace Hotel has been equipped with a little memorial park and benches. The adjacent street, Tanzimat Sokağı, boasts some fine old Ottoman houses which had been falling down until a restoration project was begun.

ELUSIVE CITY
The Bronze Age settlement of Ledra – over whose remains Nicosia was built – remains one of the most elusive ancient sites in Cyprus. Fragments of foundations and an occasional rock-cut tomb uncovered during excavation work for new buildings are all that have come to light so far.

QUIET WAY
Walking from the Selimiye Mosque along Kirlizade Sokağı, past the Lapidary Museum, the Haydarpağı Mosque (now the HP Gallery) and the Yeni Mosque, and returning by way of Eski Saray Sokağı, makes a quiet and interesting stroll through a traditional quarter of old Nicosia.

59

Quiet back streets in the city's atmospheric old Turkish quarter

The Turkish Cypriot leader does not officially exist. Despite this, he cuts a larger-than-life figure within Turkish Cyprus, where he is simply the village headman on a slightly grander scale. A settlement of the Cyprus problem will depend in great measure on his decisions.

ACID TEST

'Turkish Cypriots have to be convinced that the people...on the other side...are people who have changed in heart and who really seek peace, people who are not furthering their policy of Hellenising Cyprus by hook or by crook.'
– From an address by Rauf Denktaş to the UN Security Council.

TRYING TIMES

Denktaş was banished from Cyprus in 1964 by the government of Archbishop Makarios. In October 1967, he attempted to return clandestinely from Turkey. Because of a navigational error his boat came ashore at the wrong place and he was arrested by the Greek Cypriot police. Plans to try him for offences against the state were abandoned in the face of strong international pressure and he was re-exiled instead.

Populist approach The old harbour at Kyrenia (Girne) is one of the highlights of Cyprus. An old saloon car may occasionally be seen heading towards its elegant horse-shoe of waterfront restaurants. The harbour is a pedestrian zone, so the driver parks near by and walks the rest of the way, stopping frequently to chat or shake hands with an acquaintance. His official state limousine has been left back in Nicosia and Rauf Denktaş is doing what he likes best: being the ordinary man's politician.

It is, perhaps, as well that his friends and voters recognise Denktaş, for no government on earth, save that of Turkey, does. As president of the self-proclaimed Turkish Republic of Northern Cyprus (TRNC), Denktaş may not be exactly an international pariah but his claims on behalf of his people, by turns emotional and analytical, have elicited little response from a world community which continues to call for the withdrawal of Turkish troops and a settlement of the Cyprus problem that offers justice to the many Greek Cypriots who lost their birthright in 1974. Born in 1924 at Paphos (as it was spelt then), Denktaş himself knows the pain of separation from his roots.

School of hard knocks Denktaş's emotion comes from his experience of combating the Greek Cypriot drive for union with Greece and the traumatic experience the Turkish Cypriots suffered in their isolated, surrounded and harassed enclaves. The analysis – cold calculation some would say – comes from his lawyer's mind, trained as he was at Lincoln's Inn in London. His motives are suspected by many, although this is a common enough situation for any politician. Has he used the crisis to advance his own position? Greek Cypriots believe so and call him intransigent.

Denktaş's life is an odd mix of playing at the highest level in international politics and handling the routine affairs of a small, mainly agricultural society. Secretary-generals of the United Nations, leaders of the Security Council, NATO and various Islamic organisations have all weighed his words carefully, calculating the chances for a settlement that everyone agrees is overdue. Yet there is no movement. Denktaş is firm: if the price of a settlement is a deal that puts Turkish Cypriots back even part of the way to pre-1974 conditions, and if the penalty of being labelled intransigent is greater isolation, he will block the settlement and choose isolation every time.

Rights stuff Yet listening to Denktaş, one senses his yearning for people to understand the situation of the Turkish Cypriots. He quotes often from the American

Declaration of Independence and adds that if all men have the right to life, liberty and the pursuit of happiness, then the right to life must come first and foremost. He has proposed compromises on the territorial issue (minimal ones to be sure) involving the return of areas adjacent to the demarcation line to the Greek Cypriots. These proposals have been rejected as inadequate, yet have stirred up a hornets' nest of protest from extremist elements on his own side.

The TRNC's presidential palace within the Quirini bastion of Nicosia's Venetian walls was formerly that allocated to the vice-president of the Republic of Cyprus, a post reserved for a Turkish Cypriot under the 1960 constitution and once held by Denktaş's friend and mentor, the late Dr Fazil Kutchuk. It is a modest and informal affair for a statesman of international repute. For a photographer, however, it is quite respectable and the president is a keen amateur photographer. His subject, in art as in life, is his country and its people.

Opposite and below: members of the press watch as Rauf Denktaş leaves UN discussions in Geneva, 1974

The courtyard of the Kumarcılar Hanı (Gamblers' Inn)

SHADED SPOT
A tiny patch of ornamental garden just outside the Kyrenia Gate represents one of the few patches of greenery in the Turkish Cypriot sector of the old city. It makes a shaded place to rest, or to wait for a bus.

Modern art displayed at the converted Haydarpaşa Mosque, now the HP Gallery

▶ **Haydarpaşa Mosque** 42C3

Kirlzade Sokağı
Open: Mon–Fri 9–1 and 2–5, Sat 9–1. Admission free
The 14th-century Latin church of St Catherine joined the long parade of churches used by the Ottomans as mosques. Still an outstanding Cypriot example of the Gothic style, it has now embarked upon an interesting new career as the HP Gallery of Modern Art.

▶▶ **Kumarcılar Hanı (Gamblers' Inn)** 42B3

Asma Alti Sokağı
Courtyard accessible. Admission free
A smaller and altogether more precious – in the stylistic sense at least – cousin of the Büyük Han, this late 17th-century caravanserai is being restored and houses the Turkish Cypriot Department of Antiquities. The antiquities staff don't seem to mind people wandering into the hanı's flower-bedecked courtyard, which makes a good place of escape from a hot and busy part of the old city.

▶ **Kyrenia (Girne) Gate** 42B4

Between the Quirini bastion and Barbaro bastion of the Venetian walls
In high summer, the Kyrenia Gate in the Venetian walls, dating from 1567–70, may be the best sight in Nicosia. For it is here that the main road leads out of town to the Kyrenia (Beşparmak) Mountains and to the coast around Girne (Kyrenia), with its cooling sea breezes.

▶ **Library of Sultan Mahmut II** 42B3

Zuhtizade Sokağı
Open: Mon–Fri 9–1 and 2–5, Sat 9–1. Admission charge
A delightful little place, the domed library was built for Sultan Mahmut II and opened in 1829. It contains 1,700 books in Turkish, Arabic and Persian, including antique copies of the Koran, some as much as 700 years old.

▶ **Lapidary Museum** 42C3

Zuhtizade Sokağı
Open: irregularly; key from Library of Sultan Mahmut II. Admission free
This museum of carved stonework contains various bits and pieces salvaged from old churches and wealthy private homes, including sarcophagi, gargoyles and a pulpit. The 15th-century Venetian mansion which houses the museum is appealing in its own right.

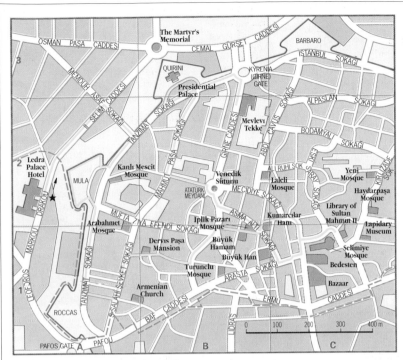

Walk

Turkish Cypriot Nicosia

Like its Greek Nicosia counterpart, this walk covers city walls, the Green Line, monuments and ordinary streets. Designed to be completed in an hour, it takes longer if you visit the places mentioned. The sights are covered in more detail on pages 57–65.

Begin at the Ledra Palace checkpoint, overlooked by the former **Ledra Palace Hotel**, now UN headquarters. Pass through the city walls, turning right on to Tanzimat Sokağı. The **Mula bastion** has been converted into a memorial park, and there is a fine view from here of the Ledra Palace Hotel and over the Green Line. Further along, once battered Ottoman-style houses have been restored.

Turn left on to Salahi Sokağı. The **Derviş Paşa Mansion▶▶▶** is situated on the right. Next, turn right along Mufta Ziya Efendi Sokağı, which leads to an area rich in historic buildings: the **Büyük Hamam▶▶**; the **Büyük Han▶▶▶**; the **Kumarcılar Hanı▶▶**; the **Bedesten▶**; the **Selimiye Mosque▶▶▶**; and the **Library of Sultan Mahmut II▶**.

Take Asma Alti Sokağı to pleasant **Atatürk Meydanı (Atatürk Square)▶▶**, the business and commercial heart of Turkish Nicosia. Mahmut Paşa Sokağı leads to the Quirini bastion, within which lies Turkish Cyprus's modest **Presidential Palace**. Near the adjacent **Kyrenia (Girne) Gate▶** is the **Mevlevi Tekke▶▶▶**, once the home of Nicosia's 'whirling dervishes' and now a museum.

The Library of Sultan Mahmut II

*Right: mementoes in the
Mevlevı Tekke, where
whirling dervishes
once danced*

►►► Mevlevı Tekke 42B3

Girne Caddesi
Open: Mon–Fri 8–1 and 2–5. Admission charge
This is the Cyprus foundation of the legendary Mevlevı
dancers, the 'whirling dervishes' who danced the mystic
rites of the Sufi sect until Kemal Atatürk banned such
practices as part of his drive to secularise Turkey in the
1920s, a policy also adopted in Cyprus. The spinning symbolised the motion of the heavenly spheres and the
dancers' stance, one palm upraised and the other pointing
downwards, man's position as a 'bridge'
between heaven and earth
with God's blessings
flowing from one to
the other. Islamic
scholars have written
approvingly of the
'saintliness' of Jalal
al-Din al-Rumi, called
Mevlana Master), the
14th-century Sufi
adept who was
responsible for estab-
lishing the rituals of
the brotherhood.

A *tekke* was a kind of Islamic
monastery and this one, founded early in the 17th
century, was the only Mevlevı monastery in Cyprus.
Located adjacent to the Kyrenia Gate, the building now
operates as the Ethnographic Museum. The disco-style
dance-floor, where the dervishes whirled themselves into
religious rapture, can still be seen, along with marvellous
old photographs which show them in action. Among the
museum's exhibits are an old HMV (His Master's Voice)
gramophone donated by the wife of President Denktaş.
More interesting historically are Koran reading-desks
inlaid with mother-of-pearl, prayer rugs, books, ornamental scimitars and traditional costumes. One wing of
the *tekke* contains the tombs of sheiks who ran the Mevlevı
order in Cyprus.

Presidential Palace 63B3

Quirini bastion of the Venetian walls
The unpretentious 'White House' of the Turkish Republic
of Northern Cyprus was formerly the vice-presidential
palace of the government of the united island. It can be
seen (but not visited) in the Quirini bastion, near the
Kyrenia Gate.

►►► Selimiye Mosque 42B3

Selimiye Sokağı
Generally open: dawn–dusk. Admission free
Formerly the 13th-century Cathedral of St Sophia, this
was one of many Latin churches which the Ottoman
Turks converted to mosques after their 1571 conquest.
The twin minarets remain the most distinctive landmarks
of the divided city, and are visible from a long way off
across the Mesaoria (Mesarya) Plain. The mosque takes its
name, though only as recently as 1954, from Sultan Selim
II, the Ottoman ruler who ordered the invasion of Cyprus.
The cathedral's foundation is dated to 1209 and its

consecration to 1326 – quite a rapid construction rate for those days, perhaps because the income of the diocese was lavished upon it to an extent that warranted a papal rebuke. Although the Cathedral of St Sophia was damaged when Nicosia was sacked by the Genoese and the Egyptian Mamelukes, subsequent repairs still left its treasury attractive enough for the Venetians to be moved by devout fervour to pocket the lot.

The mosque today seems better patronised by young Turkish army conscripts than by Turkish Cypriots. The cathedral's human and saintly images were removed, and all other Christian decoration covered up – as required by Islamic tradition. The *mihrab* (prayer niche indicating the direction of Mecca) stands in the former chapel of the Virgin Mary.

▶ Turunclu Mosque   63B1

Baf Caddesi
Open: irregularly. Admission free
Dating from 1825, this mosque has clearly taken its inspiration from the Cypriot church architecture of the period, an ironic reversal of the usual conqueror-to-conquered flow in cultural ideas. The 19th-century **Iplik Pazari Mosque** stands near by in the quarter of the same name which was once the Ottoman-era cotton market.

OFFICE BOYS
Today, the limp hand of Ottoman-inspired bureaucracy seems to taking a firm grip on the Turkish Cypriot sector. A complex of extravagant new office blocks has been built near the outskirts of northern Nicosia to house the pen-pushers in a style appropriate to their pretensions, if not to the governance of a tiny agrarian statelet.

The cool interior of the Selimiye Mosque, once a 13th-century Gothic cathedral

65

OLD SOLDIER
Before it was taken over by UNFICYP, the Ledra Palace Hotel inside the Green Line near Pafos Gate was one of the island's principal hotels, with a long and elegant colonial history. Damaged in the intercommunal fighting, it awaits the day when, perhaps, it can be returned to its original function.

COOL TIP
Few hotels in Nicosia have a swimming pool, but there are several public pools in the city. It may be wise therefore to choose a hotel near one of the municipal swimming pools, especially when you consider the intense summer heat, the dust and the sweaty tours of museums and churches that you will probably face.

Hotels are thin on the ground in Nicosia, but they do exist

Accommodation

In an island where tourism reigns supreme, Nicosia takes second place to the resort centres in terms of quantity and, to some extent, quality of hotel accommodation. Business people and a growing number of independent travellers for whom a package holiday is anathema will find that choice in the capital is limited but growing.

ROOM AT THE INN Despite the fact that Nicosia is the capital of Cyprus, hotels and other forms of tourist accommodation are not its strong suit – compared with the coastal resorts at any rate. Where the latter are knee-deep in hotels, apartment blocks and bungalows in all quality, style and price categories, Nicosia is a poor relation. Primarily this is because Nicosia is not a tourist destination. Nicosia International Airport, once the island's sole air gateway, is now a mouldering ruin, the principal base of UNFICYP (the United Nations Force in Cyprus), and a pawn in negotiations between Greek and Turkish Cypriots over the island's partition.

Nicosia is mainly a business and political destination, although it has much of history, culture and style to offer – much more than many places to which the sunseekers rush headlong. It is a real city, a real community, and offers a taste of the real Cyprus that is as genuine in its way as the most typical mountain village. (More precisely, due to the Green Line, it is two cities: one Greek, the other Turkish.) The business exists thanks to growth in tourism, agriculture, shipping and light engineering sectors; the politics arises from Cyprus's role as a focal point of international statesmanship, and the island sees a steady stream of mediators, negotiators, ambassadors and advisers doing their bit to promote so-far elusive peace and reconciliation.

NO ROOM The **Cyprus Hilton** in Greek Cypriot Nicosia is the jewel in Nicosia's crown, an assertion with which Turkish Cypriots would surely not quibble. Its star status is an indicator of the capital's place in the scheme of things, and no disrespect is intended to the Hilton, an excellent hotel, in saying so. None of the successful indigenous hotel groups have located a flagship hotel here, although the development of the Cyprus

International Conference Centre is beginning to change this, with business-oriented hotels such as the Philoxenia taking up the slack. Nicosia is, however, one of the few locations on the island where the independent traveller has much choice, all other places being given over almost entirely to package tourists.

A swimming pool to beat the heat at the top-rated Ledra Hotel

AREA CODES The choice of location in Greek Cypriot Nicosia falls into two areas: inside the Venetian walls or outside. As a rule, those inside are in older buildings, renovated or essentially rebuilt, where character of accommodation and surroundings may take the place of modern facilities and access to parking. The further downmarket you are prepared, or forced, to go, the more likely this is to be the case. Outside the old centre, the Greek half of Nicosia fades away, through the business and commercial district, into suburbs for which 'characterless' is a charitable description. On the whole, hotels in this part of town share this lack of character but compensate with more modern facilities and easier access.

Turkish Cypriot Nicosia does not have the same suburban problem, but then it does not have many hotels in the first place. In this respect it shares Turkish Cyprus's less developed tourist infrastructure, which is partly attributable to the United Nations boycott that followed the 1974 conflict. The Saray Hotel is Turkish Cypriot Nicosia's nearest equivalent to the Hilton, while mid-range hotels are equally thin on the ground. Cyprus is, however, a popular destination with mainland Turks, and the hotels that cater for them are usually characterful, friendly and cheap.

The Nicosia Hilton is generally considered to be the capital's best hotel

LOCAL FLAVOUR

Meze is king of Cyprus cuisine, although not all restaurants serve it in the laid-back, stay-all-night-if-you-want style that makes its mosaic of little dishes a joy to experience. Those restaurants which serve the best *meze* are often unencouraging, though rarely actively discouraging, from the tourist's point of view. In such places, the visitor's attitude is all-important – if you do not act like a rich, brash tourist you may well be accepted.

Ice-cream offers a welcome antidote to the sweltering summer heat

Food and drink

Nicosia's eateries are mostly designed to satisfy the city's own diners, with few of the foreigner-oriented places that crowd the coastal resorts. This means that genuine local taste, in all price ranges, is easier to find. Yet visitors who require a tourist diet can find menus to fill the bill.

FAST FOOD As befits an industrious city, Nicosia is full of fast-food eateries designed to get people back to work quickly with something filling under their belts. This may not sound appetising, but in fact it helps visitors enjoy Nicosia's status as a 'genuine' Cypriot town. Ordinary Cypriots pop into the snack-bars for an instant coffee, which goes under the generic name 'Nescafé'; as brewed in these bars, the resulting beverage is an odds-on favourite for the accolade of 'world's worst-tasting coffee'. As an accompaniment to the coffee, your choice may be a cheese-filled pie or a cheese-and-ham 'toastie', often using the slightly bitter *halloumi* cheese.

On a more substantial level, there are cafés, the most typical being those that serve lunch to workers from the many small workshops along the Green Line. The cafés are a largely unused resource as far as most tourists are concerned, because they tend to look rather rough and ready. The cooking is, however, simple, nourishing and tasty, the atmosphere convivial and the prices user-friendly.

REAL DISHES In several distinctive areas of the old city upmarket restaurants are concentrated in mutual-support enclaves, with a few individual gems scattered at random amongst them. The most important of these areas as far as the visitor is concerned is **Laïki Geitonia**, an atmospheric warren of cobbled streets mostly given over to boutiques and souvenir shops, but with an extensive alfresco restaurant quarter at its heart. Lunch is a popular time here, yet it is in the evening, when Laïki Geitonia glows with lantern-and-candle charm, that the ambience and the food are at their best.

Nicosians can be sniffy about Laïki Geitonia, seeing it as a tourist trap. The 'in' crowd are more likely to head for the **Famagusta Gate**, where off-beat bars and cafés mingle with restaurants. The latter are

Small eateries with terraces are common

smarter and tend to be more expensive than average, yet not to the extent of overcharging customers for the privilege of resting on their hallowed seats. This is dining out with a touch of Cypriot style, in streets that rub shoulders with the Green Line to lend an air of unreality to the proceedings. Elsewhere, in suburbs like **Egkomi** and **Strovolos,** and in Lebanese and Armenian restaurants, as well as Indian and Chinese, there are enough variations in taste to be going on with if the local cuisine palls.

TURKISH TASTE The Turkish Cypriot zone is similar in many respects to the Greek Cypriot, although there are fewer restaurants and less choice. The snack-bar end of the market is complemented by a greater number of shish kebab outlets, and the succulent smell of grilling lamb can be savoured in the air as well as tasted at the counter. Along the Green Line runs a string of working-class cafés whose attributes perfectly complement those a few metres – and a world – away on the other side. Freshly pressed fruit juice makes a wonderfully thirst-quenching drink on a typically sultry day, and kiosks dispense masses of the stuff.

Adjacent to the Selimiye Mosque and Bedesten are some tourist-oriented open-air restaurants little different from those of Laïki Geitonia in the Greek Cypriot sector. These establishments are clean and friendly, and the atmosphere bustling and colourful; the food has not been too far compromised to cater for international taste. On the downside, however, this is a miniature tourist ghetto, leavened with a handful of well-dressed Turkish Cypriots, which won't necessarily appeal to those seeking genuine Turkish Cypriot taste.

HOME COOKING
The best introduction to Cypriot cuisine may come if you are lucky enough to be invited to a Cypriot's home for dinner. Fresh fruit and vegetables from the market are sure to be on the menu, as are a few 'secret' recipes, handed down from mother to daughter in the way of old village traditions.

Coffee and water, the essential ingredients of a quick break

Shopping

Although not exactly world renowned for its shopping possibilities, Nicosia is the principal location in Cyprus for this popular activity.

NO PARADISE Nicosia cannot in any way be described as a chic European shopping capital, but style is available, albeit thin on the ground. Limassol and Kyrenia (Girne) offer tough competition when it comes to price tags and the range of goods available, but Nicosia does represent the island's main concentration of shops and markets.

In Greek Cypriot Nicosia, the most important shopping areas are Lidras Street and Onasagorou Street within the city walls; both are well known for their department stores, clothing and footwear outlets, as well as for electrical goods. The adjacent tourist-oriented Laïki Geitonia district is the place for souvenirs of all kinds, from postcards and key-rings to hand-made lace and jewellery. Archiepiskopou Makariou III Avenue, outside the Venetian walls, is another principal shopping artery, noted for its department stores, while some side-streets leading off it are the places for chic speciality stores.

CRAFT VIRTUES Handicrafts are big business, pushing the finest products from traditional centres in the hinterland. The excellent **Cyprus Handicraft Service** at 186 Athalassis Avenue in the city's southern outskirts gives

TOP PEOPLE'S CATALOGUE
Some famous shoppers have taken advantage of Cyprus's reputation for quality products in the past: King Agamemnon, for example, whom Homer records in the *Iliad* as wearing a cuirass of Cypriot copper; and Alexander the Great, whose favourite sword was made in Cyprus. Neither of them is known to have visited the island, however, so they must have done their shopping by mail-order.

Scent of a bargain at an antiques shop in the Turkish sector

an excellent introduction to the various handicraft types and styles, all under one roof, as well as offering the chance to buy examples in its shop. This is far from being the only outlet, and prices are likely to be keener in shops where commercial considerations take precedence over preserving threatened folk arts – such as the **Craft Box** (430 Stasikratous Street). Products recognised by the Cyprus Handicraft Service are labelled 'CHS' and are also on sale at centres in Limassol, Larnaka and Pafos.

Pots such as these may tempt the souvenir-hunter

71

Among craft-produced fabrics to watch out for are the unsurpassed hand-made Lefkara lace, or *lefkaritika*; *pafitika* loom embroidery; *lefkonika* towels, aprons and placemats; *alatjia* silky-smooth striped cotton; and hand-crocheted lace and wool. Pottery from Kornos and Foini is particularly fine, although the grand traditional clay pots called *pitharia* are probably on the large side for souvenirs. Leatherwork has a diminished range, but handbags and jackets are good value. Copper is no longer commonplace, but exquisite ornaments and even cooking pots can still be found. Gourds are transformed into plant-pots, vases, carafes and the like, while reeds are employed for basket-weaving and light furnishings. Finally, Cypriot forests provide the basic raw material for an exhaustive range of wood-carvings.

ORIENTAL COOL Turkish Cypriot Nicosia boasts many of the same products, although sales are on a smaller scale and include items with a more oriental touch, such as *hookahs* and *kilims*. Visitors used to Turkey, where haggling is a way of life, will discover that it is not so in Turkish Cyprus, even in the bazaars; this is just one of many ways in which Turkish Cypriots are more European than their cousins on the mainland. Shops in the Turkish sector are somewhat scattered, although there is an upmarket enclave around Atatürk Meydanı and a more popular one adjacent to the Selimiye Mosque in the centre, while outlying streets such as Mehmet Akif Caddesi have modern shops.

Both parts of the divided city share a mirror-image district of dingy old workshops that run alongside the Green Line. Some of these are craft workshops which produce a variety of metal and woodwork items to order.

MARKET PLACES
Markets in Nicosia are neither as numerous nor as extensive as Cyprus's vast range of fresh products and handicrafts would suggest. Yet the weekly fruit and vegetable market and the permanent markets and bazaars on both sides of the Green Line are sources of unrivalled value as well as much local colour.

A fruit-seller offers his wares at the Municipal Market

CONSUMING NIGHTLIFE

The main source of nightlife entertainment for most Nicosians is dining out, particularly at one of their own traditional and lively tavernas, where a major part of the enjoyment is the vigorous hubbub of conversation. Visitors who ignore or downplay this factor are certain to miss much of the essential atmosphere of the city.

Drama at the Nicosia Theatre Festival

Nightlife

Compared with the tourist resorts, nightlife in Nicosia is more scattered and less easily defined. In compensation, it is also less artificial, appealing much more to local people than to hyped-up holidaymakers. In the Greek Cypriot sector especially, there is some of the exuberance and style appropriate to a capital city.

GETTING THE RHYTHM The Greek Cypriot half of Nicosia works hard and plays fairly hard as well. Friday is the big release, when the discos, cafés and restaurants start buzzing for the weekend; Saturday is the weekend at its hottest; by Sunday, the spirit is still willing though the flesh has grown weak; on Monday, people go out, but more from a sense of duty than real enthusiasm; Tuesday is reserved for rest and recuperation; everyone perks up a bit on Wednesday and maybe makes a brief mid-week foray; and Thursday is taken up by more R&R. Nightlife in Nicosia follows the pattern of the city's differences from the coastal resorts in other regards, with tourist-oriented attractions almost non-existent and the emphasis firmly on what appeals to Greek Cypriot and permanent residents' sensibilities.

Dancing is the big diversion, with a sharp divide between discos and nightclubs in terms of age. The discos are filled with sultry and stylish fashion-demons who, during the day, are ordinary fresh-faced schoolchildren. The nightclubs, on the other hand, form a kind of hip senior citizens' home for the over-19s, where live music alternates with disco and traditional Greek and oriental favourites. As in other cities, the 'in' places come and go with distressing ease, responding to the mysterious 'word on the street' which either confers life or sanctions death.

LAID BACK More restrained entertainment is on offer to those that seek it. The **Municipal Theatre** on Mouseiou Street is an elegant place where classical and modern plays in both Greek and English are performed.

Experimental theatre often takes place at the **Famagusta Gate Cultural Centre**, while the **British Council** on Mousieou Avenue features chamber music and other events. The city's seven cinemas feature international films, mostly American but also Greek and other European productions, in their original soundtrack, with Greek subtitles where appropriate; the **American Center** on Omirou Avenue occasionally also has a film show. As well as the Cultural Centre, the Famagusta Gate has an adjacent enclave of trendy cafés, some with live music, which are favoured places with the city's smart set and keep going well into the wee small hours.

INFORMATION SOURCES Information on all the town's entertainment can be found in the Cyprus Tourism Organisation's free *Monthly Events* and from the free *Nicosia This Month*, produced by the municipality. All are available from tourist offices and usually from hotels, conference centres and tour operators. During the summer tourist season, Cyprus Broadcasting Corporation (CyBC) broadcasts a programme on 498m, *Welcome to Cyprus*, in English, French and German, giving a news summary and including 'what's on' information.

Traditional music is still popular, especially as an accompaniment to eating out

73

QUIETER TIME Turkish Cypriot Nicosia is altogether more restrained, so much so that many Nicosians decamp to nearby Kyrenia (Girne) at the coast for the town's discos, nightclubs, casinos and cafés, and for the all-important 'atmosphere' that makes going out at night more than a chore (drivers should be careful about drink-driving on such excursions).

Those who stay in the capital are more likely to concentrate on going out for a meal, although the restaurant may well feature some live music, even if only from a singer with a synthesiser, and, at weekends, possibly a belly dancer. The **Saray Hotel** does, however, have a casino and also features live music performances.

FUEL FOR DANCING
Greek Cypriot Nicosia's nightclubs are usually crowded by 10pm, although the action may not start for an hour or so after this. They play their share of Western disco music, but the real moments of audience participation come when Cypriot and Greek music, both modern and traditional, are performed.

Public transport is generally good, but a moped or bicycle will be ideal for getting through old Nicosia's cramped backstreets

GOOD DIRECTIONS
Guided walking tours of historic Nicosia (in the Greek Cypriot zone) leave from the Tourist Information Office on Aischylou Street in the Laïki Geitonia quarter. These offer a good introduction to the city, with access to churches which are otherwise frequently locked, and with a well-informed and enthusiastic commentary. Leaflets giving timetables and itineraries are available from the office.

Practical points

One half of Nicosia is exclusively Greek Cypriot, the other Turkish Cypriot. But within each of the two zones there is the additional contrast between the old city, inside the Venetian walls, and the modern business and residential districts.

FLYING IN Nicosia International Airport is closed and occupied by the United Nations. Its reopening is a permanent possibility as part of UN-sponsored 'confidence-building measures', but nothing has happened since 1974. Meanwhile, Greek Cypriot Nicosia is served by Larnaka International Airport, about an hour away by road; and Turkish Cypriot Nicosia by Ercan International Airport. The latter is not recognised by the International Air Transport Association (IATA), is served only by Turkish and Turkish Cypriot airlines, and is considered an illegal port of entry by the Greek Cypriot authorities.

GREEN LINE The main stumbling-block to getting around is the UN buffer zone, which in Nicosia is called the Green Line and which separates the Greek Cypriot sector in the south from the Turkish Cypriot in the north. The only crossing-point from the Greek Cypriot to the Turkish Cypriot sector is for visitors who pass through on foot before 2pm and who return by 5.30pm on a one-day permit issued at the Ledra Palace Hotel. This route is occasionally closed and, apart from returning permit-holders, movement is not permitted from the Turkish Cypriot sector to the Greek Cypriot. Movement within the zones, except immediately adjacent to the line, is otherwise unaffected.

PHOTOGRAPHY Taking pictures of the Green Line, the personnel and installations of the UN, the Greek Cypriot National Guard and the Turkish army is strictly forbidden. This restriction may be extended to adjacent points of interest.

ON FOOT Old Nicosia, within the Venetian walls, is a small and not frantically busy place, so walking is a good way to get around. The only proviso to this is that it can get desperately hot, particularly when the sun is overhead and there is less chance of 'shadow-hopping' from point to point. Outside the walls, walking can be a traffic-tormented, heat-infested nightmare, particularly as distances are great and points of interest few and far between.

CAR The going by car, outside the walls, is a lot easier than it looks, although the one-way system may call for annoyingly roundabout routes to one's destination. Nicosian drivers are relatively tolerant of tourists driving the distinctive hired cars with their red licence-plates and an initial letter 'Z', though if irritated by too much indecision their response can be explosive. Parking ought to be a problem, given the busy traffic and lack of spaces, but Nicosians 'solve' the problem by parking wherever they like, whatever the consequences. Driving is on the left in both sectors.

TAXIS These are fairly cheap and efficient, either booked in advance by telephone or flagged down from one of the taxi ranks scattered around the centre. In addition, a small group of tourists can hire a taxi for the day to tour either half of the divided city. This is both cost-effective and relaxing, with the added benefit that you will have a guide, who will normally speak English at least.

BUSES Metropolitan bus services in both sectors are adequate. Anyone visiting Nicosia for a short time will be unlikely to unravel the routing and timetable complexities sufficiently for them to be useful, although services to and from the city centre for visitors staying at an outlying hotel may prove convenient. In the Greek Cypriot sector, a free service on yellow buses is available around the old town and local environs. The main bus stations are at Dionysos Solomos Square and outside the Costanza bastion. In the Turkish Cypriot sector, the principal interchange point for buses is at the Kyrenia (Girne) Gate.

Taxis are plentiful, metered and not too expensive

PEOPLE MOVERS
Anyone planning to stay in the city for an extended period may find it worthwhile to invest in a moped, which offers a fast and efficient way of getting around, and can be sold at the end of one's stay. Of course, a bicycle is equally effective and more environmentally friendly, although it is harder on the legs.

The main highway from Nicosia is the one that leads out to the coastal resorts

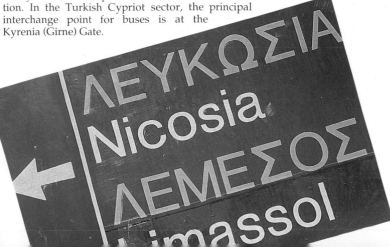

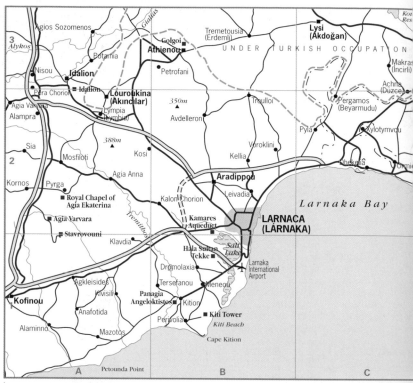

THE SOUTHEAST From Nicosia, Cyprus's main highway runs southwards, skirting the edge of the Mesaoria (Mesarya) Plain, a fast track to the bustling resorts that line the island's southern shore. In the past, before partition, this was the approach most holidaymakers would have taken.

Based on the gateway city of Larnaka, the southeast region covers a great arc of coastline, and a wedge of hilly country that can be considered as foothills of the Troodos Mountains – if only because the Troodos are so dominating that any hills within reach can be so considered. That 'within reach' helps define an important characteristic of the southeast: it is important to understand that not everywhere that is visible is within reach.

The region is unnaturally cramped on its eastern flank, but this has nothing to do with geography even if it is a physical reality on the ground. Instead, the legacy of the Turkish invasion in 1974 presses hard on this corner of the island.

The long-running division between Greek and Turkish Cyprus is ever present in the demarcation line against which the area abuts, with blue-helmeted United Nations forces holding the neutral ground between both sides' fortified positions.

Villages have expanded rapidly in the past 20 years or so, not just because of the pressure of the burgeoning tourist industry but also to accommodate all of the Greek Cypriot refugees who poured in from the Turkish zone after the invasion.

Left: looking out from the quiet, cloistered courtyard of the 16th-century Agia Napa Monastery

The Southeast

SUNNY STORY
The 3,300 hours of sunshine per year which attract people to beach resorts such as Nissi Bay and Protaras also provide them and the local population with free hot water. Solar heating systems on the roofs of Cypriot houses are almost universal, and the companies making them have established lucrative export markets in the Middle East. In summer the water can be heated to 84°C, a temperature that may fall to 35°C in winter.

ON THE BEACH From a point near the demarcation line at Deryneia, it is possible to look across to the hotel blocks and beaches of Famagusta (Gazimağusa), tantalisingly close but out of reach. Yet the contradictions of Cyprus are such that one of the Mediterranean's most vigorous beach-holiday resorts is located only a few kilometres away. Agia Napa is as artificial a construction as can be. It exists purely and simply to offer the place of escape that attracts many tourists to Cyprus in the first place – and it does so with total commitment and some style.

Even in the resort's immediate surroundings, however, life goes on much as it did in the past. This is the Kokkinochoria, or 'red villages' country, whose vivid rust-coloured soil can produce no fewer than three potato crops every year so long as it is well irrigated, which it is. Moving away from the thin commercial carapace along the shore is to move into a different kind of Cyprus.

It would be hard to get further from traditional Cyprus than in the British Sovereign Base Area at Dhekelia, with its streets named after the fields of past military glory such as Waterloo. The base, whose boundary runs from Larnaka Bay to the UN-patrolled demarcation line, permits no commercial development. Military development is something else, of course, and although more than half the area of the base is freely accessible, part of the coastline here is not.

OUT FROM LARNAKA In Larnaka, the southeast boasts a fast-expanding small city, based mainly on Cyprus's busiest airport, which serves the coast from Agia Napa to Limassol and inland to Nicosia. Larnaka contains more elements of intrinsic interest than Limassol, as well as being conveniently located for exploring the coastline and the line of hills that lies between it and Nicosia.

Unlike the Agia Napa area, the shoreline from Cape Kition west as far as Governor's Beach is scarcely developed, and there are some stretches of wild and uninhabited coast. This has as much to do with the lack of golden sands hereabouts as with any commitment to conservation, but the effect is the same for anyone in search of peace and quiet.

Between the main motorways linking Limassol, Larnaka and Nicosia lies a triangular 'island' of land, an island whose shores are made of tarmacadam. This triangle is an intriguingly isolated piece of countryside. There are a few points of tourist interest – Agia Ekaterina Chapel and Stavrovouni Monastery (see page 96), for example – and only a handful of villages. Mostly the dusty trails lead seemingly nowhere and, in the scorching heat of summer, the deserted landscape takes on an almost lunar quality. In a way this area encapsulates all that is southeast Cyprus: you can have the fast track if you want it, but the alternative is never far away.

MARCH OF PROGRESS
The red soil of the Kokkinochoria ('red villages') district around Agia Napa would be less rich were it not for constant irrigation. In the past, water was brought up from underground aquifers with the help of windmills, many of which still dot the landscape. Nowadays, diesel-powered pumps do the work, but windmills are increasingly being restored and brought back into service.

Time to relax on a spectacularly sited bench overlooking Cape Gkreko

The Southeast

DRIVER'S BLUES

Travelling from Nicosia to Agia Napa by the quickest route can be a frustrating experience. The motorway allows for rapid transit most of the way, but the need for concentration leaves little opportunity for admiring the countryside. Beyond the British base at Dhekelia, it becomes a fast, busy two-lane road passing occasionally through narrow village streets, and once again there is little opportunity for admiring the scenery. All in all it's better to be a passenger than a driver.

Agia Napa Monastery: an oasis of calm in the busy resort

After a hard day's sunbathing, Agia Napa knows how to let its hair down

▶▶ Agia Napa   77E2

What Agia Napa lacks in cool sophistication – and it lacks a lot – it more than makes up for in its single-minded commitment to being a successful holiday resort, with all that implies in terms of beaches, cafés, shops, discos and the like. The resort's own beaches, which lie on either side of the harbour and incorporate a cluster of sea caves, are complemented by those of nearby Nissi Beach and Makronisos. All are thick with sunbathers at peak times.

One point of historical interest in Agia Napa is a monastery, to which the town clings like a poor relation hoarding an inherited jewel.

However, it is not to see Byzantine monasteries that people go to Agia Napa. The formerly deserted shoreline in and around the town has become Cyprus's holiday playground *par excellence*, as the tourist industry reacted to the loss of some of its best resorts after the 1974 invasion.

Although overshadowed by tour boats and private yachts, the harbour and marina retain elements of local colour in the fishing boats that discharge their marine cargoes here. Glass-bottom and other tour boats leave from here for cruises in the direction of Cape Gkreko and Larnaka. Just behind the harbour, the tiny waterfront chapel of **Agios Georgios** now looks sadly out of place.

The new **Municipal Museum of Marine Life**►► (25 Agias Mavris street, tel: 03 723409. *Open* Mon–Wed and Fri–Sat 9–2, Thu 3–6. *Admission charge*) has displays and dioramas of sea life off Cyprus's shores.

►► Agia Napa Monastery 77E2
Adjacent to Seferi Square
Open: daily dawn–dusk. Admission free
This 16th-century monastery and its Orthodox church were once all there was to Agia Napa. Now they look lost, engulfed and surrounded by the glitter of the new resort.

► Agia Thekla 77D2
This small whitewashed chapel beside the sea a few kilometres west of the busy Nissi Bay resort area overlooks another, but smaller, tourist beach. Easily missed, however, is the original chapel hewn into the rockface beside the beach near by, its gloomy interior and a few icons illuminated by a single oil lamp. The quiet, rough road that runs between the sea and the main highway along this section of the coast makes a fine place for a walk or a bicycle tour.

► Agioi Anargyroi 77E2
Another of the small, whitewashed chapels scattered at intervals along this stretch of coastline, the building makes a nice visual contrast with the deep blue of the sea. Agioi Anargyroi's main claim to fame is that it lies at the end of a shaded pathway and represents one of the few easily accessible points of interest that can persuade sunbathers to take a break from the beach.

►► Cape Gkreko 77E1
Forming the sharp point of a peninsula southeast of Agia Napa, the cape's tip is unfortunately out of bounds because of the presence of military and civilian radio installations. The surrounding waters are excellent for snorkelling and scuba-diving, while adjacent cliffs provide a dramatic view of the rugged coastline in both directions. Dirt-bike riders favour some of the testing trails in the area of the cape, and walkers enjoy the paths through Cape Gkreko Forest Park.

► Deryneia 77D2
This village lies so close to the demarcation line that it even has a café with a viewpoint from where pictures can be taken (this is usually forbidden anywhere near the line) of the UN observation towers and the fortified military positions of either side, with Famagusta (Gazimağusa) and its resort suburb of Varosha (Maraş) beyond. Deryneia is blessed with a modern Orthodox church of such extravagant size and domed magnificence that it seems to have been built to send some kind of religious or political message to the Turkish Cypriots across the way.

ODD ATTRACTION
Boat trips leave from Agia Napa bound for various scenic attractions along the coast. The strangest of these trips goes around Cape Gkreko and along the coast towards Varosha (Maraş), a resort suburb of Famagusta (Gazimağusa) that has been entirely abandoned for more than 25 years (see page 249). The UN buffer zone extends out to sea, so the boats cannot get too close, but the sight of the town's crumbling holiday hotels and apartment blocks is still astonishing. (In recent years, a few private hire boats have reportedly been fired upon from the Turkish side after straying too close.)

81

RADIO WAVES
A transmitter of Radio Monte Carlo stands beside the sea on the point of Cape Gkreko, relaying French-language programmes to the Middle East.

Whether to swim in the azure waters of the sea or stick to the hotel swimming pool?

Hala Sultan Tekke: a little piece of Arabia on the shores of Larnaka's Salt Lake

▶ **Dhekelia** 76C2

This is the heart of the British Sovereign Base Area (one of two on the island), which, among other things, is busily employed in snooping on telecommunications traffic in the Middle East. As with Akrotiri in the west, the actual extent of military installations (which remain inaccessible to the public) is less than half of the total base area, with the remainder freely accessible. Police checkpoints on the road at either end and an armed sentry at the main base entrance are usually the only obvious formalities.

▶▶▶ **Hala Sultan Tekke** 76B1

Open: summer 9–5.30; winter 9–5. Admission free, but a donation is expected

Tucked away in a grove of palm trees on the shore of Larnaka's Salt Lake a few kilometres from the sea, the mosque is a rare monument to the period of Arab raids and conquests during the 7th and 8th centuries AD. The sight of its dome and minarets sets one's sense of place out of joint, as if a scene from The *Arabian Nights* had been shipped across the sea and landed in the Cypriot country-side. The interior of the dome is decorated with medallions inscribed with the names of Allah, Muhammad and the first six caliphs of Islam: Abu Bakr, Umar, Uthman, Ali, Hussein and Hassan.

Although the mosque dates from the early 19th century, it enfolds the tomb of the Hala Sultan, also known as Umm Haram, an aunt of the Prophet Muhammad, who died here in AD 649 (year 28 of the Islamic calendar) after falling from her mule. Her sepulchre, covered by green cloths of mourning, can also be visited. The stone sur-mounting it is said to have flown miraculously from Mount Sinai in Egypt to protect the tomb, and Muslim ships sailing within view of the shrine would dip their colours in honour of the illustrious lady.

PILGRIM'S WAY

The Hala Sultan Tekke on the shores of Larnaka's Salt Lake is reputed by Cypriots to be the third most important shrine of Islam, after the mosques of Mecca and Jerusalem. During important Islamic festivals it becomes a place of pilgrimage for Muslims travelling from far and wide.

The grandmother of King Hussein of Jordan, who had died in exile in Cyprus in 1929, is also entombed in the same mosque.

▶▶▶ Kition 76B1

This attractive but otherwise ordinary village west of Larnaka boasts one remarkable monument in its centre, as well as several points of interest in the nearby country-side, all of which are worth a detour. Fishing for trout is allowed with a permit in the small freshwater **Kition Lake▶** a few kilometres north of the village, where the Tremithos river has been dammed as part of Cyprus's extensive water-retention programme.

Somewhat misleadingly named, **Kiti Tower▶** is not actually in the village of Kition itself but beside the sea at rugged Cape Kition, several kilometres distant. The tower is a simple, fortified stone observation post built by the Venetians as part of their vain attempt to fend off an expected invasion of Cyprus by the Ottoman Turks in the 16th century. A lighthouse overlooks the sea and the steep cliffs along this coast, which is dotted with small beaches.

In addition to its more or less routine – for Cyprus, that is – panoply of murals, icons and gilt iconostasis, the church of **Panagia Angeloktistos (Our Lady 'Built by the Angels')▶▶▶** (tel: 04-424646. *Open* Mon–Sat 8–12 and 2–5, Sun 8–12 and 2–4. *Admission free*), rebuilt in the 12th century on the foundations of a 5th-century church, has a beautiful mosaic in the domed roof of the semicircular apse behind the iconostasis. The mosaic depicts the Virgin Mary carrying the infant Jesus and flanked by the Archangels Gabriel and Michael. The style and workman-ship of the mosaic, with its tiny tesserae of coloured and precious stones, stand elegant comparison to the 6th-cen-tury mosaics of the Emperor Justinian, Empress Theodora and the Byzantine court at Ravenna in Italy.

It seems certain that the Panagia Angeloktistos mosaic was the work of an imperial craftsman sent from Constantinople at a time when Byzantine mosaic art was at its height. And therein lies a mystery: why are there not more mosaics of this calibre in Cyprus, given the wealth and influence of the Cypriot church at that time?

MOSAIC PATTERNS
It is interesting to compare the mosaics of Panagia Angeloktistos with those of the earlier Roman period found at Pafos. In both cases, the motivation is religious – the one Christian and the other pagan – but although the level of craftsmanship is comparable, the styles differ vastly.

FROM RUSSIA WITH CASH
Cyprus's tourist industry is experiencing a boom in visitors from Russia, and although numbers have dipped since Russia's 1998 economic crisis, more than 100,000 arrive every year. Shopping is a popular pastime, the visi-tors spend thousands of Cyprus pounds, and pay in cash – even for seaside villas in the CY£100,000 range. Questions arise as to the origins of this largesse, but few Cypriots ask them too loudly.

83

The ornately decorated iconostasis at Panagia Angeloktistos church in Kition

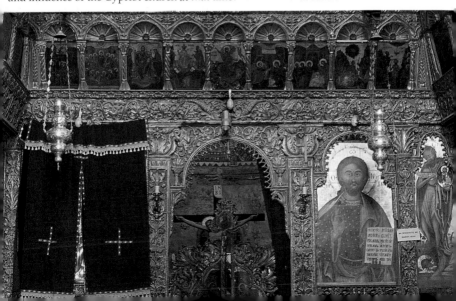

Cyprus has no shortage of that essential ingredient for marine sports: sea water. No point on the island is much more than an hour's drive from the sea, a sea that is warm and of a blue so inviting as to encourage even the most timid.

POINT OF VIEW
Glass-bottom boats, which sail from harbours in or near all the main resorts, offer certain undeniable advantages over scuba-diving when it comes to observing the local marine life: even inexperienced practitioners can breathe without the aid of cumber-some mechanical devices; it is possible to share observational data in real time (in other words, chat) with one's companions; and the picnic sandwiches don't get soggy – unless it rains of course!

The term 'marine sports', just about all of which are prac-tised around the island's shores covers a multitude of sins. Simplest of all is swimming at the beach, and even the most determined of land-bound sunworshippers may make a discovery that changes their whole vacation: the sea is warm! From there the sky's the limit.

Adventure lines At all popular beaches a line of coloured buoys parallel to the shore indicates the safe-bathing area, which power-boats are not allowed to enter and which is watched over by lifeguards. On the far side of this line lies adventure. There are enough companies eager to introduce beginners to sailing, paragliding, water-skiing, jet-skiing and windsurfing. None of these activities is exactly cheap, but cost has to be weighed against exhilaration. Experienced practitioners will find the condi-tions for these sports enjoyable, if not overly challenging. Strangely enough, sea-kayaking is not common, even though conditions appear perfect for it.

Paragliding is common and may seem risky, but it is quite safe and a satisfying experience to soar high above the crowded beaches and turquoise sea.

Snorkelling and scuba-diving are popular, thanks to crystal-clear waters and rocky sections of coastline. Submarine cliffs and valleys, coral colonies, sea-anemones and sponges, fish and sea-shells in exotic colours offer plenty of interest for divers, but note that it is illegal to remove antiquities and sponges from the seabed. Despite all this, the island unfortunately is no scuba-diving paradise in terms of the range of marine life that can be encountered.

Windsurf rigs lined up and ready to go at Nissi Beach

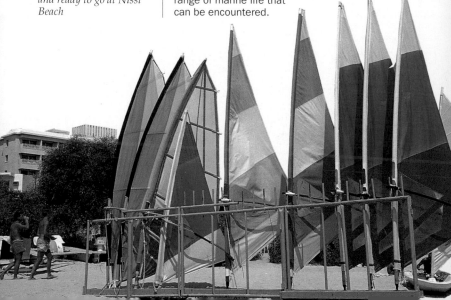

Sharks may occasionally be seen but rarely come inshore, and although some 260 different fish species frequent the waters off Cyprus, they do so only in low numbers.

Amateur sportsfishing is limited due to the lack of big game fish, although it is possible to go out on a commercial swordfishing boat. Spear-fishing, angling, and fishing with vertical lines or trolling lines with a maximum of 100 hooks and with up to three fish-traps are the only permitted sea-fishing methods; nets and other commercial gear are not allowed. Sea bream, grouper, amberjack and sea perch are among the species that can legally be caught. A permit issued by Fisheries Department district offices (see page 105) is required for spear-fishing with an aqualung, and will only be issued to certified divers.

Sporting zones The main marine sports locations are: Agia Napa–Protaras; along Larnaka Bay; around Limassol and Lady's Mile Beach, where windsurfing is particularly good; at Pafos and Coral Bay; the Polis–Latsi area; Kyrenia (Girne) and Famagusta (Gazimağusa). The waters off the Karpas (Karpaz) Peninsula are a maritime exclusion zone, and there are other restricted areas along the Turkish Cypriot coastline.

For most people, the areas listed above will offer all the possibilities they need during a two- or three-week holiday. Serious practitioners may wish to use a four-wheel-drive vehicle to reach the many isolated coves. An alternative route to out-of-the-way places is by speedboat. These can be hired at all the main resorts without the need for a special licence, or, you can hire a fishing boat with skipper. Even if you only want to swim *au naturel* in some deserted bay, having your own speedboat for a day is the ideal way of getting there.

85

GOING UNDER
There are numerous sub-aqua clubs, diving centres and underwater safari companies at the principal resort areas: Agia Napa–Protaras, Larnaka, Limassol, Polis–Latsi, Pafos, Kyrenia (Girne) and Famagusta (Gazimağusa). Tuition and guided tours are widely available. Further information is available from the **Cyprus Federation of Underwater Activities** (a member of the World Federation of Underwater Activities), PO Box 1503, Nicosia, tel: 02-454647.

Paragliding off the beach at Agia Napa

76B2

▶▶ Larnaka

LIVING LEGEND
The French city of Marseille also claims Lazarus as a former bishop in competition with Larnaka. Either possibility would surely make him the most widely travelled former corpse in antiquity.

When Nicosia International Airport was closed by the Turkish attack of 1974, Larnaka developed as Cyprus's main international gateway. Partly as a result of this, the city of 60,000 inhabitants has become an important tourist destination in its own right. It could be argued that its intrinsic merits do not entirely justify this, but Larnaka has numerous points of interest and an atmospheric old town that compensate for the haphazard development which has crowded in on the city. In addition, Larnaka is well situated as a base for exploring the coast and the eastern reaches of the Troodos Mountains, and is less than an hour by road from Nicosia.

IN THE CENTRE Agios Lazaros (Church of St Lazarus)▶▶
(Agiou Lazarou Square. *Open* Apr–Aug Mon–Sat 8–12.30 and 2.30–5. *Admission free*) is a cathedral-like 17th-century Orthodox church with a fabulous gilt iconostasis, a fabulously ugly chandelier and a soaring baroque tower. It is best known for its association with that Lazarus who, as the New Testament declares, was raised from the dead by Jesus. The next time Lazarus died he was not so lucky, and legend has it that he was buried in Larnaka (at that time called Kition). The original church was built here when the saint's supposed sepulchre was discovered in the 9th century. The sepulchre can still be seen, but the saint's remains were moved to Constantinople by the Emperor Leo VI.

In the grounds of the church is a small **Byzantine Museum** (tel: 04-652489. *Open* summer Mon–Fri 8.30–1

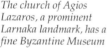

86

The church of Agios Lazaros, a prominent Larnaka landmark, has a fine Byzantine Museum

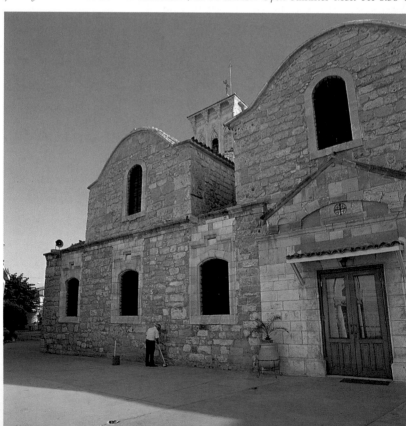

Larnaka's extensive beach runs alongside the seafront promenade

and 4–6; winter Mon–Fri 8.30–1 and 2.30–5. *Admission charge*), in which are gathered some outstanding examples of ecclesiastical art: icons, Bibles, chalices, bishops' mitres and robes. Every year on the feast day of St Lazarus, eight days before the Greek Orthodox Easter, the saint's icon is paraded through the town.

The 16th-century **Al-Kebir Mosque**►► (*Open* daily. *Admission free*, but donation expected), which is still in use) is an interesting place to visit if only to compare the extreme simplicity of its cool, columned interior with the intensely decorated places of worship then favoured by the Christians.

The **Laïki Geitonia**► area of Larnaka is a smaller version of Nicosia's award-winning district of the same name, and has been restored to create a pedestrian precinct with shops and restaurants, and a certain amount of style and atmosphere.

In the old Turkish quarter near the Al-Kebir Mosque, the fruit and vegetable market is a modest affair.

WATERFRONT ATTRACTIONS Larnaka Fort►► (*Open* Mon–Fri 9–5.30, 5 in winter. *Admission charge*) is possibly Larnaka's premier attraction. Rusting pre-World War I artillery pieces manufactured by Krups of Germany stand hub to hub in the 16th-century fort's lower level, part of which is surrounded by gardens and used as an open-air theatre. The topmost level, with its turreted battlements, offers a dominating view over the harbour and the maritime approaches to Larnaka. In its time, the fort would have been a particularly tough nut to crack for any would-be invader, and Turkish gunners manning the artillery of an earlier era must have prayed for something hostile to sail within range of their well-sited pieces. The fort also houses The **District Medieval Museum**►, displaying suits of armour and other objects of the era.

Cabin-cruisers, yachts, glass-bottom boats and excursion cruisers line up side by side in the busy marina. Situated north of Larnaka Fort, it is an important draw for boat-owners in this part of the Mediterranean.

LAST RESORT
The city's name, Larnaka, is thought to derive from the Greek word *larnax*, meaning sarcophagus, a possible reference to the great number of tombs from ancient Kition found there. It gives a whole new meaning to the expression 'This place is really dead.'

Palm trees and ornamental lamp-posts run the length of the reconstructed **Foinikoudes Promenade►►**, which follows the seafront south from the marina and makes a fine place for a stroll. The beach is usually busy, although its imported sand is certainly not the stuff of desert island dreams.

Across the way, Larnaka's efforts to improve its facilities are encapsulated in the chic hotels and restaurants which have replaced pubs and tavernas. A bust of the Athenian hero Kimon, who led a fleet to recapture Persian-occupied Kition in 450 BC and perished in the failed attempt, is back in its place of honour on the promenade now that reconstruction work is complete.

MUSEUMS Larnaka owes the outstanding collection of ancient Cypriot objects in the **Pierides Foundation Museum►►** (Zinonos Kitieios Street, tel: 04-652495. *Open* mid-Jun–Sep Mon–Sat 9–1 and 4–7; Oct–mid-Jun Mon–Fri 9–1 and 3–6, Sat 9–1. *Admission charge*) to the 19th-century scholar and archaeologist Demetrios Pierides, who ensured that many finds were not spirited out of the country. Housed in a 19th-century mansion owned by the Pierides Foundation, the collection includes pottery, ornaments, statues and the like, dating from the neolithic period to the classical era. Particularly interesting are the many delicate items of Roman glassware, and a funerary offering from 750 BC depicting a lounging nobleman.

Despite being up against some very stiff competition from the Pierides Foundation Museum in the ancient history stakes, the **Larnaka District Archaeological Museum►** (Kalograion Street, tel: 04-630169. *Open* Mon–Wed and Fri 9–2.30 and, except summer, 3–5. *Admission charge*) pulls together a noteworthy legacy from nearby sites such as Kition and Khirokitia. There are archaic terracotta figurines, ceramics from virtually all stages of Cyprus's history, jewellery, amulets, seals, bronze implements and weapons, coins, statues and funerary monuments. In the pleasant garden around the museum there is a jumble of pediments, columns and steles. The only shortcoming is a lack of 'star' exhibits.

The **Tornaritis-Pierides Palaeontology Museum►** (Evropis Square, tel: 04-658848. *Open* Tue–Fri 10–1 and 4–6, Sat–Sun 10–1. *Admission charge*) is a trip down evolution's memory lane. Housed in the Municipal Cultural Centre, its dinosaur dioramas and other reptilian resources are the kind of culture that children can get to grips with.

The bust of the Athenian hero Kimon on Foinikoudes Promenade

SEASIDE STROLL
The waterfront Foinikoudes Promenade offers the most stylish stroll in Larnaka, running as it does from the marina, past a multitude of café terraces and on to Larnaka Fort. At night it is also one of the liveliest parts of town.

ANCIENT MONUMENTS With all due respect to the 4th-century BC philosopher Zeno, whose birthplace it was, ancient **Kition►** (off Archiepiskopou Kyprianou Avenue. *Open* Mon–Fri 9–2.30. *Admission charge*) must be a strong contender for the accolade of 'world's most boring archaeological site'. Kition's decline and fall have been almost total, and the few pitiful remnants of this once important Phoenician, Greek and Roman city mostly lie under fast-expanding Larnaka. Kition once moved in the fastest circles of its day, with Mycenaeans, Phoenicians and even the Assyrians taking an interest in its progress. An 8th-century BC basalt stele found at the site bears an inscription of the Assyrian King Sargon II.

Built by the Turks in the 18th century, the 33 remaining arches of the **Kamares Aqueduct►** on the outskirts of Larnaka seem much older. The aqueduct was in use until as recently as 1939.

BACK TO NATURE The city's **Municipal Park►** is a modestly sized triangle of trees, plants and grass located beside one of the main roads out of town. Larnaka, like other Cypriot cities, lacks parks, making the ones that do exist doubly valuable.

Inside the Municipal Park, the recently established **Natural History Museum►** (tel: 04-652569. *Open* Jun–Sep Tue–Sun 10–1 and 4–6; Oct–May Tue–Sun 10–1 and 3–5. *Admission charge*) offers visitors an interesting collection of dioramas featuring scenes from the natural world in Cyprus, such as the pink flamingos that gather every winter in the salt lakes near Larnaka and Akrotiri.

89

The elegant façade of the Pierides Foundation Museum

Walk

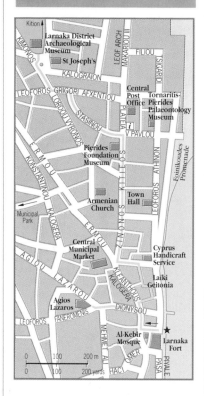

Larnaka city centre

Although not an especially attractive or interesting city, Larnaka does have several points of interest which are grouped fairly close together; this one-hour walk connects most of these sights, which are covered in more detail on pages 86–9.

From the turrets of **Larnaka Fort▶▶** look out over Larnaka Bay, the palm-tree-lined seafront promenade and the city's beach. Cross Kamil Kenan street to the **Al-Kebir Mosque▶▶**, open outside prayer times.
  Cross to Dionysou Street and continue along it through the old Turkish quarter, its narrow streets occupied by workshops and coffee shops which have been taken over by Greek Cypriots. At the end is **Agios Lazaros Church▶▶**.

Return along Dionysou Street and turn left on to Leanthous Kalogero Street; to its right lies **Laïki Geitonia▶**, a restored area now given over to shops and cafés.
  Follow Zinonos Kitieos Street to the end for the **Pierides Foundation Museum▶▶**, a mid 19th-century building housing a large collection of historical objects.
  Then turn left on to Stasinou Street, left again on to Grigori Afxentiou Avenue and then right on to Lordou Vyronos (Lord Byron) Street. Right across the square at the end there is the **Larnaka District Archaeological Museum▶**, where you can see many of the objects that have been excavated in the area.

The Pierides Foundation Museum

Few countries have had as many interesting visitors as Cyprus during the past 5,000 years or so. Just about every empire that ever dipped its toes in the Mediterranean decided it liked the island's many and varied charms so much that it wanted them all to itself.

Mycenaeans, Egyptians, Phoenicians, Persians, Greeks, Romans, Byzantines, Lusignans, Venetians and Turks: the parade has been continuous, and each has left a little piece of itself behind, providing employment for archaeologists for generations to come. One such is Marina Ieronymidou, a Cyprus Department of Antiquities archaeologist responsible for the Byzantine and medieval period. She expects that it will take her whole career to uncover all the secrets of the 16th-century Venetian sugar mill she is excavating at Episkopi. Budgets are painfully tight, allowing her only four weeks of digging each year, and Cyprus's legacy of historic sites is so rich that its handful of full-time archaeologists is drastically overstretched.

Big attraction Archaeology involves much more than 'just' uncovering the tomb of a king or an ancient temple, says Marina, and her work on the sugar mill, part of an estate owned by the last queen of Cyprus, provides valuable insights into the Cypriot economy shortly before the Ottomans took over, and into the lives and working conditions of ordinary Cypriots. Worthy as these goals are, it is still the ancient cities and their temples to pagan gods that attract the tourists: places such as Kourion, Pafos and Amathus in the Greek Cypriot sector, and Salamis in the Turkish Cypriot sector. Both sides have their problems. Projects in the Greek sector get reasonable support and international backing, but commercial considerations sometimes take precedence. Some historic sites in the Turkish zone have suffered from neglect as well as lack of resources and international backing.Despite all this, Cyprus retains a remarkable heritage, which can be experienced either free or for just a few cents or lire for a remarkable voyage of the imagination all the way back to the glory days of Greece, Rome and Byzantium.

GOING UNDER AGAIN
If an architect included in the plans for a new building a proposal for its demolition after completion, it might be considered strange. Yet archaeologists in Cyprus are beginning to think they may have to rebury some of their excavated sites in order to preserve historic treasures from the deterioration that sets in as soon as they are exposed to the elements for the first time in what may be thousands of years.

The ruins of ancient Kourion, overlooking the sea, are among the finest in Cyprus
Top: mosaic floor at Kourion

The golden sands and azure waters of Nissi Bay attract multitudes of sun-worshippers

TEETHING TROUBLES
Sharks are occasionally seen off the Cypriot coast – this is the Mediterranean, after all – but fortunately these magnificent creatures rarely come inshore. If you are worried about having your toes nibbled while you're swimming in the sea, take heart: there are no reliable reports of sharks being sighted in hotel swimming pools.

► Liopetri 77D2

Villages of the Kokkinochoria red-earth district have a reputation for basket-weaving, with many of the baskets being used for carrying the potatoes which are equally characteristic of the area. Liopetri is one of the main producers of these baskets, and local women can be seen working on them in the shade. The village's cafés and shops make for a quieter and simpler experience than those of the nearby resorts.

► Makronisos 77D2

A westerly extension of the Agia Napa tourist area, Makronisos is notable for its enclave of Hellenistic and Roman rock-cut tombs in an area otherwise dominated by beach cafés and hotels. Nevertheless, it was these local businesses which funded the excavation of the burial chambers in the late 1980s. Items from the site can be seen at the Cyprus Museum in Nicosia and in the Larnaka District Museum.

►Nissi Bay 77D2

The whole bustling panoply of a modern beach resort is spread along this and the adjacent sandy bays (one of which is actually called Sandy Bay). Golden sands, turquoise seas, guaranteed sunshine; what more could anyone want? Peace and quiet are not to be expected – except possibly during a midnight swim – in an area where square centimetres of beach space are worth their weight in golden suntan oil.

► Ormideia 76C2

The village's heyday, such as it was, dates from the last century when it was a summer retreat for officials from Larnaka. Nowadays, Ormideia is an averagely interesting village just off the main road from Larnaka to Agia Napa.

► Paralimni 77E2

Once a village, Paralimni has now grown into a small town under the pressure of the nearby tourist resorts. Its Church of the Panagia (Our Lady) is impressively built but not otherwise particularly noteworthy. The town seems to be one of those many places where nothing much happens – although it was struck by an earthquake in 1941 – yet Paralimni is the source of a rather grotesque delicacy, ambeloboulia; this is a tiny migratory songbird that is captured around the town, pickled and then eaten whole by devotees.

On the town's western edge is **Paralimni Lake**, once a proper lake which was drained on account of its malarial mosquitoes. The lake bed still fills with water in winter but dries out to a mud flat in the heat of summer.

►► Potamos Creek 77D2

Almost everywhere that fishing boats dock in Cyprus, they are virtually squeezed out by tourist craft and certainly dominated by tourist hotels and tavernas. Potamos is an exception, which is doubly welcome because it occupies such an attractive and surprising location. This narrow creek, a few kilometres from the village of Xylofagou, is the picture-postcard image of a Mediterranean fishing harbour, with blue-painted boats

coming and going from the fishing grounds, a jumble of nets on the crazily leaning wooden jetties where they tie up and swarthy fishermen downing a beer in the harbour-side café. Near the harbour is the small chapel of **Agios Georgios**, while the rocky coastline in this area makes a pleasant change from the crowded beaches elsewhere.

Paralimni's Church of Our Lady

▶ Protaras   77E2

A no-nonsense beach resort whose primary assets are sand, sunshine and a sea which is pleasantly warm in summer. Watersports are the main concern of those beachgoers who can manage to raise themselves up from the sand. The nearby resort of **Pernera▶** adds up to more of the same; the two are connected by the fine sandy beach of **Fig Tree Bay▶**, which is packed wall to wall with sunbathers at peak times.

▶▶ Pyla   76C2

Minefields, police posts and a UN watchtower over the village coffee shop tend to detract from the carefully cultivated image that all is well in this village, jammed up against the demarcation line, where Greek and Turkish Cypriots still live together in harmony. Despite the fact that Pyla is overlooked by a ridge bristling with military positions, the main business of the village – buying duty-free from the Turkish shops which import their goods from the Turkish Cypriot sector – continues, despite being illegal.

The experiment in living together is hopeful, even if disputes between the two communities can sometimes break out over, for example, repairs to the mosque or the placing of Greek emblems outside the coffee shop.

WAY OF PEACE
The coastal track that runs between the main coast road and the sea from Makronisos to Potamos Creek is little used, since almost all traffic sticks to the main road. This makes the track a surprisingly peaceful place for walking or cycling. Make use of it while you can, for in an area where new tourist developments are spreading like wildfire its tranquil days are numbered.

Ready for the morrow: fishermen's nets at Potamos Creek

Drive

See map on pages 76–7

Agia Napa to Deryneia

This short route (only 20km) begins at one of Cyprus's newest resort areas, traverses the Kokkinochoria district and ends at a viewpoint overlooking abandoned hotels across the demarcation line in the Turkish Cypriot sector. Allow a full morning or afternoon to stop off at the small coves that dot the coast for sunbathing and swimming.

The sights on this drive are covered in more detail on pages 80–97.
The 16th-century **Agia Napa Monastery**▶▶ and its Orthodox church look a little lost surrounded by the brash glitter of Agia Napa, but locals still go there to kiss the icons, light candles and pray.

Head east for the two approaches to **Cape Gkreko**▶▶; the first one leads along a rough track to a high cliff with a dramatic view of the cape, festooned with military and civilian radio masts on one side and looking back towards Agia Napa on the other. The second approach, about 200m beyond the first, leads to the cape – or as close as you can get (a fence denies access to the point itself). Adjacent rocky inlets are favoured by cabin-cruiser skippers and scuba-divers, while land-bound folks may instead decide to settle for an ice-cream from the van that is usually parked on the shore here.

Agioi Anargyroi▶, a tiny white-washed chapel beside the sea, lies at the end of a rough track from the main

Above: chapel near Fig Tree Bay
Left: basket-weaving, Agia Napa

road. A walkway leads from there to a beach bordering a shallow bay less than a kilometre to the north. The beach is probably best reached from a rough and very dusty track just before the Grecian Park Hotel, a little further along the main road. It consists mostly of sand and is a safe place to swim.

Despite – or perhaps because of – its colourful name, the narrow stretch of sand at **Fig Tree Bay▶** is likely to be packed with sunbathers lying in regimented rows under beach umbrellas. There is no lack of cafés and tavernas for anyone who needs a break or sustenance.

Midway between Protaras and Pernera, on the left-hand side of the road up the cliffside, the small church of Profitis Ilias is reached by climbing a stairway.

Pernera▶ is a modern resort, distinguished only by its beach, tiny harbour and seafront tavernas.

At the crossroads where the main road turns left towards Paralimni, a right turn leads to **Agia Trias▶**, a pleasant sandy bay which takes its name from a small shoreside chapel and which has some reasonable seaside tavernas.

Formerly a village, **Paralimni▶** has grown under the twin pressures of nearby tourist developments and an influx of refugees from the north during the 1970s into a substantial town. Its inner core retains some character, this being further enhanced by the stone-built Church of the Panagia.

From a café – called appropriately Viewpoint Café – on the northeastern edge of **Deryneia▶** and reached by a side-road with signs indicating the way, you can look beyond the Greek Cypriot, UN and Turkish military outposts to the city of Famagusta (Gazimağusa) and its abandoned suburb, the once thriving resort of Varosha (Maraş).

Church of the Panagia in Paralimni

Greek Orthodox monk taking his ease at Agia Ekaterina

▶ Royal Chapel of Agia Ekaterina 76A2

Open: irregularly. Admission free

In the dry season, the track that leads from the main road near Pyrga to the 'Chapelle Royale' of Agia Ekaterina must be one of the dustiest in Cyprus. The church is notable as much for its isolated location and scenic outlook as for its intrinsic interest and its remains. The latter are undergoing a slow process of restoration and are likely to appeal mainly to specialists. Built during the Lusignan era, which accounts for its French name and Gothic style, the Royal Chapel's vaulted interior contains some murals, including one of Queen Charlotte of Bourbon.

▶▶ Salt Lake 76B1

Like its cousin on the Akrotiri Peninsula near Limassol, Larnaka Salt Lake is filled with shallow salty water in winter but dries out to leave a hard crystalline crust in the summer. The salt used to be exploited commercially, but growing pollution levels have brought this to an end. Indeed, when seen from a distance the dried-up lake bed appears a dazzling white; from close up, however, the salt is encrusted with hydrocarbons and dirt. Pink flamingos, presumably not informed of the pollution, are among the bird species to winter here in large numbers.

▶ Sotira 77D2

The village name means 'salvation', and certainly there are enough Orthodox churches in and around it almost to guarantee this happy outcome. The best known is the **Church of the Metamorfosis (Transfiguration)▶**, rebuilt in 1533 on an older foundation, and with a finely carved iconostasis and Byzantine eagle emblem. **Agios Mamas** is several centuries older and features some reasonable murals. Just outside the town is the partially restored **Panagia Chordakiotissa** (*Open* irregularly (all three sights). *Admission free*), formerly a Latin monastery. The nearby village of Frennaros takes its name from the French for the Friars Minor (Frères Mineurs), Franciscan monks who once occupied it.

▶▶ Stavrovouni Monastery 76A1

Open: Apr–Aug daily 8–12 and 3–6; Sep–Mar daily 8–12 and 2–5. Admission free: women not allowed; dress respectfully

This is one of Cyprus's most emblematic historic places, a monastery perched on a 700m-high peak on the edge of

SALTY TALE
St Lazarus, to whom Larnaka's church of Agios Lazaros is dedicated, is also associated with the Salt Lake. Legend tells that Lazarus asked a woman from Larnaka for some of the grapes she was carrying. She replied that there was more chance of the soil yielding salt instead of wine than of her parting with any of her grapes. Lazarus replied, 'Then let it be so; from henceforth the soil shall produce salt, not the fruit of the grape.'

the Troodos Mountains, commanding a spectacular view across the Mesaoria (Mesarya) Plain to Nicosia in one direction and to the Mediterranean at Larnaka in the other. Of course, the founders of the 'Mountain of the Cross' monastery in AD 327 were not so concerned with the view – unless it was the equally fine view of heaven from such a vantage point.

The mother of Emperor Constantine the Great, the future St Helena, kept herself busy in Cyprus, between introducing snake-hunting cats (see panel on page 102) and establishing monasteries. At Stavrovouni she apparently did both, bequeathing the new foundation a relic of the True Cross which she had come across on a trip to the Holy Land. Ironically, (since the mountain-top was sacred to Aphrodite in ancient times) women can go no further than the visitors' car park.

Despite the high regard in which it holds itself, Stavrovouni has been destroyed and rebuilt so many times through the centuries that only its historical reputation – and the superb view over the surrounding plains – are really noteworthy today, the 17th-century buildings being best described as 'solid'.

The venerated relic of the True Cross, hanging beside the iconostasis in the monastery church, is lavishly covered in gold leaf and set within a silver-ornamented wooden crucifix.

Christ Pantokrator at Stavrovouni

▶ Voroklini   76B2

This village north of Larnaka has developed a reputation for its hand-woven baskets, which can be bought in local shops and indeed all over Greek Cyprus. The village is one of several in this area that has been forced to grow too rapidly, due to an influx of refugees from the 1974 conflict and some tourist development associated with the nearby coastal resorts along Larnaka Bay.

▶ Xylofagou   77D2

A Venetian watchtower stands in glorious isolation on the shore near here, reached along tracks that traverse an intensely farmed district on the edge of red-soil country. The village itself is quite attractive.

CROSS CONNECTION
In 1553, the Englishman John Locke recorded his impressions of climbing Stavrovouni: 'Upon the sayd hill is a certain Crosse, which is, they say, a Holy Crosse. This Crosse in times past did, by their report of the Island, hang in the ayre, but by a certain earthquake, the Crosse and the Chappell it hung in were overthrown, so that never since it would hang in the ayre.'

The stunning view from Stavrovouni

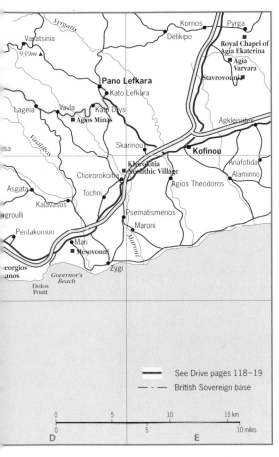

THE SOUTHWEST Southwest Cyprus covers an area based on the port city of Limassol. The region is also an important commercial and industrial hub, having been forced to develop rapidly as a replacement for Famagusta (Gazimağusa) after the Turkish invasion of 1974.

As with much of Cyprus, the sea and the mountains are never far from any point in the southwest. Another defining geographical feature of the area is the great wedge of the Akrotiri Peninsula jutting into the Mediterranean west of Limassol with its Salt Lake in the centre. Here is located one of Britain's two Sovereign Base Areas in Cyprus, a factor that has saved the peninsula from the unrestrained development characteristic of other coastal regions, but at the price of having some of its most scenic

The southwest is an area of contrasts, with sleepy villages (far left) bucking the busy port of Limassol (below)

► ► ► REGION HIGHLIGHTS

AGIOS NIKOLAOS TON GATON MONASTERY *see page 102*

AMATHUS *see page 103*

KATO LEFKARA *see page 111*

KHIROKITIA NEOLITHIC VILLAGE *see page 108*

KOLOSSI CASTLE *see page 108*

KOURION *see page 109*

KOURION MUSEUM AT EPISKOPI *see page 104*

SALT LAKE *see page 116*

SANCTUARY OF APOLLO HYLATES *see page 116*

The Southwest

NOISE POLLUTION
The fragile atmospherics of ancient sites, such as Kourion and the Sanctuary of Apollo Hylates in the Southwest, can be shattered by the arrival of a fleet of tour-buses. Not only is noise generated by the influx of people, but the drivers generally leave their engines running to keep the air-conditioning working. Yet another reason for getting to such places early, before the crowds.

stretches placed out of bounds. Although the coastline in the southwest is now the most popular in terms of concentration of tourists, and many of its businesses are owned by Greek Cypriot refugees from the Turkish Cypriot area, it has had a hard time replacing the 'lost' beaches of Famagusta and Kyrenia. Had the replacements been of comparable quality and extent, Limassol and its environs would no doubt have been equally popular in the past.

Apart from some notable exceptions, much of the coastline is rocky and those beaches which do exist can be busy. A surprising exception is the excellent Lady's Mile Beach on the eastern shore of the Akrotiri Peninsula, but as this looks out on the less than scenic installations of Limassol harbour, its relative emptiness may be understandable.

THE HILLS ARE ALIVE You can't get away from them: all of southwest Cyprus is dominated by the great bulk of the Troodos Mountains looming against the sky. Many people on holiday at the coast are sufficiently tempted by the sight to get up off the beach and head for the hills – yet they usually rush directly from the coast to the peaks, ignoring the foothills that lie between. This is a mistake, for the whole southern edge of the Troodos is filled with sleepy little villages, as far in spirit from the close-packed beaches as it is possible to imagine, even though they may be little more than 10–20km distant.

The secret of discovering the best of these villages is to get off the main roads and on to the rough tracks, slowing down to idling pace both mentally and physically. Take time to stop by the wide pools of silvery water lying amidst the dry summer landscape, where dams have been established and rod-and-line fishermen take advantage of the trout on offer.

A great swathe of the southern Troodos is given over to vineyards, and with Limassol being the main centre for

The age-old Cypriot way of life is still to be found in villages like those in the foothills of the Troodos

Greco-Roman remnant of Kourion, bathed in romantic Mediterranean light

vine production in Cyprus, traffic can be heavy at harvest time; however, as 'heavy traffic' in much of this area means two lorries on the road at the same time, the hardship is not too great. Cycling and walking are generally easier here than higher up in the mountains, and the wonder is that so few people choose to practise them.

CLASSIC TIMES The southwest has been blessed with some of Cyprus's finest and most important historical sites. The ancient coastal cities of Amathus and Kourion definitely fall into this category, especially the latter, with its dramatic clifftop location and romantic Greek theatre built into the side of a steep slope. Near to Kourion lie the remains of the Sanctuary of Apollo Hylates, the woodland god. It seems a fortunate privilege that so much of this once holy place remains for the modern visitor.

The region thus encompasses all of Cyprus's virtues: the sea, mountains, village life and history; it even has a city for those who cannot do without the urban touch.

IMPERIAL BOOST
Limassol developed at the expense of nearby Amathus partly because a Roman emperor gave his name to a new port built on an earlier settlement called Lemesos. At the end of the 4th century, Theodosius the Great, the last to rule over a united empire, named the settlement Theodosias. This act more or less guaranteed the town's prosperity, even though it went back to the future and reacquired its earlier name of Lemesos.

GETTING THE MESSAGE
During the period of British rule, so the story goes, the *muktar* (headman) of Agios Tychon village near Limassol had been pressing the authorities to build a bridge over a nearby stream, but to no avail. Then the district officer arrived on an official visit and, while crossing the stream where the bridge was needed, his horse slipped, pitching him headlong into the water. A bridge was soon forthcoming.

ÉLITE FIGHTERS

There are frequent historical references to Cyprus being overrun with poisonous snakes. Snake-fighting cats were bred at several locations, including Agios Nikolaos ton Gaton, to combat the menace. If the small numbers of remaining poisonous vipers are anything to go by, the feline special forces were victorious. The combat must have been as epic as anything in Cyprus's human chronicles, so no one should blame the cats of today for their self-satisfied airs.

102

Descendants of snake-fighting cats bask in the glow of victory at Agios Nikolaos ton Gaton Monastery

► Agios Amvrosios   98A3

This is an attractive village in the heart of Cypriot wine country, best known for the 'ecological' wine produced here from grapes grown without the 'benefit' of chemicals or pesticides. The finished product is likewise free of artificial flavouring or colouring.

► Agios Georgios Alamanos Convent   99D2

Open: daily. Admission free

Lying near the coast midway beween Amathus and Governor's Beach, this convent is a tranquil place, an attractive and bright modern construction founded on an original 12th-century cloister. Icons and honey, both produced by the resident nuns, can be purchased here. A nearby trail leads to the sea at the Agios Georgios Café, a simple eatery with a campsite and a fine location beside the rocky coast.

►► Agios Minas Convent   99D3

Open: Mon–Fri for group visits only; May–Sep closed noon–3pm

Lying in a peaceful valley between Vavla and Kato Drys, this 15th-century convent is dedicated to St Minas the Glorious, a 3rd-century Egyptian martyr. The nuns of this immaculately maintained convent, a typically tranquil religious retreat (except when it is overrun by the occupants of a passing tourist bus) make and sell icons and honey, both of which are noted for their quality.

►► Agios Nikolaos ton Gaton Monastery   98B1

Open: daily. Admission free

'St Nicholas of the Cats' owes its fame as much to the felines of its title as to the sainted Nicholas. The cats referred to are those reputedly introduced to Cyprus by St Helena, mother of the Roman Emperor Constantine the Great, to rid the island of poisonous reptiles (see panel). There are still plenty of cats at Agios Nikolaos, which was indeed founded during Constantine's reign (AD 324–37), although the present structure represents the partially, but quite handsomely, restored remnants of a 13th-century abbey abandoned to the invading Turks in 1570.

Today, the religious peace is more likely to be disturbed by howling jets operating from the nearby British air base.

►► Akrotiri Peninsula   98B1

The Akrotiri Peninsula, a thick wedge of land jutting into the Mediterranean just west of Limassol, is occupied almost entirely by one of the two British Sovereign Base Areas in Cyprus.

Although most of the peninsula is freely accessible, the military installations around Akrotiri Air Base at its tip, including the promontories at Cape Zevgari and Cape Gata, are closed to the public.

▶▶▶ Amathus

98C2

Open: summer daily 9–7.30; winter daily 9–5. Admission charge

Listed on road signs as 'Amathounda', the ancient city of Amathus is the subject of intermittent excavation, with archaeologists currently uncovering harbour remains from the Phoenician period. Occupied from around 1000 BC, Amathus chose to stick by the Persians during the Greek revolt some 500 years later, but sided with the Greeks when Alexander the Great came on the scene.

Despite being quite small, the site (overlooking the sea some 6km east of Limassol) is atmospheric yet suffers from an absence of information – beyond the simple label 'Agora' (market-place) – to add to visitors' understand its significance.

In addition to the market-place – an open area of white stone surrounded by the vestiges of colonnaded porticoes – there are indications of an early Christian basilica, baths and, on the hill rising to the east, the acropolis and parts of the defensive walls. There were temples to Hercules, Adonis and, of course, Aphrodite.

Much archaeological work remains to be done on what was once an important city-state; and although it slowly declined in influence under the Romans and Byzantines, the former used it as a district capital. In the late 6th century Amathus was the birthplace of St John the Almsgiver, later patron saint of the Knights Hospitaller.

Little remained of the city's glory by the time King Richard I of England, the 'Lionheart', landed near here in 1191 on his way to the crusades, and its stones were later used as a convenient quarry for buildings in Limassol, as well as for more distant projects such as the Suez Canal.

QUICK EXIT
The exit by car from the site of ancient Amathus is extremely dicey, as it entails joining the fast-moving traffic on the coast road just beyond a blind corner. In Cyprus, right turns in particular offer those who attempt them an excellent chance of becoming ancient history themselves.

Complex spiral patterns can be seen on some of the ruined columns at ancient Amathus

PILGRIM'S PAUSE
Roberto da Sanseverino, an Italian on pilgrimage to the Holy Land in 1458, dropped in on Episkopi and was lavishly entertained by its Venetian owner. Roberto was much impressed by the fruit growing on his host's estates, including carob beans and bananas. The bananas seemed a good omen for his pilgrimage: 'Slice them as often as you like, you will always find a cross in the centre of the fruit,' he noted in his travel diary.

Water captured from winter streams fills Germasogeia Lake

► Arakapas   98C3

This averagely pretty hill village, with its attractive open square, is most notable for the small ancient church of **Panagia Iamatiki** adjacent to a modern church of the same name with a baroque bell-tower. The latter has taken over the duties of Our Lady the Healer, and miraculous cures are attributed to her intercession, a tradition the village celebrates with a festival each September.

►►► Episkopi   98A2

There are really two Episkopis. The original one, now little more than a village, was settled by refugees escaping from nearby Kourion (ancient Curium) in the 7th century ad and grew to importance as the seat of an archbishopric. The other is 'settled' by personnel and their families from the British Sovereign Base Area's Episkopi Barracks, located a few kilometres west of the old village.

Episkopi Barracks is a little piece of Britain set down beneath the warm sun next to the blue Mediterranean, and is more like an English garden suburb modelled on a country village. The coast road from Limassol to Pafos runs through here, and generally the only formality is to stick to the speed limit when passing the police checkpoints at either end of the base.

Housed over the foundations of a building devastated in the earthquake of AD 365, **Kourion Museum**►►► (*Open* Mon–Fri 9–2.30. *Admission charge*) an excellent collection of discoveries from excavations on the site of Kourion and the nearby Sanctuary of Apollo Hylates. There are pottery, oil-lamps, coins, ornaments, amphorae, sculptures and little votive figurines.

Most poignant of all is a group of three skeletons huddled Pompeii-style against the sudden hammer blow delivered by nature to their city and lives: a young man tries vainly to shelter a woman, who is surely his wife, while she in turn attempts to protect an 18-month-old child. They all died together when the earthquake's powerful tremors demolished Kourion.

Fishermen mending their nets on the black sands of Governor's Beach

105

▶ Fassouri Plantations 98A1

Citrus groves form a dense wedge around the village of Fassouri (also spelt Phassouri), just to the west of Limassol, at the base of Akrotiri Peninsula. Guided tours are offered by the company operating the plantations, but it may be enough simply to drive or cycle around the orchards on leafy roads shaded from the sun by overhanging cypress trees, breathing in air that is heady with the tang of oranges, lemons and limes. Walking tends to be less pleasant because traffic moves fast on roads that are narrow and have no proper pavements, and it is not really possible, nor wise without permission, to walk through the orchards.

▶ Foinikaria 98C2

The small village of Foinikaria, tucked away in the hills northeast of Limassol, is a pleasant enough place for taking a quiet coffee break in the shade, but its main attraction is the shimmering **Germasogeia Lake▶** near by. Fishing for trout and other species is permitted in the lake, which is fed by springtime surges in the Germasogeia river. A permit is necessary and may be obtained from one of the Cyprus Fisheries Department's district offices at Limassol (near the old harbour entrance; tel: 05-330470).

▶ Governor's Beach 99D2

This fine, and popular, stretch of sand at the end of a rough track, east of Limassol has only one potential drawback: the sand is almost black and soaks up vast quantities of solar heat, releasing it into the soles of unsuspecting barefoot sunworshippers.

▶ Kalavasos 99D2

A pretty enough but otherwise unremarkable hill village, Kalavasos features a narrow-gauge train, comprising engine and freight cars, parked on a bridge over the Vasilikos river. Used up to the 1960s to serve iron and gypsum mines, the train is now derelict, although it is surrounded by a tracery of fairy lights. Mining history around Kalavasos reaches back almost 4,000 years to when copper was first extracted here.

ARCHAEOLOGIST'S DREAM
The rough countryside of the Vasilikos river valley around Kalavasos has become an archaeologist's dream – or nightmare – with Cypriot and international teams facing a mountain of excavation work in several hundred identified sites dating as far back as 6500 BC.

Cyprus has seen military bases come and go from its earliest days. Where once there were Greek and Roman triremes, then Venetian and Turkish galleys, today there are Royal Air Force jet-fighters. The two British bases on the island fulfil much the same role as their predecessors, projecting military power into an area still considered vital to western interests.

SUNSHINE SOLDIERING
Although the base authorities are reluctant to admit it openly – perhaps fearing that the taxpayers will take a dim view of it – most British service personnel in Cyprus seem delighted to be there. They may have to work hard but they can play in the sun – which is more than can be guaranteed at bases in Britain and Germany.

A squadron of Royal Air Force Tornado bombers shatters the calm of early morning above the Akrotiri Peninsula, a dozen jets returning from a live-fire exercise somewhere over the Mediterranean. Amidst a deafening concussion of noise they touch down out of sight at the airfield beyond the security fence. The scene is a routine and familiar one at Akrotiri, one of Britain's two Sovereign Base Areas (SBAs) in Cyprus (the other is at Dhekelia, east of Larnaka – see pages 82 and 102).

Britain's role dates back to the end of its colonial era in Cyprus in 1960, when it bowed to the violently expressed will of the Greek Cypriot people and gave up its domination of the island. In agreement with the new government of independent Cyprus, however, Britain retained two bases as important staging posts and as convenient 'watchtowers' for keeping an eye on the former Soviet Union and the unstable, oil-rich lands of the Middle East. They were employed in this role during the Gulf War of 1991 and the subsequent operations to protect Kurds and Shia Muslims in Iraq.

The bases are called Sovereign Base Areas because they remain British territory and are not part of the Republic of Cyprus. Nevertheless, Her Majesty's Government does not own most of the land on the SBAs – some 57 per cent of their total area of 250 sq km is privately owned by Cypriots

British military radar installation at the summit of Mount Olympus

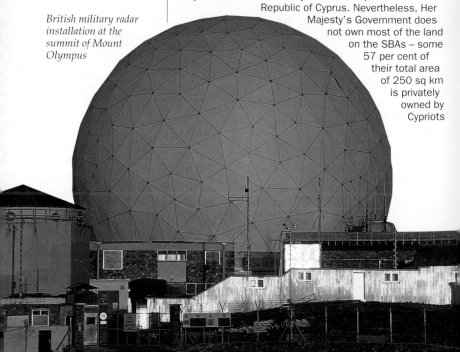

and SBA law is closely aligned with Republic of Cyprus law. The bases' irregular boundaries are accounted for by the need to exclude civil centres of population as far as possible.

OUT OF BOUNDS The only contact most visitors are likely to have with the SBAs is when they pass through on the public highways that traverse them and an occasional spot-check of traffic by police officers or base security personnel. A more annoying side-effect of their presence is that some interesting areas, located in or near military installations, are out of bounds to the public. These include the tips of the Akrotiri Peninsula and Cape Gkreko, as well as the summit of Mount Olympus, the highest mountain in the Troodos range, which is crowned by the geodesic dome of a radar station.

Some compensation for these restrictions is that only small-scale commercial activity is allowed in the SBAs, a ruling that has undoubtedly helped preserve the natural environment from destruction at the hands of 'developers' who would otherwise have filled it up with hotels and tavernas. Archaeological sites on base territory, of which there are many, including the ancient city of Kourion and the sanctuary of Apollo Hylates, remain the responsibility of the Cyprus Department of Antiquities.

LIVING STANDARDS Inside the living quarters of the bases, with their street names reminiscent of an English suburb, life goes on as normal for the 4,000 service personnel and their families. They have their own houses, shops, churches, banks and hospitals, as well as sporting facilities such as cricket fields and polo pitches. When off duty, the troops take advantage of the many sea and mountain sports that Cyprus offers all of its residents.

The British Sovereign Base areas in Cyprus represent an important asset to the island's economy, from direct and indirect expenditures as well as through offering employment.

It is logical to wonder how long Britain will want to retain these bases when it no longer has colonial possessions in the Middle East and Far East to support. The answer probably lies in how long Cyprus continues to be a convenient stepping-stone to an area that is considered vital to Western interests. A casual glance back through the pages of history suggests that the stay could very well be a long one.

LIQUID ELEMENT
In Cyprus, where water is a scarce commodity and its misuse is frowned upon, travellers passing through the British barracks at Episkopi may be outraged to note the lush green of a well-irrigated cricket field and other sports grounds in what is called Happy Valley. Aware of this, the base authorities are at pains to point out that the occupants provide the irrigation themselves, so to speak, by reusing water from the base's sewerage system.

107

Going shopping in a little slice of Britain at the Dhekelia base

Remains of Stone Age houses at Khirokitia Neolithic Village

KNIGHTS OF OLD
It was from Kolossi Castle in 1303 that the Grand Master of the Knights Templar, Jacques de Molay, returned to France to face charges that the crusader order had betrayed Christendom and engaged in all manner of vile infidel practices. Despite the knights' courageous record in the Holy Land, many were subjected to torture, imprisonment and execution. De Molay was burned at the stake. The rumour persists that the Templars survive to this day as a secret and influential underground society.

▶▶ Khirokitia Neolithic Village
99D2

Open: summer daily 9–7.30; winter daily 9–5. Admission charge

The historic site of Khirokitia Neolithic Village (dating from around 5800 to 5500 BC) is located adjacent to the modern village of Choirokoitia, some 6km from the sea in the foothills of the Troodos Mountains. Khirokitia's round, stone-built dwellings, heaped together in neighbourly profusion, climb the slopes of a steep promontory around which curls a loop of the Maroni river. The geography of the site provided both isolation and protection for the agricultural community which settled here, and the complex construction of the dwellings indicates that a high degree of social organisation existed.

Excavations have revealed that the people of this aceramic (literally 'lacking pottery') culture buried their dead under their cramped huts. High infant mortality and a lifespan of between 25 and 40 years ensured that there was no shortage of occupants for this city of the dead. For the living, however, life is thought not to have been too bad: the conditions for farming, livestock and hunting were favourable, while warfare seems not to have been a problem. The nearby village of Choirokoitia was the scene of a battle in 1426 in which Egyptian Mamelukes defeated the Cypriot forces of the Lusignan kings.

▶▶▶ Kolossi Castle
98A2

Open: summer daily 9–7.30; winter daily 9–5. Admission charge

A romantic castle in bright stone, with a fine view over surrounding orchards from its turreted battlements,

Kolossi Castle was a place of refuge for crusader knights fleeing from their latest abortive mission to the Holy Land. An original structure on the site was granted to the Knights Hospitaller (the Order of the Hospital of St John of Jerusalem), who located their Commandery here after being driven definitively from Palestine in 1291. The Hospitallers engaged in a tug-of-war over Kolossi Castle with the equally footloose Knights Templar, the dispute being resolved, to the Hospitallers' satisfaction at any rate, when their rivals were proscribed by papal decree in 1311. The present structure was built by the French Grand Commander of the Hospitallers, Louis de Magnac, around 1454.

Kolossi's romantic ruins make it easy to imagine crusader knights striding around in flowing capes emblazoned with the Holy Cross. Its stout walls must have given its defenders confidence to make fun of Genoese and Mameluke besiegers, discounting the unlikely chance of their breaking in. The Hospitallers concentrated on peaceful pursuits, accepting the bounty of their wheatfields, cottonfields, sugar-cane plantations and vincyards. The latter are recalled in Commandaria, a sweet red dessert wine.

In addition to the central keep, there are the remains of a basilica, sugar-cane factory and aqueduct. The fleur-de-lis symbol can be seen carved on walls and fireplaces, and the entrance hall has a medieval mural of the Crucifixion, damaged by time and 20th-century vandals.

Crusaders found life at Kolossi Castle easier than fighting in the Holy Land

▶ Kornos   99E3

Although noted for its production of ceramics, and especially the large traditional Cypriot pots called *pitharia*, which are shaped by hand rather than being turned on a wheel, no evidence of this activity is to be seen by the casual visitor. The village is otherwise unremarkable and scarcely worth diverting for.

▶▶▶ Kourion   98A2

Open: summer daily 8–7.30; winter daily 8–5. Admission charge

Architects of the ancient world had an advantage over their modern counterparts when it came to designing cities: the best locations were all freely available. Kourion's builders made full use of this: the ruined city occupies a stunning clifftop setting overlooking the Mediterranean west of Limassol.

HISTORY According to Herodotus, Kourion was founded in the 14th century BC by Greek colonists and became an important city-state. The 12th-century Egyptian pharaoh Ramses III wanted Kourion to come under his dominion, and its kings later paid homage to Assyria.

The Romans brought Kourion (Curium in Latin) to the peak of its prosperity and, as with the rest of Cyprus, it soon embraced Christianity. An early bishop, Philoneides, was martyred during persecutions by Emperor Diocletian at the end of the 3rd century AD. Kourion was shattered by the earthquake of 365 and, although rebuilt, was finally abandoned following Arab raids during the 7th century.

SOLE MATES
The remains of a neolithic settlement contemporaneous with that at Khirokitia has been found at Kastros, at the very tip of the Karpas (Karpaz) Peninsula in the Turkish Cypriot zone.

TURNCOAT CITY
Kourion played a pivotal, if shameful, part in the Greek revolt against Persia in 498 BC. In his *Histories*, Herodotus wrote that its king, Stasenor, changed sides, abandoning the Greek cause and helping to deliver Cyprus into Persian hands.

The last rays of the sun illuminate the benches of Kourion's theatre

JUST THE TICKET
Evening performances at the Kourion theatre during the summer include historical Greek tragedies and comedies, and works by international and Greek Cypriot dramatists, both historical and modern. In addition, there are classical and modern music, ballet performances and a *son et lumière*. The programme varies from year to year. Full details are available in the local press and from tourist information offices, tour company representatives and hotel information-brochure racks. There is no on-site ticket office, but tickets are available from tourist information offices or from theatre booking offices. Vital accessories are a cushion for sitting through long performances on the ancient theatre's hard stone benches, and a light sweater or windcheater for warding off the cool evening breeze that wafts up the cliffs from the sea.

SIGHTS The ruins of Kourion that can be seen today are dealt with in order from east to west. For the adjacent Sanctuary of Apollo Hylates, see page 116.

'Enter for the good luck of the house' was the inscription that welcomed visitors to the imposing patrician dwelling known as the **House of Eustolios**►►. It takes its name from one Eustolios, praised in an inscription dating from the end of the 4th century AD for not leaving his fellow citizens in 'abject misery', but who donated his baths and an annexe of the house to the earthquake-stricken city. The Christian nature of the house is attested by another inscription, referring to the 'venerated signs of Christ', and a mosaic of a young woman with the Greek legend ktIcic, symbolising the Creation.

Built into the side of a steep gully overlooking the sea, the **Theatre**►►► must have presented its audiences with a dilemma: to concentrate on the show or on the magnificent view, a difficulty that continues to this day as it again features theatre, ballet and music performances (see panel). Originally built during the Hellenistic era for presenting Greek plays, the theatre was transformed into an arena by the Romans to satisfy their passion for blood-letting as a spectator sport, before being restored to theatrical use in the Christian era. At its best when the late afternoon sun showers its white stones with rosy light, the theatre is a spectacle in itself, conjuring up the ancient world by the sheer drama of its setting.

The 5th-century **Early Christian Basilica**►►► complex includes on its clifftop site the main church, a chapel, sacristies, annexes and the bishop's palace, testifying to the power of the Christian Church less than a century after it had become the official religion of the Roman Empire. Bishop Zeno, who represented the Cypriots at the Council of Ephesus in AD 431, is thought to have been responsible for the basilica's construction.

The **Roman Forum**►► is the subject of continuing excavation, with numerous constructions coming to light, including medieval lime-kilns. In this jumble of stone behind the basilica are a Hellenistic-era water reservoir, a Roman nymphaeum (which seems to have been Kourion's main water distribution centre) and other public and private structures.

The **Achilles Mosaic**►► is a damaged mosaic in a 2nd-century AD public building near the main road. The mosaic itself depicts the dramatic moment when Odysseus unmasks Achilles – who has been disguised as a girl by his mother to prevent him going to the Trojan War – by producing a sword and shield which Achilles cannot resist grasping. Near by is the **House of the Gladiators▶▶**, a large private dwelling undoubtedly owned by a wealthy patrician. The house takes its name from the mosaics found there depicting gladiators in combat.

Located 3km west of the main excavation site, the elongated **Stadium▶** (*Open* permanently. *Admission free)* was an arena for track and field events, with an estimated capacity of 6,000 spectators. Little remains of the stadium apart from the lower courses of its exterior wall.

▶▶ Lady's Mile Beach　　　98B1

This fairly good stretch of beach not far from Limassol, just outside the closed area of the Royal Air Force base at Akrotiri, was named for the place where the colonel's wife's horse was walked during the balmy days of the British Empire. Despite being generally all but deserted, the beach is supposed to be popular with service personnel from the base and some of its cafés will serve you only if you are, or at least look like, a soldier. Frequent strong winds in this area make the waters an excellent place for windsurfing, but the major drawback is that the view – across to the cranes of Limassol harbour – can hardly be described as scenic.

▶▶▶ Lefkara　　　99D3

There are two Lefkaras, located about 1km apart, thanks to the common Cyprus practice of having a 'Pano' (Upper) version of a village and a 'Kato' (Lower) one. In this case it is relatively unspoiled Kato Lefkara that rates three stars, while more commercial Pano Lefkara merits two.

Lace is the attraction here, the traditional local style being called *lefkaritika* (see page 113). This cannot be described as a pattern as such because no two designs are repeated, each being a unique creation of one of the village women who sit outdoors in the shade painstakingly

stitching the intricate designs, generally backing them on to pieces of Irish linen. Silverware and *loukoumia* (Turkish, or Cypriot, delight) have become other specialities of the two villages.

Kato Lefkara is a particularly attractive mountain village with its pastel-painted houses giving a picture of idyllic charm. Although it clearly thrives on its lace sales the approach is low key, making a stroll around the village a pleasant experience. Pano Lefkara has much more of a tourist infrastructure in the way of shops, tavernas and parking places, so inevitably it gets thronged at peak periods.

CURTAIN CALLS
A Greek theatre such as the one at Kourion seems to bring out the exhibitionist in people. Visitors cannot resist posing in a manner they consider to be reminiscent of Aristophanes; brides and bridegrooms like to be photographed there before embarking on the theatre of life; and both British and Greek Cypriot soldiers turn it into a kind of theatre of war for unit photographs.

PICTURE PERFECT
Few places in Cyprus are as beautiful in springtime as the countryside around Kato and Pano Lefkara. The two villages, along with the varicoloured floral patterns on the hills and in the fields, make up a photogenic combination that is hard to beat.

Left: Kourion's ruins crown the top of a cliff overlooking the sea

Above: Petra tou Romiou, better known as Aphrodite's Rock

Boat trip

Limassol to Aphrodite's Rock

This trip can be done either on one of the excursion boats that leave from Limassol, or by hiring a boat at the harbour, with or without a crew. The time spent depends principally on the kind of boat you have, but it is as well to allocate a whole day.

Leaving Limassol's busy Old Harbour, you pass the even busier commercial port, the principal maritime gateway to Cyprus, with a constant procession of cargo ships coming and going. From there you run alongside the sandy stretch of **Lady's Mile Beach**▶▶ on the eastern flank of **Akrotiri Peninsula**▶▶, with the **Salt Lake**▶▶▶ visible behind. Not much can be seen of the military facilities at the British Akrotiri air base behind its screen of dunes and vegetation – presumably this is how the Royal Air Force likes it – but you may see Tornado or Jaguar jets heading out into the Mediterranean for a live-fire exercise. Rounding Cape Gata, then Cape Zevgari, you sail along the western arm of Akrotiri Peninsula. Keeping close inshore guarantees a spectacular view of the cliffside at **Kourion**▶▶▶ where the ruins of the Greco-Roman city bask in the sun (see pages 109–10).

Pissouri Bay▶▶ makes a fine place to come close inshore and perhaps moor to enjoy the sandy beach.

The best way to approach **Petra tou Romiou**▶▶▶, otherwise and more famously known as Aphrodite's Rock (see page 177), is from the sea. After all, this was the same route the goddess herself took when she was born in the foam and borne ashore by the gentle west wind. More mundanely, with only stony beaches in the area, it is generally a reasonably quiet destination, however approached.

Making lace by hand in the twin villages of Pano and Kato Lefkara is a generation game, with mothers passing on their skills to their daughters. Lefkara lace is sought both by royalty and by the many humbler visitors who come here.

The women sit outdoors in the shade, chatting, while their fingers move nimbly and with painstaking care over pieces of linen. Their needles seem to have a life of their own as they pull the thin strands of mercerised cotton. Delicate patterns – naturalistic or abstract – slowly take shape, patterns which exist only in the mind of their creator, and which might never again be repeated. 'How long will it take to make?' a visitor asks a woman working on a particularly intricate piece. 'A year,' she replies.

Lace has been made in Lefkara for centuries, even before the village became a retreat for wealthy Venetians seeking relief from the heat of summer. The Venetian women brought embroidery with them and worked on it while the village women worked on theirs. The legacy of these two embroidery traditions is now in demand the world over.

Man's work The men were no doubt quite content that their womenfolk were gainfully employed. As time passed, the gain from this employment exceeded that from the men's farms, and Lefkaran men became sales representatives for the graceful products made by their wives, mothers, sisters and daughters, travelling abroad with samples while the women remained at home stitching.

Generation game The tradition of mothers passing on their skill to their daughters has been partially disrupted by modern social and employment trends. Visitors to Lefkara can, however, still watch several generations of the same family working through their repertoire of stitches: buttonhole stitch, stem stitch, back stitch, satin stitch, and so on. Watch the patterns unfold from the needle points: geometric motifs and a characteristic zigzag called 'the river'. Natural patterns are also employed, with butterflies and flowers being favoured.

MILANESE PIECES
Leonardo da Vinci is said to have visited Lefkara in 1481 to obtain lace hangings for Milan Cathedral. No evidence exists to substantiate this claim. Leonardo might never have been to Lefkara, but he should have!

113

A Lefkaran woman practises the painstaking art of making lace

BRITISH TOUCH
Thanks to Limassol's large expatriate British population, its proximity to the nearby British military base at Akrotiri and its many British holiday-makers, pubs and fish 'n' chip shops seem about as thick on the ground as tavernas in some districts. Even though many British visitors turn their noses up at this, presumably the establishments would go out of business if they were not popular.

Limassol's 13th-century castle was later strengthened by the Venetians

▶▶ Limassol 98B2

Although the fastest growing and most popular tourist centre in Cyprus, as well as its key industrial and commercial hub (thanks mainly to its excellent port facilities), it takes quite a stretch of imagination to describe this city of 140,000 as 'attractive', even if it does consider itself to be the 'Paris of Cyprus'. Yet Limassol has its points of interest as well as being a good base for exploring the southern coast and the Troodos Mountains.

In addition, the city has an active and occasionally sophisticated nightlife scene, which is an important contributory factor to Limassol's popularity. Whether it makes economic sense (it certainly makes no environmental sense) to fill up the adjacent coastline with cheek-by-jowl hotels remains to be seen.

OLD TOWN SIGHTS Occupying a commanding position near the Old Harbour, **Limassol Castle▶▶** (tel: 05-330419. *Open* Mon–Sat 9–5, Sun 10–1. *Admission charge*), which dates to the Lusignan era in the 13th century, with later modifications by the Venetians, Turks and British, provides present-day visitors with an excellent viewpoint from its battlements. Its main claim to fame now, however, is that it houses the **Cyprus Medieval Museum** in a series of Gothic-arched halls deep in its interior. The museum complements this gloomily atmospheric setting with exhibits that consist mainly of funerary monuments. The higgledy-piggledy houses of the former Turkish Quarter are clustered around Limassol Castle, making it an excellent district in which to wander, browsing in the

numerous small boutiques and workshops that have sprung up.

The quietly distinguished little Orthodox church of **Agios Antonios▶** can be found in this part of the city. Notable also is the adjacent mosque. Unlike the church, however, this is closed for renovation.

A fairly sleepy corner compared with the frenetic activity of the modern commercial port, the **Old Harbour** retains elements of colour in the many fishing boats tied up gunwale to gunwale. Private yachts and cruisers are also moored here, and this is the starting-point for cruise excursions up and down the coast. The seafront promenade starts from near the harbour and makes for a pleasant, shaded stroll beside the Mediterranean.

Lounging around on the beach is a popular way of life at Limassol

TO THE NORTH Heading north from the old town along Agiou Andreou street will take you to the **Folk Art Museum▶** (253 Agiou Andreou Street, tel: 05-362303. *Open* Jun–Sep Mon–Wed and Fri 8.30–1.30 and 4–6.30, Thu 8.30–1.30; Oct–May Mon–Wed and Fri 8.30–1.30 and 3–5.30, Thu 8.30–1.30. *Admission charge*), housed in a fine 19th-century mansion. The museum displays an interesting and varied collection of typical objects, ornaments and costumes of everyday use in Cyprus during the more recent past, as well as a range of wedding dresses which point to the importance of these special occasions.

Continuing along this street and then turning right on to Tornariti street will take you to the **Municipal Gardens▶**. Although not especially big, the gardens represent a welcome patch of greenery and shade, being almost unique in Limassol in this respect. They contain the Municipal Open Air Theatre and the Municipal

Limassol Zoo, inside the shaded oasis of the Municipal Gardens

Zoo. The Limassol Wine Festival takes place in the park during September is a great open-air party, with free wine flowing and throngs of people taking full advantage of the opportunity.

To the north of the Municipal Gardens is the **Limassol District Archaeological Museum▶** (corner of Kanningos street and Vyronos street, tel: 05-330157. *Open* Mon–Sat 9–5, Sun 10–1. *Admission charge*). The museum is well placed for sources of exhibits – Amathus and Kourion both lie near Limassol – and its extensive collection of ceramics and pottery dating from Mycenaean to Roman times is well worth the visit. Highlights are the bust of Aphrodite and statues of Egyptian and Phoenician gods.

TO THE SOUTH Since 1974, Limassol has developed as the island's premier port, growing to keep pace with the economy's rapid development. All the activity of a major port can be seen to the south of town towards Lady's Mile Beach, with merchant ships coming and going constantly.

EVERGREEN PLEASURE
Greenery is conspicuous by its absence in Limassol, so if you want to take advantage of what little there is, combine it in a short stroll. Walk through the Municipal Gardens to the seafront, and then continue south along the palm-tree-shaded promenade.

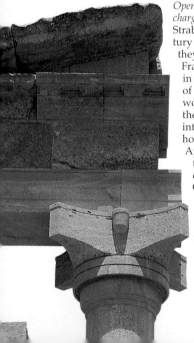

In summer, the Salt Lake dries out to a hard crystalline sheen before filling up when the rains come again

Partially restored column and pediment from the temple which dominates the Sanctuary of Apollo Hylates

▶▶▶ Salt Lake   98B1

For half of the year this is more salt-flat than salt lake, but with November comes rain to fill the shallow basin, attracting the first of many migratory birds, including pink flamingos. Feeding on small crustaceans that flourish in the salty water, the birds present quite a spectacle in large numbers, a pink splurge of motion in the middle of the lake (see panel). During the dry season, the glittering salt-flat in the heart of Akrotiri Peninsula makes for a fine cross-country run if you have a four-wheel-drive or dirtbike. The Salt Lake is just outside the closed area of the British base and, as with the lake near Larnaka, the salt is no longer fit for human consumption.

▶▶▶ Sanctuary of Apollo Hylates   98A2

Open: summer daily 9–7.30; winter daily 9–5. Admission charge

Strabo, a Greek geographer writing early in the 1st century AD, refers to a promontory near Kourion 'from which they hurl those who have touched the altar of Apollo'. Fragments of the altar referred to by Strabo are strewn in a pile of rubble at the heart of the sanctuary 3km west of the main Kourion site. This was among the classical world's holiest places. Broken walls mark the house of the priest of Apollo. The temple's roof has vanished into the blue Mediterranean sky; yet the wonder is not how much has disappeared, but how much remains.

Apollo's sanctuary, in continuous use from the 7th century BC until the middle of the 4th century AD, when classical pagan cults were abolished in favour of Christianity, has completed its journey through the succeeding centuries in a remarkable state of preservation. Originally there were two entrances, with the Kourion Gate and the Pafos Gate, the modern entrance lying between them. The dormitories and display halls can clearly be identified, as can a *palaestra* (gymnasium), a baths complex and the remains of the priest's house and the strongroom which held the temple treasury.

The heart of the sanctuary consists of some remarkable monuments: the archaic *temenos*, or precinct of the god; the Temple of Apollo, partially restored, and reached by the long, narrow Sacred Way; and votive pits into which were thrown masses of surplus offerings, many of which can be seen in the island's museums. One monument is unique in the Mediterranean: a circular area of rock pitted with holes which archaeologists speculate was the scene of ritual dances around a cluster of trees and bushes sacred to Apollo.

SHOCKING PINK
Most European flamingos migrate to Africa for the winter, but a sizeable flock regularly overwinters on Cyprus at the salt lakes near Akrotiri and Larnaka; they are eagerly awaited by both serious birders and casual observers. The shallow brine lakes are among the most important feeding areas in the eastern Mediterranean for this bird, which filters minute organisms from the water with its bill – the pink colouring comes from the prawns the flamingos consume. Other species that can be seen at the lake at various times between October and April include the black-winged stilt, dunlin, ruff, little stint, marsh sandpiper, little egret, grey heron and little-ringed plover.

117

At the end of the Sacred Way, the Temple of Apollo retains the romance of antiquity

DOWN THE PIT
Pilgrims came from all over the Mediterranean to the famed Sanctuary of Apollo Hylates at Kourion, particularly during the Roman Empire. They left so many votive offerings at its altars that the priests were forced constantly to clear them out to make space for new ones. This they did by depositing less valuable items in a specially dug pit on the sanctuary grounds. Thousands of these, most of them small terracotta figurines representing people and animals, have since been recovered by archaeologists. A selection can be seen in archaeology museums at Nicosia, Limassol, Pafos and Episkopi.

▶ **Zygi**　　　　　　　　*99D2*

This little coastal village between Limassol and Larnaka has developed a reputation as a seafood centre, popular with visitors and Cypriots alike, with many of its fish restaurants lined up along the shore. Unlike many such places in Cyprus, the seafood here is mostly fresh rather than frozen. At some tavernas, such as Apovathra, you choose your own fish and eat it right beside the water, although the nearby electricity plant and concrete factory may put you off.

Above: Agios Minas Convent

Drive

See map on pages 98–9

Limassol to Lefkara

This 50km route begins at the coast and winds into the foothills of the Troodos Mountains. Passing through some attractive villages on the way, the drive route terminates at one (or rather two) of Cyprus's most interesting villages. The sights on this drive are covered in more detail on pages 103–17.

Limassol's major attraction, from the point of view of this drive is that it is fairly easy to escape to the east. The quickest route out of town is via the A1 motorway, but the B1 coast road is more attractive: in the long term its sea view seems certain to be sacrificed to a sea-wall of hotels.

Above: loukoumia, *or Turkish delight, from Lefkara*
Below: the church and village of Pano Lefkara

The ruined ancient city of **Amathus**▶▶▶ lies alongside the coast road just beyond the sprawl of Limassol's beach-hotel district. Its air of rather forlorn majesty and the ongoing excavation of its Phoenician harbour and Greek acropolis make for a fascinating stroll through history.

Beyond the undistinguished village of Parekklisia, the road climbs steadily, opening up a superb view over terraced hillsides to the distant Mediterranean. Some of the surrounding rocky landscape has been partially reafforested, and the intermittent green canopy of leaves adds to its attraction.

The church of Agios Georgios in **Kellaki**▶, ensconced like a miniature Parthenon on a rocky outcrop at the summit of the village, has a fine gilt iconostasis and a priest who is happy to show it off to visitors. By now you are into 'hairpin bend' country, which is characteristic of much of Cyprus as you drive away from the coast.

Zoodhokos Pyghi▶, the 'Monastery of the Life-giving Spring', sits on a spur outside Eptagoneia, visited seemingly by no one despite its handsome modern aspect.

A popular place for a break with tourists travelling between Limassol and Nicosia, **Agios Minas**▶▶ is well worth the stop. The convent is beautifully maintained and the nuns are welcoming to visitors.

Kato Drys▶, an attractive mountain village whose narrow streets are crowded with typical old houses, some painted blue, as well as some fine villas, is the home village of the Cypriot-British millionaire Sir Reo Stakis, who made his fortune in restaurants, hotels and casinos. Just beyond it is the Plane Tree Restaurant, whose owner is the proud possessor of what he claims is the largest plane tree in Cyprus, planted by one Mr Cavecas in 1906.

The twin villages of **Lefkara**▶▶▶, separated by only a kilometre (they are also connected by a steep, narrow road which is more interesting and challenging than the main road), are particularly famed for their lace and silverware.

119

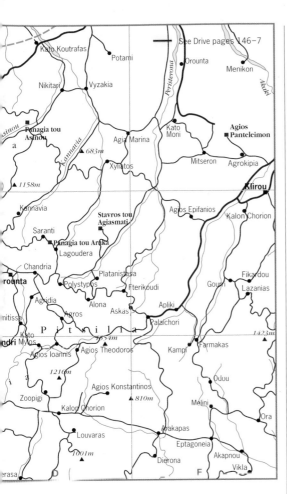

THE TROODOS MOUNTAINS

THE TROODOS MOUNTAINS It is not a great exaggeration to say that, geographically, Cyprus consists of the Troodos Mountains and a few other fragments. The range dominates the western half of the island, a citadel that guards well its treasures of nature, religion, agriculture and human life.

From all but the most distant points of Cyprus the mountains are unmissable. They rise up virtually from the shoreline in a steepening swell that gathers momentum the higher it reaches, until it crests on the 1,952m-high Mount Olympus, the fittingly named abode of Aphrodite (not to be confused with its namesake in Greece where the Olympians dwelt). The summit is a military base but the slopes attract skiers in winter.

Of course, the mountains date from a far earlier era than classical antiquity. Long before the island existed in its present form, the mountains were there, the product of volcanoes that erupted tens of millions of years ago. Erosion has been working on them ever since, wearing them down slowly but inexorably to remnants of their former glory; even so, the Troodos will be around for some time to come.

Left: mountain sunset seen from a point near the Archbishop Makarios III tomb on Throni Hill

▶▶▶ REGION HIGHLIGHTS

AGIOS NIKOLAOS TIS STEGIS
see page 124

CEDAR VALLEY *see page 125*

COMMANDARIA REGION
see page 126

MARATHASA VALLEY
see page 133

MOUNT OLYMPUS
see page 134

**PANAGIA TOU KYKKOU
(OUR LADY OF KYKKOS)**
see page 142

SOLEA VALLEY *see page 149*

STAVROS TOU AGIASMATI
see page 149

**TOMB OF ARCHBISHOP
MAKARIOS III** *see page 150*

The Troodos Mountains

Typical village house, Koilani

WORLD CLASS
UNESCO has included nine historic Byzantine churches in the Troodos Mountains in its World Cultural Heritage Site classification. They are:
- **Agios Ioannis Lampadistis** (page 132).
- **Agios Nikolaos tis Stegis** (page 124).
- **Archangelos** (page 126).
- **Panagia tou Asinou** (page 141).
- **Panagia tis Podythou** (page 126).
- **Panagia tou Araka** (page 140).
- **Panagia tou Moutoullas** (page 135).
- **Stavros tou Agiasmati** (page 149).
- **Timios Stavros** (page 148).

COOL STUFF
Throughout southern Cyprus, heading for the Troodos is the answer for those who just have to escape the scorching summer temperatures elsewhere on the island. While the temperature in Nicosia can soar above 40°C and 35°C is not uncommon around the coast, Mount Olympus rarely goes higher than 27°C. The average temperature in the high mountains is 15°C lower than that of Nicosia.

Department of Forests information sign

At a more mundane level, the Troodos are the subject of much head-scratching over road maps. All roads but the coast road lead to the mountains, and there, for the most part, they run out in twisting byways or rough trails that add hours to any cross-island journey and subtract years from the life of drivers determined enough to attempt them. And yet there the mountains are. Crane your neck from a prone position on any beach and you will see them staring straight back down at you, cool, green and imperious, masters of all they survey. Sooner or later most visitors to Cyprus ask themselves: 'I wonder what it's like up there...?'

What it's like is a breath of fresh air, as the sultry Mediterranean zephyrs are magically transmuted by altitude into cool, sharp-edged breezes. Cypriots knew all about this before the

tourists, of course, and perhaps the hardest thing for them to bear is that the visitors have pursued them to their mountain hideaways. Even the president's summer residence is the target of tramping tourists whose curiosity has got the better of them.

High times There is, however, enough room in the Troodos for everyone, provided they stay away from the choke-points where the few good trans-mountain roads converge. Hiking trails, which are at once educational and scenic, have been marked out by the Forestry Department at several locations around the upper reaches, and in most places there are no obstacles, apart from obvious physical ones, to striking out into the forests on deep-penetration hiking expeditions.

Today's forests are relative newcomers to the Troodos. The Forestry Department is continuing the task begun by the British to restore the tree cover laid low by centuries of over-felling. Restoration has more than an aesthetic value, because the Troodos are the island's principal watershed, the reservoir of a precious resource diminished by forest loss and erosion. Cyprus's main rivers rise here. Fed by the heavy winter rains, they plunge wildly downhill before running into as many dams as the authorities can muster to capture the flow before it disappears in summer's drought.

Sporting life Sport is a big attraction in the Troodos – even if most people get sufficient exercise staring out their car or tour-bus window at the passing view. As well as hiking, both cycling and mountain-biking are challenging possibilities. Their difficulty on steep gradients and rocky paths, aggravated by altitude and heat, should not be underestimated, yet why go to the mountains if not to get closer to nature? In winter there is even skiing (always assuming there is snow).

Considering how many people head for the hills to find a different Cyprus, it is ironic that the Troodos first gained popularity for their isolation from the coast. Orthodox monks, in particular, chose this path to escape the temptations and dangers of the plain, with its worldly towns and threat from invaders and pirates. When the stars crowd into the night sky like jewels scattered on a black velvet background, framed by tree-covered peaks, it seems as if the monks chose wisely and that heaven is not far away.

MOUNTAIN TIME
'The country we traversed is charmingly picturesque, a series of plains sloping gently towards the hills, all beautifully green. Above the hills rises a chain of high mountains, whose summits are crowned with snow.'
– *Travels of Ali Bey* (1806)

123

Selling the famous Marathasa Valley cherries

Agios Nikolaos tis Stegis, one of the delightful Troodos churches recognised by UNESCO as a World Cultural Heritage Site

►►► Agios Nikolaos tis Stegis   *120C2*

Open: Tue–Sat 9–4, Sun 11–4. Admission free

Like several other historic Troodos Mountain churches, this small 11th-century edifice 5km south of Kakopetria has two roofs: an outer one that protects the church from heavy winter snowfalls, and an inner one in the classic domed Byzantine style. Indeed, the 'tis Stegis' part of its name means 'of the roof'. A combination of its age, construction and, especially, the suite of superb religious frescoes in its interior has given Agios Nikolaos the status of a UnescoWorld Cultural Heritage Site.

Dating from the time of the church's construction to the 17th century, the murals depict some of the key moments of the Christian faith, including the raising of Lazarus from the dead, Christ's entry into Jerusalem and the Assumption of the Virgin. In addition, there is a finely rendered Christ Pantokrator gazing down from the dome – always a vital Orthodox symbol – and a painting of St Nicholas, for whom the church is named. The situation of Agios Nikolaos tis Stegis in the shadow of the mountains along a narrow side-road in the scenic Solea Valley, as much as the stellar quality of its decoration, attracts frequent visitors.

►► Agios Theodoros   *120C3*

Easily one of the most picturesque of Cypriot villages, Agios Theodoros has become both a subject for artists and an artists' retreat. The rugged Pitsilia region forms the painterly backdrop, with its forested peaks rising above the village's own 1,000m-hilltop altitude. The fine villas dotting the vineyard-studded surroundings testify to the wealth that can be gleaned from agriculture and local business, as well as art. The 16th-century church of the **Panagia►** (Our Lady) (*Open* irregularly. *Admission free*) contains a superbly preserved iconostasis of the following century, with a silver-gilded icon of Our Lady, prayers to which are said to be efficacious whenever rain is needed – in Cyprus that means just about always.

FROM THE ROOFTOPS

Some Troodos Mountain villages can be disappointing to look at from a distance because their houses may lack the red-tiled roofs that fit so well the image of a rustic lifestyle and complement the green of hills and forests. From close up it can be seen that roofs are often made of corrugated iron, an entirely romance-free material but one that is practical in an area of heavy snowfalls.

Have you tried to speak Greek?

Greek is the language spoken in Cyprus, but English is spoken almost everywhere

Helllo/Good-bye	Ya-soo
Hi	Ya
How are you?	Ti kanis/iss-eh kala?
I'm fine	Imm-eh kala
Good	Kala
Good morning	Kali-mera
Good night	Kali-nicta
Please	Se para-kalo
Thank-you	Ef-haristo
Yes	Neh
No	O-hee
Today	Sim-mera
Tomorrow	Av-rio
Where (is)	Pou (inn-eh)
What (is)	Ti (inn-eh)
When (is)	Po-the (inn-eh)
Why	Ya ti
I want/would like	Thelo
Toilets	Tou-alletta
Restaurant	Estiatorio
Hotel	Kseno-tho-hee-o
Police	Astee-nomia
Hospital	Noss-ock-oh-mioh
Water	Nero
Wine	Krass-ee
Beer	Beer-a
Cheers!	Is igee-a!
One	Ena
Two	Thee-o
Three	Tree-ah
Four	Tess-era
Five	Pen-deh
Six	Ex-ee
Seven	Ef-tah
Eight	Octo
Nine	Enn-ay-a
Ten	Th-ekka

Useful Information

EMERGENCIES

POLICE/FIRE BRIGADE/FIRST AID/AMBULANCE 112/199
FOREST FIRE REPORTS 1407

SERVICES

GENERAL HOSPITAL 22801400
MAKARIO HOSPITAL 22405000
APOLLONIO PRIVATE HOSPITAL LTD 22350022
EVANGELISTRIA MEDICAL CENTRE 22671580
ADVISORY BUREAU ON AIDS 22305155
SUPPORT AGAINST DRUGS ABUSE 1410
OVERNIGHT PHARMACIES 90901412
DOCTORS ON CALL 90901432
POLICE 22802020
ELECTRICITY FAULTS 90901420

USEFUL TELEPHONES

CYPRUS TOURISM ORGANIZATION - CTO
Head Office: 19, Limassol Avenue 22691100
TOURIST INFORMATION, *Laiki Yitonia* 22674264
NICOSIA MUNICIPALITY, *Eleftheria Square* 22797000
CENTRAL POST OFFICE, *Eleftheria Square* 22303123
IMMIGRATION OFFICE, *Government-Complex Bldg* ... 22305458
CYPRUS BROADCASTING CORPORATION, *Aglandjia* ... 22422231

TELEPHONE SERVICES

NATIONAL DIRECTORY ENQUIRIES 192
INTERNATIONAL DIRECTORY ENQUIRIES
(country codes, trunk codes, rates) 194
INTERNATIONAL CALLS *(through operator)* 198
EXACT TIME .... english 193 / greek 195
TELEGRAMS BY PHONE 196
MON.-FRI.:7.15A.M.-1.45P.M./SAT.:7.15A.M.-12.45P.M./
SUN.:7.15A.M.-1.15P.M.
FAULTS REPORT 197
CUSTOMER CALL CENTRE 132

AIRPORTS

LARNAKA INTERNATIONAL AIRPORT 77778833
(49km from Nicosia)
PAFOS INTERNATIONAL AIRPORT 77778833
(146km from Nicosia)

▶ Agros   121D2

Various kinds of liquid inducements exist for making a visit to Agros. There is a choice of three – rose-water, mineral water and wine – for which the village is world famous, in Cyprus at any rate. Agros is both well sited and handsome, its inhabitants doing their best to keep it a living, and even flourishing, entity.

▶ Arsos   120B1

The houses of Arsos with their red-tiled roofs hug the side of a valley on the southwestern Troodos slopes. This is a Krassochoria (wine district) village, famed for its deep-red wines as well as the fiery zivania spirit, and is characteristic of the smaller villages of the area. Most of the younger people have moved to jobs in the cities and at the coast, so Arsos gets by on the hard work of its old folk. Legend gives Arsos a romantic beginning: it was reputedly named after Cleopatra's younger sister, Arsinoë, who was banished from Egypt by Julius Caesar in 47 BC.

▶▶▶ Cedar Valley   120A3

In times past, the phrase 'cedars of Lebanon' was a household expression and a romantic image of that country. The cedars of Cyprus may not have attained such popular acclaim, but there is no doubting the romantic appeal of this valley on the western slopes of the Troodos, filled with serried ranks of the distinctive trees. All the trails to Cedar Valley, from any direction, are sufficiently rough for it to be as well that both the journey and the final destination are scenic enough to make the experience worthwhile.

The variety of cedar, *Cedrus libani brevifolia*, is indigenous to Cyprus. Most of the island's 50,000 or so cedars are here in the **Tripylos Nature Reserve▶▶▶**, between Kykkos Monastery and Stavros tis Psokas in the Pafos Forest, alongside pine, plane and golden oak. They stand tall and proud, their symmetrical branches rising in horizontal order and their cylindrical green cones standing straight up like Christmas-tree ornaments.

WILD AT HEART
A reserve for the rare and previously endangered moufflon has been established in Cedar Valley, although these wild mountain sheep may also be found higher up in the Troodos. Cyprus Airways has adopted the moufflon as its emblem.

Call of the wild in Cedar Valley

125

Cedars of Cyprus are the attraction in this rugged valley

The Troodos Mountains

▶▶▶ Commandaria Region   120C1

A narrow sliver of the southern slopes of the Troodos is given over to the production of grapes, from which are made Cyprus's distinctive Commandaria sweet red dessert wines. There is little, in fact, to distinguish this area from the neighbouring Krassochoria wine district in terms of landscape or climate, but the tradition of its unique suitability for Commandaria is fixed.

▶ Foini   120B2

This small village nestles in the bottom of a valley near Kato Platres. Its steep-sided streets boast several traditional pottery-makers; in times past the village was an important producer of the large *pitharia* pots, but now it specialises in smaller pieces. There is a small but interesting **Pottery Museum▶**, whose exhibits recall the village's pottery-making history.

▶▶ Galata   120C3

Situated just off the main road from Nicosia, where it climbs through the Solea Valley towards the Troodos peaks, Galata is a pretty village in its own right, consisting of a cluster of white-painted houses set down on the green valley floor. Its restored Ottoman-era **Hani Kalliana Inn▶** adds to its interest. Besides this, there are no fewer than four fine churches in and around Galata, two of them being on UNESCO's list of World Cultural Heritage Sites.

Agios Sozomenos▶ in the village centre dates from the early 16th century and its post-Byzantine frescos make for an interesting comparison with the much older ones in UNESCO-classified churches elsewhere in the Troodos. Similarly, among the fields just outside the village, is 16th-century **Panagia tis Podythou▶▶**, a UNESCO-recognised site particularly notable for its triangular rendering of the Crucifixion and its superb Our Lady as the Queen of Heaven in the narthex. The small timber-roofed church of **Archangelos▶▶**, near by, has simpler but still impressive post-Byzantine frescos. Finally, there is **Agia Paraskevi▶**, a small 16th century church situated on the old road from Galata to Kakopetria (All churches are *open* irregularly. *Admission free*).

Not all the Orthodox churches in the Troodos are of venerable age: this one at Galata is modern

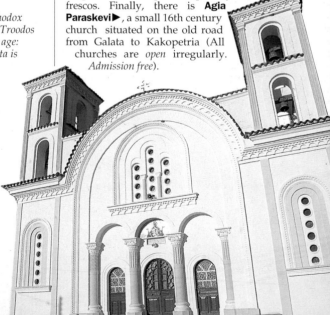

▶▶ Kakopetria   *120C3*

On the road to Troodos from Nicosia, Kakopetria is the first indication that you are entering a totally different environment. As the road begins to climb, you can turn off towards the village, whose historic and somewhat ramshackle old centre is considered so typical of Cyprus that it is being preserved and restored. Kakopetria is a fast-growing resort, with a fine view over fertile valleys, and well equipped with hotels and restaurants. The village is located on the northern edge of the mountains, but is close enough to be convenient for exploring them.

▶▶ Kaledonia Falls   *120C2*

Visions of a Cypriot Niagara Falls must be put firmly out of mind. Indeed, a dispassionate observer looking at this diminutive cascade tumbling all of 20m into a shallow pool might wonder if the description 'waterfall' is not overdone. These objections noted, however, Kaledonia Falls is still a worthy phenomenon, if only for its unique-ness in being fed by a perennial stream, known as the Kryos. The signposted 2km Kaledonia Trail follows a pretty route through the forest to the falls from a point near Troodos village.

▶ Kaliana   *120C3*

Certain small villages seem, in an unforced, unrestored way, to be characteristic of the old way of life in Cyprus. This one, situated in a narrow side-valley on the western edge of the Solea Valley, is in addition representative of the area's agricultural richness, surrounded as it is by orchards, vegetable plots and vineyards. Nothing much ever happens in Kaliana: it is a charmingly tranquil little place whose 16th-century church of **Agioi Joachim ke Anna** (*Open irregularly. Admission free*) is its most notable asset, containing some murals from the same period.

Kakopetria village

GOING WITH THE FLOW
Virtually all of Cyprus's rivers originate from the snow and rain that falls on the Troodos watershed. Apart from the waters that flow over Kaledonia Falls, however, few survive much beyond the spring. Yet in the past the streams had a more abundant and long-lasting flow. Cyprus's first regular supply of electricity came from a hydroelectric plant at Kakopetria.

Kaledonia Falls

As long as your chosen sport does not depend on white water, Cyprus is surely an outdoor sports enthusiast's paradise. Trails leading through the Troodos and Kyrenia (Beşparmak) mountains allow serious hikers and mountain-bikers to push themselves to the limit, while gentler routes around the coast cater for the more easy-going.

Above: hikers in the Troodos. Below: soaring above the coast near Kition

128

Active vacations are said to be getting more popular by the minute, although this does not seem to be the case if you compare the numbers of mountain-bikers in the Troodos to those of sunworshippers at Fig Tree Bay. Mountain-biking in the Troodos is no picnic: the hills are high, the trails rough, the sun hot, and any effort to overcome these difficulties involves perspiration in disheartening amounts. Cycling along the coast is at least easier, although caution is needed on the busy coast roads, and cyclists should stick to the less frequented coastal tracks. Facilities for renting touring bikes are available in all main resorts, and mountain-bikes can be hired at Pano Platres in the Troodos. Further information on cycling possibilities is available from the **Cyprus Cycling Federation**, 20 Ionos Street, PO Box 24572, 1301 Nicosia tel: 02-663344.

Walking away Many of Cyprus's outdoor activities are free: hiking, for example, or even just walking and admiring the flowers and the scenery. Several nature trails have been established by the Forestry Department around Troodos village, Pano Platres and Mount Olympus in the Troodos Mountains, and in the wild and lonely Akamas Peninsula on the northwest coast, ranging in length from 3km or so to over 20km.

Rock-climbers near Trooditissa Monastery

In the Kyrenia (Beşparmak) Mountains there are also numerous trails. One runs across the spine of the mountains from Voufaventon (Buffavento) Castle to the Halevga (Alevkaya) Forest Station. All involve some huffing and puffing, but for an averagely fit person it would be an overstatement to call them hikes.

Real hiking is all about going in search of moufflon in the Pafos Forest, with a compass, a large-scale map (these can be obtained from some bookshops, although some of the highly detailed military survey maps are unavailable for security reasons; in the Turkish Cypriot zone no such maps are available), and a good supply of food and water. The Akamas has almost equally difficult terrain but is more popular with walkers because of its proximity to a beautiful section of the coast. The experience of traversing such hard-boiled landscapes, knowing that few other people

are willing to do so, may be satisfaction enough. In summer, clothing should be light but offer adequate protection against the sun, and footwear should be sturdy at all times of the year.

Assisted passages Horse-riding may be preferable to cycling or walking, since the horse does most of the work. Cross-country trekking is available at bigger resorts such as Pafos and Limassol, and outside Nicosia; tuition is offered by various local horse-riding centres. Further information is available from the **Cyprus Equestrian Federation**, PO Box 24860, 1304 Nicosia tel: 02-472515 or 349858.

Dirt-bikes can be hired in all the holiday resorts. All across Cyprus, moreover, there is rough non-agricultural country where dirt-bikes come into their own. Some of the rugged trails in the Akamas Peninsula and the Troodos Mountains are ideal, but not for the little mopeds that most riders hire.

Fishy pursuits As Cyprus compensates for diminished rainfall by damming its rivers, freshwater lakes have been created and stocked with trout, carp, catfish, silver bream and perch. At some dams, these reservoirs can be fished year-round. In both cases a permit from the local Fisheries Department district office in Limassol, Larnaka or Pafos is required (see page 105). Further information is available from the **Ministry of Agriculture and Natural Resources, Fisheries Department**, 13 Aiolou Street, 1101 Nicosia tel: 02-807830/80781.

WALK OF LIFE
Inasmuch as walking can be considered an outdoor sport, an excellent account of walking in Cyprus is given in Colin Thubron's book, *Journey Into Cyprus*, recording a 1,000km tour of the island he made on foot in 1972, before partition.

129

FOOTBALL GLORY
The Cypriots' own sporting passion is reserved almost exclusively for soccer, originally introduced by the British. Each season, the Greek Cypriot First Division alone accounts for the equivalent of one ticket sold for every man, woman and child. The sport is organised by the Cyprus Football Association, which controls the four top divisions and 12 minor divisions. Turkish Cypriots are no less fanatical about the game.

A sea-angler tries his luck near Agia Napa

By bike

road for any particularly keen mountain-bikers, although some sections of the road are rough enough to make this seem superfluous. Individual sights on this tour are covered in more detail on pages 126–50.

Going downhill at the start of the trip means that the last leg will also be downhill – which may be an important consideration by then if you are on your last legs. Starting from **Pano Platres►►**, head downhill towards **Kato Platres►**, passing the church of **Faneromeni** on the way.

Still heading downhill, you enter the strikingly situated small village of **Foini►**, which is noted for its pottery production – both traditional Cypriot ware and modern varieties – and which also has a small **Folk Art Museum►**. Beyond Foini the road begins to climb up through open countryside.

The experience of cycling uphill in the thin mountain air, under the strong Cyprus sun, will provide an insight into the exertion required to complete the whole route; if you decide this is not for you, take the track which runs off to the right at the chapel as this will drastically shorten the trip.

This trail leads to **Trooditissa Monastery►►**. On its rough surface, however, even the few downhill stretches seem like uphills (though they are not quite as physically demanding as the uphills), so it is not necessarily an easy option.

If you choose not to take the short cut, continue on the main road, now lined with woodland, towards Timios Stavros village or detour to the left through the steeply sited village of Agios Dimitrios. In this segment you emerge from the forest cover and the true impact of the Troodos range can be seen, as the view opens up across

Through the Troodos

Fresh air and marvellous views are among the attractions of the Troodos Mountains, and what better way to experience them than from the saddle of a bicycle? This 40km round trip is, however, quite demanding and you should be confident of your fitness and stamina.

There are several shops in Pano Platres that hire mountain-bikes, advertising that they do so on their windows. Numerous trails lead off

Testing time for the mountain-biker high in the Troodos

The church at the scenically sited Trooditissa Monastery

131

forest-covered peaks and down into the open valleys with tiny villages pinned to the slopes.

If you are so fit that the route so far has seemed like no more than a mere jaunt, you may wish to push things a little further by detouring to the left at Lemithus, down into the church-dotted valley and the hamlet of Treis Elies. Otherwise, it's best to stick to the itinerary.

Climbing again, you move back into the forest cover in the direction of the Troodos summit, but turn away from it at the high-altitude village of **Prodromos▶**. A Forestry College and Agricultural Station near Prodromos show the importance attached to both

activities in this area. If the route so far has seemed hard, relief is close at hand: Forestry Department picnic sites along the way make ideal places for a break and the road soon begins to head downhill. A short diversion, to the right this time, again leads to Trooditissa Monastery, overlooking a steep gorge.

The final stretch is an exhilarating downhill run on a sharply curving road all the way back to Pano Platres. Because this road slices past the village and joins the main road 1km below the town, be sure to follow the signs for Platres and not race past them; otherwise the final stretch will be an unwelcome uphill one.

A mosaic at the entrance to the Trooditissa church

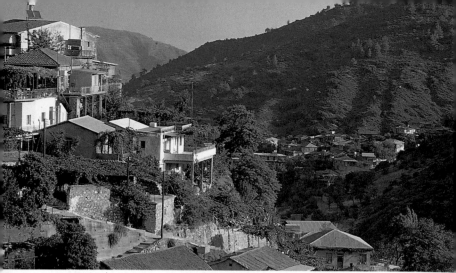

Looking towards the village of Kalopanagiotis

FIRE RISK
Fire can be a serious hazard in the mountains, particularly when the long, dry summer creates tinderbox conditions in the forests. The consequences of a blaze can be devastating to the reafforestation effort. It ought to go without saying that no one travelling in the Troodos should take the slightest risk of setting off a fire.

► Kalopanagiotis 120C3

This village, in the heart of the Marathasa Valley on the northern slopes of the Troodos, used to be a noted spa resort thanks to its sulphur springs. Nowadays, its closest connection with water is in the **Kalopanagiotis Dam►** a few kilometres outside of town. The village still attracts visitors, however, who come to see the former monastery of **Agios Ioannis Lampadistis►►►** *(Open* daily 10–12 and 3–6. *Admission free)*, whose remarkable church, really three churches in one, is a UNESCO World Cultural Heritage Site.

The three churches stand side by side under an outer snow-roof. Each is painted with frescos depicting images of the saints and the life of Christ and the Holy Family. Those of the domed middle church, 11th-century Agios Irakleidios, have faded drastically with time, but the remaining two, a 12th-century Orthodox church and a 15th-century Latin chapel, both with vaulted ceilings, have retained their frescos more or less intact. If the church is locked, you may well find the priest who looks after it in the café next door, playing backgammon.

► Kampos 120B3

The northwestern corner of the Troodos takes some beating as a rough-country area traversed by some very poor roads. This apparent disadvantage can be seen as a positive advantage, however, if you are looking for isolation and wilderness. Not many tour buses make the mountain-goat trek into this quarter. Kampos village is

Relaxing in the shade of a café terrace at Kampos

one of the few centres of any size in the area, with a hotel, tavernas and coffee shops, and marking a dividing line between the rugged higher ground and the gentler lower slopes. The surroundings of Kampos are dotted with ruined Byzantine churches, and with forest stations and picnic areas.

►► Koilani   120C1

A charming small village in the heart of the grape-growing, wine-making district on the southern Troodos slopes, Koilani has not allowed its commitment to Bacchus to divert it entirely from the path of righteousness. Proof of this lies in the **Koilani Ecclesiastical Museum►** (*Open* irregularly; ask at village kafenion. *Admission charge*). Given that a great deal of Cyprus's cultural heritage rests in its Byzantine and Orthodox religious tradition, a museum like this helps put some perspective on an otherwise potentially bewildering array of churches and treasures. It's collection includes icons spanning six centuries (from the 13th through to the 19th), religious vessels and ornaments (including some outstandingly crafted in silver) and antique prayer books.

► Kyperounta   121D2

This small village lies in rough country off the eastern face of the Troodos at an altitude of 1,080m, and makes an interesting diversion for travellers touring the environs of the upper mountains. Its small 16th-century church of **Stavros (The Holy Cross)►** (*Open* irregularly. *Admission free*) has some restored frescos and a group of paintings depicting the discovery of the True Cross.

► Louvaras   121D1

For *aficionados* of Byzantine mural art, the village's 15th-century **Agios Mamas►** (*Open* irregularly. *Admission free*) church boasts some frescos by the noted artist Philippe Goul, a Christian from what is now Lebanon, who achieved renown in Cyprus for his work at the time of the Lusignan kings (see panel on page 149). Goul was also responsible for important works at Stavros tou Agiasmati church near Platanistasa (see also page 149).

► Mandria   120B1

Mandria is best known as a crossroads village for travellers descending from the mountains and seeking an alternative, more scenic route to the coast. It is also a market-gardening centre in an area of large farms. Taking the right fork here leads to Pafos, while the left fork leads to Limassol. Apart from the road, tiny Mandria itself is so peaceful sometimes that all its inhabitants seem to have tiptoed away.

►►► Marathasa Valley   120B2

While much of the Troodos Mountains consists of wild and rugged country, there are several valleys of almost fairy-tale charm, besides providing important access routes to the high mountains. One of these is Marathasa Valley, set in a green, fertile landscape dotted with agricultural villages on the northwestern slopes of the Troodos. Marathasa is renowned for the quality and quantity of its cherry harvest.

Honey is just one of the products of the Marathasa Valley

FRUIT-PICKING

Anyone wanting to take part in fruit-picking, either of cherries or of the many other fruits grown in Cyprus – oranges, grapefruit, grapes, apples, bananas, melons – is advised to contact the Ministry of Agriculture, Natural Resources and Environment, Louki Akrita Avenue, Nicosia tel: 02-805520, or the local authorities of the fruit-producing villages. Local tourist information offices and national and international offices of the Cyprus Tourism Organisation can also provide advice.

A television tower takes advantage of Mount Olympus's towering altitude

TREKKING TIP

Unusual nature treks (as well as archaeological tours) deep into the Troodos Mountains and Akamas Peninsula are organised by the highly committed personnel of Exalt Tours in Pafos who can be reached at Box 337, Pafos Street, Pafos tel: 06 243803.

The restored and revitalised main street in Omodos

▶▶ Mesa Potamos Monastery   120C2

Situated about half-way along a very rough track between Pano Platres and Kato Amiantos are the ruins of 14th-century Mesa Potamos Monastery, with rebuildings from later centuries. It overlooks a steep gorge where the Mesa Potamos riverbed plunges downhill (the river also plunges down, but only in winter). This trail makes for an enjoyable, if by no means easy, mountain-biking expedition from Pano Platres, where the bikes needed for such an undertaking can be hired.

▶▶▶ Mount Olympus   120C2

Military bases, both old and new, occupy some of Cyprus's finest locations. However, it does seem particularly cruel that the 1,952m summit of the island's highest mountain, Mount Olympus (also known as Mount Khionistra), should be out of bounds. The white geodesic dome of a British radar installation is the *trompe-l'oeil* occupying a position once sacred to Aphrodite. Tyre-traps, security fences and guards complete the dismal picture. Occupying the high ground has always been a military priority, but too many of Cyprus's priorities are military ones.

Elsewhere around the summit, there is a Cyprus army bunker, a fire-watch observation tower and red-and-white-painted television masts. In between it is just possible to enjoy the benefit of Olympus's altitude in the superb view across the surrounding mountains. The 7km Artemis Trail, a signposted nature trail established by the Forestry Department, begins at a point a little way downhill from here and describes a circumference of the summit, featuring information panels that point out interesting examples of flora, geology and geography on the way (see page 137).

Some heaps of rubble off the western summit are thought to indicate the ancient settlement of Palaia Khoria. The stones were apparently piled up to form a defensive wall by Venetian troops planning a last-ditch stand against the 16th-century Turkish invaders who had already captured Famagusta (Gazimağusa) and Nicosia. Not much came of this do-or-die resolution, however, and the Turks were soon in control of the entire island.

In winter, the snows of Olympus create a skier's playground, with several ski-lifts serving the pistes.

▶▶ Moutoullas
120C3

Located in the cherry-rich Marathasa Valley, Moutoullas is an attractive village noted for the frescos and handsomely carved doors of its tiny 13th-century Byzantine chapel of **Panagia tou Moutoullas**▶ (*Open* irregularly. *Admission free*), one of the nine historic churches in the mountains acclaimed by UNESCO.

▶▶ Omodos
120B1

This, the largest of the Krassochoria wine villages, has taken some fairly shrewd steps to preserve its traditional character, while cashing in a little on the tourist boom that has tended to pass the mountain villages by – as well as contributing to the drain of their young people to the resort towns. Part of the village centre has been restored and developed as a street-stall and café centre, while some residents will invite visitors in for a guided tour of their traditional homes, albeit for a fee.

It seems mean-minded to badmouth the restoration effort, which included replacing the asphalt in the village square with cobbles, but the outcome for this otherwise attractive place, appears to be neither fish nor fowl, a split-personality village unable to decide which way it wants to go. Nevertheless, Omodos's new-found vigour causes the Cypriot authorities to count it a success story in the restoration and preservation drive.

Among the goods for sale are pieces of local lace (called *pipilla*), and the ring-shaped bread called *arketana*, a speciality of Omodos that is now sold all over the island. The restored house interiors, hung with gourds and kitchen utensils beside the traditional oven, also have a cellar where the large earthenware pots called *pitharia*, formerly filled with wine, are stored. In addition, among the rustic and traditional items in the village's **Folk Museum**▶ is a restored 15th-century wine press.

Omodos's **Stavros Monastery**▶▶ (*Open* daily. *Admission free*), founded in AD 327, is another of the religious foundations favoured by St Helena, mother of the Roman Emperor Constantine, who scattered around Cyprus numerous sacred relics she had collected on a pilgrimage to the Holy Land. The church has one golden cross containing hempen fibres said to be from the ropes that bound Jesus to the cross, while another is said to contain a fragment of the True Cross.

Cherries ripen through the lazy days in the Marathasa sun

CHERRIES BLOSSOM
Cherries, such as those grown in the Marathasa Valley, are a relatively recent Cypriot product, but one which has caught on quickly. Roadside tables, market stalls and shop counters throughout Cyprus, but particularly in the valley, groan under the weight of this top-quality fruit during its short spring and early summer season. Most of the cherries are eaten fresh, though some are used in preserves.

LIFE FROM DEATH
Dead and rotting trees are prized almost as much as live ones in the sparse forests around Mount Olympus. This is because rotting trees provide a food source for microbes and other organisms, which play an essential role in forest ecology and, therefore, in the reafforestation process.

The monasteries of Cyprus are storehouses of Greek Cypriot tradition and the Orthodox faith. Ironically, these religious foundations, intended as refuges from the world, are now among the island's foremost tourist attractions.

136

OH, WHEN THE SAINTS...

Name days, the feast days of the various saints for whom most Cypriots are named, take the place of birthdays in Greek Cyprus (although birthdays are becoming more popular). Monasteries are often 'hosts' of name-day feasts, with stalls and entertainments set up in their grounds. Some examples:

- **Agios Antonios** (St Anthony), 17 January.
- **Agios Neofytos** (St Neofytos), 24 January.
- **Agios Georgios** (St George), 23 April.
- **Agioi Petros & Pavlos** (St Peter & St Paul), 29 June.
- **Agios Ioannis Lampadistis** (St John Lampadistis), 4 October.
- **Agios Loukis** (St Luke), 18 October.

Top: detail of the iconostasis, Panagia Chrysorrogiatissa. Below: Christ Pantokrator, Panagia tou Kykkou

More so than even the churches, the monasteries are the fountainhead of the faith. Their fortunes have ebbed and flowed with the tides of history, but their commitment to Orthodoxy, to the memory of Byzantium and to the emotional claims of Hellenism has never wavered. A visit to those monasteries that have not been turned into museums will show that the fires of faith still burn bright.

Throughout Greek Cyprus, 2,000-year-old Orthodox traditions are being maintained in work and prayer. Icons are being painted; hymns, church music and prayerbooks written; and fields, orchards and vineyards tended. And, because the religious men and women reconcile differently the requirements of hospitality and tranquillity, tourists are either being welcomed or fended off. The monasteries' ageless atmosphere is no accident; they have taken the worst that the ravages of time and the hand of man could impose, and yet they are still there.

High society A constellation of proud foundations holds the great ideas in trust: Panagia tou Kykkou (page 142) and Trooditissa (page 150) high in the Troodos Mountains; Machairas (page 190) atop the foothills of Pitsilia; Stavrovouni (page 96) on the heights above Larnaka; Panagia Chrysorrogiatissa (page 176) amidst the Pafos Forest; Agios Neofytos (page 158), with its cliffside chambers, overlooking Pafos. There are the humbler, more human convents, where nuns make honey and tend their flowers: Agios Nikolaos ton Gaton (page 102), overrun with pampered cats; reclusive Agios Georgios Alamanos (page 102); flower-bedecked Agios Minas (page 102); deeply spiritual Agios Irakleidios (page 188).

In the Turkish sector of Cyprus, the last monks have departed from glorious Apostolos Varnavas (page 232) near Salamis, now an archaeological museum; rustic Agios Mamas in Morfou (Güzelyurt – see page 216) is also a museum; and the most spectacular of all, that of the Apostolos Andreas (page 230), beside the rocky cape of the same name and with its blessed spring, drifts towards the same end.

Above: a dying tree marks a milestone along the Artemis Trail

Walk

The Artemis Trail

Named after the goddess of the forest, this marked trail circles the upper reaches of Mount Olympus, where the Forestry Department is working to restore Artemis's realm. At just over 7km, the walk can be completed in about two hours, although with more time you will be better able to enjoy the view and the flora.

Black pine trees are the main constituent of the forest, with some of the plant species around them – barberry, St John's wort and catmint, for example – being identified on information panels. Other points of interest along the route are mineral formations. Panel 6 points to a group of black pine trees that have been struck by lightning.

Other species which can be seen are fir trees and, around panel 11, where reafforestation is under way, cedars of Lebanon. Shortly after that there is a test quarry for chromite. The 'Walls of the Old Town' at panel 22 coincide with the site of ancient **Palaia Khoria►**, and are said to have been used by Venetian soldiers planning a last-ditch stand against invading Ottomans.

The slopes are steeper here and shows the effects of erosion which are proving difficult to reverse. Panel 29 indicates a giant black pine.

The views from beyond the ski-lift look out across the plains around Morfou (Güzelyurt) in the Turkish zone. From here the trail soon returns to its starting point.

Imagine a chill wind in your face, the swish of skis on snow and an exhilarating downhill rush through a white-painted world. Cyprus's winter charms stretch a long way from the doubtful warmth of the beach, to the ski slopes of the Troodos Mountains.

Skiing in the morning, swimming in the sea in the afternoon. This tempting and, on the face of it, surprising prospect is possible in Cyprus, although it may involve a fair amount of driving and some wishful thinking about snow and warm seas. The Mediterranean island, with its 300 or so days of sunshine every year, may not be the obvious destination for a skiing holiday, yet in the Troodos Mountains, specifically on the uppermost slopes of 1,952m-high Mount Olympus, skiing is eminently possible and skiing in the sun an odds-on probability.

In a good year (or a bad one, depending on which way you look at it) there may be enough snow to permit skiing from December to April, but more usually the season lasts from January to March. Given their altitude, the slopes are frequent candidates for snow, but given their latitude, rain is at least as likely. Nevertheless, the snows of Olympus do exist and can reach a depth of up to 3m, although a good deal less than that is more usual, yet still adequate.

Allowances needed At such times enthusiasts get their skis on and head for the pistes. The Troodos Mountains are not the Alps, however, and the facilities in terms of lifts, runs, equipment hire, on-site refreshment and après-ski are limited. In the nearly 40 years that skiing has

138

COOL IDEA
In the Ottoman era (and doubtless before then as well), the snows of Olympus were put to a more practical use than as a medium for swift motion. Snow was transported to Nicosia and other towns in those pre-refrigerator days to be used as a cooling agent for drinks and food. In effect, the mountains became a giant ice-making machine.

Practising those all-important turns

been practised in Cyprus, it has been growing steadily in popularity, and genuine enthusiasts will happily make allowances for the minimal possibilities so long as they have an opportunity to ski at all. In any case, there are cafés located near by with log fires, mulled wine and the other essentials after a day on the pistes.

There are four ski-lifts on Mount Olympus, serving the runs at Sun Valley and the North Face, which are clearly signposted on the approach roads. The former offers downhill stretches more or less corresponding to beginner and intermediate levels, while the latter features more testing descents of between 1km and 1.5km. Instructors from the Cyprus Ski Federation are on hand for beginners and intermediate-level skiers who want to get started or improve their technique. Several cross-country trails snake through the scenic pine forests from Sun Valley. Lift passes come with either seasonal or temporary membership of the Cyprus Ski Federation, obtainable on site, while equipment – skis, poles and boots – is available for hire and accessories for sale at Sun Valley.

Alpine breaks Given that the distance to Mount Olympus from the coast is not great, the only problem in getting there is that most of the roads are none too good. Driving in winter during sudden snow showers can be particularly difficult, but in fine weather and when the roads have been cleared it presents few problems. It is also possible to stay in the mountains and combine an alpine break with skiing. The main resorts are Troodos village, which is also the closest to the pistes, and Pano Platres, a little further down on the southern slopes. Both of these are important year-round resorts, and Pano Platres in particular has plenty of accommodation, restaurants and other facilities.

An international skiing competition takes place in February, with top skiers from other countries taking part, and several lower-level competitions as well. There are other attractions to being in the mountains at this time of year: tobogganing, for example, or taking part in snowball fights. Hiking, surrounded by Christmas-card scenery, is another kind of Cyprus treat.

WINTER CAMOUFLAGE
With names like Edelweiss and Vienna, the hotels and chalets of Platres can have one reaching for the map, just to check which country this is. These alpine-style names work well enough in winter but in summer they do seem a mite strange.

139

Skiing in the morning and swimming in the afternoon is the Cyprus promise

Tranquil Panagia tou Araka Monastery in the Troodos foothills

HILL STATIONS
The British, in their colonial heyday in India, loved their 'hill stations', little pieces of the motherland parked atop breeze-cooled heights to which they would withdraw before the withering heat of a real Indian summer. Being of fixed habits, they simply translated the institution to Cyprus. Pano Platres (see page 143) developed as just such a mountain retreat in the late-19th century, initially for convalescent soldiers, then for genteel society seeking relief from Nicosia. Cypriots followed the trend, so that Platres was a flourishing holiday resort long before anyone thought of dipping their toes in the Mediterranean.

▶ **Palaichori** *121E2*

Seen from the head of the mountain pass leading to it, the village of Palaichori, with its white-painted houses and red-tiled roofs, looks like a frozen avalanche suspended in the act of tumbling down the steep hillside on which it perches. From close up the image is less alarming, but the Byzantine-era village is no less pretty. Orchards, vineyards (which produce a fine red wine), almond trees and vegetable patches form its pastoral backdrop, softening the rough contours of the surrounding hills. These are irrigated by water from nearby Palaichori Dam, which is filled on a seasonal basis by the poplar-lined Peristerona stream. The 15th-century church of Sotiros (The Saviour) contains an early cycle of frescos (1466) by the noted artist Philippe Goul (see panel on page 149).

▶▶▶ **Panagia tou Araka**
(Our Lady of Araka) *121D2*

Open: daily 10–4. Admission free, donation welcome

The priest who welcomes visitors to this monastery shows no sign of diminished enthusiasm for his work, despite the regular flow of tourist buses, and greets visitors to the church with incense and holy water. His pride is understandable, although the 12th-century Byzantine monastery dedicated to Our Lady of Araka is in no sense a grandiose affair. Its modest bearing is enhanced by the trellised verandas overlooking its courtyard and its hilly situation near the village of **Lagoudera,** in the easternmost reaches of the Troodos.

UNESCO has granted World Cultural Heritage status to the establishment, principally for the unparalleled frescos (dating from 1192) that adorn its church. Artists were commissioned from Constantinople itself, capital of the Byzantine Empire. The Christ Pantokrator gazing down from the dome of heaven is particularly fine, with an expression that seems sadly resigned to human weakness, and eyes that appear to follow the observer, their gaze penetrating to the soul.

Other scenes include an image that imparts both great tenderness and wonder at the birth of the Saviour: a midwife washes the holy infant while Mary looks on. In an Annunciation scene, the Archangel Gabriel steps down from a heaven that looks like a Byzantine palace to deliver to Mary his message of the miraculous birth to which she can look forward.

►►► Panagia tou Asinou (Our Lady of Asinou)

121D3

Open: daily 9–3. Admission free, donation welcome

Also known as Panagia Forviotissa, this ought to be among the most tranquil mountain churches, thanks to its forest location near **Nikitari** village – and would be, except for a nearby taverna's chugging diesel generator. This is a pity, because 12th-century Panagia tou Asinou is considered the finest Byzantine church in the Troodos, heading the list of UNESCO World Cultural Heritage Sites.

The tiny church is filled with dazzling frescos representing the zenith of Byzantine religious art. Some date from 1105, including those depicting the Last Supper and the Ascension, painted by artists from Constantinople. The classic Orthodox image of Christ Pantokrator, who looks down from the dome as if from a window in heaven, has one of its noblest representations here. Repainting and restoration has been carried out through the centuries, most recently in the 1960s.

Asinou is in some respects typical of Cyprus's Byzantine churches. Generally, these are located in remote places and are mostly unimpressive from the outside when compared with, say, a Gothic cathedral. Several bear a more than passing resemblance to a barn because of the sloping roof and unadorned walls that protect them from the elements. Their real beauty, however, lies inside.

LODES OF UMBER

Mines in the Troodos supply a material that has been highly prized by artists, from ancient Egypt through the Italian Renaissance to modern times. The material is umber, an iron oxide mineral pigment, and Cypriot lodes are reckoned to yield among the best quality in the world. Umber is found at the interface between a layer of sedimentary chalk formed over millions of years and underlying solidified lava. Several locations in the Troodos produce umber from the so-called Pera Pedi Formation.

141

The tiny church of Panagia tou Asinou plays host to a superb suite of religious frescos

►►► Panagia tou Kykkou
(Our Lady of Kykkos)
120B3

Modern mosaics provide an indication of the wealth of imagery in Panagia tou Kykkou monastery

Open: daily dawn–dusk. Admission free; admission charge for museum

Photography is emphatically not permitted in the church of this proudest and richest of all Cyprus monasteries, dedicated to Our Lady. Visitors who sneak a quick snapshot of its icons and glittering ornamentation, expecting at most to be admonished by the guardian, are liable to find themselves grabbed by the scruff of the neck and bundled unceremoniously out of the door. Kykkos is as impressive as its haughty self-image implies, and, as with the Kingdom of Heaven, entrance is dependent on good behaviour.

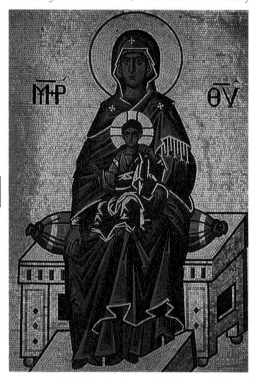

The present structure dates from the 19th century, previous foundations having succumbed regularly to fire since its establishment in the 10th century. It might have made the monks humble to wonder why their venerable institution has so often been burnt to a crisp, but this doesn't seem to be so. In any case, their most treasured possession, an icon of the Virgin said to have been painted by St Luke, and donated to Kykkos by the 12th-century Byzantine Emperor Alexius I, has come through all the blazes intact. Enclosed in tortoiseshell and mother-of-pearl, it stands on the iconostasis.

Most of the monastery's wealth is invested in land, much of it donated by the faithful as a means of avoiding Ottoman inheritance taxes in previous centuries. The museum displays some of the monastery's more liquid assets: ecclesiastical vessels, ornaments in gold and silver, and intricately embroidered vestments. Modern icons and murals are characteristic of Kykkos, particularly on the outside walls, and it remains to be seen how well these withstand the challenge of time. Kykkos is renowned throughout the Orthodox world, and has temporal power also, having been instrumental in maintaining Greek Cyprus's Hellenism through centuries of foreign occupation. Archbishop Makarios, the republic's first president, was a novice at Kykkos, and the monastery's counsel still reaches deep into the heart of Greek Cypriot government.

► Pano Amiantos
120C2

This village on the eastern face of the Troodos should be notable for little more than its pleasant character, an unremarkable place and no doubt happy to be so. Between here and its sister village **Kato Amiantos** further down the mountain, however, is a 'monument' of which no village

VIEWPOINT
The views from the mountain around Kykkos are perhaps the most spectacular in Cyprus, which is no mean commendation for an island that appears to have been deliberately designed with spectacular views in mind.

could be proud: a lifeless landscape that looks like the dark side of the moon. The installations of the Amiantos asbestos mine are unused now, crumbling into mementoes of industrial archaeology, but the mountain will take a long time to recover, if ever, from the depredations wrought across its surface.

▶▶ Pano Platres   120C2

The principal resort of the mountains, Pano Platres is an alpine-style village at an altitude of 1,100m. It was formerly a mainly Cypriot holiday hideaway, but has become popular with foreign tourists as they search for something more exciting than the traditional beach holiday. The result of these two streams of visitors, plus the village's position at an important crossroads, means it gets busy at peak times, up to and including the unwelcome phenomenon of traffic snarls. Still, it never quite loses its charm even then. At calmer times, in the magical early morning for example, the mountain stillness is interrupted only by the sound of rushing water, as the Kryos stream, tunnelling under the streets, goes charging downhill.

All the amenities of 'civilisation' – hotels, restaurants, cafés, shops, supermarkets, banks, exchange bureaux, a petrol station, a tourist information office – can be found in Pano Platres, most of them lined up along the steeply curving main street. These may be welcome to anyone who has been hiking along the hot and dusty mountain trails around the village, particularly in those areas where forest cover has not been re-established and there are no shading branches to ward off the sun. Day-old European newspapers are available for anyone who can't stand to be out of touch.

The main tourism role of Pano Platres is as a base for exploring the mountains. For those who take the time to do it properly – by mountain-bike or on foot – the way may be hard but the rewards are great. When the tourist buses and day-trippers in jeeps have pulled out for the night, groping their way down the narrow, twisting roads back to the resorts along the coast, Platres belongs to those who live there, however temporarily. The sharp-edged mountain air invigorates, and the substantial Cypriot food and crisp Cypriot wine taste all the sweeter.

DROPPING A LIGHT
A large tract of the forest running downhill to the west from Kykkos is quite visibly of more recent origin than its surroundings. This is because although warnings about the dangers of summer fires are widespread, no one thought to inform the Turkish air force, which in August 1974 dropped napalm on the forest, incinerating an enormous area and setting the re-afforestation programme back by a generation.

143

TROODOS CENTRAL
There are no 'attractions' as such in Pano Platres. Rather, it is the village, its character and location in the mountains that attract visitors. Pano Platres lies at the heart of the mountain web. Trails from here climb up through the forest to Kaledonia Falls, and beyond to Mount Olympus; downhill, following the course of the Kryos stream, to the Pera Pedi Forest and Pera Pedi Lake; and eastwards, under the 1,629m-high South Shoulder, towards Mesa Potamos Monastery. Mountain-bikes can be hired in several shops along the main street for tough expeditions along forest trails or steep mountain roads.

Catering for visitors to Panagia tou Kykkou, this shopkeeper does a heaven-sent trade

In both Greek and Turkish Cyprus the process of reafforestation that was begun by the British continues today. Not only do local industries, wildlife and water supplies benefit, but tourists find among the trees a ready-made shelter from the summer sun and a holiday experience far different from the traditional beach model.

Cyprus's forests are among the island's glories. In the dog days of summer, when heat smothers the plains, the forests of the Troodos and the Kyrenia (Beşparmak) Mountains act like magnets, drawing people upwards to the cool scent of eucalyptus, cedar and pine. So extensive are the forests in both ranges, and so rugged the terrain on which they grow, that they represent the last great place of escape on the island. No other country in the Levant boasts such wide-ranging and dense forest cover, yet the green canopy shading the mountains is but the straggly remnant of its former glory.

144

Trees struggle to retain a grip on an almost deforested slope

The main tree varieties on Cyprus are Aleppo pine, black pine, cypress, eucalyptus, juniper, plane, oak and cedar, the latter most notable at Cedar Valley in the Pafos Forest. In addition, cultivated trees not generally found in the forests include walnut, olive, carob, almond, citrus (orange, lemon, grapefruit and tangerine), fig, pomegranate, loquat, mulberry, apricot, damson, date palm and banana.

Fallen giants In ancient times the fame of Cyprus's forests spread far and wide – and people came from far and wide to chop them down. Cypriot trees went into the fleets with which Phoenicians, Persians, Greeks and Romans formerly dominated the Mediterranean, and into copper smelters to fuel Bronze Age civilisation. Natural regeneration was unable to keep pace with demand, yet even as late as the Ottoman period the island's forests covered not only the mountains but extended to the coastal plains. Excessive felling, overgrazing of young shoots which would have eplaced the fallen giants, clearance for agriculture and fires all conspired to lay the forests low.

The British were horrified at the destruction and took steps to reverse the process. They created the first forestry station, at Stavros tis Psokas in the western Troodos in 1884, to re-establish the Pafos Forest, which is still at the forefront of the reafforestation programme. In 1907, Winston Churchill, who was then a junior government minister, visited Cyprus and determined to aid the work with additional funds. It was not merely a question of aesthetics: loss of trees led to soil erosion and to climate changes. Streams dried up in summer and underground aquifers were depleted, a problem that remains serious today.

Extreme devastation High in the Troodos Mountains, the traveller may suddenly come upon a scene that looks like the end of the world. Around the village of Kato Amiantos the forest vanishes and a great swathe of mountainside lies desolate. The Amiantos asbestos mine is no more, but its legacy has permanently scarred the mountain, an extreme example of the devastation wrought by ill-considered exploitation. Not far away is the Forestry College at Prodromos, where students learn the skills of replanting and caring for the trees.

There is no equivalent to this level of devastation in the Kyrenia (Beşparmak) Mountains of Turkish Cyprus, although there are quarries in the foothills. Woodcutters are active enough in the higher reaches, but the exploitation is on a small scale and the forests seem well able to cope. In any case, even more so than the Troodos, the Kyrenia Mountains are sparsely populated and have only minimal tourist facilities. Reafforestation continues in both Greek and Turkish Cyprus, with determination but with a long way to go. It may be that Apollo Hylates, the woodland god whose sanctuary stands on the coast between Pafos and Limassol, would be mollified, if not exactly ecstatic, at the knowledge that the glory of his realm is being re-created, tree by tree.

FOREST STATIONS
There are forest stations scattered all over the Troodos Mountains, covering not only the high peaks, but reaching all the way to the lowest foothills in all directions. The Stavros tis Psokas Forest Station (see page 179) in the western Troodos foothills has a guest-house, while most have information panels, and picnic and barbecue areas. Some have nature trails, such as the Artemis Trail on Mount Olympus (see page 137).

The Kyrenia (Beşparmak) Mountains of Turkish Cyprus have a network of similar forest stations. A forest trail runs from Agios Ilarion (St Hilarion) Castle to Kantara Castle, and there is an important forest station at Halevga (Alevkaya), with a restaurant and a forestry museum.

145

CLEAR IMPROVEMENT
The ancient Greek geographer and astronomer Eratosthenes wrote that when Cyprus was first occupied by man it was so overgrown with trees that cultivation was impossible, but that the inhabitants at last cleared the ground and cultivated it. Their labour, he wrote, was richly rewarded, for the island was transformed from a wilderness into one of the most fertile and delightful countries on earth.

Athalassa Forest near Nicosia: a nursery for the reafforestation effort

Above: Panagia tou Kykkou

146

Drive

See map on pages 120–1

Kato Platres to Throni

This 50km drive is spiritually soothing, both for the lofty outlook and champagne air of the high mountains and for the emblematic Byzantine monastery at its end. Two hours of leisurely driving would complete it, but longer should be allocated for savouring the experience and exploring some of the side-trails. The sights on this drive are covered in more detail on pages 124–51.

Take the road north out of Kato Platres and, as the open slopes of the Troodos Mountains' southern approaches give way to thick pine forests, you arrive at **Pano Platres**▶▶, boasting a plethora of hotels and restaurants which have not, however, detracted overmuch from its alpine charm. At the first T-junction on the edge of Platres turn right for Troodos, then left at the second T-junction.

It may be a little early in the itinerary for walking, but if not, the short trek to the **Kaledonia Falls**▶▶ is recommended for its immersion in the forest air, with perhaps a free shower under the trim little waterfall as well. A **trout farm** is situated beside the restaurant at the start of the walk. At the next junction follow the sign for Troodos.

Still climbing, you pass a cluster of government lodges on the left, and somewhere off to your right, hidden among trees on the steep eastern slope, the president's summer palace. Shortly afterwards there is the first of several picnic areas that dot the route. **Troodos**▶▶ village is not exactly idyllic, with its souvenir shops and fast-food outlets, but its popularity depends on precisely those assets. At the far end of Troodos village turn left, following the sign for Prodromos.

A subsequent left turn puts you on the short diversion to **Mount Olympus**▶▶▶. The summit is out of bounds, but the outlook from nearby viewpoints is spectacular, which compensates for the limited view obtained from the tree-lined road up to this point. Return to the main road and turn left for Prodromos.

Now head downhill, passing the Hera ski-lift to the left, followed by the Prodromos reservoir. This rectangular, stone-lined basin of water is not especially grand, but its banks make for a pleasant enough picnic site. At the hairpin bend at the entrance to Prodromos either carry straight on to explore the village or bear right towards **Pedoulas**▶, a busy yet

attractively sited resort. As forest gives way to open countryside, the views into the rugged valleys become more spectacular.

Note the colossal **Holy Cross of Pedoulas** to your right. From here the road to Kykkos widens, following a winding course into the eastern fringe of Pafos Forest.

The great bulk of **Panagia tou Kykkou**▶▶▶, with its church and extensive outbuildings, dominates the landscape when seen from a higher viewpoint, but as you arrive along the road it emerges suddenly and unexpectedly from behind the forest cover. All the power and glory of Cyprus's Greek Orthodox Church is evident in the imposing foundation of its most powerful monastery.

From here continue uphill towards Throni for the **Tomb of Archbishop Makarios**▶▶▶, the final resting-place of the nation's first president. At the summit of 1,318m Mount Kykkos, the tomb amply fulfils Makarios's desire to look out across the land whose independence he secured.

147

Head for the hills...

▶ Pedoulas
120C2

Early summer brings a fabulous harvest to this village in the Marathasa Valley. As the valley is famous for its cherries, it isn't hard to guess what the harvest is. Roadside stalls are filled with the dark fruit, piled up in baskets like heaps of precious stones. The village's small 15th-century church of **Archangelos Michael▶** (*Open* irregularly. *Admission free*) has three silvered domes and some interesting murals, while a short distance along the road to Kykkos is the modern **Holy Cross of Pedoulas**, a huge cross visible from a long way off.

148

The tower and dome of the church of Archangelos Michael in Pedoulas

▶ Pelendri
121D2

Somewhat off the beaten track to the east of the upper mountains, Pelendri overlooks the greener lower slopes from its 880m vantage point. It was once a royal estate, the property of Jean de Lusignan, son of the 14th-century king of Cyprus, Hugh IV. It is still distinguished for its church of **Timios Stavros▶▶** (*Open* irregularly. *Admission free*), a UNESCO-classified site. Dating from 1360, the church has a suite of fine frescos depicting a wide range of biblical scenes.

▶ Pera Pedi
120C1

Dominated by the **KEO winery**, conveniently sited for processing the grapes that are the key element of the local economy, Pera Pedi lies south of Platres.

A kilometre north of the village, the **Pera Pedi Dam** on the Kryos river makes a fine target for a walking excursion and a scenic picnic site on arrival. Its churches of **Agios Nikolaos** and **Agios Ioannis** have some interesting 16th-century icons.

▶▶▶ Pitsilia
121D2

This vaguely defined but extensive area on the eastern flank of the mountains is the wild side of the Troodos, with few specific points of tourist interest. Scattered villages hanging on its slopes make their living from vineyards and almond and hazelnut orchards. The best roads in the Troodos either stop, as if in fright, when they hit Pitsilia or bypass it. This makes it perfect for aimless wandering.

▶ Prodromos
120C2

Perched at an altitude of 1,390m, Prodromos commands a spectacular view across the Troodos Mountains. Indeed, it offers a better panorama than can be gained from many points higher up, mainly because of its position overlooking a constellation of tiny villages on the western slopes in an agricultural area that has not been heavily forested. The sense of greater vision is no doubt helpful to students of the Cyprus Forestry College at Prodromos.

▶▶▶ Solea Valley 121D3

Also known as the 'valley of apples', on account of the preponderance of orchards in its agricultural make-up, the Solea Valley carries the main road from Nicosia via Peristerona into the Troodos Mountains. It is a sad fact that the lines of traffic making this journey generally bypass the valley, as if the end of the road were more important than the attractions en route. Bordered by the **Adelfi Forest ▶▶** and watered, in winter at any rate, by the Karyotis stream, the Solea forms a green carpet across the steadily climbing landscape.

▶▶▶ Stavros tou Agiasmati 121D2

Open: irregularly. Admission free
Located 8km by road from the village of Platanistasa (4km of them along a dusty track), this little mountain church has developed into something of a minor village industry, as groups of tourists scour the coffee shops for the keyholder. When the keyholder finally appears, he turns out to be an inspired guide, although his only language is Greek. Any initial disappointment on arriving at the drab-coloured, strikingly situated structure is soon dispelled. The 15th-century frescos, some by the Lebanese artist Philippe Goul (see panel), which fill the Church of the Holy Cross, recount just about every significant episode from the New Testament, with a few from the Old Testament thrown in as well. The beautifully rendered Virgin in the half-dome behind the iconostasis might alone have persuaded UNESCO to include the church in its list of World Cultural Heritage Sites.

MURAL-MAKER
An inscription in the church of Stavros tou Agiasmati near Platanistasa dates its frescos to 1494 and records the name of their creator as Philippe Goul, a Lebanese Christian whose family achieved wealth and influence in Cyprus under the Lusignan kings and whose name derived from the old French word *gueules*, a heraldic term meaning 'red'. Goul's work employs a lively palette, of which red is indeed the most vibrant. His cycle of frescos at Stavros tou Agiasmati is considered the finest surviving example from the 15th century in Cyprus. Goul's contemporaneous work, from 1495, also graces the church of Agios Mamas at Louvaras (see page 133), while an earlier suite of frescos, from 1466, can be seen in the church of Sotiros at Palaichori (see page 140).

149

Magnificent frescos in the remote church of Stavros tou Agiasmati

The Troodos Mountains

Village time moves at its own leisurely pace in the mountains

▶▶▶ Tomb of Archbishop Makarios III   120B3

Open: daily 9–3. Admission free

On Throni hill, 2km from Panagia tou Kykkou, the first president of the Republic of Cyprus, Archbishop Makarios III, who died in 1977, rests in a tomb surmounted by a black marble slab and watched over by an honour guard of the Cyprus National Guard. It was Makarios's wish that he be buried here, at the top of a mountain that commands an unparalleled view across the island. A simple and not especially attractive modern chapel dedicated to him stands at the summit of the nearby hillside, amply fulfilling his wish to look out in eternity across the land he loved. Mountains march away into the haze, rimmed by the silver gleam of the sea.

▶▶ Trooditissa Monastery   120B2

Rarely open for visitors

Trooditissa is alpine in character, thanks to its design and location among the pine forests overlooking a steep gorge some 5km from Pano Platres, and more user-friendly than Kykkou and Machairas. The present buildings date from the 1700s, and the church boasts a priceless icon, a silver-gilt work of the Virgin, and a leather belt decorated with silver medallions, which is reputed to cure infertility.

▶▶ Troodos   120C2

Troodos village is one of those rare tourist resorts which, considering it consists mostly of gift shops, tavernas and car parks, should not be attractive, yet is. Perhaps the reason for this is its situation near the forested roof of the mountains and the feeling of well-being that is imparted by the fresh air; or perhaps the obvious pleasure that the tourists take derives from being among a crowd as a reward for the loneliness of the mountain trails. Two nature walks, the 9km **Atalanta Trail** and the 3km **Persephone Trail**, leave from Troodos, taking different trajectories through the forests around the village.

During the British period, Troodos was a mountain resort and an army summer base for colonial administrators and troops, influenced by the British tradition in India of fleeing to the mountain 'hill stations' to escape the scorching heat of the plains. The governor's summer residence (now belonging to the president of the republic; closed to the public) is hidden away in steeply sloping, dense forests a few kilometres south of Troodos.

▶▶ Vasa
120B1

A wine-making village in the Krassochoria district, Vasa is a red-roofed crown on a hilltop in the southwestern Troodos, below Omodos. Wine is not the only drink for which Vasa is renowned, for mineral water is bottled here from the village's excellent spring.

The village once belonged to the Catholic Knights Hospitaller, whose commandery was at Kolossi (see pages 108–9); the village's church of **Agios Georgios** was apparently built in the 14th century by Orthodox monks who had been expelled from their monastery by the Hospitallers. Roman-era tombs in the area suggest that this may have been a mountain hideaway some 2,000 years ago; their treasure of coins, jewellery and amphorae can be seen in Nicosia's Cyprus Museum. The house of the Cypriot poet Lipertis, who died in 1937, has been restored and can be visited.

▶ Vouni
120B1

Like many of the mountain villages, Vouni had, until recently, known better and richer times – not necessarily richer in terms of money, but richer in the life of a community whose young people had not yet drifted away to the towns in search of jobs. And like many of them still, it whiled away the drowsy hours of the long summer days, as if dreaming of those better times. Now, with preservation orders, art and craft workshops and outside investment coming in, Vouni has awoken from its sleep and is taking action to break the cycle of decline. Red-tiled roofs and cobbled streets maintain the feel of its past.

RIMBAUD TOO
The French poet Arthur Rimbaud was employed as foreman during construction of the British governor's (now the president's) summer residence at Troodos. Rimbaud arrived in Cyprus in 1879 and worked in a quarry at Potamos Creek near Agia Napa. Typhoid forced his return to France in May the following year. A year later he was back, at Troodos. In a letter home he complained: 'It is always necessary to travel by horse; transport is terribly difficult, the villages very far away, the food very dear.' He complained of cold and of feeling ill, but admitted 'the air is very healthy'.

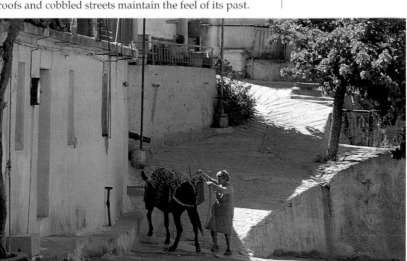

▶ Zoopigi
121D1

One of the villages which produces the Commandaria dessert wine, Zoopigi is a brightly coloured village, which is, naturally, surrounded by vineyards in a dazzlingly green area far off the main slopes of the Troodos. Dotted with villas and pretty villages, the grape-growing country has an ambience somewhat reminiscent of classic European wine-producing regions such as Tuscany and Rioja.

In Zoopigi village, a donkey still carries the weight

Cypriot wines were renowned for their quality in ancient times. Today, wine is once again one of Cyprus's most important exports, with great stretches of land given over to viticulture.

VINTAGE CHAMPAGNE
Cypriots say that it was from their vines that the Champagne grape was first grown, and that these were taken from Cyprus at the time of the crusades, when the Count Thibaud of Champagne visited his cousin, the Lusignan Queen Alice, in Cyprus.

152

Right: Georgios Yiallouros, owner of the Ecological Winery at Agios Amvrosios, displays the fruit of his natural talent

It is a late afternoon in autumn, and golden light washes over the vineyards that carpet the southern and western foothills of the Troodos Mountains. Thick bunches of ripened grapes weigh down the vines, awaiting the picker's hand. The whole village has turned out, it seems, pickers of all ages bent double under the sun and piling up grapes in bags ready for collection. Soon, Cyprus's narrow roads will be busy with lorries moving vast quantities of grapes to the wineries. 'Next year's wine is the sweetest,' goes the Cypriot expression, but this year's seems sweet enough.

Wine is among Cyprus's most important exports, with both production and sales growing by leaps and bounds. Britain is the principal overseas market, but sales in continental Europe are growing, even in such wine-producing citadels as France and Italy. Cyprus wines draw on a reputation that reaches back to ancient times, when they were commended by Homer. King Solomon, too, had a way with words which are music to a modern wine-marketing executive's ears: 'My beloved is unto me as a cluster of Cyprus grapes in the vineyards of Engadi.'

Producer's choice Georgios Yiallouros looks more like a Viking warrior than a Cypriot wine-grower, but that has proved no disqualification for owning one of Cyprus's most interesting wineries. His Ecological Winery at Agios Amvrosios in the southern Troodos produces, as its name implies, ecologically sound wines from its organically grown grapes. They also taste good. Georgious, who is a welder by profession, and his wife Joanna, set up their winery in the late 1980s, initially supplying only friends and neighbours. The business developed quickly and is today a

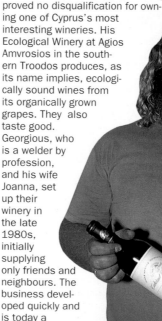

respectable cottage industry producing up to 60,000 bottles a year in five brands: Ambelidha dry white; Oenanthi rosé; and Agravani, Agrambeli and Cabernet Sauvignon red.

Monks also have their feet in the wine press. Panagia Chrysorrogiatissa monastery, near Pano Panagia, has won respect for its high-quality Monte Royia wines. An estimated 30,000 families (mostly in the Greek section of Cyprus) are involved in grape production, with nearly 10 per cent of the island's surface area given over to this crop. Yet, although production from small independent wineries like the Ecological Winery and Panagia Chrysorrogiatissa is growing fast, the bulk of wine-making is dominated by four giant wineries in Limassol: KEO, ETKO, LOEL and SODAP.

Vineyards near Pafos are the source of a light, fruity wine

Festival time Limassol is the scene of the industry's showcase, the Limassol Wine Festival, held in the city's Municipal Gardens in September. This can turn into quite a riot, as all the island's wineries are present and all give away free wine as fast as their staff can fill up festival-goers' plastic cups. Not much considered oenology gets done at this event, but everyone has a high old time. Cyprus wines run the gamut from light, sparkling whites to full-bodied reds, with most popular attention being focused on the former as they go so well with the climate and with an alfresco taverna dinner.

153

CYPRUS WHISKY
The village peasant's waste-not-want-not philosophy has provided Cyprus with a distinctive product, *zivania*, or 'Cyprus whisky'. Made from the grape remnant after wine fermentation, distilled in a copper pot called a *kazani*, the result is an alcohol so fiery that Cypriots drink it in frugal moderation, even employing it as rubbing alcohol for soothing aches and tired muscles. The alcohol is used in the production of local gin, sherry and brandy, and much of it is exported. Zoopigi and Kalon Chorion are important village producers of *zivania*.

Cypriot wines: all bottled up and ready to go

Just desserts A wine that has experts reaching for their superlatives is Commandaria, the heir to a wine that was drunk in ancient times at festivals in honour of Aphrodite. In its 'modern' form, it originated in the 13th century with the crusader Knights Hospitaller, who produced it at their Grand Commandery, the estate they owned and operated from Kolossi Castle, west of Limassol. A dark, ruby-red, sweet dessert wine, Commandaria is made from grapes picked at the last possible moment, then sun-dried, from vineyards above 1,000m around the villages of Zoopigi, Agios Konstantinos and Kalon Chorion.

154

See Drive pages 180–1

0	5	10	15 km
0	5		10 miles

Map labels:

Mazaki Island

Cape Arnaoutis

Fontana Amoroza

Chrysochou Bay

Akamas

Baths of Aphrodite

Latsi

Neon Chorion

Marion
Polis

Prodromi

Relathousa

Akamas Forest

Androlikou

Chrysochou

Ster

Fasli

Skoulli

Lara Bay

Drouseia

Choli

Turtle Hatchery

Kritou Tera

Ineia

Avgas

Avgas Gorge

Pano Arodes

Mihou

Agioi Anargyroi

Sim

Aspros

Cape Drepanon
Geronisos Island

Agios Georgios

Kathikas

iolou

Theletra

Pegeia

Akourso

Stroumpi

Pole

Mavrokolympos Lake

Coral Bay

Koili

Letymou

Agios Neofytos

Tala

Tsada

Kalleper

Kisonerga

Chloraka

Empa

Mesogi

Panagia Chryseleousa

PAPHOS
(PAFOS)

Armou

Anavargos

Geroskipou

Konia

Episkop

Kato Paphos

Koloni

Acheleia

Timi

Pafos International Airport

Mandria

A   B

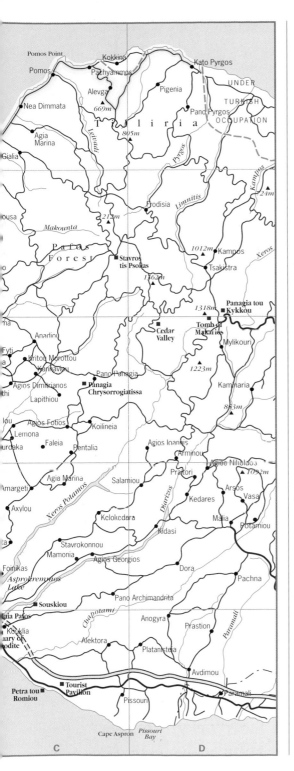

ROAD SENSE

Many roads between the coast and the Troodos Mountains are only of sufficient width for one-and-a-half vehicles to pass each other; two vehicles (a more usual combination) won't fit. This leads to some interesting situations, particularly as Cypriot farmers have learned that by driving their pick-ups straight at tourists' Z-registration hired cars they can, as if by magic, be left with the whole road to themselves. It is as well to be cautious.

THE WEST From the sun-gilded lower slopes of the Troodos Mountains where grapes ripen in profusion during the long summer days, to the wild shores of the Akamas Peninsula, western Cyprus has a romantic quality scarcely matched anywhere else on the island. This, after all, is where Aphrodite was born, carried ashore by the west wind at the rock called Petra tou Romiou. Her favourite haunts are dotted all over the region and here her spirit lingers still.

In Pafos, the west boasts Cyprus's newest resort area, thanks to the government's decision to build Pafos International Airport as a spur to developing this section of the coast. One can only hope that the lessons learned from older resorts are not being entirely ignored at Pafos. The town retains some elements of its former charm and has its own intrinsic merits as a holiday resort, despite the complaints of those who react sniffily to even the slightest hint of commercialism. It must be said, however, that tourism development and conservation rarely sit well together and the prognosis is for more of the same.

Coral Bay, north of Pafos, is one of the best beaches on the island

RISK FACTORS The battle lines in this debate have shifted northwards, to the coast at Polis and Latsi, to the ruggedly beautiful Akamas Peninsula with its Baths of Aphrodite and to the beach at Lara Bay where endangered turtles come ashore to lay their eggs. At the latter, the development offensive has been slowed, if not halted. The government's tourism policy is effectively on trial in this area, which many people – Cypriots and tourists alike – consider to be the last refuge of the natural world along the coast. The omens are not good, though, and the government recently approved a 'relaxation' in zoning regulations to allow construction of a giant resort hotel, by a company partly owned by the family of a government minister, on the edge of the Akamas Peninsula, an area that is supposed to become a national park. Going some way towards balancing the account, Friends of the Earth's Laona Project sponsors 'low-impact' tourism in villages bordering the Akamas, allowing local people to benefit financially from tourism without ruining their villages' traditional character. Though there is powerful opposition, locally and nationally, to any attempt to slow the development juggernaut in the Akamas area, the project at least offers an alternative. This, and the long-awaited establishment of an Akamas Peninsula National Park, seem the only way to secure the survival of what has been called 'the last truly Homeric landscape in the Hellenistic world'.

Smooth sea, rough country: the distinctive signature of the Akamas Peninsula

History has left its mark here. Pafos was an early capital of the island, and the seat of the imperial governor during the Roman Empire and into the Byzantine period. The ruins of its patrician houses and public buildings have yielded a remarkable harvest of mosaics and other archaeological finds. At Old (Palaia) Pafos, now the village of Kouklia, an earlier city still bears scars from Greek wars with Persia; here also are the moving vestiges of the Sanctuary of Aphrodite. Byzantine monasteries and churches are as thick on the ground as everywhere else.

ROUGH COUNTRY The long sweep of near-deserted northern coastline from Polis to the demarcation line at Kato Pyrgos is a glimpse of another Cyprus, of the island before tourism crossed its shores. Between coastal plain and mountain the picture is similar: those lime-green hills bathed in lemon light look deceptively mild from a distance. Here are some of the roughest tracks on the island, and the rare moufflon (wild sheep) has its stamping ground in an area now being painstakingly reafforested.

Sunset belongs to the west, and an appreciative audience is always on hand to watch it. As the sun touches the shining surface of the sea, like a ripe peach resting on a silver platter, casting a shimmering red luminescence across the waves and setting the sky aflame, it is easy to believe that the Mediterranean remains the realm of gods and heroes, and that the wind still sighs in the rigging of a triple-banked galley sailing just over the horizon.

157

GOING BANANAS
The climate and soil of western Cyprus are ideal for the production of bananas. You can see extensive plantations along the coast north of Pafos, easily identifiable even to the agriculturally challenged by the many bright blue plastic bags in which bunches of bananas grow. Smaller than their Caribbean cousins, Cypriot bananas have a strong local following and after the harvest you are sure to be given them at the end of a taverna meal.

Sky and sea form the stage for the sunset's daily spectacle

SWEET-TOOTHED BUFFALO
Cyprus's sugar is said to have been so sweet that Egyptian buffaloes, which had somehow acquired a taste for that delicacy and also discovered where it came from, were apparently in the habit of swimming across the sea just for a nibble.

MOIST ZEPHYRS
Rainfall in the west is higher than in the rest of the island, which accounts for the noticeably lusher vegetation hereabouts. This is a result of Homer's 'moist west winds' hitting the barrier of the Troodos Mountains, causing the clouds to unload their cargo of water. The difference in average precipitation may be discernible to meteorologists, but the average tourist is unlikely to be deluged.

Agios Neofytos Monastery, founded by the ascetic hermit St Neofytos

▶ **Acheleia** *154B2*

Until competition from the Caribbean began to overwhelm it during the Venetian period, western Cyprus had an important sugar industry, with processing plants in villages from here to Episkopi exporting their sweet-toothed product all over Europe. Acheleia's sugar connection is no more, and its two Byzantine churches – the 12th-century **Agios Theodosios**, modernised in the 1930s, and the 16th-century **Agios Georgios** – are its only points of special interest for visitors; there are some faded murals in the former and icons in the latter. The village is in the heart of a government-sponsored cluster of experimental farms aimed at improving yields and broadening the range of products in cultivation. Several such farms are indicated on road signs around Acheleia.

▶ **Agioi Anargyroi** *154B3*

Open: Apr–Sep 9–1 and 2–6; Oct–Mar 9–4. Admission charge
The sulphur springs near this village are reputed to be efficacious in cases of arthritis, although the works seem somewhat arthritic themselves and have clearly seen better days. A modern hotel with swimming pool has been built adjacent to them. The nearby village of **Giolou** is perhaps better appreciated, if only for its rich farmland surroundings and an Onion Festival in July.

▶ **Agios Neofytos** *154B3*

Churches in caves are a minor speciality of Cyprus, and the tiny 12th-century church of Agios Neofytos Monastery near the village of Tala is one of the more outstanding, being crammed with spectacular murals. Its founder, the ascetic would-be hermit St Neofytos, could be described as a failed recluse. Having successfully side-stepped an arranged marriage, he carved himself a cave in the Melissovouno hill overlooking Pafos, but instead of escaping to the quiet hermitic life, he found himself becoming a kind of religious superstar, his writings

attracting followers from all over the Orthodox world. Neofytos is said to have lived in a coffin filled with skulls of deceased followers. In any case, the *encleistra* (enclosure) carved into the cliff-face by the 12th-century saint, and covered with murals, is well worth seeing.

The bay near Fontana Amoroza, source of legendary love

▶▶▶ Akamas Peninsula 154A5

This wild and lonely peninsula is frequently cited as the last piece of genuine wilderness left in Cyprus – an indication of the anti-development passions this area arouses. It is beautiful indeed, with a rugged coastline bordered by azure waters and a backbone of forested hills. Difficult of access, to put it mildly, its terrain is so testing for four-wheel-drive vehicles, mountain-bikes and dirt-bikes that few people chance it (although it is possible to cross the tamer parts in an ordinary car). As a result, its ecology has remained largely intact and it seems certain that a national park will be established to protect it in perpetuity, although there is some opposition from local communities and commercial interests.

The fruit of a reafforestation programme, **Akamas Forest▶▶** is spreading through some of the roughest terrain on the peninsula. It is, however, traversed by a fairly good trail, beginning at the coast about 6km north of Lara Bay and ending at Neon Chorion (or vice versa), which makes it easier to get to grips with its rugged charms.

Fontana Amoroza▶, the 'Fountain of Love', is no more than a muddy pool near the tip of the peninsula. Its association with Aphrodite is tenuous but tantalising, since anyone who tastes its water will immediately fall in love. Wrote Italian Renaissance poet Ludovico Ariosto: 'Thanks to the goddess, young people and old experience the ardour of love to the last hours of their lives.' Aphrodite, gives the ultimate compliment to her own gender: 'In this place, every woman and girl is more desirable than in any other place on earth.'

Steep and narrow, the roads of **Neon Chorion▶▶** village witness some interesting moments when four-wheel-drive vehicles heading into and out of the Akamas encounter one another. The villagers seem quite used to traffic snarls (sometimes involving three or even four jeeps) and are always ready to leave their café tables to assist. If Neon Chorion has something of the feel of a frontier town, it is hardly surprising, for the Akamas Peninsula is, after all, the wild west. (See also pages 162–3.)

COUP DE FOUDRE
Visitors to the Fontana Amoroza in the Akamas Peninsula might wish to be careful about who they go with, as legend has it that anyone who drinks from the pool will fall instantly head over heels in love with the first person they see.

159

Selling fresh-picked oranges in the Akamas Peninsula

The West

PREOCCUPIED SAINT
The St George of Agios Georgios Church at Cape Drepanon must be one of the busiest saints in the Christian canon. He is consulted by lovers who want to know where their relationship is headed and, when not engaged in this delicate task, is employed by shepherds who have misplaced their sheep or goats.

The Baths of Aphrodite, sacred to the goddess of love

► **Asprokremmos Lake**   *155C2*
This large freshwater lake on the lower reaches of the Xeros river was created by the government's dam-construction programme to preserve scarce water supplies. As at many of the island's dams, fishing is permitted for trout and other species, but only with a permit issued by a Cyprus Fisheries Department district office (see page 105).

►► **Avgas Gorge**   *154A3*
Hikers need to get their boots on for this spectacularly jagged gorge, between Cape Drepanon and Lara Bay, which makes testing ground for a stroll. Only go there when it is dry, however, for in the rainy season the Avgas river comes charging through the gorge, and rain and wind may dislodge rocks from the cliff sides.

►► **Baths of Aphrodite**   *154A5*
Near the beginning of the Akamas Peninsula, this tiny freshwater pool half-hidden by a cave and a grove of trees is one of the more easily accessible locations in the area, being five minutes' walk from the car-park at the end of the approach road.

Ordinary mortals are forbidden to enter the cool waters of the spring-fed pool where the goddess of love is said to have bathed. As its waters are said to confer eternal youth, this is perhaps not surprising.

► **Cape Drepanon**   *154A3*
Uninhabited **Geronisos Island**►►, one of Cyprus's handful of diminutive islands – islets really – lies just off Cape Drepanon's rocky shore; there are faint remains of a Roman-era settlement and military camp. Cape Drepanon itself is a scenic spot, with a small fishing harbour overlooked by the domed church of **Agios Georgios** (*Open daily. Admission free*) (built in the 1920s), and a rocky shore favoured by sunbathers. The area appears to have been quite important in imperial Roman times, and archaeologists have uncovered

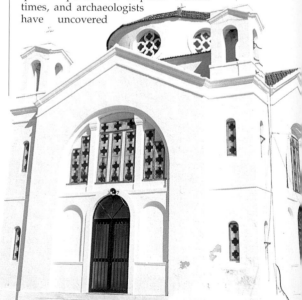

Modern Agios Georgios basks in the sun at Cape Drepanon

160

rock-tombs and scattered traces of monumental architecture. The Christians picked up where the pagans left off, and Agios Georgios has three predecessors, dating from the 6th to the 14th centuries, jumbled together on a nearby excavation site.

▶ Chlorakas   154B2

On the shore near here, amidst newly built hotels, stands a museum containing the Grivas Boat. The Greek army Colonel (later General) Grivas landed here in 1954 to form EOKA and lead the struggle against the British for Enosis (union of Cyprus with Greece). The caique displayed is not the boat in which Grivas sailed, but a similar one.

▶▶ Coral Bay   154A3

Situated a few kilometres north of Pafos, this bay has one of the longest and finest stretches of golden sand in the area. Because of this, a small resort has grown up around it and the beach can get very busy at peak times. Out of the main season, and even into winter, it is quieter and remains a good spot for bathing. In the hills overlooking Coral Bay is the fast-expanding village of **Pegeia**, which is recorded in a Cypriot folk song thanks to its village spring, To Vrysi, and is notable for half a dozen excellent tavernas in and around its square..

▶ Geroskipou   154B2

This village has come a long way since it was the Sacred Garden of Aphrodite, and the journey has been mostly downhill. Aphrodite relaxed here after amorous adventures, in a garden watered by a spring. Flowers, olive trees and fruit trees, including pomegranate trees, which were sacred to Aphrodite, grew there. Nowadays myth has to deal with the reality of a nondescript, fast-growing village, virtually a suburb of Pafos.

However, Geroskipou does have points of interest. The five-domed church of **Agia Paraskevi,** dating originally from the 9th century but frequently rebuilt, is a rarity simply for those five domes, and contains an important icon of the Virgin besides. Geroskipou's **Museum of Folk Art▶** (tel: 06-240216 *Open* Mon–Fri 9–2.30. *Admission charge*), in the house of Hadji Smith (a Cypriot appointed by the British as their vice-consul in 1800), displays a moderately interesting collection of period domestic items and costumes. Geroskipou is also reputed for pottery and *loukoumi* (Turkish delight, or, as it is known in these parts, Cypriot delight – see panel).

161

A shepherdess leads her flock to pastures new

The wild and wonderful Akamas Peninsula is nature's last stronghold in Cyprus. Isolated, rugged and beautiful, it is a treasure even more valuable than the Troodos Mountains. Many people believe that granting the peninsula national park status is the only chance to preserve some vestige of the island's natural heritage.

NAKED TRUTH
The virtually unfrequented beaches of the Akamas, although mostly composed of pebbles or rock, are among the best places in the island for sunbathing and swimming in the tradition of Aphrodite and Adonis. The only drawback to going nude – apart from binocular-equipped hikers admiring the peninsula's wildlife and scenery – is that some of the rocks just under the surface are razor sharp. The more remote beaches are best reached by power-boat, which can be hired in Latsi.

Diving off the Akamas Peninsula

Manoeuvring a four-wheel drive vehicle in the Akamas can be as much a test of human nerve as of mechanical endurance. The slopes you tackle can at times seem vertical, and the rock-fields you negotiate may seem as sharp as razor-blades to your tyres.

Nature protects herself with formidable defences in the Akamas Peninsula, a thick slice of rock jutting out into the sea in the far west, and until now humans have not mounted the kind of full-scale commercial assault needed to break down the walls and sack the citadel. If the increasingly vocal, not to say desperate, environmental lobby in Cyprus has its way, they never will. The idea of creating the Akamas Peninsula National Park was mooted many years ago; its time seems to have come, although some sharp-edged ridges remain to be crossed before the Cypriot government passes legislation to establish it.

Crucial decision The conservationists have allies in an unlikely place. Hoteliers in Agia Napa, where nature has been relegated to the spaces between apartment blocks and nightclubs, look to the Akamas and add their voices to the clamour for protection. Some say they aim to pre-empt the opening of a competitive resort area, but they deny this and claim they want somewhere for their guests to experience a different kind of Cyprus. Clearly a crucial decision has to be made, one whose outcome will determine not only where Cyprus stands on conservation, but also the fate of the peninsula which takes its name from Akamas, son of Theseus, and a hero of the Trojan War.

Back to nature Some 530 plant varieties, almost one-third of Cyprus's indigenous species, call the Akamas home, and in springtime the colours are those of a giant impressionist palette. Forests of Aleppo pine mixed with Phoenician juniper bushes crown the rough range of hills that runs along the peninsula's spine. Birds, too, are numerous, with some 168 species having been observed in the area. Snakes and other reptiles get along just fine, and butterflies add their dash of colour.

162

Explosive company Another visitor to the Akamas is the fighter-bomber; Britain's Royal Air Force, astonishingly, has practice bombing and strafing rights in the peninsula. For an area slated to become a national park this might seem like a sick joke were it not for the signs that have been placed around it telling people to stay out when the warning flags are flying and not to pick up strange objects, which may explode and kill them.

Most of the time, however, tranquillity and the Akamas go together like peaches and cream, and the best way to experience this blissful reality is to load up a small backpack with a picnic and walk. There are a few specific points of interest: the Baths of Aphrodite, Fontana Amoroza, Pyrgos tis Rigaenas, Neon Chorion village, the Akamas Forest, the ancient necropolis of Agios Konon and the wreck of a grounded boat on the northern shore. In addition, the Cyprus Forestry Department has established two nature trails, the Aphrodite and the Adonis, which range across interesting geology and flora in the setting where the goddess and the golden shepherd boy carried on their ill-fated romance. There are many unmarked trails to follow, and no reason for not pushing into the rough countryside. To hike as far as the mystic blue of the sea at Cape Arnaoutis is quite a trek, but the sense of peace and wilderness is ample compensation.

163

COUNTING SPECIES
Some 530 plant species have been recorded in the Akamas Peninsula, of which 126 are endemic. Varieties which can be observed from the Aphrodite and Adonis nature trails include: Aleppo pine, cypress, Phoenician juniper, spiny broom, thorny burnet, bramble, carob tree, lentisk, terebinth, myrtle, virgin's bower, kermes oak, gorse, caper, headed thyme, Cyprus thyme, Cyprus woodruff, marjoram, sage, wick weed, Spanish hedge-nettle, fig tree, royal oak, alaternus, storax, olive tree, eucalyptus, strawberry tree, oleander, gromwell, golden drop, rock roses and various *Cistus* species. Of fauna, 168 bird, 12 mammal, 20 reptile and 16 butterfly species have been identified. Birds to look out for include: Eleonora's falcon, turtle dove, crested lark, Cyprus warbler, Cyprus pied wheatear, Bonelli's eagle and Scops' owl.

Tranquillity and the Akamas Peninsula go together hand in glove – except when the area is used for target practice by the Royal Air Force

The West

LIVING DOLL
The legendary Pygmalion was said to have ruled over Palaia Pafos. He was both king and sculptor, and fell in love with the statue of a beautiful young woman he had created; the goddess Aphrodite brought the statue to life and Pygmalion married the woman, named Galatea. The child of their union was named Paphos.

CLOSE SHAVE
It doesn't fit with Aphrodite's image of celestial beauty, but there is a suggestion that she may have been worshipped as a bearded goddess, Aphroditos, at several locations in Cyprus, including Amathus. The 5th-century AD Roman antiquarian Macrobius wrote in his *Saturnalia*: 'There is in Cyprus a bearded statue of the goddess with female clothing but with male attributes, so it would seem that the deity is both male and female.'

▶▶ Kato Pyrgos   155D5

Although situated only some 60km from Nicosia as the crow flies, Kato Pyrgos is one of the most inaccessible locations on the whole island, thanks to the conflict of 1974, which cut it off from easy communication with the capital. The direct road now runs through some of the roughest sections of the Troodos Mountains, and visitors from Nicosia usually prefer to go the long way, via Limassol, Pafos and Polis. Its isolation, one of the village's attractions, saved it from being overwhelmed by the by-products of tourism. Tranquil little Kato Pyrgos is favoured by vacationing Cypriots, and there are several reasonable hotels, cafés and tavernas to serve them.

▶ Koloni   154B2

Cyprus is not famously noted for its pottery, with the exception of the giant, hand-thrown red pots called *pitharia* which were popular in the past and which can still be found today. Nevertheless, a pottery tradition does exist, and has been carried on to a certain extent. At this village south of Pafos pottery can be seen being made as well as purchased.

▶▶▶ Kouklia   155C1

This would be an otherwise ordinary Cypriot village were it not surrounded by the fragmentary remains of an ancient city and the most important temple of Aphrodite, the goddess who made Cyprus her own. Pausanias, a 2nd-century AD travel writer, attributed the founding of **Palaia (Old) Pafos▶▶** to King Agapenor, a legendary hero of the Trojan War. Its vestiges date from the Bronze Age to the end of the Roman Empire's pagan era. At the Marcello hill outside Kouklia, archaeologists have uncovered part of the ancient city walls, revealing a dramatic scene from the Cypriot rebellion against Persia in 498 BC: a Persian siege mound reaches up to the walls in preparation for troops to storm them; the defenders tunnelled desperately to undermine the mound and there was heavy fighting. Herodotus wrote that the Persians retook all the rebel cities, and the fate of their inhabitants can only be guessed at.

Mosaic of Leda and the swan at the Sanctuary of Aphrodite, near Kouklia

One's sense of expectation on entering the **Sanctuary of Aphrodite ▶ ▶ ▶** (tel: 06-432180. *Open* summer daily 9–7.30; winter daily 9–5. *Admission charge*) cannot quite survive the reality of finding its remnants sparse and hard to interpret. An impossible effort of imagination is needed to fill the spaces between vanished walls and broken columns with glimpses of the scene to which ancient writers allude: youthful handmaidens of Aphrodite giving themselves willingly to visiting pilgrims, who arrived in colourful processions, dancing, singing and wearing garlands of narcissus and myrtle. Nevertheless, this was the shrine of the goddess of love, Homer's 'golden Aphrodite', whose *temenos* (sacred precinct) and incense-burning altar were renowned in the ancient world.

The temple comprised two halls, connected by porticoes and rooms for administration and guests. One part of the complex dates from the late Bronze Age around 1200 BC, the other from the Roman period, until the Emperor Theodosius abolished the pagan cults in the 4th century AD. Evidence from coins, analysis of the remnants and commentaries from antiquity prove that this was not a temple in the traditional Greek style, such as the Parthenon in Athens, but was more like an oriental shrine consisting of an open enclosure, of which the archaic sanctuary was only a small part.

Holes gouged in the walls of the *temenos* have no obvious purpose, and it is speculated that they were made by robbers searching for the 'treasure of Aphrodite'. A shallow basin in the floor was probably filled with holy water and used by worshippers for ritual ablutions. The later hall shows the interest the Romans took in the shrine. The Emperor Titus dedicated an altar in AD 69, while in the next century Trajan repaired earthquake damage.

The on-site museum is housed in a Lusignan manor called the Château de Covocle, which was itself incorporated into a Turkish-era farm called the Chiftlik. Several important finds from the sanctuary are on display, including a conical stone which is thought to have been the archaic cult idol of Aphrodite.

Inside the museum of Palaia Pafos, where remains from the Sanctuary of Aphrodite can be seen

NAUGHTY GIRL
Aphrodite's extra-curricular activities frequently landed her in trouble. In the *Odyssey*, Homer tells how, upon her release after being caught *in flagrante* with her lover Ares by her husband Hephaestus, 'laughter-loving Aphrodite [fled] to Pafos in Cyprus, where she has her sacred precinct and an altar fragrant with incense. There the Graces bathed her and anointed her with the imperishable oil that the immortals use. And when they had decked her out in her lovely clothes she was a marvel to behold.'

The West

Lara Bay, home to endangered turtles

FATAL ATTRACTION
Newly born turtles emerge from their nests at night and head instinctively for the sea, attracted by the luminescent glow of the water. A tragic aspect of tourism development at many of Cyprus's beaches is that the neon lights of nightclubs are brighter than the sea's lumines-cence. The effect is that the young turtles head instinctively for the near-est disco. For them, it is a fatal attraction.

▶▶▶ Lara Bay   154A4

Located between Pafos and the western shore of Akamas Peninsula, sandy Lara Bay is the next logical item on the tourism development agenda. This will be bad news for the endangered loggerhead turtle if environmentalists should lose their battle to prevent the development sce-nario being enacted. Female turtles will only come ashore to lay their eggs on open, quiet beaches, of which few now remain in Cyprus – or indeed anywhere in the Mediterranean. A conservation programme, the Lara Turtle Project, has been established by the Cyprus Department of Fisheries on the Lara Reserve to protect the turtles' nesting grounds and to ensure the highest possi-ble rate of survival of fledgling turtles.

Lara is not exactly hard to get to, but the track that takes over from a tarmacadamed road is bumpy and dusty enough to discourage casual visitors, who are not in any case greatly desired at the site during the nesting and hatching season. Mesh fences are placed in the sand around the trenches dug by female turtles to house their eggs. A public information tent containing display cases of baby turtles being prepared for release has also been established to help explain the project to visitors and, it is hoped, to gain their co-operation in keeping the nest-ing site undisturbed.

The coast on either side of Lara Bay is a mixture of rocky and stony beach, and is also part of the Lara Reserve. In the reserve area sunbeds, beach umbrel-las, caravans, tents and the like cannot be taken on to the beach, and visitors cannot stay on the beach after sunset. Also banned are fishing, other than with a rod and line, using or anchoring a boat without a permit and driving any vehicle onto the beach. The 'Turtle Protected Area' extends to a distance of 90m from the shore, and to a depth of 20m in the water.

As might be expected of a village with a busy fishing harbour...

▶▶▶ Latsi   154B4

Formerly a sponge-diving centre, until the sponge supply ran out a few years ago, the last resort on the northern road into the Akamas Peninsula is essentially a fishing

harbour with ambition. That ambition may have to be curtailed if the Akamas is to remain the largely unspoilt wilderness it is today. The problem is that Latsi attracts tourists who consider themselves more enlightened than their fellow holidaymakers soaking up the sun on the beaches of, say, Agia Napa. Alas, even enlightened tourists appear to need hotels, restaurants, gift shops, Coca-Cola with ice, suntan lotion, cars, jeeps and motor-bikes – and that in the end makes them seem not quite so enlightened after all. The development versus preservation contest is at its sharpest here, and the outcome is still in doubt. Hotels are, so far, restricted in number and capacity, thus loading the dice in favour of conservation.

Taken on its own merits, however, Latsi is an attractive and colourful place, its harbour the liquid gateway to the Akamas, and beautifully situated in the heart of sweeping Chrysochou Bay. Scuba-diving is particularly popular in the area, with several schools teaching the art to beginners, not so much at the village itself but along the rocky Akamas coastline. A fringe of mostly excellent tavernas specialising in seafood graces the harbour, and the adjacent beaches are popular with tourists getting their suntans in order before striking out on hiking expeditions into the Akamas.

...seafood is high on the menu at most tavernas in Latsi

► Mavrokolympos Lake — 154B3
Trout may be on the menu after a successful fishing expedition to the lake, which has been created by a dam on the Mavrokolympos river a few kilometres inland from Coral Bay. Fishing is permitted here, for trout and other species, but only with a permit issued by the Cyprus Fisheries Department (see page 105).

► Pachyammos — 155C5
Pocket-handkerchief-sized beaches are the main attraction of this tiny village on the northern coast, near the point where the the coast road begins its spectacular climb into the lower peaks of the Troodos Mountains to avoid the fortification-ringed Turkish Cypriot enclave at Kokkina (Erenköy).

The icon is the principal religious art form of the Orthodox faith and the very image of Byzantium, the Christian empire whose capital was Constantinople (modern Istanbul). For almost 2,000 years icons have transmitted to the faithful their message of the holiness of the saints and the glory of God.

PICTURES AND EXHIBITIONS

Icons can be seen at a vast number of locations all over Cyprus, mostly in churches. Among the best of these are:

- **Agios Trypiotis** (page 47)
- **Panagia Chrysaliniotissa** (page 55)
- **Agios Lazaros** (page 86)
- Stavrovouni (page 96)
- **Panagia tou Kykkou** (page 142)
- **Agios Irakleidios** (page 188)
- **Machairas** (page 190)

The museums with the best icon collections are:

- the **Byzantine Museum** (page 47) in Nicosia
- the **Byzantine Museum** (page 172) in Pafos

In the Turkish Cypriot zone, there are fine collections at:

- the **Icon Museum** (page 213) in Kyrenia (Girne)
- **Apostolos Andreas Monastery** (page 230)
- **Apostolos Varnavas Monastery** (page 232)

Cyprus's Orthodox churches are treasure chests of icons

As the wellsprings of the thousand-year-old classical civilisation dried up in the 4th century AD and the Roman Empire staggered into its decline and fall, a new force rose to the forefront. Christianity, formerly the reviled superstition of slaves and the ignorant poor, became the official state religion of the new Byzantine Empire. In art, the classical preoccupation with the human form gave way to stylised images of the introspective, spiritual dominion of the new religion. Man was no longer the measure of all things; the Christian God and his saints held the keys to the kingdom of heaven and eternal life.

The icon, from the Greek word *eikon* (image), is the perfect mirror of this change. Representations of Christ, the Virgin Mary, angels and saints, and scenes from liturgical history are venerated, not – at least in theory – for themselves, but as aids to devotion and channels of God's blessing. The traditional medium used by Byzantine painters was egg tempera on gesso over wood; oils are a comparatively recent introduction from Western Europe. Sometimes gold leaf is employed, and intricate gold or silver covers are placed over the images.

Venerated symbols Cyprus's importance in the history of icons lies in the number and quality of surviving images and the island's role as a sanctuary for icon-makers during periods of 'iconoclasm', notably in the 8th and 9th centuries, when doctrinal disputes based on the second commandment's prohibition of the worship of images flared up and icons were destroyed in vast numbers. Icons are not the only signs of the true faith: domed churches, murals, mosaics, and ecclesiastical garments and vessels also have their place. But they are the most important in the eyes of the faithful, and kissing the icons is a key element in the rituals of the Orthodox Church. It is this element of loving veneration that the secular or non-Orthodox tourist is most likely to lack. To view an icon purely as a work of art is to remove all sacred content from it, leaving it a surface impression only. Of course, there is a hierarchy of aesthetic worth among icons and the church authorities are well aware of the value of the pieces they hold. In this they are not alone: international art thieves are as devoted to icons as the most pious church-goer.

Images of eternity Perhaps the most obvious characteristic of icons is the immobility of the subjects. Although the painters must reach deep into their own spirituality to transmute paint into an image of transcendent faith, following centuries-old patterns, there is little of ordinary humanity in the result. Christ, the Virgin and the saints, who were all at one time human, are captured frozen in eternity, gazing far beyond the everyday world to the celestial city of God. The occasionally more naturalistic example is all the more refreshing for its rarity.

Cyprus's churches are great storehouses of icons in all sizes and from all periods of Byzantine history. Some are faded almost beyond recognition; some have been disastrously 'restored'; others, particularly precious or sacred, are hidden away from sight. The iconostasis, an often elaborately carved and gilded screen separating the nave of the church from the inner sanctuary, is the main 'exhibition area'. Icons still pour forth from monasteries, convents and churches, the motive for their creation being the same as impelled the evangelist Luke, 19 centuries ago, to paint the first examples, one of which is said to rest in the church of Panagia tou Kykkou monastery (see page 142): the veneration of God and his holy saints.

ICONS AS WEAPONS

Icons play a part in the war of words between Greek and Turkish Cypriots over the island's cultural patrimony. Following the Turkish invasion of 1974, it is clear that icons were looted and destroyed. This seems not to have been a deliberate Turkish policy but rather the result of fighting, undisciplined actions by troops and the work of art thieves – who have also struck in the Greek sector. It is difficult to arrive at objective conclusions, but the Greek Cypriots have been forced to buy icons taken from monasteries and churches in the north and sold on the international black market.

FROM RUSSIA...

Basil Grigorovich Barsky visited Panagia tou Kykkou in 1727 and reported the monks' tourist patter about the miracle-working icon: 'The icon, so it is said, is painted on some rare wood from the Tree of Paradise, but not by modern methods. Rather it is done with a sort of wax and mastic. This is impossible to verify because of the silver covering... They carry the icon up to the mountain-top in times of drought and reveal her face upon which rain miraculously falls.'

This superb rendering of Christ can be seen at Panagia Chrysorrogiatissa

CONFLICT OF THE GODS
Some scholars have interpreted the mosaic of Apollo and the musical shepherd in the House of Aion at Pafos as a pagan allusion to the inevitable triumph of the old gods over the upstart Nazarene who had inflicted Christianity on the world. If this analysis is correct, the pagans were soon to be proved much mistaken.

170

Taking the camel trail in Pafos

▶▶▶ Pafos   *154B2*

Pafos is, in many respects, the most attractive of Cyprus's major holiday resorts, partly because development has not overwhelmed it and the coast is still relatively open. Its historic resonance dates back to the Roman Empire, when it was the island's capital, ruled by an imperial proconsul (governor) whose palace has been uncovered by archaeologists. So rich is Pafos in cultural treasures that it is included in UNESCO's list of World Cultural Heritage Sites. The spelling of the town's name is gradually changing from Paphos to Pafos; there is Kato (Lower) Pafos, where the main tourist area is located near a picturesque harbour, and Upper Pafos, also called Ktima.

Ancient sites The **Mosaics of Pafos**▶▶▶ (tel: 06-240217. *Open* summer daily 8–7.30; winter daily 8–5. *Admission charge*) were discovered in a cluster of buildings of the Roman period, principally the 3rd century AD. They form a major historical treasure, with a range of subject matter and quality of workmanship that alone would guarantee their worth, and their vigorous treatment of pagan myths contradicts the belief that the wellsprings of classical art dried up as Christianity gained the ascendancy. The mosaics are in four main locations.

The **House of Dionysos** makes for a dazzling journey through pagan mythology: Narcissus, who fell in love with his own reflection; Dionysos in triumphal procession; the twin heroes Castor and Pollux, offspring of the union of Leda and Zeus; the tragic tale of Phaedra and Hippolytos; Ganymede being carried off by lecherous old Zeus; the love between Pyramos and Thisbe; Neptune and Amymone; and Apollo and Daphne. Also discovered, at a lower level, was a 3rd-century BC mosaic pavement made from black and white pebbles instead of tesserae.

The **House of Orpheus** is named for a mosaic depicting Orpheus playing his lyre, surrounded by wild beasts enchanted by the music. Hercules appears in the first of his labours, where he fights the lion of Nemea. An Amazon is also shown.

The **Villa of Theseus** awaits further excavation for mosaics which are undoubtedly there to be uncovered. This seems to have been the palace of the Roman proconsul (governor) and bids fair to be the richest of all. Mosaics showing Theseus battling the Minotaur; Poseidon, god of the sea, riding the waves on a sea monster, accompanied by Amphitrite; and the first bath of the infant Achilles, give some idea of the marvels to be expected.

The **House of Aion**, adjacent to the Villa of Theseus, has yielded a five-panelled mosaic showing Leda being approached by Zeus in the shape of a swan; the infant Dionysos being handed to his future tutor Tropheus; a beauty competition between Cassiopeia and the nereids, watched over by Aion; Dionysos leading a procession of maenads and satyrs; and Apollo condemning the flute-player Marsyas to death for daring to challenge him to a musical contest.

Although the 2nd-century AD **Odeion**▶, close to the mosaics, suffers from comparison with the larger and more spectacularly sited theatre at Kourion, it retains considerable charm within its semicircle of limestone blocks –

In the Tombs of the Kings

enough to be in use still for summer musical and theatre performances after 18 centuries (ticket information is available from the Pafos Tourist Information Office). Next to the auditorium, though not easily recognisable, are the remains of the agora, the main public square of ancient Pafos.

The **Tombs of the Kings**▶▶▶, (tel: 06-240295. *Open summer daily 8–7.30; winter daily 8–5. Admission charge*), beside the sea at the northern end of Kato Pafos, are a complex of rock-cut tombs, where leading citizens of Pafos (not royalty) were interred during the city's Hellenistic and Roman periods (3rd century BC to 3rd century AD). Their carved steps leading down to the burial

BATTLE OF WORDS
During the 1974 conflict, Turkish warplanes rocketed the archaeological zone beside the harbour in Pafos, damaging some of the priceless mosaics in the process. Opinions naturally differ as to whether this was a case of the pilots simply missing their intended targets (vessels in the harbour bringing military supplies from Greece) or a deliberately vandalistic strike against an important Greek cultural monument.

171

chambers were indeed the pathway to the underworld. Archaeologists are still busy, and will be for many years to come, uncovering the *tumuli* (mounds) that have accumulated over the tombs and digging down to the graves. Several tombs have impressive *atria* (courtyards) surrounded by Doric pillars, and were decorated with paintings and other ornamentation.

A late pagan mosaic in the House of Dionysos

Excursions leave Pafos southwards to Aphrodite's Rock and northwards to the Akamas Peninsula

SCHOOLBOY FIGHTERS
The modern gymnasium (high school) on the outskirts of Pafos, although not a tourist 'attraction' as such, is an impressively grand (or grandiose) construction, a symbol of the classical foundation that still inspires Greek education. A relief in the schoolyard depicts a young boy attacking a lion with a stone; many of the EOKA guerrillas who fought, and died, for union with Greece against the British in the 1950s were, literally, schoolboys, and the monument honours their struggle and sacrifice.

MUSEUMS Given the rich archaeological harvest of the Pafos area and western ▶ Cyprus, **Pafos District Archaeological Museum**▶▶ (tel: 06-240215. *Open* Mon–Fri 9–5, Sat–Sun 10–1. *Admission charge*) has no shortage of treasures, from prehistoric to Venetian times. These include pottery, sculpture, coins and jewellery. That the Romans found Cyprus chilly in winter is shown by a set of moulded clay hot-water bottles.

Near the bishop's palace, the **Byzantine Museum**▶ (tel: 06-231392. *Open* Jun–Sep Mon–Fri 9–7, Sat 9–2; Oct–May Mon–Fri 9–5, Sat 9–2. *Admission charge*) concentrates on Orthodox religious art, particularly icons, dating from the 12th to the 18th centuries. There is a fine gilt statue of the Virgin and Child.

The **Ethnographical Museum**▶ (tel: 06-232010. *Open* May–Sep Mon–Fri 9–1 and 3–7, Sat 9–1; Oct–Apr Mon–Fri 9–1 and 2–5, Sat 9–1. *Admission charge*) contains a diverse, although not extensive, range of exhibits, from neolithic tools and ancient funerary sculptures, to local costumes and everyday household objects. This small, privately operated museum is in Pano Pafos (Ktina).

Pafos Aquarium▶▶ (Dionysou Street, tel: 06-253920. *Open* daily 10–8. *Admission charge*) makes a good place to give children a break. Its display tanks mainly feature Mediterranean marine life but include colourful saltwater and freshwater creatures from around the world.

Churches The church of **Panagia Chrysopolitissa**▶▶ is a 13th-century construction standing amid the ruins of a colossal early Christian basilica, the largest on the island. Long-term archaeological research is being conducted on the site so it is frequently closed to the public, a great disappointment to many who wish to see St Paul's Pillar, where the apostle is said to have been scourged with 39 lashes during his evangelising visit to Cyprus in AD 45 – presumably before he converted the Roman proconsul, Sergius Paulus, to Christianity. Panagia LimeniotissaP is a ruined and partially excavated 5th-century Christian basilica near the seafront. Our Lady of the Harbour proved to be too conveniently sited in the path of 7th-century Arab raiders, who laid it low.

Today a damp and mysterious underground chamber, the catacomb of **Agia Solomoni►** (*Open*: permanently. *Admission free*) was a refuge for early Christians. A sacred tree, said to have the power to cure disease, stands near the entrance.

The **Theoskepasti Church►** is modern and stands where there was once an early Christian church of the same name, which means 'veiled by God'. A miraculous fog apparently shrouded the church, making it invisible to Arab raiders, who then destroyed the less favoured Panagia Limeniotissa at the other end of the harbour.

THE HARBOUR AREA The harbour is an ideal picture-postcard Mediterranean fishing harbour, with gaily painted craft tied up in rows, glass-bottom boats, private yachts and cruisers joining them. Taverna terraces stretch to the water's edge and the scene is animated at all times of the day. Remains of the ancient breakwater can be seen at the harbour's eastern end.

Pafos Fort►► (*Open* summer daily 9–7.30; winter daily 9–5. *Admission charge*)was built by the Ottoman Turks to protect the harbour. It is similar to the forts at Limassol and Larnaka, but smaller, and stands on the site of the earlier castles built by the Byzantines, Lusignans and Venetians, with turrets and gloomy halls.

Also known as the Byzantine Castle, **Saranda Kolones►►** (*Open* permanently. *Admission free*) takes its principal name from the Greek for 'forty columns', a reference to the many ruined columns found near by. The castle, close to the Odeion and the complex of Roman-era houses where the mosaics were found, was built during the Lusignan period in the 12th century on the foundations of a Byzantine fortification. The Lusignans had scarcely finished the place when an earthquake struck in 1222 and destroyed it again. Byzantine, Lusignan, or just plain ruined, the castle makes a fine place for scrambling over walls and battlements. There are two **Municipal Gardens►**, one in Kato Pafos and one in Ktima.

173

HARBOUR STROLL
Unquestionably the most atmospheric place for a stroll in Pafos is around the old harbour, with its colourful fishing boats. Start at the fort and continue past the former harbour warehouses, now waterfront tavernas, towards the souvenir shops at the eastern end.

The catacomb of Agia Solomoni, shaded by a tree decked with votive offerings

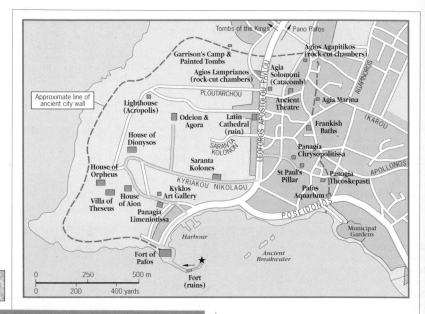

Walk

Pafos Fort, built by the Ottomans, was declared an ancient monument in 1935

Historical sites of Pafos

As capital of Cyprus during the Roman Empire, Pafos developed a brilliant urban lifestyle. The walk traverses some of the excavated highlights and lasts about four hours if visits to the sights are included (the sights themselves are covered in more detail on pages 170–3).

Begin at the end of the pier. Across the harbour are the remains of the ancient breakwater, and adjacent are the scant ruins of an early fort. The harbour is devoted to fishing boats and pleasure cruising. As you walk towards the town you pass **Pafos Fort►►**, which replaced an earlier one near the end of the mole.

Turn right along the seafront promenade (Apostolou Pavlou Street), then left along the lane behind the cafés. To your left is the ruined early Christian basilica **Panagia Limeniotissa►**, and to your right the modern **Kyklos Art Gallery►**. Continue to the end of the lane where

four Roman-era buildings contain the **Mosaics of Pafos►►►**, one of the island's most marvellous ancient scenes. The four buildings, all excavated ruins, are the Houses of Aion, Theseus, Orpheus and Dionysos. From the House of Dionysos, walk east along the lane called Sofias Vembo Street (or Kyriakou Nikolaou Street on local maps). A short detour to the left leads to the **Odeion►**. Continuing straight ahead, you pass the ruined Byzantine Castle, or **Saranta Kolones►►**, on your left. Turn left on to Apostolou Pavlou Avenue, then first right to the early Christian basilica and **Panagia Chrysopolitissa►►**. Finally, return to Apostolou Pavlou Street and turn right for the **Agia Solomoni Catacomb►**.

Christendom's white wedding retains elements of fairy-tale – even if its solemnly sworn vows are honoured more often in the breach than the observance. Cyprus's divorce statistics are rising, but couples still get married with the best of intentions and a certain unforgettable style.

One's first sight of a Cypriot wedding can be an irritating experience. You may be driving along a deserted road far from anywhere when, suddenly, you find yourself stuck in the mother of all traffic jams. When Cypriots wed, they like as much of Cyprus to be there as possible.

During the church service, the bride will be required to fear her husband, an undertaking she appears to forget pretty quickly. The duties expected of a couple entering into the holy state of matrimony having been agreed to, the bride and groom move to the icing on their wedding-cake, otherwise known as the traditional Cypriot wedding feast. They start out married life as they aim to continue: happily ever after. One participant who probably has a tough time celebrating is the bride's father, who has had to shell out for his daughter's dowry; a house is generally considered acceptable.

Fertile imagination Fertility is assured by the 'spreading of the mattress', when the married women sew the bed linen to it and a baby boy is rolled along it. The feast itself is the product of at least a day's cooking by the women guests – after all, the whole village has been invited. Feasting, singing and dancing are the order of the evening, along with various good luck rituals. 'Pinning on the money' is one of the final rituals, when the bride and groom dance alone and their parents, relatives and friends pin banknotes to their clothes. No doubt Aphrodite watches over the proceedings with great satisfaction.

175

Wedding portrait at Kourion Theatre

BIG DAY
In previous years, weddings could only take place on a Saturday, but that regulation has now been relaxed and Sunday weddings are becoming more common.

Wedding-day bliss, or blues: marriage is a serious business

*Monk on the move,
Panagia
Chrysorrogiatissa
monastery*

▶▶▶ Pafos Forest 155C4

Winston Churchill took a hand in the creation (or re-creation) of this forest, although there is no evidence that the renowned British statesman went so far as to get his hands dirty. However, in 1907, while a junior minister with responsibility for colonial affairs, Churchill began the process of reafforestation which has continued to this day, with the Cyprus Forestry Department slowly restoring to a huge area the tree cover that vanished into the shipyards and foundries of the ancient world.

▶ Panagia Chryseleousa 154B2

Open: irregularly. Admission free
Located in the village of Emba, near Pafos, this church dates back to the 11th century and was restored fairly recently. It has a noteworthy fresco of Christ Pantokrator gazing down from its dome.

▶▶ Panagia Chrysorrogiatissa Monastery 155C3

Open: daily dawn–dusk. Admission free
This monastery, 'Our Lady of the Golden Pomegranate', is one of the most dramatically sited in Cyprus. Its flower-bedecked courtyard and its fine view over the surrounding forests commanded the attention of the young Makarios Mouskas, living in the village of Pano Panagia just below; the boy would grow to fame and glory as Archbishop Makarios. The monastery also commands a certain amount of fame and glory for its high-quality wines, particularly its Monte Royia, and for an icon of the Virgin found by St Ignatius in the 12th century, now kept in a silver case.

▶▶ Pano Panagia 155C3

The late Archbishop Makarios, first president of the Republic of Cyprus and a figure of international reputation in the non-aligned movement, was born and raised in this isolated mountain village overlooked by the great monastery of Panagia Chrysorrogiatissa. His movingly plain family home has been preserved and maintained as a shrine in honour of this complex and controversial figure, who saw no contradiction between his religion and his politics and who is revered by many Greek Cypriots as the father of the country.

*Heavenly view across the
country from Panagia
Chrysorrogiatissa*

►►► Petra tou Romiou
(Aphrodite's Rock)

155C1

This unusual rock formation standing in shallow sea water beside the Limassol–Pafos road must be the most famous spot in Cyprus. The name means 'Rock of the Greek' and comes from the legend of the Byzantine hero Dighenis, who hurled enormous rocks at Arab invaders and destroyed their fleet.

However, the rock's fame stems from a more ancient and timeless myth, for it was here that Aphrodite, goddess of beauty and love, first set foot in the world. Homer well knew the story and told it in his *Hymn to Aphrodite*:

> I will sing of stately Aphrodite,
> gold-crowned and beautiful,
> whose dominion is the walled cities
> of all sea-set Cyprus.
> There the moist breath of the western
> wind wafted her over the waves
> of the loud-moaning sea.

This favourite child of Zeus was met on the shore by her handmaidens, the Horae (Hours), who received her with joy, decked her out with precious jewels, set on her immortal head a crown of gold, and gave her earrings of gold and copper. Botticelli's diaphanous *Birth of Venus* (Venus was the Roman equivalent of Aphrodite) is undoubtedly the best-known image of the moment when the goddess was borne ashore on a seashell. Petra tou Romiou is a virtual place of pilgrimage for romantic couples, particularly at sunset when a gentle breeze ruffles the surface of the 'loud-moaning sea'.

Aphrodite came to Cyprus as an adaptation of the Phoenician Astarte, who was a soul-sister of the Assyro-Babylonian Ishtar. When she could spare time from her primary duties, she was also Aphrodite Pelagia, goddess of the sea; Aphrodite Pontia, of seafarers; Aphrodite Euploia, who guaranteed prosperous voyages; and Aphrodite Gelenaia, goddess of fair winds. She was happiest playing the sweet game of love as Aphrodite Urania: her raunchier side showed through in Aphrodite Pandemos and Aphrodite Porne. Finally, she settled down as Aphrodite Nymphia, the protector of marriage.

Aphrodite's Rock, a place of pilgrimage for romantic couples

177

ACTING THE GOAT
The insatiably nipping teeth of the humble goat have taken much of the rap for deforestation in Cyprus, presumably because humans prefer to blame a dumb animal rather than look too closely in the mirror. One (rather pompous) authority on the subject wrote: 'Goats and reafforestation are irreconcilable; and the authority of some tribunal should intervene to sentence them not only to legal separation, but to irrevocable divorce.'

TRAUMATIC BIRTH
The early Greek writer Hesiod provided an earthy account of the birth of Aphrodite in his *Theogeny*. The goddess was created, he wrote, when Cronos castrated his father Uranos and cast his genitals into the sea, where they floated to the surface to produce a white foam, from which arose Aphrodite.

**ROUGH
NEIGHBOURHOOD**
In 1879, the British colonial administrator for the
Pafos district excoriated
the people of the area in
and around Polis for the
extraordinarily high
number of thieves and
cut-throats among them.
Fortunately their descen-
dants have turned to more
benign pursuits and the
chance of having one's
throat cut in modern Polis
does not seem excessive.

*With the working day in
Polis over, the serious
business of the coffee shop
can begin*

▶▶ Pissouri Bay   155D1

On a stretch of the coast where sandy beaches are few and
far between, Pissouri Bay's golden sands guarantee its
popularity. Reached via a long side-road from the main
Limassol–Pafos highway, Pissouri is basically a beach and
very little else, although there are some reasonable tavernas around the bay. In the countryside behind, where
upmarket tourist and expatriate accommodation is being
developed, vineyards still hold sway.

▶▶▶ Polis   154B4

The principal resort north of Pafos, Polis is still essentially
a village that has taken on the role of a resort without sur-
rendering itself to it entirely. It is a laid-back sort of place,
with lots of old-fashioned nooks and crannies in addition
to a central pedestrian area mostly given over to tavernas
and shops. If the scarcely developed northern coastline
has a metropolis, Polis is it, and its size and leisurely pace
are a welcome sign of just how different things are in this
part of Cyprus.

Arriving at Polis from the south, you are presented with
a choice: turning left leads to the wild Akamas Peninsula
and its mythological associations with Aphrodite; turning
right takes you along the all-but deserted north coast,
around the broad empty sweep of Chrysochou Bay,
towards the Turkish Cypriot enclave of Kokkina
(Erenköy) and the main military demarcation line beyond
Kato Pyrgos.

Polis's ancient predecessor, Marion, was an important
Greek port city, thanks mainly to its proximity to rich copper mines. The future holds a great deal of work for
archaeologists charged with separating the story of
Marion from the tangle of undergrowth in which its
remains are embedded. Preliminary work has uncovered

CAMEL TRAIN
In the area south of the Pafos Forest, camels used to transport copper from the Troodos mines to the sea at Pafos. It was the Venetians who established the Camel Trail through this exceedingly rough terrain and who built bridges over the rivers to accommodate it.

Life in the fields is not always idyllic

a Hellenistic necropolis as well as the remains of public and private dwellings, but not much of Marion is visible to reward the visitor who goes searching for it. You can see some of what's left at the new **Archaeological Museum▶** (tel: 06-322955. *Open* Mon–Fri 7.30–2.30. *Admission charge.*).

179

▶▶ Pomos 155C5

This attractively located fishing village on the hilly north coast is flanked by Pomos Point, a small but sharp-edged peninsula jutting into the sea. Pomos is a little oasis of cafés on this quiet stretch of the north coast.

▶ Souskiou 155C2

The church of Souskiou is modern, and its silvered icon of Christ on the Cross disappeared during a time of troubles, only to turn up in nearby Ariminou. The latter's devout inhabitants blithely maintain that the icon travelled to their church under its own steam – an explanation which makes up in imagination for what it no doubt lacks in veracity. There is a chalcolithic-period cemetery near the village, with faint traces of early human habitation.

Polis is on a user-friendly scale – even its churches are of modest dimensions

▶▶ Stavros tis Psokas 155C4

Reaching this abandoned 18th-century monastery in the Pafos Forest is liable to break the hearts of all but the most determined; even its monks pulled out in the 19th century. The tracks that connect the monastery to the outside world add several new dimensions to the word 'rough', and it seems that half the dust in the world has been purposely deposited on them, prior to blowing into the eyes, noses and mouths of travellers venturing this way. If you desire solitude, it is worth the journey, for Stavros tis Psokas is now a forest station with a restaurant and guest house surrounded by wilderness.

▶ Timi 154B2

Near Pafos International Airport, this might be the best place to pick up a last consignment of *haloumi*, the traditional cheese of Cyprus, which is particularly tasty when grilled. The village's **Agia Sofia** church represents a rare instance of a mosque being transformed to Christian use in the aftermath of the 1974 Turkish invasion.

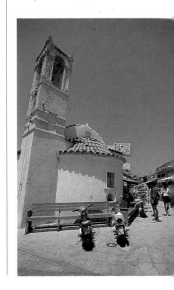

Drive

See map on pages 154–5

Polis to Kato Pyrgos

The attraction of this drive is that there is virtually nothing to see, in an area largely free of the mass tourism that reigns elsewhere, and there are no 'sights' in the conventional sense. Covering some 40km, it could be raced through in less than an hour, but that would be to miss out on the spirit of the coast.

The few sights encountered on the drive are covered in more detail on pages 164–79.

Polis►► is a town with a choice to make. The outcome will determine if it is to retain any elements of the down-at-heel charm which, up to now, has made it a welcome place of escape for lovers of the 'real' Cyprus, or if it will grasp the nettle of mass tourism and give up its identity in the process. The signs are mixed, but the pressure to open up another resort area for Cyprus is heavy and Polis has already

changed enough to persuade 'purists' to pass it by.

The main road eastwards out of Polis hugs the long eastern sweep of Chrysochou Bay, with fine views to the west towards the Akamas Peninsula and, in clear weather, Cape Arnaoutis at its tip. A short way out of town is a disused pier.

A worthwhile diversion is to **Makounta** village, on a road which climbs up through orchards and olive groves. The dusty track on the left, about half-way to Makounta, ends at a small dam.

Back on the coast road, the next village is a coastal extension of the small inland village of Argaka – a kind of Argaka-on-Sea, dominated by the looming mass of the Troodos Mountains. The beaches on either side of Argaka are stony, with rough brown sand; they are not the stuff of picture postcards, yet they have charm in a sense that nature is at work on its own agenda here, not merely acting as an adjunct to a tourist brochure.

Continuing northeast along the coast road, in an area dotted with

Looking towards the sweeping curve of Chrysochou Bay

The coastline near Polis

small seaside churches and farms whose fields reach almost to the water's edge, the coastal hamlets, very much smaller cousins of inland villages, are more notional than real – blink and you'll find you've already passed through.

With so many near-deserted beaches, swimmers may take the opportunity to do a little nude bathing. However, there are some parts of the coastline that are spoilt by piles of abandoned rubbish.

The small fishing village of **Pomos▶▶** is one of the prettiest on the coast, which is now more rocky, leading to the distinctive hump of Pomos Point. Fishing boats and an occasional cabin-cruiser make lazy circles in the shallow turquoise waters just off shore.

At **Pachyammos▶**, you can visit the modern, seaside church of Agios Rafaelis and see its extensive covering of contemporary murals inside. Beyond this, the sad realities of modern conflict intrude on an otherwise idyllic scene and force the traveller away from the coast. Cyprus National Guard, United Nations and Turkish army positions climb into the hills around the Turkish Cypriot enclave of Kokkina (Erenköy). Photography is, of course, forbidden just where the spectacular scenery persuades even a rank amateur to reach for his or her camera. Nevertheless, the enforced detour is a memorable one, and there is no law preventing you from stopping to admire the view.

A busy and dusty little resort, **Kato Pyrgos▶** is much favoured by Greek Cypriot holidaymakers seeking an escape from the foreign tourists who have taken over every other resort on the island.

A walk on the wild side of Cyprus can turn up a surprising variety of both indigenous and visiting fauna. Some species have to be protected if they are to survive the loss of habitat brought on by a fast-growing economy.

DONKEY WORK

The once universal donkey, that long-suffering symbol of traditional Mediterranean village life, is as rare now as baggy breeches on its owners. Yet they may still be seen in remoter areas, although any villager rash enough to display such a venerable symbol of local colour is liable to be mobbed by strangers with video cameras. Meanwhile, wildlife biologists are researching the 'wild donkeys' of the Karpas (Karpaz) Peninsula in the Turkish Cypriot zone, an alarming sounding creature that, if not mythical, is surely the stuff of which nightmares are made.

182

It is a sight that could make a conservationist out of the most hardened cynic: baby loggerhead turtles, tiny bundles of frantic energy and haste, scrabbling over the sand on their first journey. The turtle-ettes don't know it but they have a guardian angel, a host of guardian angels in fact, who have protected and nurtured them and now watch with delighted satisfaction as their little charges obey the mysterious dictates of evolution and leave them for the warm embrace of the sea.

Time was when such creatures did not need the help of the Lara Bay Turtle Project to make their way in life; but time also was when the golden sands lay deserted under the sun and beach hotels were a nightmare of the future. Nowadays, female turtles will not even come ashore at most of their favourite beaches on the west coast to bury their eggs: water-skiers, swimmers, sunbathers and cafés do not make for the required tranquil birthplace. As a result, the loggerhead turtles are on a fast descent to oblivion. The Lara Project aims to reverse their slide.

Protection racket On Cyprus, the animal kingdom is retreating before the spreading tide of humanity and all its works, penned into ever-diminishing scraps of habitat until nature concedes defeat and sounds the death-knell of extinction. Not all Cypriots, nor tourists, are willing to accept that the island's wildlife heritage must be sacrificed on the altar of economic progress. The battle to save the turtles is one example of their commitment. There are others.

While driving through the western slopes of the Troodos Mountains, it is a good idea to stop from time to time, turn off the engine and

Top: the rarely sighted moufflon. Below: newly hatched turtles head across the sand towards the sea at Lara Bay

listen. There may be nothing to hear but the chirp of bird-song and the wind sighing through the pine branches; but there may be the sharp clatter of rocks tumbling down scree-covered slopes, signifying that a moufflon is trying to put as much distance between itself and you as its legs will permit.

This wild mountain sheep is the star of Cyprus's wildlife show. A shy, retiring creature, its less-than-flattering attitude to humans is: if you can see it, you're too close. Travelling normally in pairs, they head north like, well...like the proverbial mountain goat, taking the punishingly steep hills in their stride, stopping only to check whether they can still see you before disappearing among the trees. Spotting a moufflon is a memorable experience – while it lasts.

Wildlife parade Cyprus has much to delight on its wildlife roster. Griffon vultures soar on updrafts in the Kyrenia (Beşparmak) Mountains; pink flamingos crowd the salt lakes at Larnaka and Akrotiri when winter rains restore their waters; monk seals,

Southern festoon butterfly: one of many species that take full advantage of Cyprus as the 'island of flowers'

183

although rarely seen, cavort off the remote Akamas Peninsula; loggerhead turtles nest on protected beaches. No fewer than 55 butterfly species, including the painted lady, speckled wood, brown argus, Cleopatra and two-tailed pasha, have been identified.

Migrating birds can't seem to pass Cyprus by: the swallow, swift, little ringed plover, Eleonora's falcon, bee-eater, hoopoe, Cyprus pied wheatear, masked shrike and black-headed bunting are just a few of the species that either pause on their migration route or remain to breed. The venomous blunt-nosed viper should ideally be avoided, but most snakes are non-poisonous and anyway are rarely seen.

SERPENTINE ROADS
Snakes, such as three varieties of whip snake and the Montpelier snake and viper, are most likely to be observed flat as pancakes and dried to a crisp after being caught under the wheels of passing cars while attempting to cross the road. This is a sight which even the Roman Emperor Constantine's mother, St Helena, a determined reptile-hater who introduced snake-fighting cats to Cyprus, would surely have abhorred.

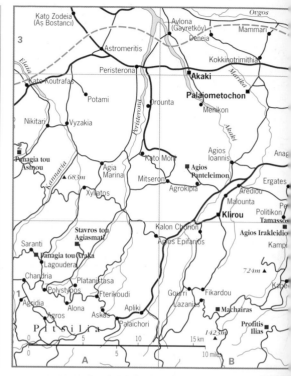

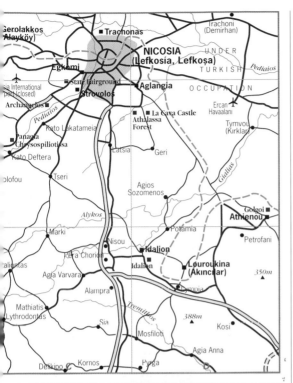

Left: the products of
irrigation and good land
Far left: the desert-like
central plains in the
summer heat

THE CENTRE Central Cyprus may seem like the bit left
over when all the more popular places have been covered,
but it has its own quiet charm – a quality some of those
other places have traded for fool's gold.

Yet outside Nicosia this is the region most badly affected
by the harsh reality of conflict and division. In normal circumstances it would form a squashed circle around the
capital, reaching north towards the Kyrenia (Beşparmak)
Mountains and south to the Troodos, taking a bite out of
the Mesaoria (Mesarya) Plain to the east and the Morfou
(Güzelyurt) Plain to the west. Instead, the circle has been
slashed in two by the barbed-wire scar of the UN military-
demarcation line that cuts across the island's middle,
splitting it in two.

▶▶▶ REGION HIGHLIGHTS

*Handicrafts on sale in a
restored traditional
dwelling*

Time was when all roads running through this area led to Nicosia, a capital with at least some of the graces that make living in a hot and dusty plains city tolerable. Now the highways have been amputated; central Cyprus is filled with roads that lead nowhere, or at best to a check-point manned by a bored but determined rifleman. With no sun-hallowed beaches or sharp-tanged mountain air to commend it, central Cyprus is left with only its farms and workaday villages to distract the senses and divert attention from that dismal line.

REAL THING Well, not quite. No part of Cyprus is so weighed down by this time of troubles as to forget that life goes on. And amid the constellation of farming villages, which in any case share the characteristic restful welcome of all Cypriot villages, there are enough bright stars to more than justify pulling off the main highway from Nicosia to the coast. Because this area is not one for which tour guides and tourist brochures employ the nearest handy superlatives, it is in some respects far closer to the 'real Cyprus' than many places more favoured.

The immediate vicinity of Nicosia is filled with a mess of suburbs and, more poignantly, permanent refugee villages: hastily built housing projects for Greek Cypriots who got out of the north just one step ahead of the advancing Turkish army in 1974. A little further away, however, is a bewilderingly large and all-but-deserted landscape that rolls and wanders to nobody's whim but its own.

Finally, the central area butts up against the Troodos foothills and the coastal plains, and hands the torch on to its competitors.

GETTING LOST Travel this area by the main roads and you pass through as if in a bubble, traversing familiar-looking fields and villages, and insulated from its true impact. Turn off the main roads on to the narrow side-roads, then stony tracks and dusty trails, and a new experience awaits, one that has little to do with route maps and easily followed itineraries. In other words, you're going to get lost. Count on it. Of course, getting lost in Cyprus is a relative concept: it rarely takes long to get found again.

ROAD WITH A VIEW
The main road west from Nicosia through Peristerona to the Troodos Mountains runs alongside the UN buffer zone for most of its length, providing a good view of 'the other side'. You can see across the fertile Morfou Plain to the town of Morfou, a centre of the citrus industry, and beyond it to the dark mass of the Pentadaktylos Mountains.

Yet to drift through this sometimes barren, always dusty region is to glimpse another Cyprus, one as distinctive in its own way as parts which are better advertised.

It may be just as well that the ridges and valleys of the central region offer enough of interest to the casual transient, because the traditional tourist 'attractions' are thinner on the ground than elsewhere. The package does, however, include an ancient city or two (thoroughly ruined of course), some venerable monasteries and surprising old Byzantine churches.

The closer you get to the mountains, the more rugged the landscape becomes, but paradoxically also more green and fruitful thanks to underground water sources and reservoirs. The heartland has its moments too.

Houses at Fikardou conservation village, shuttered against the sun

187

DUST DEVIL
The kind of dry and dusty tracks that the Troodos foothills specialise in hold a special peril for the occupants of open-topped jeeps, which otherwise can take most obstacles in their stride. The dust gets everywhere, so that not only do the occupants need frequent showers, but so does the inside of the jeep.

PLAYING WITH FIRE
In the farming country around Nicosia it is not uncommon to see miniature 'forest fires', as farmers clear and prepare the land for the next crop. This can pose a danger to traffic, as thick smoke reduces visibility to zero. It can also pose a danger to the farmers' own houses, if a wind pushes the flames in an unintended direction.

Machairas Monastery, one of the principal seats of the Orthodox faith in Cyprus

Murals depicting saints at Agios Irakleidios Monastery

▶▶▶ Agios Irakleidios Monastery
184B1

Open: daily dawn–dusk. Admission free

The nuns of this monastery are among the most relaxed towards visitors in all of Cyprus, which is perhaps just as well, seeing that they get so many of them. They have their treasures to display: the whitened bones of St Irakleidios's hand, and his head too, the latter mercifully placed out of eyeshot inside an ornate gilt reliquary.

Of notable icons and murals the monastery church has an elegant sufficiency, and in a smaller adjoining chapel there is a Roman-era tomb which is thought to be that of the saint.

It may be that the nuns' simple handicrafts, icon souvenirs, confectionery and honey, and the bougainvillea-bedecked peace of their cloister, exert as much of an attraction as the more mystical powers ascribed to the relics of Irakleidios, who was an early bishop of nearby Tamassos and a martyr for the faith. The present foundation dates from the 18th century, although a monastery has existed on the site since the 5th century, having been destroyed and rebuilt several times.

▶▶ Agios Panteleimon Monastery
184B2

Rarely open for visitors. Admission free

This simple, flower-bright 18th-century monastery is set in good farming country near the village of Agrokipia in the low foothills of the Troodos Mountains. The villages around here stand between two of the important secondary routes from the mountains to Nicosia, which make for interesting alternatives to the main road through Peristerona and Kakopetria.

▶ Agios Sozomenos
185D2

Wide open countryside around this village southeast of Nicosia is mainly given over to sparsely populated farmland, eventually jutting up against the demarcation line. Abandoned hamlets in a state of shell-scarred dereliction are eerily empty reminders of the island's troubled recent history and that even now Cyprus is not all sweetness and light.

► Archangelos Monastery 185C2

Open: daily. Admission free

Dedicated to the Archangel Michael, this monastery is situated a very short drive from Nicosia and makes for a pleasant quick excursion from the city. The palm-tree-bordered foundation dates back to the Byzantine era, but was rebuilt in the 18th century, since when it has been owned by the wealthy and influential Kykkos Monastery of the Troodos Mountains.

►► Athalassa Forest 185D2

Something doesn't quite add up with this nature park just outside Nicosia. It is attractive enough and certainly welcome in the environs of a hot and busy capital not noted for its wealth of green spaces. But a military base, a weather station and an agriculture and forestry research institute take up a fair part of the available area, and access to the public space is far from simple. Nevertheless, shaded walks and picnics are possible and there is an artificial lake, while the research institute creates enough pleasant scents from its range of exotic plants to mask at least some of the city's diesel fumes.

Buffer Zone 185D2

While it may be in poor taste to consider this a tourist attraction – and certainly no Cypriot would so consider it – it exists and exercises a peculiar fascination, just as the Iron Curtain once did. In any case, it is hardly possible to get there before being stopped by a warning notice, or Greek Cypriot or United Nations checkpoint (a determined attempt to get into the zone may lead to arrest and should not be attempted).

The array of observation posts and flag-decorated defensive positions looks toy-like and innocuous from a distance, an image enhanced by the fact that Greek Cypriots farm right up to the limit of what is permissible – and occasionally, to the distress of the UN, beyond.

NO PICTURES PLEASE
The UN shares the picture-shyness of the Greek Cypriot, Turkish and British troops on the island. Understandably, none of these forces wants to become a tourist attraction, and there are legitimate, even vital, security reasons for restricting photography, however ridiculous these may seem if you are behind the lens.

189

The tree-shaded grounds of Agios Panteleimon Monastery

The highlight of Gourri village is its church

HOLY OLIVES
The olive trees around Idalion are said to have a holy provenance, having apparently sprung from olive-stones the apostles Paul and Barnabas spat out when they stopped to enjoy a spot of lunch.

The present structure of Machairas Monastery dates from the early 20th century

▶▶ Fikardou
184B1

This attractive village, well out on the road towards the Pitsilia region of the Troodos Mountains, has been declared an ancient monument and conservation zone to preserve the wooden balconied houses dating from the Ottoman period and the general rustic charm of an entirely unspoiled Cypriot village.

This folk architecture heritage brings the village under the gaze of Cyprus's Department of Antiquities, which may not please all of its inhabitants.

▶ Golgoi
185D2

Located right next to the military positions of the demarcation line, this ancient Greek colony of Corinth has itself settled into the rolling countryside southeast of Nicosia. Golgoi now awaits better days and fatter archaeological budgets before delivering up its secrets.

▶ Gourri
184B1

Although it has Ottoman-era houses with carved wooden balconies equal to those in nearby Fikardou, this village has not been declared a conservation zone and ancient monument.

▶ Idalion
185D1

The Bronze Age city-state of Idalion is one of many locations where the golden shepherd boy Adonis, who dallied once too often in pastoral idyll with Aphrodite, is said to have met his end at the tusks of a wild boar sent by the goddess's outraged husband, Hephaestus. It is difficult to relate soap-opera Greek mythology to the few stumps of Idalion that remain above ground at this location 19km south of Nicosia near the modern village of Idalion. Only minimally excavated, Idalion has nevertheless yielded traces of temples to Aphrodite and Athena, as well as great ashlar blocks from the walls which protected the city until its demise around 400 BC.

▶ Kokkinotrimithia
184B3

The name of this farming village amidst rich red soil close to the demarcation line recalls the Kokkinochoria, or red-earth country, around Agia Napa which is renowned for its excellent potatoes.

▶▶▶ Machairas Monastery
184B1

Open: for group visits Mon, Tue, Thu 9–12. Admission free
This is a favoured location for capturing the mysterious romance of Cyprus's Greek Orthodox monasteries, which have borne the spirit of Byzantium

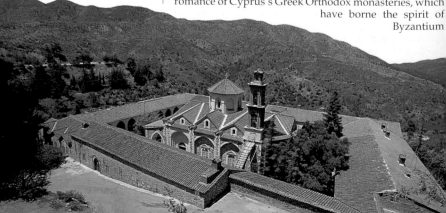

The pristine-looking interior of the Machairas Monastery

down through the centuries since the island was detached from the empire. Partly this is because it is a handsome-looking place, especially when the warm late-afternoon light washes its walls; partly because it commands magnificent views (in one direction reaching all the way to Nicosia); and partly because of its association with EOKA, the guerrilla organisation that fought the British in a savage and almost mystically inspired campaign to unite Cyprus with Greece.

Although the monastery's history stretches back to the mid-12th century, when an icon of the Virgin is said to have been found on the site, the present buildings date from the early 20th century, when the monastery was rebuilt after a disastrous fire ravaged the place in 1892. The result is an almost pristinely modern foundation which appears to re-create the graces of ancient Byzantium but without the patina of age that would make it look venerable as well. The church has, however, hung on to its important icon, covering it with a silver shell to add to the mystery.

Nicosia International Airport 185C3

This was once Cyprus's gateway to the world; now its only international connection is that it acts as the main base of the United Nations Force in Cyprus (UNFICYP). During the 1974 conflict, the airport was attacked by Turkish paratroopers who were repulsed by Greek Cypriot troops. UN sentry posts ring the base, and there are wrecked aircraft beside the runways.

The airport is one of the places whose reopening for business is regularly proposed by UN goodwill ambassadors as a measure to raise confidence between the island's divided communities, but the minimal level of confidence needed to get even the proposal, never mind aeroplanes, off the ground has never been forthcoming.

PRO PATRIA...
Gregoris Afxentiou, a deputy commander of EOKA in the fight against the British during the 1950s, was killed in a cave near Machairas Monastery. Brought to bay by British troops, he shot one of them, then died himself when the soldiers set fire to his hiding-place. The flag-bedecked cave is a popular place of pilgrimage for Greek Cypriots.

Eating out in Cyprus is a great social event, and traditional Cypriot cuisine lends itself to the experience. Lingering over an alfresco dinner in the scented evening air, or crunching into a village salad at lunchtime, can make the hard work of a holiday seem well worthwhile.

BRANDY SOUR
The recipe for this popular and refreshing Cyprus cocktail is: pour a liberal dash of angostura bitters into a tall glass, followed by a good measure of brandy and an equal amount of fresh lemon juice; add sugar and ice, fill the glass with soda and garnish with a slice of lemon.

192

If Cypriots thought eating and drinking had as their sole purpose the sustaining of life, they might give them up as a bad deal. As it is, they regard them as life-enhancing to an extent that it is hard to see how they find time for other things. This is most notable on family outings, especially if *meze* is on the menu – an avalanche of little dishes that cascades onto the table in a seemingly endless torrent, each one a traditional favourite to be savoured and discussed. With an unrivalled storehouse of fresh products to draw on from its farms and orchards, Cyprus can afford to pamper its collective stomach.

That doesn't mean diners always strike edible gold. Another tradition exists alongside the Greek, Turkish and purely Cypriot one. It may rather loosely be described as 'international', although 'awful' would do about as well. This second tradition is found in many holiday hotels where the lowest common denominator is considered adequate, and in a multitude of tourist restaurants and tavernas where the Cypriot touch has been left at the kitchen door. It is not a question of price: the smug equation that cheap equals bad and expensive equals good does not always add up, and Cypriot cuisine can be excellent value at all price levels. It is more a question of attitude.

Good influence Cyprus stands at the crossroads of three continents and has

This village salad looks as colourful as a still-life painting

absorbed culinary influences from all three, but Greek and Turkish antecedents adapted to Cypriot tastes are the strongest. *Meze* provides the best possible introduction, with 20 to 30 dishes ranging from dips and raw vegetables to fish and meat in richly flavoured sauces. Such a meal is a test of appetite and endurance, another reason why Cypriots linger so long over it. A restaurant which piles on the *meze* dishes, allowing some to get cold before they can be tasted, then follows up rapidly with the bill, is best avoided next time. Seafood and vegetarian *meze* are also available in some places.

Typical items on the Greek Cypriot meze list and as individual orders are: *haloumi* (goat's milk cheese flavoured with mint, which is often served grilled); *kolokithakia* (stuffed or plain courgettes); *koupepia* and *dolmades* (vine leaves stuffed with rice and meat); *lountza* (smoked pork which has been marinaded in red wine); *tahini* (a sesame dip mixed with lemon, garlic and parsley); and *hummus* (an Arab-style dip made from chickpeas, garlic and lemon juice). Main dishes include such favourites as *afelia* (chunks of pork stewed in a red-wine sauce and sprinkled with coriander seeds); *keftedes* (fried meatballs); *kleftiko* (lamb or goat meat roasted in an earthenware oven); *souvlakia* (lamb or pork grilled on a skewer); and *moussaka* (a layered dish of aubergines or potato and minced meat in a béchamel sauce).

Turkish Cypriot variants of these and other dishes are available, the most important difference in the meat department being the absence of pork. Desserts tend towards the sweet-toothed, liberally spread with honey. Fresh fruit of excellent quality is a standard item, but vegetables, despite their wondrous variety, take a back-seat to meat dishes.

Liquid refreshment Cypriot wines make an ideal accompaniment to a meal, but are not available in the Turkish zone, where good-value labels from Turkey predominate. Commandaria, a sweet red dessert wine with a history dating back to medieval times, is one of Greek Cyprus's most notable products. Sherry, too, is a local stalwart, while Greek *ouzo* and Turkish *raki* are popular on both sides of the divide. Cyprus's distinctive contribution to the world of cocktails is the refreshingly sharp brandy sour.

SWEET TEMPTATION

A traditional Cypriot confection is *soujoukko*, which looks like a long waxy string of giant beads. Genuine *soujoukko* is made from almonds laced on strings and dipped repeatedly into heated grape juice until a thick covering congeals in layers around the almonds. The string is hung up in the sun to dry. Its taste and consistency are not unrelated to that of rubber, but it is surely more healthy than modern sugary confectionery.

Snack bars are often the source of simple but tasty Cypriot food

193

►► Panagia Chrysospiliotissa
185C2

Open: daily. Admission free

One of the strangest of all Cyprus's Orthodox churches, Panagia Chrysospiliotissa, some 11km southwest of Nicosia near Kato Deftera village, is also one of the most attractive, with a simple, almost childlike charm. Our Lady of the Golden Cave stands half-way up a cliff-face in an enlarged natural cavern that recalls the catacombs of the persecuted early Christian churches; it may indeed have been used as such since the 1st century. The barely illuminated interior, reached by a steel stairway, is decked with votive offerings, including wedding dresses.

The votive-filled interior of the cave-built church of Panagia Chrysospiliotissa

► Pera Chorion
185C1

This small village near Idalion is noted for its 12th-century Byzantine church of **Agioi Apostoloi►**, containing colourful frescos, including a fine (but damaged) image of Christ Pantokrator in the dome.

► Peristerona
184A3

The village stands in orchard country near the demarcation line west of Nicosia on the road to Troodos. Peristerona is symbolic, in Greek Cypriot eyes at any rate, of the peaceful relations that used to exist in former times between the island's now divided communities. Two religious foundations, a 19th-century mosque, which is no longer in use, and a church, stand almost side by side in the centre, suggesting a solidarity that has now passed away. The church, the superbly multi-domed 10th-century **Agioi Varnavas ke Ilarion**, stands by the usually dry riverbed.

ANTIQUE VIRTUES
Strabo, in his *Geographica* (AD 23) wrote: 'Such then is Cyprus in point of position. But in excellence it falls behind no one of the islands: for it is rich in wine and oil, and uses home-grown wheat. There are mines of copper in plenty at Tamassos, in which are produced sulphate of copper and copper oxide useful in the healing art.'

►► Profitis Ilias
184B1

Some wild and wonderful forest trails criss-cross the country around this rustic monastery at the far end of a 6km track west of the village of Lythrodontas. There are views into a beautiful valley below, filled with cypress trees. The

194

monastery, with its two-storey array of monks' cells and an old monastic church, is no longer operational, and a forest station occupies its grounds.

Apart from attending an occasional baptism in the church, few pilgrims make the journey for any reason other than to light a barbecue or enjoy a picnic in the cool glades around the monastery.

▶ Strovolos 185C2

Typical of the villages being swallowed whole by fast-expanding Nicosia, Strovolos still has a recognisable village centre and retains some country atmosphere despite the intense pace of new construction. This was the birthplace of Archbishop Kyprianou, a Greek Cypriot hero almost on a par with Archbishop Makarios. Kyprianou was executed by the Ottomans in 1821, along with many leading Greek Cypriots, when they were accused of conspiracy during the mainland Greek revolt against Turkish rule.

▶▶ Tamassos 184B2

Open: Tue–Fri 9–3, Sat–Sun 10–3. Admission charge

At first glance this appears to be one of those ancient Cypriot cities that have just barely survived their journey through the millennia and have come down to us as a seemingly indecipherable muddle of stones. A second glance tends to confirm that initial unpromising assessment, and it is unfortunate that neither the archaeological nor the tourism authorities have done much by way of providing information to fill in the details.

Tamassos has, however, a rich history, with references to its wealth dating back to Homer. The Roman poet Ovid also sang its praises as the 'best part' of Cyprus. The wealth was based, as was so often the case in ancient Cyprus, on the mining, smelting and working of copper.

Systematic excavation of the site began only in 1975, and since then a temple, thought to have been dedicated to Aphrodite, has been uncovered. Most notable of all and described by a leaflet available at the ticket office are two royal tombs with carved and decorated walls, dating from the 7th century BC. When the tombs were discovered in 1890 there were three of them, but local villagers, less impressed than archaeologists by Cypro-Archaic Period II royal tombs, destroyed one and used its stones for building materials.

GIFT OF APOLLO
In 1836, a local peasant found a life-size bronze statue of Apollo while ploughing a field near Tamassos. The man was so pleased with his wind-fall that he cut up the statue, which must to all intents and purposes have been priceless, and sold it for scrap.

195

The scant remains of ancient Tamassos, once an influential city

For almost 40 years, soldiers answerable to the United Nations secretary-general in New York have held the line between Cyprus's two communities. Their experience runs the gamut from boredom to death by hostile fire, a variety of sacrifice designed to give politicians time to end the island's tragedy.

VOLVO IN MIND
It has not been all hardship for soldiers assigned to peacekeeping duties with the UN in Cyprus. Members of the Swedish contingent (which has since been withdrawn) were so well paid for their six-month tour of duty in Cyprus that they called it the 'Volvo posting', because the first thing they would do when they went home was buy a Volvo with the money they had saved.

UNFICYP armoured car on patrol along the Green Line in Nicosia

Sightings of Cyprus's peacekeepers are liable to be disjointed: a relaxed, blue-bereted sentry at the Pafos Gate checkpoint in Nicosia, who politely but firmly waves away all requests for a picture; a white-painted jeep sweeping through the countryside near the demarcation line, the UN pennant on its aerial snapping in the wind; observation towers in the buffer zone, calmly flying the UN flag between hostile positions where Greek Cypriot and Greek flags engage in a kind of semaphore war with Turkish Cypriot and Turkish flags across the way.

Though few in number, the United Nations Force in Cyprus (known by the acronym UNFICYP) is ubiquitous. Its job puts it in harm's way between the two potential combatants. Its role is to defuse situations of tension long before the point where either side reaches angrily for its holster. If the reality of the mission is that sunburn and tedium are more often a greater menace than flying bullets, that has not always been the case. Some UN soldiers have paid the ultimate price asked of them by the world community they serve and whose desire for peace in Cyprus they uphold.

Out of control Four years after Cyprus gained its independence from Britain, UNFICYP was set up. Power-sharing between Greek and Turkish Cypriots collapsed in 1963; fighting erupted in Nicosia, then spread throughout the island. British troops in the capital set up the Green Line separating the two commun- ities there, but the island.wide situation was out of control. The UN authorised a peacekeeping force on 4 March 1964 with troops from Austria, Britain, Canada, Denmark, Finland, Ireland and Sweden.

In its first 10 years, UNFICYP's complex task was to look after minorities threatened by the other side. In practice, as Turkish Cypriots withdrew into enclaves surrounded and occasionally attacked by Greek Cypriot forces, this usually meant protecting the Turkish Cypriots, which raised cries of bias against the peacekeepers.

In 1974, the situation changed drastically with a Greek-inspired coup against the Cypriot government – which President Makarios called an invasion of Cyprus by Greece – and the subsequent Turkish military intervention. Eight UN soldiers were killed and more than 60 wounded during the fighting that followed this disastrous sequence of events.

Observer status When the smoke of battle had cleared and the immediate humanitarian crisis of prisoners of war and refugees had been dealt with, UNFICYP's revised task, while no less onerous, was at least simpler. Its forces now man a series of observation posts in the UN buffer zone beween each side's ceasefire line, running from Kokkina (Erenköy) in the west and meandering across the island, through the Green Line in Nicosia, to a point south of Famagusta (Gazimağusa) in the east. The observers ensure that neither side intrudes militarily beyond its ceasefire line and that civilians do not enter the UN buffer zone, either of which might provoke a response from the other side.

As talks between the communities constantly fail to reach agreement, some national governments have grown disillusioned at the lack of progress and the cost and have with drawn their contingents, although others have taken their place. The UN has many more serious problems in other parts of the world and,the generally peaceful situation in divided Cyprus has focused its efforts elswhere, Yet one only has to see the level of military force on either side of the demarcation line to realise that the peace in Cyprus is fragile and to hope that UN member states recall that peacekeeping is far easier than peacemaking.

A British peacekeeping soldier in Cyprus makes his transfer to UN command in 1964

197

Cape Kormakitis
(Koruçam Burnu)

Livera
(Sadrazamköy)

Orga
(Kayalar)

Vavylas
(Güzelyalı)

Kormakitis
(Koruçam)

Vasileia
(Karşıyaka)

Karavas
(Alsancak)

1024m

Kyre
(Kery
Gir

Palaia
Kastro

UNDER

Diorios
(Tepebaşı)

Myrtou
(Çamlıbel)

Lapithos
(Lapta)

Agios Georgios
(Karaoğlanoğlu)

Agia Eirini
(Akdeniz)

Agios
Pandeleimon

Karmi (Karaman)

Agios
Hatton

888m

93

TURKISH

Asomatos
(Ozhan)

Kontemenos
(Kiliçaslan)

Agirta
(Ağirdağ)

Atoupos

Morfou Bay
(*Güzelyurt Körfezi*)

Kato
Pyrgos

Syrianochori
(Yaylar)

Toumba
tou Skonrou

Kalon Chorion
(Kalkanli)

Profitis Ilias

Skylloura
(Yılmazköy)

Fota
(Dağyolu)

Kato Dik
(Aş Dik

OCCUPATION

Serrachis

Morfou
(Güzelyurt)

Agia Marina
(Gürpınar)

Agios Vasilios
(Türkeli)

Gonyeli

Vouni
(Vuni)

Pentageia
(Yeşilyurt)

Argaki
(Akçay)

Orgos

Ortaköy
(Ortaköy)

Trac

Soloi
(Soli)

Karavostasi
(Gemikonağı)

Kato Zodeia
(Aş Bostancı)

Katokopia
(Zumrutköy)

Gerolakkos
(Nayköy)

Ampelikou
(Bağlıköy)

Lefka
(Lefke)

Petra
(Taşköy)

Astromeritis

Egkomi

Fidia

Peristerona

Akaki

Strovolos

Xeros

Skarolos

A

B

C

NOXIOUS WEED
A strand of seaweed may look like a dull, unintelligent creature but it knows enough to get a bunch of its pals together and head for the nearest beach. Some beaches, in particular those on the northern coast, attract great carpets of seaweed that can make any attempt to enter the water seem like a scene from *The Day of the Triffids*.

TO GO OR NOT TO GO...?
That is the question. In international law, the Turkish Cypriot zone is illegally occupied by the Turkish army. The Turkish Cypriots have their own side of the story to tell and there are strong touristic reasons for going there, but the salient fact of its occupied status ought not to be forgotten.

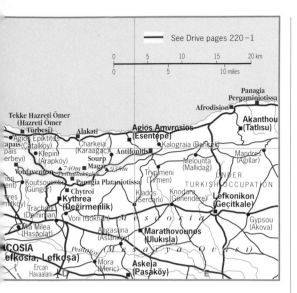

THE NORTH For the purposes of this book, 'the north' refers only to the northern part of the island, that is the northern coast, the Kyrenia (Beşparmak) Mountains and the adjoining area. This is an imprecise geographical concept, not a political one. Nevertheless, for practical reasons the north lies wholly within the territory called by its inhabitants the Turkish Republic of Northern Cyprus, although it does not cover all of it (there remain the east and Turkish Cypriot Nicosia). It is for others to decide whether they approve of this distinction or not.

With its friendly people, beaches and forest-clad mountains, castles, abbeys and churches, farming villages and a fishing harbour, all northern Cyprus lacks is the kind of tourist overexploitation that has marred some other sections of the island. However, few visitors will complain about that.

Based on the handsome port town of Kyrenia (Girne), the north lays claim to being the most beautiful and least 'spoiled' part of the island, with long stretches of glorious, unspoiled sandy beaches.

The long, jagged blade of the Kyrenia Mountains saws at the sky along much of the region's length. This range has an excessive number of names, being known also as the Beşparmak Mountains, the Pentadaktylos Mountains and the Gothic Range, for the castles and abbeys dotting its slopes. The Castle and Harbour of Kyrenia (Girne) are fascinating structures from the Byzantine era.

Far left: Kyrenia (Girne) Harbour
Below left: packing charcoal in Turkish Cyprus

*Inside the ramparts of
St Hilarion Castle*

WHAT'S IN A NAME?

Place-names, as well as being essential for letting people know where they are, may be a political statement. Official Greek and Turkish names exist for all localities on the island. Now only Greek names are used in the Greek Cypriot sector and Turkish in the Turkish Cypriot sector. The Greek-speakers accuse their Turkish neighbours of changing the names in their sector as part of a strategy to eliminate the Greek cultural heritage there. The Turkish-speakers disagree, of course.

Coffee shop, Bellapais

DURRELL COUNTRY Other writers have applied their pens to the history, culture and people of Cyprus, but few have illuminated them better – or at a more critical time – than the Englishman Lawrence Durrell. His book *Bitter Lemons* captures the moment when Greek Cypriots decided that violence would loosen Britain's hold on Cyprus and win union with Greece, while Turkish Cypriots determined that the former goal was undesirable and the latter unthinkable. Durrell's presence, by turns riotously funny and hauntingly sad, touches much of the north, particularly Kyrenia, the mountains and the village of Bellapais (Beylerbeyi), where he lived from 1953 to 1956.

The north is more than a tourist paradise or writer's creation, of course. Real people reside there, earning a hard living from the soil, sea and mountains. Many hail from southern Cyprus, refugees who made the doleful journey north in 1974 from homes that were too hard pressed to retain, just as their Greek Cypriot counterparts were heading south. Others are immigrants from Turkey, poor Anatolian farmers for the most part, taking the chance for a better life, yet regarded with condescension by some Turkish Cypriots and with impotent fury by the Greek Cypriots. Despite this tragic background, however, the north is not fixated on the past.

BETTER TIMES The dazzling harbour at Kyrenia is the jewel in the northern crown. In good weather (which means almost always), the semi-circle of upmarket cafés and restaurants housed in its magnificent old warehouses spread their terraces on to the quayside. The customers flock to these cafés, to the glittering constellation of casinos in and around Kyrenia, and to the discos. Yet, despite its lively sense of fun, the town of Kyrenia still manages to be a quiet place by the standards of most other resorts in the Mediterranean.

If you are seeking an even quieter time, then an even quieter time you will find. All along the windy heights of the Kyrenia Mountains there are nature trails so lonely that it seems as if the rest of the human race has packed up and left. And the numerous Latin and crusader castles and abbeys that give the mountains their Gothic tag are perched in places so far from being accessible that it is clear their builders never spared future tourists so much as a passing thought. Much of the long coastline is a living showcase of what the Mediterranean must have been like in the days when holidays abroad were the exclusive province of the idle rich. So for goodness' sake don't tell everyone about it!

201

The road leading out of Nicosia to Kyrenia (Girne) passes the capital's Venetian Kyrenia Gate

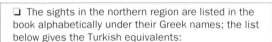

❏ The sights in the northern region are listed in the book alphabetically under their Greek names; the list below gives the Turkish equivalents:

Akdeniz (Agia Eirini) page 202
Alsancak (Karavas) page 208
Beylerbeyi (Bellapais) pages 207–8
Çamlıbel (Myrtou) page 218
Çatalköy (Agios Epiktitos) page 202
Değirmenlik (Kythrea) page 216
Gemikonağı (Karavostasi) page 209
Girne (Kyrenia) pages 210–14
Güzelyalı (Vavilas) page 224
Güzelyurt (Morfou) pages 216–17
Kalkanlı (Kalo Chorio) page 208
Karaman (Karmi) page 209
Karaoğlanoğlu (Agios Georgios) page 202
Koruçam (Kormakitis) page 209
Lapta (Lapithos) page 216
Lefke (Lefka) page 216
Mount Beşparmak (Mount Pentadaktylos) page 218
Taşkent (Vounon) page 225
Tekke Hazreti Ömer (Hazreti Ömer Türbesi) page 224
Yeşllyurt (Pentageia) page 218 ❏

ON THE HORN
Anyone who has considered Cyprus's often vicious recent history might expect Cypriots to have horns – an accusation that was in fact made against them in ancient times. In reality, few people are more hospitable. This can be seen even at the sharp end of the divide, in the armed forces. Most Greek Cypriot conscripts are sun-wilted kids, pulling sentry duty while wondering how soon they can get away to the disco; tourists may be saluted by the Turkish military policeman turning them away from some restricted area. Horns are not readily discernible.

The North

LONESOME ROAD
The narrow road that runs along the northern coast from a point east of Agios Epiktitos (Çatalköy), virtually in the sea for long stretches, is a delight to drive, cycle or walk. Little in the way of facilities of any kind will be encountered and the whole area retains a wild feel that speaks of former days in the Mediterranean.

202

*The Peace and Freedom
Monument, on Yavuz
Çikarma*

► **Afrodision** 199E2

Despite its intriguing name, this once-important Greco-Roman city has become one with the dung-covered fields hereabouts and awaits the belated attentions of archaeologists. A few kilometres east on the coast lies the crumbling structure of the 12th-century Panagia Pergaminiotissa Church.

► **Agia Eirini (Akdeniz)** 198B2

In a ravine outside this agricultural village, fossilised bones of Cyprus's extinct pygmy hippopotamus have been found. On the nearby shore are the remains of Palaia Kastro, an ancient temple site at which masses of terracotta votive offerings were discovered; they are now in the Cyprus Museum in Greek Cypriot Nicosia. Unfortunately, at the time of writing neither of these sites is accessible as they both lie within an extensive military zone, and the harsh sound of soldiers' whistles greets any attempt to penetrate the area.

► **Agios Epiktitos (Çatalköy)** 199D2

The church of St Epictetus, dating from the 1830s and named after a 12th-century Christian hermit who took up residence in a cave near the town, is now a mosque. Large villas in the surroundings provide evidence of the village's popularity with well-heeled expatriates.

► **Agios Georgios (Karaoğlanoğlu)** 198C2

Renamed by the Turkish Cypriots for a high-ranking Turkish army officer killed during the 1974 invasion, this little seaside village west of Kyrenia (Girne) was formerly noted for its fossils of Cyprus's extinct pygmy hippopotamus (see panel). Just beyond the village, the beach of **Yavuz Çikarma►**, where the Turkish force came ashore, is marked by the rather grotesque concrete Peace and Freedom Monument, as well as a Turkish military memorial displaying Greek Cypriot tanks and other heavy weaponry knocked out during the operation. Ironically in view of its grim associations, the beach is also known as Bambi Beach. Off shore lies tiny **Snake Island**, one of Cyprus's retinue of diminutive islets.

▶▶▶ Agios Ilarion (St Hilarion Castle)   198C2

St Hilarion Castle, perched 700m above the road

Open: summer daily 9–5; winter daily 9–4. Admission charge
Midway between Nicosia and Kyrenia, and occupying a
strategic position 700m above the road, St Hilarion is the
picture-book image of a crusader castle – or was until the
Venetians partially dismantled it in the 16th century.
Nevertheless, more than enough remains intact for the
picture to be scarcely affected. So powerful are the castle's
layered defences that as recently as the 1960s Turkish
Cypriot militiamen in occupation easily beat off determined attacks by the Greek Cypriot National Guard. The
more romantic crusader and Lusignan period was the castle's heyday, however, when its cool mountaintop
position made it an ideal summer residence for the
Lusignan kings; the French knights called it the Dieu
d'Amour (God of Love) Castle, perhaps in a misguided
macho appreciation of Cyprus's very own Aphrodite.

This is the most impressive of the three crusader castles
in the Kyrenia (Beşparmak) Range, with three separate
defensive systems of crenellated walls and towers culminating in a craggy redoubt. It was fortified in two major
stages, beginning with the Byzantines in the 12th century.
The castle was surrendered by the Byzantine usurper
Isaac Komnenos to England's King Richard the Lionheart,
while the latter was on his way to join the Third Crusade.
Under several of the Lusignan kings, the castle was greatly
strengthened during the following three centuries.

Entering the bailey (the courtyard enclosed by the
walls), the visitor climbs past the stables and barracks of
the garrison, and through another gate to the royal apartments, with a Byzantine church, a dining hall and more
barracks. Still climbing, the final destination is the upper
enceinte, with more apartments, a dining hall and
kitchens. At the summit is a tower from which one
aggrieved blue-blood, the Prince of Antioch, had his
Bulgarian bodyguards pitched to their deaths for
allegedly plotting against him.

▶▶ Alakati Beach   199D2

Several fine beaches lie on either side of this one, some
18km east of Kyrenia, at what was a Mycenaean-era settlement. Further east, one of these beaches has been put
permanently out of commission by the eyesore of Turkish
Cyprus's first, and badly needed, electric power plant
(until it opened in 1994, all power had to be imported
from the south, and cuts at peak times were a far from rare
occurrence). In this area is also **Turtle Beach**, where
Cyprus's rare loggerhead turtles come ashore to lay their
eggs. Although some tourist developments – including a
troops-only beach – have been established in this area, the
coast is mostly wonderfully unexploited.

203

THEM BONES
At several points on the
northern coast, including
Agios Georgios
(Karaoğlanoğlu) and Agia
Eirini (Akdeniz), the
fossilised bones of
Cyprus's extinct pygmy
hippopotamus have been
found. Pious villagers
got there before the
palaeontologists, however,
and, believing the bones
to be those of St
Fanourios, ground them
up, added the powder to
water and drank the con-
coction for its supposed
medicinal value.

WHITE KNIGHTS
St Hilarion Castle is said
to have provided the Walt
Disney studio's animators
with an inspirational
model for the castle in
Snow White.

With its varied landscape and climate, Cyprus offers much to interest both the scientist and the amateur botanist. The full range of flowers on the island has yet to be catalogued entirely, with more than 1,700 species already observed, 126 of these endemic. To the casual observer, the sheer quantity and variety of flowers is a truly unforgettable visual treat.

BLOOD AND TEARS
The legend of Aphrodite and Adonis is associated with the anemones that carpet great tracts of Cyprus in the spring. Red anemones sprang forth from the blood of the golden youth who was killed by a wild boar while hunting, and white anemones originated with the tears of Aphrodite at the death of her lover.

Spring is an early visitor to Cyprus. Already in January the first orchids are blooming, the prelude to a tidal wave of floral colour and fragrance that flows across the island for the next five months until it recedes under the intense heat of summer. Few of the island's flowers are adapted to the near-drought conditions that apply in summer, so they take their chance to bloom and seed when winter's rains have restored moisture to the soil. The burgeoning flowers create an astonishing display in fields, orchards and meadows, as well as in less promising locations, such as roadside verges and rocky slopes.

Cyprus in springtime merits its description as 'the scented isle'. March, April and May are the best months, when the species on display read like a florist's catalogue: tall white asphodels, poppies, chrysanthemums, tulips, hyacinths, narcissus, marigolds, irises, crocuses, peonies, cyclamens, anemones and many others, all of them in the wildest profusion. In *Bitter Lemons*, Lawrence Durrell wrote of the cyclamens and anemones around Klepini (Arapköy) in the Kyrenia (Beşparmak) Mountains 'glittering like young snow, their shallow heads moving this way and that in the sea-wind so that the fields appeared at first sight to be populated by a million butterflies'.

The Hottentot fig, now common throughout the Mediterranean, was originally introduced from South Africa

Hard times Even from July to the end of September though, some hardier plants and flowers hold their own during the scorchingly hot and dry days. There are thistles in a rainbow of pastel tones, while the white flowers and purple stamens of the caper bush are no strangers either. These are joined in different locations by myrtle, pink-flowered oleanders and tamarisk. But the prevailing colour at this time of year is the brown of shrivelled-up plants and grass; delicately petalled things keep their heads down.

Flower power Some flowers have a connection with ancient mythology and actual historical events. Inside the stem of the giant fennel, whose yellow floral heads can reach up to more than 3m, Prometheus is said to have hidden and delivered to man the fire stolen from heaven.

Pafos, the 'flower town', celebrates all Cyprus's love-affair with flowers in its annual Anthestiria Flower Festival in May, whose antecedents reach back to the ancient floral rites in honour of Aphrodite and Dionysos. Nicosia, Larnaka, Limassol and Paralimni also hold flower festivals, a tradition that is spreading.

Orchid paradise Cyprus is a treasure trove of wild orchids, mostly growing in the Kyrenia Mountains and, to a lesser extent, in the Troodos, but with others at home in coastal areas. The sensuous orchid has acquired a collector's value almost on a par with the illegal trade in antiquities, even though some varieties are among the 'strictly protected floral species' designated by the Council of Europe. Venal collectors will often put their possession of a rare orchid ahead of the survival of the species, or even just of its natural beauty when alive and well in its own environment.

Of Cyprus's 45 orchid species, subspecies and varieties, three are threatened with extinction and survive in only a few locations, while others are in trouble as a result of loss of habitat to cultivation, reafforestation and tourist developments. Common lowland varieties are the yellow bee orchid, the wavy-leafed monkey orchid, the bug orchid and the holy orchid. High in the Troodos can be seen the eastern violet helleborine and other rare species. It goes without saying that none of these should be picked or stepped on.

Bindweed

205

BEE LINE
It can be a fairly intimidating experience to turn a corner in the Cypriot countryside and encounter a heap of boxes buzzing like a squadron of World War II fighters on a strafing run. Bees are big business on the island, for between the flowering and fruiting seasons there is no shortage of pollen. Fortunately, the little critters have their own business to attend to.

Delicate oxalis

Vandalised and looted, Antifonitis Church and its unrivalled murals are mouldering away

▶▶▶ Antifonitis Church 199E1

Generally open. Admission free

Getting to this highly symbolic place is no easy task – by the end of the trail even a jeep finds the going hard. Founded in the 12th century, the domed Byzantine church lies in a rugged valley near Agios Amvrosios (Esentepe), where the Kyrenia (Beşparmak) Mountains tail off towards the east. It is in a sad and grim condition that is little short of a scandal. If the tattered remnants of its frescos are anything to go by, they must have been among the finest in Cyprus. Now, weeds flourish in the grounds. However, the worst is still to come: its finest frescos have been looted and the remainder vandalised.

The Turkish Cypriot authorities point out that much of the graffiti is in Greek and predates their control, and that Greek Cyprus appropriates all international assistance, leaving them only their own limited resources on which they have too many demands.

At least they have made a start in cleaning up by sealing the windows and carting away the goat droppings that carpeted the floor. Any recovery, however, can by now only be partial at best. Antifonitis's 17th-century iconostasis has vanished, and the once-renowned frescos of the Tree of Jesse and the Last Judgement can only be admired by the criminal who paid for their removal.

Visitors can see the colours still glowing on the Archangels Gabriel and Michael in the livery of Byzantine court officials. And they can turn their gaze into the dome, where the damaged image of Christ Pantokrator seems to bear an expression of bewildered sadness.

CULTURAL CONFLICT
Controversy over the treatment of cultural treasures such as Antifonitis is matched by Turkish Cypriot claims that 117 mosques were destroyed by Greek Cypriots between 1955 and 1974, as part of a determined attempt to eliminate their religious heritage.

The exterior of Antifonitis, overgrown and crumbling

▶▶▶ Bellapais (Beylerbeyi)   199D2

The village of Bellapais, set among citrus groves beneath the Kyrenia (Beşparmak) Mountains and overlooking the sea, is almost as emblematic of a vanished Cyprus as the sanctuary of Aphrodite. Here, the writer Lawrence Durrell lived from 1953 to 1956 among a memorable cast of characters whose island was just beginning its descent into tragedy, as recounted in his travel book *Bitter Lemons*. The Tree of Idleness is there, in the square in front of Bellapais Abbey, as is Dimitri's café, where the villagers passed their leisure hours. So too is the house 'made for some forgotten race of giants' that Durrell bought from the cobbler's wife, with invaluable assistance from the 'Turkish gentleman' Sabri.

Were Durrell alive, he might recognise in today's villagers fellow spirits of those he portrayed with an affection that only now seems tinged with condescension. The denizens of Dimitri's café, lounging in the shade of the Tree of Idleness, 'whose shadow incapacitates one for serious work', were 'mostly grandfathers wearing the traditional baggy trousers and white cotton shirts...a splendid group, grey-bearded, shaggy-haired, gentle of voice and manner'.

But. Bellapais is now Beylerbeyi to its Turkish Cypriot inhabitants, many of them refugees from anti-Turkish pogroms in Greek Cyprus. Dimitri's café is a Turkish coffee shop, while a modern restaurant stands opposite the Tree of Idleness. The steep, narrow streets through which Frangos chased his cows lead to Durrell's house, which sports a plaque recording his stay there but which has been vilely modernised. In a way, this is typical of the transformation wrought in village life by the passage of time to a more worldly age, with villagers being well aware of the commercial benefits to be gained from Bellapais' situation.

Relatively small and personable holiday developments dot the surrounding hillsides: villas, cottages and restaurants. None of these can be said to overwhelm the atmosphere, but there is no doubt that Bellapais is now changing.

The magnificent 800-year-old ruined **Abbey of Bellapais**▶▶▶ (*Open* summer daily 9–6; winter daily 9–5. *Admission charge*) could not easily be changed by the passions of a few violent decades and still lies 'like some great ship at anchor'. ('Bellapaix', Durrell insisted, was the best modern approximation of its original name, Abbaye de la Paix: the Abbey of Peace.)

Plaque on the wall of Lawrence Durrell's former house

WRITE IMAGE
Bellapais (Beylerbeyi) may be an object lesson in the mixed blessings that can accrue to a simple country village once a well-known writer has turned his or her pen on it. In the course of a brief visit, few places can live up to the picture created in one's imagination by a writer who has been inspired or seduced by it and its people. Bellapais is still wonderful; but Lawrence Durrell's 'Bellapaix' exists beyond time and place.

Icons glow in the dimly lit church of Bellapais Abbey

STONE CERTAINTIES
Bellapais village owes its existence to Bellapais Abbey in more ways than one: many of the stones used in building the village houses came from the abbey's ruins, thus ruining it further while adding to the architectural charm of the village.

TREASURE TROVE
A hoard of early 7th-century Byzantine silver plates was found in 1902 by villagers quarrying stone on the site of Lambousa. The plates, depicting scenes from the biblical story of King David, had been walled up in a niche, probably to protect them from Arab raiders.

Ruins of the great Gothic Abbey of Bellapais

Bellapais Abbey is entered via the ticket-booth beside the Tree of Idleness, through a once-fortified and moated gateway. To the right is the 13th-century abbey church, a tough-minded example of the French Gothic style. Icons glow amidst the gloomy interior, which is often locked. The sacristy and chapter-house are to the northeast of the church.

Directly ahead through the gateway are the remains of the *cellarium* and kitchens, below which is the crypt, while at ground level to their right is the cloister. Four giant cypress trees stand centre-stage inside the cloister, of which only fragments remain of the ornately carved arches that supported the arcades where once monks strolled in contemplation. In the northwest corner of the cloister are two Roman marble sarcophagi at which the monks washed, apparently unconcerned by their original purpose.

The abbey's cloister is bordered to the north by the magnificent refectory, whose entrance is marked by the arms of the Lusignan kings. The enormous hall, its soaring vaulting still intact, is lit by six great windows commanding a superb view over the steeply sloping landscape (and the swimming pools in the gardens of villas further downhill) all the way to Kyrenia (Girne) and the sea. Stairs lead up to a carved pulpit, from which suitable texts would be read to the monks while they ate.

Outside again, more stairs lead up to the open sky, where once stood the dormitories in which the monks of St Norbert had their cells – and to which they later brought their wives and children after succumbing to the worldly lures of Levantine life.

▶ **Kalon Chorion (Kalkanlı)**   *198B1*
Driving from Kyrenia (Girne) to Morfou (Güzelyurt), the road passes through this village and drops steeply away into the Morfou Plain. From the village's edge, a superb view is in prospect over the plain towards the Troodos Mountains.

▶ **Karavas (Alsancak)**   *198C2*
A cluster of historic sites lying on the coast just north of this village were, at the time of writing and clearly for some time to come, unreachable as they lie within a Turkish army base. These include the ancient city of **Lambousa**, apparently founded by Spartans in the 12th century BC (remarkable if true, as the Spartans, unlike other Greeks, were not noted colonisers). It continued into Roman and Byzantine times before it was wiped from the map by Arab raiders in the 7th century. Despoiled for building materials since medieval times, Lambousa cannot be visited at all, while the domed 12th-century **Achoiropoiitos Monastery** and the 15th-century **Agios Evlambios** church, both visible from the base boundary, look to be in miserable condition.

► Karavostasi (Gemikonağı) 198A1

On Turkish Cyprus's otherwise scenic northwest coast, the port of Gemikonaoğı presents an astonishing scene of industrial dereliction. Jetties with loading facilities where cargo ships once took on copper and iron ore now stand abandoned and rusting, while the hulk of an old coastal freighter is in a similar condition on the beach itself. The copper mines lie on the wrong side of the island's Greek–Turkish divide and are worked out anyway. The wasteland should, of course, be cleaned up, but while it remains it is worth seeing as an object lesson in decay.

► Karmi (Karaman) 198C2

Government-sponsored renovation has made this one of the most attractive villages on the northern slopes of the Kyrenia (Beşparmak) Range. It has also made it popular with well-heeled expatriates, who appreciate its charm and fine location.

► Kormakitis (Koruçam) 198B2

The people of this village near Cape Kormakitis (Koruçam Burnu) are mostly ageing Maronite Christians of Lebanese origin. The young people leave Turkish Cyprus for better prospects elsewhere.

The small Orthodox church of **Panagia** on the edge of the village is dilapidated, but the Maronites' **Agios Georgios ►** church in the centre, dating from 1940, is alive and well, its decoration and statues of the Virgin and saints with illuminated haloes imparting an air of almost childlike innocence. From the needle-pointed cape itself, you can make out the Taurus Mountains of Turkey on a clear day.

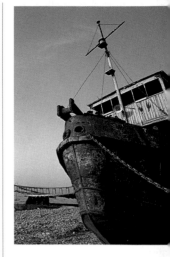

Derelict port installations spoil the shoreline at Karavostasi (Gemikonağı)

209

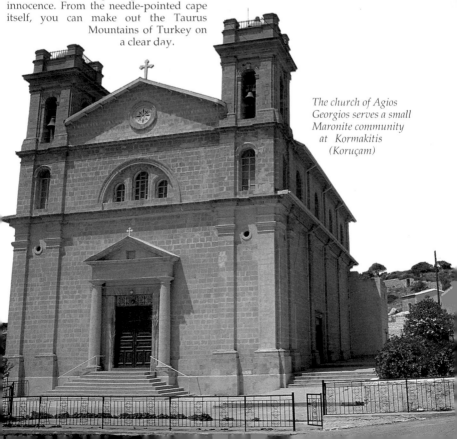

The church of Agios Georgios serves a small Maronite community at Kormakitis (Koruçam)

The long sloping ramp that leads to the interior of Kyrenia Castle

▶ ▶ ▶ **Kyrenia (Girne)** *198C2*

Called Kerynia by its first inhabitants, the little town (population 6,000) has a history stretching back to the Achaeans in the 10th century BC. In more recent times, it was common to escape the scorching heat of a Nicosia summer by driving north over the Kyrenia (Beşparmak) Mountains to cool off in the town's harbourside cafés. Today, by way of a Saudi-financed highway, the drive from Nicosia to Kyrenia takes just 20 minutes, well within the timescale even of tourists from the south crossing the Green Line on a one-day pass and taking a taxi to the coast. Today, thanks mainly to its characterful old harbour and Venetian castle, Kyrenia would be among the front-runners in any contest for Cyprus's most picturesque town.

THE CASTLE Like most ancient military structures in Cyprus, **Kyrenia Castle** ▶ ▶ ▶ (*Open* summer daily 9–7; winter daily 9–5. *Admission charge*) has undergone transformation at the hands of successive owners driven by the need to update the fortifications to match developments in the craft of siege warfare. However, one thing that has never changed, even as recently as 1974, is that the castle controls the harbour.

The original Byzantine structure was a fairly simple one of four towers connected by curtain walls, elements of which were incorporated into the strengthening works undertaken by the Lusignans. It was the Venetians who gave the castle its current look, building massively thick walls intended to withstand artillery. They worked frantically to perfect the defences in the face of an expected Ottoman invasion but then lamely surrendered in 1571 without a fight.

The entrance is in the northwest corner, where a 12th-century Byzantine church, St George of the Castle, stands inside the walls to the left. Where once there was a simple drawbridge at the end of the moat, the Venetians created the elaborately protected entrance that can be seen today, beyond the bridge that leads over the now dry moat. Towards the end of the tunnel leading up to the parade ground is the green-cloth-covered tomb of an Ottoman admiral, Sadık Paşa, who was killed during the conquest of the island. The parade ground is a wide open space surrounded by guardrooms, stables and visitors' quarters.

Ramps give access to defensive positions on the upper wall, while steps lead up to what were probably the Lusignan royal apartments and a small Latin chapel. In the other direction, downwards, there are dungeons, storage rooms and powder magazines. Parts of the battlements are in fairly poor condition, so anyone making a circuit of them has to be cautious. The magnificent view over the harbour, the town and the Mediterranean, as well as to the jagged peaks of the Kyrenia Mountains, makes any potential risk worth taking. You will also find the Shipwreck Museum in the castle (see pages 212–13).

THE HARBOUR It is as well that **Kyrenia Harbour▶ ▶ ▶** is horseshoe-shaped, because at peak times in summer visitors need all the luck they can get to find a vacant seat at one of the waterfront café terraces. Kyrenia aspires to being something that not much else in Turkish Cyprus, mercifully you might think, cares a great deal about – chic. A little of what you fancy can go a long way, however, and the harbour area's style is possibly more welcome as a result of its rarity. The romantic atmosphere is enhanced by the knowledge that those (relatively) high-priced restaurants and bars were once humble carob warehouses, storage depots for the bean-shaped edible seed-pod of the carob tree, which, as a substitute for chocolate, was formerly a key Cypriot export.

North Cyprus is not a great yachting centre, but what yachts there are inevitably find their way to the harbour at Kyrenia, where they tie up alongside cruise boats and strictly work-oriented fishing vessels. The harbour tower was part of the city's fortifications, from which a chain gate stretched across the old entrance, sealing it against hostile vessels. A customs house, breakwater, marina offices and the tourist information office complete the rest of the harbour's facilities.

Coats of arms, Kyrenia Castle

BESIDE THE SEA
An evening stroll along the waterfront in Kyrenia is the perfect end to a day, starting from a point near the Dome Hotel and finishing at a harbourside café terrace.

211

Boats moor alongside the waterfront café terraces in Kyrenia Harbour

The North

Marine relic: the 2,300-year-old remains of a Hellenistic merchant vessel that once plied the seas between Greece and Cyprus

SHIP SHAPE
The Kyrenia shipwreck was the subject of a remarkable act of co-operation between the two communities, in the very aftermath of the devastating conflict of 1974. The Greek Cypriot archaeological authorities transferred to Kyrenia temperature- and humidity-control equipment for the newly completed museum, without which the priceless recovered ship would have been in grave danger.

MUSEUMS Some time around 300 BC, a trading vessel plied the coast of Asia Minor. The boat and its crew put in at Samos and collected a consignment of wine stored in amphorae (large pottery jars which were the standard containers of the time). They continued to Kos for a load of millstones; these were for sale but were also carried to provide ballast. The vessel's last port of call was Rhodes, where more wine-laden *amphorae* were added to the hold. Finally, the four-man crew pointed their ship's prow to the open sea and headed for Cyprus. They never arrived. Caught in a heavy storm, the wooden vessel foundered outside Kyrenia harbour.

Thus do modern historians and archaeologists re-create the ill-fated final voyage of the Hellenistic merchant ship that is the remarkable star exhibit of the **Shipwreck Museum**▶▶▶, based inside the castle. For in a sense the Kyrenia ship did arrive, 2,300 years behind schedule, as the result of a massive marine archaeology recovery project during the late 1960s and early 1970s. The remains of this, the oldest recovered ship in the world, are a truly memorable and moving sight. A fair amount of the ship's 14.3m-long hull, made from Aleppo pine sheathed in lead, has survived the millennia and is displayed in a temperature- and humidity-controlled environment. More than

400 wine amphorae were brought up from the seabed, along with the millstones and four each of the simple utensils – cups, plates and spoons – that the crew used.

A supply of 9,000 time-blackened almonds were intended for the crew's diet, to be supplemented by fish caught *en route*. Radio-carbon analysis places the almonds at 288 BC (± 62 years) and the ship's timbers at 389 BC (± 44 years), suggesting that the ship may have been about 100 years old when it sank. The Kyrenia ship is a unique time-capsule, affording a glimpse of everyday life at sea shortly after the time of Alexander the Great; it should not be missed.

A moderately interesting collection of paintings and ceramics is about all the **Fine Arts Museum▶** (*Open* daily 9–1 and 2–5. *Admission charge*) has to offer, although its location in an old villa on the western edge of the town, overlooking the sea, suggests something more promising. More interesting is the **Folk Art Museum▶** (*Open* daily 9–1 and 2–5. *Admission charge*), housed in a converted carob warehouse with entrances on the harbourside and, one level up, in the street behind. This is one of the few buildings fronting the harbour that has not been turned into a café or restaurant. It contains a modest collection of traditional household goods, farming and milling implements, fabrics and clothing. These include an olive press, a primitive but effective threshing board, bridal chests and a traditional Ottoman bed. More interesting in a way is the building itself, which has not been prettified like all its neighbours and gives a good idea of the construction methods used in these warehouses.

The **Icon Museum▶▶** (*Open* daily 9–1 and 2–5. *Admission charge*) was formerly the church of Archangelos Michael, built in 1860. Its tall baroque bell-tower, white-washed steps and echoing courtyard were well known to Lawrence Durrell. Nowadays it has a different distinction: it is one of the monuments pointed to by the Turkish Cypriot authorities in response to Greek Cypriot charges that they have destroyed the Christian heritage of the part of the island they control. The church is in excellent condition and its use as an Icon Museum seems entirely appropriate. The iconostasis has been preserved, and many icons displayed have been brought from isolated churches for safekeeping.

CHURCH AND MOSQUE

Dating from the 10th century, the rock-cut Byzantine chapel of **Agia Mavra▶** is almost lost in an area of jumbled rock and ruins east of the old harbour. Its neglected interior contains the sad remains of some ancient frescos. Named after an Ottoman commander, the late 16th-century **Jafer Paşa Mosque▶**, with its ablutions spring, stands in a quiet backstreet above the harbour.

213

Icons in the former Archangelos Michael Church, now Kyrenia's Icon Museum

Walk

Above: looking over the entrance to the harbour from the ramparts of Kyrenia Castle

See map on page 210

Kyrenia (Girne)

Kyrenia is a small town. Even on foot you don't dare blink too often or you may miss it. What it lacks in size, however, it makes up for in charm. The sights on the walk are covered in more detail on pages 210–13.

Begin at the eastern end of the harbour and climb the steps to **Kyrenia Castle►►►**. A stroll around its battlements and bastions and a tour of the **Shipwreck Museum►►►**, with its 2,300-year-old remains of a Hellenistic merchant ship and its cargo, form a vital part of the Kyrenia experience. Exit from the upper level, pass the police station (marked Polis) and turn immediately right, to the green-painted entrance of the **Jafer Paşa Mosque►**, before retracing your steps slightly and descending the alley on your left, to the harbour.

At the eastern end of the harbour a narrow causeway leads to the harbour tower, from which a gate once stretched to the western end, permitting or denying entrance to ships outside. Heading westwards along the sweep of the harbour, to the left are former warehouses, now converted into restaurants and cafés. Fishing boats, yachts and tour boats are moored to the quayside, filling the available space. You may occasionally see a sunken vessel beside the tower, victim of fierce northerly gales that blow in winter.

Midway along the harbourside is the **Folk Art Museum►**, and at its end is the marina and customs house. The breakwater stretches out to cover the harbour from the north, with a beacon at its end.

Following the shore road west, you will see on your left the dazzling white bulk of Archangelos Michael Church, now the **Icon Museum►►**. The narrow streets of this area incorporate the old quarter, where much local colour can be seen. Below the Icon Museum, the Hotel Liman café terrace is shaded by the entwined branches of the 'Loving Trees'. Finally, the venerable Dome Hotel occupies the next headland along, and Kemal Atatürk's statue is in the square beyond.

The coffee shop is the centre of village life in both the Greek and Turkish parts of Cyprus – for the menfolk at least. It is a place of relaxation, of gossip and political debate, and of escape from the outside world.

'Come in, sit down. Welcome. How do you like your coffee?' Hospitality is the hallmark of the Cypriot coffee shop and this is easily extended to tourists hesitating in the doorway, uncertain whether to penetrate to the heart of the deep mystery within. In more worldly places by the coast, it will be accepted that tourists pay for their own, but in remoter villages rarely touched by the tour-bus the coffee may well be on the house.

Strong coffee it is too, the kind that puts hairs on your chest (perhaps another reason why women don't frequent these establishments). Given the sad division of Cyprus, it is as well not to call the drink by its correct name – Turkish coffee – in Greek Cyprus, but to speak instead of Greek or Cyprus coffee. Nowadays, *ouzo*, *raki*, brandy and even beer have all found their way into the coffee shop as well.

Fun time Politics, village gossip, the weather and the prospects for harvest are important staples of conversation, but only after the principal topic – soccer – has been exhausted. Card games and backgammon, played with vigorous gestures and bewildering speed, fill in the idle moments. Television, of course, has forced its way into the coffee shop, although it is generally only switched on for a football match or a racy film.

Starting the day at dawn with a strong cup or two, popping in at lunchtime for some more and settling down at the end of a day's work form an essential part of life's routine. And the younger men can look forward to their retirement, when they need never leave the coffee shop's warm, smoky embrace.

COFFEE TIME
Turkish coffee – or Greek coffee, if you prefer – is called *kafé* in Greek and *kahve* in Turkish. Made from fresh-ground coffee beans, it is prepared in a small pot, either with or without sugar according to taste. The steeped coffee grounds are then poured into a cup. The result is a thick, strong-tasting coffee, which should be sipped slowly, but only as far as the 'muddy' residue in the bottom of the cup.

215

TAKEN BY *TAVLI*
Coffee-shop denizens whizzing through a game of *tavli* (backgammon) are engaging in an activity that began some 5,000 years ago in Mesopotamia and was popular with the teenage Egyptian Pharaoh Tutankhamun, if the evidence from his tomb is anything to go by.

The coffee shop is a venerable and much-loved institution on both sides of the Cypriot divide

VEGETABLE LEGACY
Kythrea (Değirmenlik) is said to have been the source of the cauliflower, which was introduced from there to a doubtless ecstatic Europe in 1604.

GROOVY FELINE
The distinctive pottery cats of Lapithos (Lapta) began their career when a British army officer ordered one for his house. More British residents followed suit, and soon a minor marketing phenomenon was under way. Other potteries joined in with their own styles, and cat-lovers from other countries placed orders. Since 1974, production has been transferred to south Cyprus, but the Lapithos cats' allure remains.

Statue of Kemal Atatürk at Lefka (Lefke)

▶ Kythrea (Değirmenlik)　　　199D1

Water from Kythrea's spring of Kephalovryso used to make the long journey by aqueduct across the parched Mesaoria (Mesarya) Plain to ancient Salamis, where it filled the pools and fountains of the city's elegant Roman-era baths.

The aqueducts have long since crumbled to the ground, and Kythrea has declined also to a sprawling township on the southern slopes of the Kyrenia (Beşparmak) Mountains. The Turkish Cypriot government has , however, assigned funds for the restoration of Ottoman-period houses in the town, and some of these are very fine indeed.

Several kilometres north of Kythrea lie the remains of the ancient Greek city of Chytroi, founded around 1200 BC and cited by the 2nd-century ad geographer Ptolemy, in his *Geographica*, as one of the principal Roman cities of Cyprus. To the southeast of Kythrea, at the village of Voni (Gokhan), was found the magnificent bronze statue of the Roman emperor Septimius Severus, which is now one of the principal exhibits of the Cyprus Museum in Greek Cypriot Nicosia.

▶ Lapithos (Lapta)　　　198C2

Situated in the foothills of the Kyrenia (Beşparmak) Mountains overlooking the sea, this farming village has become popular with expatriates. Surrounded by lemon and lime groves, which owe their richness partly to the perpetual springs rising in the mountains that lie behind the town, Lapithos was one of Lawrence Durrell's favourite Cypriot villages; in *Bitter Lemons* he notes that it was famous for its 'woven stuff and silk'. To these can be added pottery. The village was settled by refugees from ancient Lambousa, who abandoned their coastal city in the face of constant Arab depredations in the 7th century and headed inland for greater security.

▶ Lefka (Lefke)　　　198A1

A spectacular equestrian statue of the Turkish statesman Kemal Atatürk greets visitors to this pleasant university town looking across a fertile plain towards the nearby UN buffer zone and the distant Troodos Mountains. Lefka has always had a strong Turkish community, even in Cyprus's pre-partition days. All the bitterness of the events that led to the island's division is captured in a stark cemetery with a memorial to 'unarmed and defenceless civilians' massacred by Greek Cypriot and Greek 'thugs'. Yet Lefka is a peaceable place and well worth a casual wander through its streets – even though the Turkish army is much in evidence.

▶▶ Morfou (Güzelyurt)　　　198B1

Deep in the heart of citrus territory, this handsome town, whose Turkish name means 'lovely country', is the third most important in the Turkish sector of Cyprus. The town's **Agios Mamas Monastery▶▶**, although no longer in use, is maintained in excellent condition by its current guardians. Built over an early Christian church, which itself replaced a Roman temple, Agios Mamas was rebuilt in the 15th and 18th centuries. It contains the tomb of the 3rd-century

Agios Mamas Monastery in Morfou (Güzelyurt), now a museum

hermit St Mamas, the tax-dodgers' friend. Outraged at being taxed when he lived in a cave, so the story goes, St Mamas of Morfou refused to pay. As he was being hauled before the Byzantine duke, he saw a passing lion attacking a lamb. Mamas subdued the lion with a gesture and, weary of walking, hopped up on to its back for the balance of the trip. The duke was sufficiently impressed to cancel the saint's taxes.

Güzelyurt Museum▶ (*Open* summer daily 9–1.30 and 4.30–6.30; winter irregularly. *Admission charge*), installed in the adjacent bishopric, houses on its ground floor a curious collection of stuffed birds and animals, most of them indigenous to Cyprus. The stuffing has been done with less than commendable skill, giving the creatures a ragged look, as if they have just been dragged through a hedge. Upstairs is a small but altogether more impressive archaeological section, displaying finds from the locality stretching from the Stone Age, through the Bronze Age to classical times. Particularly impressive are a terracotta figure of a bird-faced goddess and a statue of Artemis.

Some 3km north of Morfou is **Toumba tou Skourou▶**, a Bronze Age site famed for its copper industry. Excavations have uncovered faint traces of temples and other buildings.

TAX DODGERS
During Cyprus's centuries of occupation by the Ottoman Turks, many Christians engaged in a tax-dodging scheme that would have warmed the heart of St Mamas of Morfou. They became *linobambakoi*, Christians who pretended to be Muslims to avoid paying tax. The word means 'flax-cottons', a strange mixture of substances, because they retained their Christian faith, practising it in secret and presumably skipping over the commandment 'Thou shalt not bear false witness...'

View over the Morfou (Güzelyurt) Plain, towards the distant Troodos Mountains

The five distinctive indentations of Mount Pentadaktylos (Mount Beşparmak)

HOLDING ON

Part of the north region, in a political though not geographic sense, is the Turkish Cypriot enclave at the port village of Kokkina (Erenköy) west of the main demarcation line. This is now a purely military zone, all the civilians having been evacuated to Aigialousa (Yenierenköy) in the Karpas (Karpaz) Peninsula.

▶ Mount Pentadaktylos (Mount Beşparmak) *199D1*

The Byzantine hero Dighenis (not to be confused with the EOKA leader Grivas, whose *nom de guerre* was also Dighenis) once apparently leapt from Asia Minor to Cyprus while escaping from the Arabs, leaving the impression of his fingers in this 'five-fingered' mountain as he landed. This is among the roughest terrain in the Kyrenia (Beşparmak) Range, and rewards properly equipped hikers with some tough but satisfying walks in the scented mountain air. There are trails to Mount Pentadaktylos from the vicinity of Klepini (Arapköy) and Trapeza (Beşparmak), and from the point where the Kythrea (Değirmenlik) road is crossed by the rough road from Voufaventon (Buffavento) Castle to the Halevga (Alevkaya) Forest Station.

▶ Myrtou (Çamlıbel) *198B2*

The Turkish army is exceedingly active in this area, a fact that has led to the abandoned 16th-century **Agios Panteleimon Monastery** being out of bounds to visitors. About 1km south of Çamlıbel, following an unmarked track to the right, stand the remains of the Bronze Age sanctuary of **Myrtou-Pigadhes**, with a *temenos* (sacred precinct) and an altar.

▶ Pentageia (Yeşilyurt) *198A1*

This was an important town in medieval times, and near by it preserves the remains of the 12th-century **Xeropotamos Monastery**, with fragments of colonnades and marble from ancient Soloi. Pentageia also boasts Turkish Cyprus's only golf course, an eccentric but lovingly maintained seven-hole affair, on which enthusiasts will search in vain for a green among the sun-scorched grass.

▶ Profitis Ilias *198B1*

Near the village of Skylloura (Yılmazköy) and beyond, to Agia Marina (Gurpınar), the road seems to run through an almost unbroken series of restricted military zones, one of which has swallowed up this monastery.

►► Soloi (Soli) 198A1

*Open: permanently. Admission usually free, otherwise
Admission charge*

Occupying a position among fields beside a beautiful
stretch of shore marred only by the rusting remains of
copper-ore loading terminals, the ancient city of Soloi was
the subject of slow excavation before 1974. Soloi apparently got its name when King Philokypros was persuaded
by the Athenian philosopher and statesman Solon to
relocate an existing city, which the king did,
renaming it in Solon's honour. Now the site
has a slightly forlorn look, as if it has
been abandoned once again as it was in
the 7th century AD.

Little remains above ground of what
were until the last century extensive ruins of
the Hellenistic and Roman city, for the British
found its ancient stones to be just the thing
they needed for construction purposes in the
Suez Canal. However, there is an early Christian
basilica with some fine mosaic floors depicting
birds and fish, but how long these will remain
intact is uncertain for they lack even simple overhead cover. This basilica, like most of Soloi, was razed
to the ground by Arab raiders in the 7th century, and in
the 12th century a smaller church was built within the
ruins. Near by is a Roman-style theatre, partially restored
in the 1930s in an unattractively blocky style, like a
Prussian interpretation of a Roman theatre's graceful
lines. Among the sheep-fields are the paltry remains of
temples and other buildings.

*Mosaic floor in the
basilica at Soloi (Soli)*

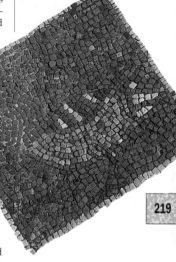

219

*Partially restored Roman
theatre at Soloi (Soli)*

Drive

Above: the ruins of Buffavento

See map on pages 198–9

The Kyrenia (Beşparmak) Mountains

Driving along the Kyrenia (Beşparmak) Range involves several flanking opera-

tions and outright retreats in the face of Turkish army bases, but crusader castles show military power to be no newcomer to these slopes. The section suggested here ideally requires a day, although it could be done in about four hours as a non-stop drive. The sights on the drive are covered in more detail on pages 202–25.

Take the coast road eastwards out of Kyrenia (Girne), turning inland and

Admiring the view from Mount Pentadaktylos

following the sign for **Bellapais (Beylerbeyi)**▶▶▶. The road snakes up through lemon groves, just as Lawrence Durrell described it in *Bitter Lemons*. You arrive in the village square at Durrell's Tree of Idleness, with the great Gothic **Abbey of Bellapais**▶▶▶ laid out before you. Driving up the steep, narrow main street to the house where Durrell lived is possible but not recommended in view of the difficulties of the ascent and the disastrous modernisation of the house.

About half-way back down the hill, a road turns off towards **Agios Epiktitos (Çatalköy)**▶, where Durrell and his Cypriot friend Panos ran into an arms search by British troops. After the village, the main road turns south towards Kythrea (Değirmenlik), climbing again into the mountains as it does so. An interesting diversion at this point is to branch off towards **Klepini (Arapköy)**▶. Durrell and Panos came this way to collect flowers a few days before Panos was shot dead by EOKA.

For **Voufaventon (Buffavento) Castle**▶▶, a public right of way ends at the signs indicating a Turkish army base, so either park the car or turn right up a much rougher slope to park beside a monument to those killed in an air crash here. From this point, if you want to play crusader knight, you must first play mountaineer. Actually, the track leading up to the castle is not so bad and the climb takes about half an hour.

Mount Pentadaktylos (Mount Beşparmak)▶ has five impressions along its summit, said to have been made by the fingers of the Byzantine hero Dighenis. The trail winds along through forest beneath the mountain. Somewhere out of sight to the right are the ruins of **Panagia Plataniotissa Monastery**, while near the end, to the left, are the slightly more visible ruins of the 10th-century Coptic and later Armenian monastery of **Sourp Magar**. A little further is the **Halevga (Alevkaya) Forest Station**, at the confluence of several forest trails. Another 300m downhill to the right is a herbarium and a small restaurant.

Where the main road turns sharply to the left just before Agios Amvrosios (Esentepe), a rough track leads off to the right, toward the 12th-century Byzantine monastery of **Antifonitis**▶▶▶, which is downhill to the left at a cross-roads of forest trails. Its disastrously dilapidated church, filled with the vandalised remnants of once-superb frescos, is worth seeing, if only to have a better idea of what neglect can do to a priceless cultural treasure. A furious debate rages over which community is responsible for Antifonitis's sad state; meanwhile the monastery disintegrates.

Bellapais Abbey

221

Holiday beaches are the stuff of dreams. The dream does not always match the reality, however. In the most popular parts of Cyprus, the picture is one of overexploitation of the good beaches and a growing risk that the undeveloped ones will go the same way.

222

ON THE BEACH

Finding a deserted beach, even at peak holiday times, is not impossible. The main ones are in the Turkish Cypriot zone, particularly along the Karpas (Karpaz) Peninsula, where there are great stretches of undeveloped, but also unsupervised beaches. Most are easily found, lying as they do alongside the northern and southern coast roads. At the northern end of Famagusta Bay (Gazimağusa Körfezi), from Bogazi (Boğaz) onwards, some beaches can be found by taking one of many dirt trails running seawards from the inland stretch of road.

In the Greek Cypriot zone, the northern coast from Polis to Kato Pyrgos offers good possibilities, although the beaches are not wonderful. The Akamas Peninsula is better, but with beaches more difficult to reach. Parts of the coast between Larnaka and Limassol have beaches which, if not exactly deserted, are a lot quieter than those in the resorts.

Endangered turtles have their protectors

Cyprus has few outstanding beaches. A holiday paradise without paradisaical beaches is a difficult sell, so the brochures are filled with praise of places that, as described, do not appear to exist. Of course, it all depends on what is meant by 'good'. There is no Ipanema, no Bondi, no Malibu – but there are stretches of fine golden powdery stuff warmed by near-perpetual sunshine and washed by an azure sea. Yet it is hard, when trying to find a couple of free square centimetres at Fig Tree Bay, Agia Napa or Coral Bay, to avoid the conclusion that most beaches are on the diminutive side of small.

In some parts of Greek Cyprus, the shortage of beaches has been tackled by shaving a few million years off nature's own beach-making process and delivering them by truck instead, creating the seaside equivalent of a moth-eaten fireside rug. Limassol and Larnaka beaches fall into this category, as do many of the pocket-handkerchief-sized beaches fronting resort hotels. The standard model, however, is a bay of modest dimensions whose beach is the major selling point of rather too many hotels, a familiar enough state of affairs throughout the Mediterranean.

Positive thinking None of this necessarily means that a beach holiday will be a disappointment. On the plus side, the facilities in terms of tavernas, beach cafés and watersports are good, the sea is warm and the sun is all but guaranteed. The atmosphere on the beaches is friendly, and there is little likelihood of theft of personal belongings. Besides, any parent knows that their children only need a few square centimetres of beach to call their own and access to the sea to be as happy as sandboys right through from dawn until dusk.

Too many people in one place can even be good for other places. One of the best beaches, Lara Bay near the Akamas Peninsula in the Greek Cypriot sector, is reserved for turtles, which prefer quiet, sandy beaches when the time comes to do their duty by the next generation. This makes them unpopular with entrepreneurs, who take the view that if God had wanted turtles on the beaches, He would have provided them with money for hiring loungers. Yet Lara Bay is a vital environmental resource, and there are other fine beaches, in the so far unspoiled Akamas Peninsula particularly, that need protection. If Cyprus can withstand the pressures for more development it will be doing the natural world a great service.

Beach invasion Turkish Cyprus is better off when it comes to beaches. One of the Greek Cypriots' most bitter complaints about the island's division is that they lost the best holiday areas, around Kyrenia (Girne) and Famagusta (Gazimağusa). Some beaches in the Turkish sector are open only to the Turkish army, either for military or recreational purposes. The Turkish troops may be duty-bound to blow their whistles at tourists who wander into unimportant places like tank depots and headquarters map-rooms, but they get seriously irritated if you go anywhere near their beaches.

A typically long, all-but-deserted beach along the Karpas (Karpaz) Peninsula

223

Deciding whether or not to bungee jump at Agia Napa... (she didn't)

SOLAR WARNING
Scientists at the National Council for Atmospheric Research in Boulder, Colorado, say that ozone cover over the northern hemisphere is down by 6–10 per cent, implying a 15 per cent increase in ultraviolet levels and a 20 per cent increase in the incidence of skin cancer, although the explosion in such cases may have as much to do with excessive sunbathing as with increasing UV exposure. In any case, it makes sense to limit sunbathing and use high-protection-factor suncreams.

   In compensation, the Turkish Cypriot zone has long stretches of wild and lonely golden sands with nary a hotel, nor a Coca-Cola stand, nor a lifeguard within 50km. Their only visitor, apart from an occasional tourist trying to find a hotel, a Coca-Cola stand or a lifeguard, appears to be a slovenly giant who spends half the year gathering up rubbish in black plastic bags and the other half spreading his collection along the shore. Maybe it is fortunate that beach holidays are going out of style.

The Tekke Hazreti Ömer, dedicated to seven Islamic martyrs, clings to a rocky foreland

►► Tekke Hazreti Ömer (Hazreti Ömer Türbesi)　　199D2

This important Ottoman-era Islamic shrine is dedicated to seven Arab soldiers killed in a 7th-century raid on Cyprus and considered martyrs for the faith. The whitewashed mosque stands on a rocky headland beside the sea, forming a simple but hauntingly beautiful scene. Its guardian can recite the outline of its history in several languages.

Beside the road to the shrine is a Turkish ambassador's residence, incorporating the little church of Agios Georgios, cracked and crumbling, and the 'Fortuna' villa that belonged to Lawrence Durrell's friend Marie.

► Vavilas (Güzelyalı)　　198C2

A farming village so close to the sea as to be in it as much as beside it, Vavilas has little to recommend it other than its perfect situation, its tranquil character and a little seaside restaurant.

►► Voufaventon (Buffavento) Castle　　199D1

Open: permanently. Admission free

Lodged atop a 940m-high crag on the southern face of the Kyrenia (Beşparmak) Range north of Kythrea (De¿irmenlik), Buffavento is reached via a rough track from the Kyrenia (Girne)–Kythrea road. Getting there involves a climb, either from a parking area beside a military base, or from a little higher up, beside a memorial to all those who died in an airliner crash there in 1988. The exhilaration of the half-hour climb, with its widening vista of the Mesaoria (Mesarya) Plain, may be augmented by the desire not to step on one of the many poisonous vipers in the area.

GIVING UP GRACELESSLY
Poor old Isaac Komnenos. For a rough, tough usurper who defied the Byzantine government in Constantinople, he put up a pathetic show after insulting Richard the Lionheart's betrothed. There is scarcely a medieval location in Cyprus that is not said to mark one of his defeats or surrenders. The picture gained is of him fleeing from one doomed strongpoint to another, before being hauled before his tormentor in chains. At Voufaventon (Buffavento), his daughter did the surrender honours.

Buffavento, 'buffeted by the winds', is a bit disappointing, especially given the exertion required to get there, but the view makes up for this. The castle was surrendered in 1191 by the daughter of Byzantine usurper Isaac Komnenos to England's King Richard the Lionheart. The Venetians later dismantled it when they concentrated their anti-Ottoman firepower at Nicosia (Lefkoşa) and Famagusta (Gazimağusa).

Visible far down the valley, although no more than a few kilometres away as the swallow flies, is the 11th-century monastery of **Agios Ioannis Chrysostomos**, one of Cyprus's finest – or so it was reputed before the Turkish army established a base in and around it after 1974. Now it is a binocular-range attraction marked by an enormous cypress tree, and its icons have been evacuated to Kyrenia. Equally inaccessible, out of sight to the west, is the church of Panagia Koutsovendis.

The climb to Buffavento Castle starts here

▶ ▶ ▶ Vouni (Vuni)   198A1

Open: permanently. Admission free

Say what you will about the ancient Persians, they knew a good place for a palace when they saw one. High above the Mediterranean, the great fortress-cum-palace at Vouni commanded more than a scenic outlook, for it loomed large above the nearby Greek city of Soloi, which had rebelled against Persia in 498 BC, encouraging the locals' loyalty by the constant reminder of its presence. This wasn't enough, and by the middle of the century the Greeks held both city and palace.

Each set of owners gave something to Vouni: an oriental architecture subsequently altered by the addition of Greek forms. Today's visitor is liable to have difficulty distinguishing between them, thanks to the minimal vestiges left behind by two-and-half millennia of looting and decay. This does not seem important, however, as the main attraction of Vouni is still its superb location overlooking the sea and the fragmentary remains of Soloi

Left: Vouni Palace

▶ Vounon (Taşkent)   199D1

This village, formerly a Maronite community, now hosts the **Martyrs' Museum**, dedicated to Turkish Cypriots massacred by EOKA, whose mass grave was exhumed by the Red Cross. Outside the village, the mountainside has been inscribed with a colossal Turkish Republic of Northern Cyprus flag and a declaration of Turkish pride by Kemal Atatürk, founder of modern Turkey: highly visible symbols understandably considered provocative by Greek Cypriots.

North of the village lies the Byzantine monastery of **Panagia Absinthiotissa**, rebuilt in the 15th and 20th centuries, whose treasures have been looted.

TURKISH DELIGHT
For anyone whose Turkish is a little rusty, the slogan of Kemal Atatürk beside the giant Turkish Republic of Northern Cyprus flag on the hillside near Vounon (Taşkent) is '*Ne Mutlu Turkum Diyene*', meaning 'How fortunate is the person who can say "I am a Turk."'

Agios Andro
(Yeşilköy
Leonarisso
(Ziyamet)

Galounia
Eptakomi
(Yedikonuk)

Davlos
(Kaplıca)
Komi
(Büyükkonuk)

Karp

Panagia
Pergaminiotissa

Galateia
(Mehmetçik)

Afrodision
Flamoudi
(Mersinlik)

Kantara

Agios Amvrosios
(Esentepe)

Akanthou
(Tatlısu)

Patriki
(Tuzluca)

Agios Theodoros
(Çayırova)

Alakati

Kalograia (Bahçeli)
2 km

Agios Epiktitos
(Çatalköy)

Charkeia
(Karaağaç)

Antifonitis

Gastria
(Kalecik)

Agios Ioannis

Vouraventon

Mandres
(Ağıllar)

Gerani
(Turnalar)

Knidos
Cape Elaia
(Zeytin Burnu)

740m

935m

Melounta
(Malıdağ)

UNDER

Bogazi
(Boğaz)

Pentadaktylos

Trypimeni
(Tırmen)

TURKISH OCCUPATION

Kythrea
(Değirmenlik)

Kiados
(Serdarlı)

Knodara
(Gönendere)

Lapathos
(Boğaziçi)

Trachoni
(Demirhan)

Lefkonikon
(Geçitkale)

Trikomon (İskele)

Mia Milea
(Haspolat)

Mesaoria

Gypsou
(Akova)

Marathovounos
(Ulukışla)

Geçitkale
Havaalanı

Milia (Yıldırım)

Angastina
(Aslanköy)

Peristerona
(Alaniçi)

Famagusta Bay
(Gazimağusa Körfezi)

Pedieos

Mora
(Meriç)

(Mesarya ovası)

Genagra
(Nergisli)

Agios Sergios
(Yeniboğaziçi)

Ercan
Havaalanı

Tymvou
(Kırklar)

Askeia
(Paşaköy)

Stylloi
(Mutluyaka)

Salamis

Gialias

Kırklar Tekke

Sinta
(İnönü)

Prasteio
(Dörtyol)

Apostolos Varnavas Monastery
Eğkomi (Tuzla)

Vatili
(Vadili)

Agios Spyridon

Lysi
(Akdoğan)

Eğkomi
(Enkomi-Alasia)

Famagusta
(Ammochostos, Gazimağusa)

Athienou

Kontea
(Türkmenköy)

Kalopsida
(Çayönü)

Varosha
(Maraş)

Trimithos

Tremetousia
(Erdemli)

Makrasyka
(İncirli)

Acheritou
(Güvercinlik)

Louroukina
(Akıncılar)

Troulloi

Pergamos
(Beyarmudu)

Achna
(Düzce)

Avgorou

Deryneia

Tympia

Pyla

Paralimni

A
B
C

1
2
3

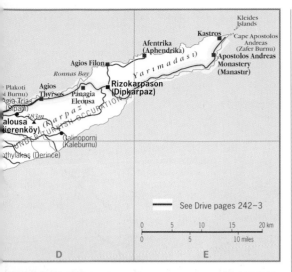

THE EAST One by-product of war and Turkish Cyprus's diplomatic and commercial isolation is that the coastline from Famagusta (Gazimagusa) all the way to the tip of the Karpas (Karpaz) Peninsula at Cape Apostolos Andreas (Zafer Burnu) is virtually a tourist-free zone. This is not by choice, however, and, like a Levantine Rip Van Winkle, it is slowly waking from its long sleep.

In former times, pre-1974, eastern Cyprus represented the single most important slice of the country's tourism pie. Specifically, this was concentrated in the hotel-and-beach playground south of Famagusta, in the days when a Mediterranean holiday meant quite simply sun, sea and sand. Now, solitude can be added if you want to get away from the sunworshipping beach-goers for an activity-based or 'green' vacation.

Crowds, if they ever were a problem in this part of Cyprus, are one no longer. Famagusta's resort suburb Varosha (Maraş) is a ghost town, its once-proud holiday hotels ruined and collapsing after more than 25 years' abandonment, and its golden sands deserted under the summer sun. There are proposals to reopen the town as part of a UN attempt to find a settlement but so far no agreement has been reached. Tourism is getting started again in eastern Cyprus, yet there is no flood of visitors nor, it seems, any desire for one.

Left: old shoreside church at Agios Thyrsos
Far left: a fisherman in the harbour at Bogazi (Boğaz)

A shoeshiner in Famagusta (Gazimağusa)

228

LUSIGNAN JEWEL Famagusta is the town on which the east is based. The walled city has lost much of its sparkle since the 14th century when, under the Lusignan kings, it was the jewel of the Levant, Christendom's forward outpost once the crusader tide had ebbed from Islam's shore. Europe's trade with the orient passed through here, and profits from spices, silks, precious metals and stones filled the city's coffers so that Famagustan merchants matched the lifestyle of royalty.

'I dare not speak of their precious stones and golden tissues and other riches,' wrote one awestruck visitor, 'for it were a thing unheard of and incredible.' The poet James Elroy Flecker (1884–1915) captured the city's romantic image:

I have seen the old ships sail like swans asleep
Beyond the village which men still call Tyre,
With leaden age o'ercargoed, dipping deep
For Famagusta and the hidden sun
That rings black Cyprus with a lake of fire.

Shrunken and diminished as it is, Famagusta still wears its history like a glove. The Lusignans' Latin legacy stands out in ruined churches, although only a tiny fraction remains of the more than 300 churches to which travellers of that period refer. Nor has the city neglected publicity, especially the favourable notice penned by William Shakespeare. Famagusta has taken on the mantle of *Othello*, based on Shakespeare's scene-setting note for the play: 'A port in Cyprus'.

PERFECT PEACE The further from Famagusta one travels, the emptier of people the landscape gets. There are the remains of ancient towns and cities dotted along Famagusta Bay (Gazimağusa Körfezi) and out into the long, narrow Karpas Peninsula, the 'panhandle' of Cyprus, but almost nothing in the way of tourist development. Instead, wild donkeys roam the Karpas and are the subject

INCOMERS
Many of the immigrants from Turkey who came to northern Cyprus after the 1974 invasion live in the sparsely populated and mainly agricultural Mesaoria Plain (Mesarya Ovasi) and Karpasia Peninsula (Karpaz Yarımadasi). The result is that these areas have a much more pronounced Turkish, as compared with Turkish Cypriot, character.

Bastion and gateway in Famagusta's powerful defensive walls

of scientific research. By the time the windy tip of Cape Apostolos Andreas is reached, with Syria and Turkey just across the way, the solitude is absolutely complete.

On the extensive spirit-level-flat plain called the Mesaoria (Mesarya Ovası), agriculture continues to be the mainstay for the inhabitants of a hundred little villages, and even then it can only be practised in winter and spring when the rains have brought life to what would otherwise be a region of semi-desert.

Put all of this together and it can be seen that eastern Cyprus commands one of the 20th century's most precious resources: nothing, and plenty of it.

The coastline near Cape Apostolos Andreas (Zafer Burnu)

MARRIAGE TROUBLES
During the coronation of Cyprus's Lusignan ruler, Peter II, the representatives of Genoa and Venice had an argument about who should take precedence in the procession. The Venetians won the argument, so the Genoese invaded Cyprus in 1372, capturing Famagusta (Gazimağusa).

229

CURIOSITY KILLS
Turkish Cypriot dogs, particularly in the Mesaoria (Mesarya) Plain, seem fatally prone to wondering what it would be like to go for a stroll in the middle of the highway. The result is that the roadsides are peppered with canine corpses. Cats, on the whole, seem less interested in walking on the road. The instinct of many animal-lovers will be to swerve or brake sharply to avoid striking a dog. They should be aware that other traffic – which may include heavy military vehicles and fast-moving buses and trucks – is liable to be unforgiving of such manoeuvres, no matter how noble the cause.

▶ Afentrika (Aphendrika) 227E3

Archaeologists will, eventually, no doubt reveal much from the site of this important settlement of the Hellenistic period, one of Cyprus's main cities in the 3rd century BC, according to Strabo, who was writing in the 1st century AD. An extensive area along the shore north-east of Rizokarpason (Dipkarpaz) throws up some slight evidence of its former glory in the remains of a citadel, traces of an ancient harbour and clusters of tombs. The best that can be said now is that its founders chose the setting wisely, the shoreline still presenting a memorable prospect today.

Church on the coast road at Agios Thyrsos

▶ Agia Trias (Sipahi) 227D3

This is one of the villages populated by recent (post-1974) Turkish immigrants to Cyprus. It is most notable for the ruins of the 6th-century Christian basilica of Agia Trias. Near by on the shore is **Agios Thyrsos**, a hamlet so small that the Turkish Cypriots haven't bothered to rename it. The salient points of Agios Thyrsos, apart from a fine prospect of the sea and coastline, are two neglected Orthodox churches, dating from the 10th century and the 15th century, the older of which stands under the cliff-face beside the sea.

▶▶ Aigialousa (Yenierenköy) 227D3

The Turkish Cypriots have named this village after the enclave of Erenköy on the northwest coast, whose handful of defenders in 1964 repelled (with help from the Turkish air force) an all-out onslaught of Greek Cypriot troops led by General Grivas. Aigialousa is a quiet enough farming village surrounded by fine countryside and is one of the few centres of shops, petrol stations and cafés in the Karpas (Karpaz). The beaches at Cape Plakoti (Yassi Burnu) north of the village are particularly fine, so much so that loggerhead turtles nest here. Soon after Aigialousa, the road to Cape Apostolos Andreas (Zafer Burnu) narrows as if in sympathy with the peninsula, which likewise narrows towards its tip, providing views of the sea on either side.

WATCHFUL PRESENCE
A Turkish Cypriot policeman notes the names and car licence-plates of all visitors to Apostolos Andreas Monastery. Access has improved greatly since the days when the Karpas was a restricted military zone, however, and the monastery is well enough cared for, although a wasteland of rusting cars and appliances and scattered trash surrounds it. The nuns at Apostolos Andreas, though ageing, are every bit as welcoming to visitors as their counterparts in Orthodox establishments in Greek Cyprus.

▶▶▶ Apostolos Andreas Monastery (Manastır) 227E3

Open: irregularly. Admission free, but donation welcome
Cyprus has no shortage of dramatically sited monasteries, but it could be that Apostolos Andreas (the Apostle Andrew) occupies the finest position of all. Dazzlingly whitewashed, it stands on the shore at a rocky headland a few kilometres short of needle-tipped Cape Apostolos Andreas (Zafer Burnu), where the Karpas (Karpaz) Peninsula points towards Turkey and Syria. The approach is through some magnificent countryside, with views on either side of the sea washing alternate stretches of deserted sand and jagged rock.

When the Mediterranean is in angry mood, waves crash over the rocks, drenching anyone at the spring said to

*Inside the church of
Apostolos Andreas, still
used by the isolated Greek
Cypriot community at
nearby Rizokarpason
(Dipkarpaz)*

have been brought forth by St Andrew. The apostle was
sailing for Palestine in a ship with a one-eyed captain
which (perhaps not surprisingly) went off course and
came ashore at this point. St Andrew struck the rock with
his staff, the spring gushed forth and the captain's full
sight was restored. An alternative explanation is that the
spring already existed and the apostle's ship merely put
in for water. In any case, the spring became a major place
of pilgrimage and miraculous cures. A small chapel dating from the 15th century stands by the shore, while a less
noteworthy 18th-century church lies at the heart of the
19th-century monastery buildings.

In 1974, a small population of Greek Cypriots at nearby
Rizokarpason (Dipkarpaz) remained behind during the
flight from the Turkish army. As its young people grow
up and depart to the south for jobs, the population has
been ageing. Few pilgrims come now to Apostolos
Andreas, only tourists who are greeted by a few elderly
nuns and an old Greek Cypriot caretaker, and the
monastery's future role seems likely to be that of
a museum.

231

SLEEP-IN
In *Journey into Cyprus*
Colin Thubron describes
the miraculous healing of
a paralysed girl at
Apostolos Andreas shortly
before his own visit to the
monastery in 1972. She
had dreamt that the apos-
tle told her that if she
slept the night in the
chapel there she would be
cured. The practice of
'incubation' (sleeping in
the temple of a healing
power) goes back to the
rites of the pagan god of
medicine, Asclepius,
whose devotees
overnighted in his
sanctuaries.

*Apostolos Andreas
Monastery and its
sacred spring are now
all but deserted*

The East

BROTHER MONKS

The monastery of Agios
Varnavas used to be
noted as much for three
of its monks as for its
associations with St
Barnabas. The three
monks were brothers in
the family as well as the
religious sense. Chariton,
Stephanos and Barnabas
remained at the
monastery for three years
after the Turkish army
occupied this area in
1974, but were finally
evacuated to Stavrovouni.

*The Icon Museum at
Apostolos Varnavas
Monastery*

►►► Apostolos Varnavas Monastery   *226B1*

Open: daily 8–8. Admission charge

On the road from Salamis to Egkomi (Tuzla), the
monastery is dedicated to the Apostle Barnabas, a native
of Salamis, who, along with St Paul and St Mark, founded
the Christian church in Cyprus. It was here in AD 488 that
Archbishop Anthemius of Salamis, facing a threat to the
Cypriot church's independence, opportunely discovered
the burial-place of Barnabas, containing a Gospel of St
Matthew written in Barnabas's own hand and placed
there by St Mark! Anthemius sent the gospel to the
Emperor Zeno at Constantinople, who was so impressed
that he confirmed Cyprus's religious autonomy and
authorised the archbishop to carry an imperial sceptre in
place of a pastoral staff, to wear robes of imperial purple
and sign his name in imperial red ink. The good archbishop was either extraordinarily fortunate, or a shrewd
hand at poker.

The foundation no longer functions as a monastery, but
houses instead an Icon Museum in the church and an
Archaeology Museum in the monks' former cells around
the cloister. Both are well presented, particularly the
archaeology section, in which the exhibits are arranged
chronologically through the cells from the neolithic
period to the Byzantine. The cloister, a pleasant stroll, is a
blaze of well-watered flowers, with shade   available
under trees. Items in the Archaeology Museum include
Stone Age tools, Greek pottery in both the black-on-red
and red-on-black styles, jewellery, Roman glassware and
statuary. Many of the finds come from the archaeological
zone surrounding Agios Varnavas, Salamis and Enkomi-
Alasia being the main locations.

▶ ▶ Bogazi (Boğaz)   226C2

The harbour of this delightful little fishing village commands some sweeping views across Famagusta Bay (Gazimağusa Körfezi), although these are spoilt in one direction by a cement plant and oil-storage tank. Not surprisingly, most of Bogazi has been devoted to the preparation and sale of fish, in a string of seafood restaurants along the main street and shoreline.

For travellers heading into the Karpas (Karpaz), Bogazi is one of the last locations where facilities are concentrated in a single place.

▶ ▶ ▶ Cape Apostolos Andreas
(Zafer Burnu)   227E3

It seems entirely appropriate that there should have been a temple of Aphrodite at this emblematic piece of coast, the furthest limit of the Karpas (Karpaz) Peninsula, complementing her principal sanctuary in the far west at Palaia Pafos. It is also appropriate that the Christians should have razed the temple and named the point after one of their own heroes, the Apostle Andrew. It remains to be seen if the Turkish name Zafer Burnu will stick.

Reached along a rocky track from Apostolos Andreas Monastery (Manastır), the cape is as wild and lonely a spot as any on Cyprus, pounded by the sea and echoing with the plangent cries of seabirds. It looks out across a flotilla of tiny islands towards the distant shores of Turkey and Syria. In the neolithic era, contemporary with Khirokitia in Greek Cyprus (see page 108), the settlement of Kastros was one of the first known human habitations in Cyprus.

BIRTH OF A NOTION
The little village of Trikomo (Iskele) near Bogazi was the birthplace of General George Grivas (also known as Dighenis), the leader of the pro-Greek Cypriot movement EOKA. You can be sure that there is no celebration of this fact in the Turkish Cypriot village.

233

View off Cape Apostolos Andreas (Zafer Burnu)

▶ ▶ Egkomi (Enkomi-Alasia)   226B1

Near the village of Egkomi (Tuzla), ancient Enkomi is on one level an archaeological treasure trove containing priceless knowledge about Cyprus's most important city of the second millennium BC; on another it is a confusing jumble of old stones. Enkomi is thought to have been the 'Alasia' referred to in the Tel el-Amarna tablets, recording letters sent by foreign kings to the Egyptian pharaohs Amenophis III and Akhenaten. It was an important centre of the copper industry. The city seems to have been a victim of the mysterious and violent 'peoples of the sea', and an earthquake in 1075 BC finished the job they had begun.

▶ Eptakomi (Yedikonuk)   226C2

This village marks the last dying gasp of the Kyrenia (Beşparmak) Mountains, before the Karpas (Karpaz) Peninsula proper begins, and it is notable for its 18th-century Orthodox church of Agios Loukas.

BIRD SANCTUARY
The tiny Klidhes (Zafer) islands off the tip of Cape Apostolos Andreas (Zafer Burnu) are the haunt of the rare Audouin's gull. This whole area has, however, been declared a maritime exclusion zone by the Turkish armed forces, and sailing is not permitted here.

RAIL LINK
Famagusta used to be the terminal of the Cyprus Government Railway which ran from Morfou (Güzelyurt) through Nicosia and was used principally for transporting copper from the mines around Morfou to the port at Famagusta. The railway was closed in 1951 after operating for 50 years.

▶▶▶ Famagusta (Gazimağusa)   226B1

Turkish Cypriots still call it Famagusta, although the word is nowhere to be seen on road signs. Whatever its name, the city's great days are firmly behind it, a history that dips and soars gracefully through Byzantium, the Lusignan period and even the rule of venal Genoese and despotic Venetians. Under the Ottomans and the British, Famagusta went into hibernation and seems never to have woken up.

Refugees from the earthquake-stricken and Arab-ravaged city of Salamis (Constantia) moved in the 7th century to the small town of Arsinoë, which was to develop as Famagusta. During the crusades the town became a forward base, a safe haven after defeat in the Holy Land and finally a retirement home for washed-up crusaders. By the 14th century, Famagusta was renowned for its ostentatious wealth, not necessarily a prudent development in what was a rough neighbourhood. Muggers, in the shape of the Genoese and the Venetians, were not long in striking. The Venetians, with the Ottoman Turks breathing down their necks, ringed the city with the powerful walls that continue to enclose it today. In 1571, after an epic ten-month siege, Famagusta, under the command of Marco Antonio Bragadino, surrendered to the far more numerous Ottoman forces of Lala Mustafa Paşa.

Nowadays, old Famagusta fits more than comfortably inside its walls. There is a curious mismatch between the import of those great walls and the dusty, down-at-heel city in their charge, dotted here and there with crumbling or ruined structures (mostly churches) from the good old days. Yet present-day Famagusta has an undeniable charm, a refined and leisurely Turkish Cypriotness that exists in parallel with the grandiose monuments and could easily get along fine

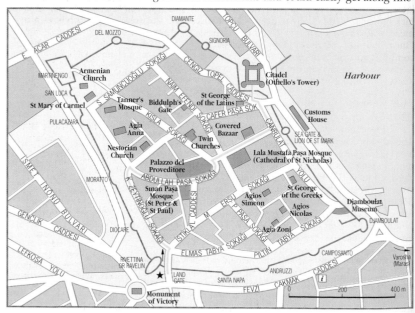

without them. Beyond the walls lie the usual nondescript suburbs that you find in any city, but within them is a historic gem attractively dulled by time and circumstance.

THE DEFENCES AND HARBOUR

Famagusta's Citadel▶▶ (*Open summer daily 8–6; winter daily 8–4. Admission charge*) was originally a moated castle built on the seaward side of the city in the 14th century and later massively strengthened by the Venetians to withstand artillery fire. It is also known as Othello's Tower – actually, mainly known as Othello's Tower, which is judged to be a better tourist draw than plain old 'Citadel'. A few bits and pieces of ancient columns and statues 'adorn' its lower level, and a stroll around the battlements and through the galleries is an interesting diversion, but the Citadel's main attraction, to anyone other than medieval citadel buffs, must be its superb view over the harbour, which still has some of its medieval structures more or less intact.

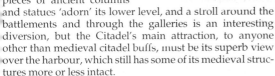

The Citadel's connection with Shakespeare's *Othello* is purely speculative, although the play's stage directions speak of 'a port in Cyprus' and 'Cyprus, the citadel'. It has also been suggested that the bard's 'valiant Moor' in the service of Venice, the Most Serene Republic, may have been modelled on either Cristoforo Moro, a 16th-century lieutenant-governor of Cyprus, or Francesco de Sessa, a later Italian mercenary in Cyprus who was apparently nicknamed 'the Moor'. Shakespeare penned the play more than 30 years after the conquest of the island by the Ottomans, so he needed no great prescience when he composed the statement:

> ...When we consider
> The importancy of Cyprus to the Turk...
> We must not think the Turk is so unskilful
> To leave that latest which concerns him first.

The Ottoman Turks laid siege to Famagusta in 1570 with an army reportedly 200,000 strong facing 8,000 Venetian defenders across the city's stone walls. Ten months later, the Turks were still on the wrong side of the 5km defensive circuit and had lost 50,000 men in the process of discovering just how stoutly built the walls were. Starvation and attrition of the small garrison achieved what direct assault could not, and finally forced Famagusta's surrender on 1 August 1571.

The original walls were built by the Lusignans when arrows and an occasional catapulted rock were the primary threat. By Venetian times, powerful siege artillery required a redesign and vast increase in their strength. A tour of the walls leaves one in no doubt about that strength. The siege has left little visible trace.

Turkish Cypriot Freedom Monument recording the 1974 siege of Famagusta

235

HIDDEN MEANINGS

Gazimağusa, the Turkish name for Famagusta, means 'unconquered' and refers to the unsuccessful siege of the Turkish Cypriot quarter by Greek Cypriot forces in 1974. The city's original name was Ammochostos, meaning 'sunken in the sand', when it was founded in the 3rd century BC by the Hellenistic ruler Ptolemy Philadelphus of Egypt.

SHOPPING LIST – 1343

Joan Benet, a Catalan merchant, made a business trip to Famagusta in 1343 to buy luxury goods for resale in Barcelona. His account book lists: pepper, cinnamon, ginger (from Sri Lanka and Mecca), lac (a resin for varnishes and red dye), incense, borax (for medicinal use), cloves, cinnamon flowers, sugar, cotton and a conserve of black plums called myrobalans (also for medicinal use).

ROUGH INJUSTICE

The Venetian commander of Famagusta's garrison, the valiant Marco Antonio Bragadino, having surrendered to Lala Mustafa with full military honours in 1571, was double-crossed by the Ottomans. Once in Lala Mustafa's power, his nose and ears were cut off and, after two weeks of further horrific tortures, he was flayed alive as a reward for the skill and heroism of his ten-month defence of the city.

Some of the fiercest fighting of the 1570–1 Ottoman siege of Famagusta took place around the Rivettina bastion at the southwest corner of the walls. The Turks eventually captured it, at which point both bastion and conquerors were blown sky high by the Venetians. Further up the line, the arrow-shaped Martinengo bastion was clearly designed to skewer any outfit unwise enough to try storming it, and the besiegers left it well alone. Between the main bastions, the defences are dotted with smaller strongpoints equipped with side-mounted cannon ports from which flanking fire could sweep any force attacking the wall.

The best view of the **Harbour▶** can be had from the Citadel (Othello's Tower), from where a comparison between the various old prints of its galley-era operations and today's rust-bucket merchantmen may be made. Ferries connect Famagusta with Turkey, while cargo ships from all over the world tie up at the quays. The city is considered an illegal port by the Greek Cypriots, and any ship's captain who subsequently turns up at Limassol or Larnaka in the Republic of Cyprus is liable to arrest and imprisonment.

CHURCHES AND MOSQUES The church of **Agios Simeon▶** is the remnant of Famagusta's Byzantine cathedral, which was heavily damaged by the Turkish cannonade of 1570–1.

Once the foundation of the Christian Nestorian sect from Syria, the mid 14th-century **Nestorian Church▶** is now a cultural centre operated by the Turkish Cypriot University of the Eastern Mediterranean.

St George of the Greeks▶ was once Famagusta's Orthodox cathedral. The Byzantine basis of the 14th-century church was added to in Gothic style, making it a rare, but ruined, specimen of this hybrid form.

St George of the Latins▶ is the ruined stump of a 13th-century Gothic-style church, which still displays some signs of its former glory.

It would be interesting to know how much Christian forbearance was displayed by the congregations of the **Twin Churches▶**, two side-by-side 14th-century crusader churches. One was owned by the Knights Templar and the other by the Knights Hospitaller, whose sworn enmity towards the infidel hordes defiling the Holy Land was matched only by their hatred of each other. The Templars' church is now an art gallery and theatre; the Hospitallers' church is a music conservatory.

Famagusta's Ottoman conquerors so admired the imposing Gothic lines of the Lusignans' great 14th-century Cathedral of St Nicholas, where the Kings of Cyprus had been crowned also as Kings of Jerusalem (Cyprus being a safer location for this ceremony than Saracen-occupied Jerusalem), that they added a

St George of the Latins, one of the city's many Gothic remnants

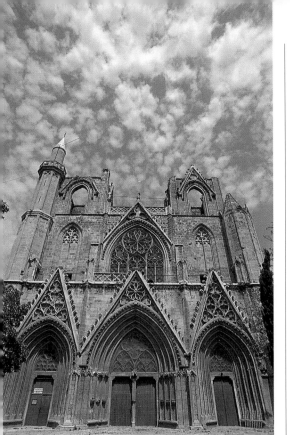

Lala Mustafa Paşa Mosque, formerly the grand cathedral of the Lusignan kings

minaret and a *mihrab* and converted it to a mosque, the **Lala Mustafa Paşa Mosque▶▶** (Generally *open* dawn–dusk. *Admission free*, but donation expected). The muezzin's cry still wails forth from the minaret, summoning the faithful to prayer – although if the response to the summons is anything to go by, the faithful of Famagusta have other things to occupy their time. Inside, the cool silence and simplicity of the mosque compete harmoniously with the Gothic vaulting, columns and rose windows of the underlying cathedral.

The **Sınan Paşa Mosque▶** (Generally *open* dawn–dusk. *Admission free*, but donation welcome), formerly the 14th-century Church of St Peter and St Paul, is a more visitor-friendly place than the more imposing Lala Mustafa Paşa Mosque.

ITALIAN PALACE Little remains of the **Palazzo del Proveditore▶** (*Open* permanently. *Admission free*), the proud structure built by the Venetians over the existing Lusignan royal palace around 1550 to house their governors in style. In later years it was used as a police station and prison, and today it is more like a small ornamental park decorated with ancient columns and sculptures. The building includes the tiny prison of the 19th-century Turkish poet Namik Kemal, who criticised the sultan in his works and lived to tell the tale – if only to his guards.

BEYOND THE WALLS
An interesting location for a stroll in Famagusta is through the dry moat beside the walls on the landward side. This gives an attacker's-eye view of these formidable defences, as well as being a fairly pleasant, grassy and, in parts, tree-shaded place.

Walk

See map on page 234

Within the walls of Famagusta

Famagusta is not very big and is lightly populated, so a stroll within its Venetian walls does not degenerate into a struggle against traffic fumes and crowds. This walk is a short one: allow an hour at the most. The sights on this walk are covered in more detail on pages 234–7.

Start at the seemingly impregnable **Rivettina bastion** (also known as the Ravelin). In 1570, Famagusta's Turkish besiegers apparently saw some weakness in its design or construction and concentrated their anti-Venetian firepower there. Walk north on Kemal Zeytinoğlu Sokağı. This short stretch allows for a view of the walls more or less as the Venetian defenders saw them as they hurried from one threatened sector to another. Two bastions, Diocare and

Above: Famagusta's small but colourful bazaar

Moratto, are on this section, and by climbing to the walls one can see how they are mutually supporting, taking any force assaulting the space between them under enveloping fire. Turn right along Abdullah Paşa Sokaği, which leads eventually to the monumental heart of Famagusta, but begins with an ordinary section of housing. You arrive at the Latin Church of St Peter and St Paul, now the **Sınan Paşa Mosque▶**. Its quiet interior may be visited. To the mosque's left are the ruins of the **Palazzo del Proveditore▶**, once the royal palace of the Lusignans, taken over and rebuilt by the Venetians.

Continue in this direction and next in view is the Latin Cathedral of St Nicholas, now the **Lala Mustafa Paşa Mosque▶ ▶**, an imposing Gothic structure with a minaret attached. Finally, you arrive at the walls again, beside the sculpted Lion of St Mark standing before what was formerly the city's Sea Gate.

Turn left on to Canbulat Yolu, and beyond a traffic oval is the **Citadel▶ ▶ ▶**, otherwise known as Othello's Tower.

At harbours all around Cyprus, fishermen still go through the age-old late afternoon ritual of putting to sea in high hopes of a good catch. By dawn, the fruits of their labours are heading for dining tables all over the island.

Stock take Fishing is not nearly so important an industry in Cyprus as one would expect of a Mediterranean island. The problem lies with marine conditions in the eastern Mediterranean basin rather than with any lack of piscatorial enterprise on the Cypriots' part. Yet at ports all round the island, fishermen may still be seen tending their nets and scrubbing their brightly coloured boats before heading out into the wide blue yonder to harvest the deep.

Therein lies the problem. The eastern Mediterranean is deep, and situated at the furthest possible remove from the nutrient-rich tides flowing through the Straits of Gibraltar from the cold Atlantic Ocean. The reduced freshwater flow from the River Nile since construction of the Aswan Dam is also said to have had a negative impact on fish stocks. The waters around Cyprus simply do not contain sufficient plankton, the basis of the marine food chain, to support vast numbers of edible species. In partial compensation, the plankton-poor, unpolluted waters make for excellent scuba-diving conditions.

Fleet operations The main fishing-fleet bases in the Greek Cypriot area are Pafos, Latsi, Potamos Creek, Limassol, Larnaka and Agia Napa, as well as some smaller locations dotted around the coast. In the Turkish Cypriot zone, there are fishing harbours at Kyrenia (Girne), Famagusta (Gazimağusa), Bogazi (Boğaz), Koma tou Gialou (Kumyalı) and some smaller places. The ordinary boats go after such species as sole, red mullet and whitebait, while specially equipped vessels sail in search of that well-armed knight of the pelagic depths: the swordfish. Octopus and squid are also picked up for the menu.

Some fish come from the dry land, in a manner of speaking: freshwater trout, for example, from reservoirs and fish farms using perpetual springs in the Troodos Mountains. The hard fact is, however, that most fish consumed in Cyprus are imported.

FISHY STORY
Long hot summers, dried-up riverbeds and chronic water shortages meant that until recently freshwater fish were strangers to Cyprus. The construction of dams to retain the rains of winter, combined with the opening of the Department of Fisheries Experimental Station at Kalopanagiotis in 1969, have been the basis of Cyprus's new-found appetite for freshwater fish. The station has been responsible for introducing such species as trout, eel and crayfish.

239

Still the boats go out

A newly built mosque dwarfs the houses of Galounia

TOILET TRAINING
Devotees of sanitary technology may be interested to compare the sophisticated Roman system in the gymnasium at ancient Salamis with the rough-and-ready crusader facilities of Kantara Castle. In the former, the citizenry performed their toilet in a purpose-built marble-and-brick chamber, whose plumbing was sluiced by constant running water, watched over by statues of the gods and prominent persons. In the latter, the knights did the needful from a windy latrine that was basically a hole in the castle wall. If developments in plumbing are any indicator of civilisation – and there is good reason for supposing that they are – Cyprus had been going backwards, so to speak, for the best part of a thousand years.

The windy heights of Kantara Castle still dominate the surrounding plains

► **Galounia** 226C2

Little remains above ground of this ancient city on the north coast of the Karpas (Karpaz) Peninsula which some scholars believe to have been the capital of Cyprus's Hittite kingdom from 1450 to 1200 BC, when it was destroyed by the mysterious 'peoples of the sea'.

► **Gastria (Kalecik)** 226C2

Faint traces of a ruined 12th-century Templar castle stand on the shore near an oil terminal and factory complex south of here, as does a ruined Byzantine church, **Agios Ioannis**, dating from the 11th century.

►►► **Kantara Castle** 226C2

Open: permanently. Admission charge, occasionally free
Every bit as isolated among the Kyrenia (Beşparmak) Mountains as its cousins Agios Ilarion (St Hilarion) and Voufaventon (Buffavento), Kantara Castle retains all the romance associated with the crusaders, even though, like the range's two other examples, it was partially dismantled by the Venetians. Begun in the 9th century under the Byzantines, Kantara was greatly strengthened in succeeding centuries, particularly by the Lusignans in the 14th century. The climb to its battlements is not so steep or long as at Voufaventon, but even so one can't help feeling sorry for the knights' horses, which had to carry their armour-plated masters to the present-day car park!

Outside the castle gate is a large water-cistern, well covered by arrow-slits in the nearby towers – presumably as a deterrent to illicit dipping. It is interesting to compare the rough-and-ready facilities of such a place with those of Greek and Roman installations elsewhere in Cyprus, dating from a thousand and more years earlier. The crusaders' primitive toilet and sleeping arrangements give some idea of how far living standards had declined since the heyday of classical civilisation (see panel).

Within its elaborate battlements the castle contains living quarters, storage rooms and stables, as well as a high watchtower and a beacon platform from which signals could be transmitted westwards across the mountains to Voufaventon and Agios Ilarion. Kantara village is surrounded by picnic and barbecue sites of a forest station.

▶▶▶ Karpasia (Karpaz Yarımadasi) *227D3*

The region of Karpasia, comprising the Karpas (Karpaz) Peninsula, must have been one of the most heavily populated parts of the island at the high point of classical Greek and Roman civilisation, with the ancient writers Strabo and Ptolemy both recording important cities in the area during this period. Unfortunately, such places as Afentrika (Aphendrika), Afrodision (Aphrodision), Carpasia, Galounia and Knidos have left few visible traces. The contrast with today's virtually unpopulated, entirely agricultural peninsula could hardly be more pronounced. Yet the Karpas is a ruggedly beautiful part of the island, a colourful tessera in Cyprus's mosaic of people and places.

▶ Kırklar Tekke *226A1*

Near the village of Tymvou (Kırklar), in an area of restricted access lying close to the buffer zone between Nicosia and Famagusta (Gazimağusa), the Tekke is a little 19th-century mosque dedicated to 40 unknown martyrs.

▶ Knidos *226C2*

The wreck of an old coastal vessel lies rusting on the rocky coast at scenic Cape Elaia (Zeytin Burnu), almost the only identifiable landmark in an area where the olive trees come down virtually to the sea. The ancient Phoenician harbour town of Knidos, inhabited from the 5th century BC to the 2nd century AD, is buried here at the end of a track from Agios Theodoros (Cayirova), but only fragmentary remains can be seen.

▶▶ Mesaoria Plain (Mesarya Ovasi) *226B1*

This great agricultural plain extends from Nicosia eastwards towards the sea and the Karpas (Karpaz) Peninsula, and northwards towards the Kyrenia (Beşparmak) Mountains. Thoroughly dried up in summer except in areas where irrigation has been established, the Mesaoria comes into its own in winter, when wheat, potatoes and other crops are grown in abundance. Three things stand out about the Mesaoria: it is spirit-level flat, it is enormous and the fields that cover it are also huge.

For the visitor, after these impressive characteristics have been absorbed, the most interesting thing about the Mesaoria is its people's total commitment to ordinary everyday life, usually involving a great deal of hard work in the fields, followed (for the menfolk at least) by concentrated rest and recuperation at the local coffee shop. The simple, and often ragged villages are just an indication of how many of Turkish Cyprus's unfailingly hospitable people live. Both Turkish Cyprus's two airports, Ercan and Geçitkale, are in the Mesaoria.

PARKS DEPARTMENT
Greek Cyprus has its ongoing debate about making a national park of the wild and unspoiled Akamas Peninsula, so it seems only fair that Turkish Cypriots should be debating the merits of a similar solution for the Karpas (Karpaz) Peninsula at the opposite end of the island. Although not so leg-numbingly rugged as the Akamas, and more affected by agriculture and village development, the Karpas is bigger and has its share of wild spaces, including unspoilt beaches and hilly areas where wild donkeys roam.

241

LOOTED TREASURE
The Church of Panagia Kanakaria at Lythragkani (Boltashli) in the Karpas (Karpaz) Peninsula was the source of a landmark legal ruling in America in 1989. The church's 6th-century apse mosaic of the Virgin and Child was ruled to have been looted since the Turkish intervention after it appeared on the international art market. It was ordered to be restored to the Republic of Cyprus.

Wild and isolated, the Karpas (Karpaz) Peninsula gives a hint of what the Mediterranean was like before tourism was invented

Drive

See map on page 226–7

Famagusta to Cape Apostolos Andreas

The Karpas (Karpaz) Peninsula, the 'panhandle' of Cyprus, is an extensive, sparsely populated area bordered by a coastline that is alternately wild and rugged or carpeted with long stretches of open, deserted beach. It is almost totally untouched by tourist development. This is an exhilarating but long (all-day) return drive, so don't attempt to do more than a couple of the suggested

Window on two worlds – Greek and Turkish – in Rizokarpason (Dipkarpaz)

diversions. The sights on the drive are covered in more detail on pages 230–49.

Roughly 10km out of Famagusta (Gazimağusa), on the main highway heading north, a cluster of historic sites can be visited. First, on the left of the coast road, is **Apostolos Varnavas Monastery**▶▶▶, now a superbly maintained and presented museum of icons and archaeology. A little further along this side-road through the countryside, at Egkomi, are the ruins of ancient **Enkomi►►**, also known as Alasia, a settlement that was founded around 2000 BC and which flourished under the Mycenaeans some 500 years later.

Return to the coast road and continue north. Soon you arrive at the entrance to ancient **Salamis►►►**, the ruins of a city with a rich history under the Greeks and the Romans, and whose finest monuments date from the late-Roman period following extensive destruction caused by earthquakes. Little of the city has been excavated, yet what there is gives a good idea of how wealthy Salamis was in its heyday. From here the road curves around the broad sweep of Famagusta Bay (Gazimağusa Körfezi), through a mostly agricultural country, passing occasional modestly sized tourist developments on the way.

Near the bay's northern end lies **Bogazi (Boğaz)►►**, a small fishing village with a fishermen's wharf and a cluster of seafood restaurants. (Bogazi is also the ideal place to divert north to **Kantara Castle►►►**, high in the easternmost edge of the Kyrenia (Beşparmak) Mountains, but the diversion, although interesting, costs considerable time followed by a fair amount of twisting and turning to regain the main road.)

Head north from Bogazi towards **Aigialousa (Yenlerenköy)►►**. You now enter the Karpas Peninsula proper and the road, which has been quiet enough up to now, slides still deeper into tranquillity. The scenery opens up into a rolling green picture-postcard image of the ideal pastoral landscape, dotted with sleepy and rather ragged-looking villages whose inhabitants wave cheerily as you pass. Curving northwards towards Aigialousa, furthermore, the landscape gets more rugged as the trailing edge of the Kyrenia range is reached, and the road shifts from hugging the southern coast to skimming the northern one.

At Aigialousa take the direction for **Rizokarpason (Dipkarpaz)►**. Here live the last remaining Greek Cypriots in the Turkish Cypriot zone, an elderly community watched over by a UN detachment and whose days, in the absence of a comprehensive settlement between the two communities, are inevitably numbered by the slow but sure process of ageing. The coast from Aigialousa to Rizokarpason is dotted with Byzantine churches, none of them in a good state of repair.

Beyond Rizokarpason follow the road to the Apostolos Andreas Monastery (Manastır). As the peninsula narrows towards its tip, spectacularly rugged vistas open up on either side and the narrow road dips and soars on its own wild course. The empty beaches draw like a magnet, but ahead now can be seen the brilliant white gleam of the **Apostolos Andreas Monastery►►►**, clinging to the rocky and wave-battered coast. After this, the peninsula's needle-tipped point at Cape **Apostolos Andreas (Zafer Burnu)►►►**, with its escort of rocky islets, is almost anticlimactic – but forms a definitive end of the road.

You can divert north at the fishing village of Bogazi for Kantara Castle

Although tourism is the main foreign-exchange earner, and manufacturing, shipping, banking and business services are important economic sectors, agriculture remains a vital industry. Hard-working farmers also give the Cypriot countryside its distinctive flow of life and colour through the seasons, and keep the island's village roots alive.

DRUG DEALER
Cyprus was an early centre of the drugs trade, at least in the sense that it produced and exported opium. Ancient Egypt was one of the countries on the delivery list.

244

Olives ripening nicely for the press

Water shortage Early morning and late-afternoon showers casting shimmering rainbows through the golden sunlight are as characteristic of summer in Cyprus as bathing suits and suntan lotion. Not that there is likely to be the tiniest amount of precipitation falling from the clear blue sky; it's just farmers spraying precious drops of water on their crops. Irrigation is an essential ingredient of almost all agriculture on this sun-parched island, the factor that makes the difference between life and death for the farmer's produce and business.

Stocks of vital water are monitored with the kind of care more usually associated with gold or oil production. Reservoirs, underground aquifers and the few perennial springs are drawn on heavily from spring to autumn, and when the first rains begin, usually in November, a Cypriot will observe the deluge with great satisfaction even if late-season tourists may have a more jaundiced opinion. As well as guaranteeing the survival of agriculture in the following summer, the rains also make possible winter crops that form an important part of production.

Market strategies A visit to a market gives an idea of how successful the strategy can be. Cyprus is a cornucopia of fresh fruit and vegetables. Just to list the main ones is to range across the gamut of fragrance and taste and to show that Cyprus deserves its reputation as a vegetarian paradise: grapes, melons, tomatoes, aubergines, peppers, cucumbers, figs, peaches, cherries, strawberries, apricots, oranges, apples, lemons, limes, artichokes, avocados, celery, onions, carrots, potatoes. Then there are bread, cheese, pulses and nuts. Lamb

Sowing the seeds of future wealth in the fields near Kition

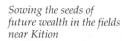

and chicken are the principal meat products (beef is available but is not nearly so common).

Around 70 per cent of agricultural production is exported, mainly to the European Union – to which the Republic of Cyprus is progressing towards membership, though without the agreement of the Turkish Cypriots, who are not opposed to membership but who want to be an equal partner with the Greek Cypriots in any negotiations. Much of the added value in agricultural produce comes from additional processing rather than the basic commodity (for example, from making and packing fruit juice instead of just exporting the fruit).

On location Cyprus's geography is sufficiently varied for there to be different kinds of agriculture suited to different locales. The principal areas in this repect are the Mesaoria (Mesarya) and the Morfou (Güzelyurt) plains. The Mesaoria is a primary source of winter wheat. In summer, it dries up to a state not far short of a desert. The Morfou Plain west of Nicosia is a more rolling landscape but also rich in winter crops. Both areas are in the Turkish Cypriot zone, a situation that creates one of the angriest Greek Cypriot complaints about partition.

Equally impressive is the great sweep of the southern and western Troodos given over to vineyards. Although many of the grapes are destined for wineries or dried for raisins, they are every bit as satisfactory just as grapes. In addition, the Marathasa Valley in the northwest Troodos is renowned for its cherries; the Kokkinochoria, or red-earth district, around Agia Napa produces three crops of potatoes in a year; tobacco is still produced, on a small scale, in the Karpas (Karpaz) Peninsula; bananas make their appearance along the coast north of Pafos; olives and carobs are all but ubiquitous; and market gardening is squeezed in wherever there is space – and irrigation, of course.

Crops near Agia Napa

245

DUSTY DEATH
Great tracts of the Cypriot countryside are as dry as a stick during the long, hot, rain-free summers. An inevitable side-effect of this is dust, which thoughtless drivers exacerbate by speeding along dusty tracks, kicking up great clouds of the stuff. Apart from the literal irritation this causes farmworkers busy in the fields near such tracks, the dust lands on crops, clogging the plants' pores and reducing their growth.

Grapes today, wine tomorrow – although it takes a little longer

Agios Filon, on the coast near Rizokarpason (Dipkarpaz)

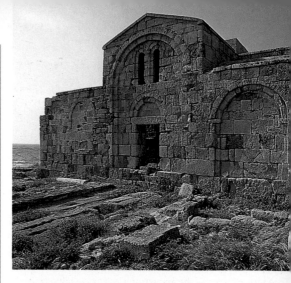

MOTIVE FORCES
The inhabitants of ancient Salamis would no doubt have been astonished to learn that one day, in the far future, mechanical transportation devices (cars) would provide visitors to the remains of their homes and shrines with a lazy person's way of getting around. Walking is practical but not a lot of fun in these open spaces amid the intense heat of summer. There is room to feel a little ashamed at driving between the excavated locations, but Salamis is spread over such a wide area, some 1.5 sq km, with the individual sites widely spaced. This, combined with the lack of public transport even of the *train touristique* variety, makes driving the only sensible option.

Intricate mosaic at the Kampanopetra Basilica, Salamis

▶ Rizokarpason (Dipkarpaz)   227D3

Rizokarpason is a fading ember of Greek Cypriot culture in Turkish Cyprus, with an ageing population provided for by the United Nations. Although no obvious physical pressure is placed on the community, and their church of **Agios Synesios** is still operating, the steady loss of young people to Greek Cyprus tells its own story.

In the immediate vicinity are the fine beach at **Ronnas Bay▶▶**; the small 16th-century church of **Panagia Eleousa▶**, whose frescos have been whitewashed over; and the 10th-century **Agios Filon▶▶** on the shore, the fittings of which have been removed, apparently by tourists. Finally, there are some ruins and traces of the Roman-era harbour of ancient **Carpasia▶**, whose high point was in the 4th and 3rd centuries BC, during the Hellenistic period of the Ptolemies. The city flourished into Roman times before declining under the Byzantines and finally succumbing to the Arabs in the 9th century.

▶▶▶ Salamis   226B1

Open: daily sunrise–sunset. Admission charge

Legend tells that Salamis was founded by Teucer, a Greek hero of the Trojan War, and named after his native Salamis, an island near Athens. The city joined the revolt against Persian rule in 498 BC but by changing sides at a critical moment ensured the Greeks' defeat. Salamis made amends under King Evagoras, a pro-Greek usurper who united most of the island under the Greek banner.

During the Roman period, Salamis remained wealthy and important. In AD 342, however, an earthquake levelled it. Rebuilt under Emperor Constantius, the city was renamed Constantia and became the seat of the Byzantine governor and Orthodox archbishop. In the 7th century, Arabs attacked, and the city never recovered.

The site of the ancient city is spread over a considerable area along the coast north of Famagusta (Gazimağusa). Most of the remains continue to lie buried beneath a forest of acacias and tangled undergrowth.

THE RUINS The colossal 4th-century marble basilica of **Agios Epiphanios▶▶** even in ruins gives some idea of the power and glory of the Christian church in Cyprus at a time when it was taking over the reins as state religion from paganism. The tomb of St Epiphanios, archbishop of Salamis, can be seen but his remains were removed to Constantinople in the 10th century by the Emperor Leo.

The **Agora**► of Salamis is said to have been the largest monumental public market-place of the Roman Empire, marked by long colonnades of which only fragments remain. An inscription found here records that the agora was restored by the Emperor Augustus. At its end is the ruined Temple of Zeus, in which an inscription honouring Livia, the wife of Augustus, was found.

The **Harbour**► of Salamis was one of the most important in the ancient eastern Mediterranean. Now its secrets lie under the sands of 13 centuries, awaiting the hand of the archaeologist. Some sections of its sea wall and of installations along the shore can still be discerned, and the sand is jumbled with sherds of sea-smoothed pottery, as well as bricks and stone.

As impressive as the ancient city's main basilica, the **Kampanopetra Basilica**►► commands a wonderful location beside the ancient harbour. Its ruins contain a vivid mosaic of concentric circles rendered in a complex pattern of coloured marble tiles, a beautiful work which, sadly, is suffering from exposure to the wearing effects of the elements.

The **Gymnasium and Baths**►►► are a photogenic image of classical civilisation, also providing unmistakable evidence of Salamis's straitened circumstances following the 4th-century earthquake. The exercise yard is surrounded by a peristyle whose columns have been salvaged from other demolished buildings rather than built anew. In the southwest corner is a fascinating piece of history: a semicircular latrine with places for 44 people who presumably shared the latest news from Constantinople while sitting side by side engaged in their business. The public baths are an institution of such marble-lined grandeur, such a complex of pools, fountains and hot and cold rooms, that visitors to the 16-centuries-old ruins can only lament the fact that there is nothing like them in Cyprus today. Also called the Byzantine Cistern, Salamis's **Roman Cistern**► is an underground water reservoir used as a place of refuge by early Christians, who left wall-paintings as a record of their stay.

HARD TO PLEASE
Teucer, the heroic founder of Salamis, was less than a hero to his father, Telamon, who banished his son because although he had fought valiantly in the Trojan War, he had returned without the ashes of his brother who had been killed in battle.

247

The Roman theatre at Salamis is still used occasionally for musical, dance and artistic performances

248

The Roman-style **Theatre▶▶▶**, built on the site of an Augustan Age (late 1st century BC) amphitheatre, has been partially restored, with rows of seating ascending in steps from the proscenium, and 'back-stage' installations also visible.

Tombs for heroes and paupers Outside the main Salamis site, near the village of Egkomi (Tuzla), the **Tombs of Salamis▶▶▶** are in two sections: the Royal Tombs, destined for prominent soldiers and citizens, and the ordinary folks' tombs, called the Cellarka, both dating from the 7th and 8th century BC. The former are an astonishingly vivid confirmation of the burial ceremonies of Mycenaean heroes described by Homer in the *Iliad* for the funeral games of Patroclus. There are several large *tumuli* (mounds) inside which the monumental tombs of noblemen were discovered. Each has a trapezoidal *dromos* (entranceway), where the skeletons of sacrificed horses and other funerary tributes were excavated. The burial chambers are made from limestone blocks and are entered via an ornamental *propylaeum* (porch). One tomb was built up with limestone blocks during the Roman period, and tradition is that the building became the prison of St Catherine of Alexandria, an early Christian martyr.

NOT JUST THE TICKET
The regular curator of the tombs of Salamis is a man of considerable enthusiasm for his work and for the history of the site in his charge. He is happy to pass on his knowledge of its history as opposed to just taking visitors' money and handing them tickets.

A restored chariot, recovered from one of the Mycenaean-era Royal Tombs at Salamis

Some distance away from the Royal Tombs is the poor people's necropolis, a partially excavated mass of burial chambers carved in the rock.

▶ Trimithos 226A1

This was recorded by the Roman-era geographer Ptolemy as being among the principal cities of Cyprus. Now the Turkish Cypriot village of Tremetousia (Erdemli) covers whatever traces of the ancient city remain, and a Turkish army military zone in this area beside the demarcation zone makes movement difficult. Also out of bounds is the 7th-century Byzantine monastery of **Agios Spyridon**, named after a local shepherd-boy who became a bishop and who is now patron saint of Corfu. The monastery was formerly a centre for icon restoration and many important works remain there, apparently in good condition according to independent experts.

▶▶ Varosha (Maraş) 226C1

Varosha is awesome. A tour of the outer fringe of this town on the southern edge of Famagusta (Gazimağusa) leaves one open-mouthed at a scene reminiscent of a science-fiction film in which the earth's population has been wiped out by some deadly disease. Before 1974, it was a mainly Greek Cypriot resort town with a permanent population of 40,000 and in those days it was the focus of Famagusta's – indeed, of Cyprus's – tourism industry.

Varosha's population fled from the Turkish army, and although the town lies inside the Turkish ceasefire line it has never been occupied since. For more than 25 years, Varosha has been disintegrating. Its hotels and houses are derelict and collapsing; a jungle of weeds, flowers and plants has sprouted; and rusting irrigation windmills creak eerily as their blades turn idly in the sea breeze. The beach, once the most popular in Cyprus, is deserted. Varosha is isolated by a barbed-wire fence marked with stern warnings that it is a first-degree military zone, with photography and entrance strictly forbidden.

Varosha cannot be visited, but it can be seen. At night, its dark mass looms against the surrounding street lights like a black hole in space. By day, it is a ghostly but gruesomely fascinating sight, a festering sore incongruously superimposed on a background of blue sea and sky, bordered by ordinary houses where people carry on with everyday life. One of Turkish Cyprus's most stylish hotels, the Palm Beach, stands beside the barbed-wire fence, and tourists sunbathe a few metres away.

Reopening Varosha is one of the 'confidence-building measures' regularly proposed by the United Nations as part of the search for agreement between Cyprus's divided communities, but in the absence of an overall settlement this has never happened. In any case the entire town would now need to be demolished and rebuilt from scratch.

Baskets are the stock-in-trade at this shop in Tremetousia (Erdemli)

LOST CITY
In his book *Cyprus: Images of a Lifetime* (1992), Reno Wideson looks back in anguish on his memories and photographs of Famagusta and its resort suburb Varosha (Maraş): 'It is difficult to believe and accept that this happy, busy, blossom-scented small town I have known, where visitors came in their thousands and where the sound of Orange Festival songs filled the air, is now an uninhabited ghost town. I hope and pray that sanity will prevail in the not-too-distant future and that Famagusta will be restored to its previous happiness and glory.'

Despite the rapid growth of the island's cities and resorts, Cypriot society is still very much grounded in the village. Experiencing the warmth of an unaffected village far from the tourist track is a quiet privilege, whose memory will remain long after the suntan fades.

SATURDAY NIGHT FEVER
Saturday night is usually the best night to be in the hill and mountain villages. Families are reunited as the younger people return from their jobs in the cities or at the coast, and the local tavernas are at their liveliest.

In a way, all villages in Cyprus are remote: if not physically distant from the cities and tourist centres, they are sufficiently far removed in spirit to merit the description. Self-contained, close to the land and unhurriedly engaged in the simple life, if not necessarily the good one, villages are the great undiscovered country of Cyprus.

Or at any rate they used to be. Inroads are being made by tourist and expatriate developments, in both Greek and Turkish Cyprus, into the most scenic villages and those most conveniently located for the holiday areas, while sparing their incomer occupants the distress of mingling with the common-or-garden package-holiday tourist. Omodos and Arsos fall into this category in the Greek Cypriot area, and Beylerbeyi (Bellapais) and Lapta (Lapithos) in the Turkish.

Shared experience In areas far from the main roads and further still from casinos and discos, Greek and Turkish Cypriot villagers have more in common than they might expect and would immediately recognise their shared experiences if only they were able to share them. The coffee-shop is everywhere the centre of the village universe, with the church or mosque somewhere near by.

Young people in both areas leave for the bright lights and fatter pay-packets of the resorts and cities. Yet the fields, orchards and vineyards remain the keys to prosperity and continued life for the village.

Remote villages can be found everywhere: in the Karpas (Karpaz) Peninsula and Tilliria, among the peaks of the Troodos and Kyrenia (Beşparmak) Mountains, in the Solea Valley and the Mesaoria (Mesarya) Plain. They are best approached on foot or by bicycle, rather than by jeep or roaring dirt-bike. This is a Cyprus that works to another agenda and moves at its own pace and rhythm. The residents may sometimes be surprised to see you – but they are always hospitable.

Threatened by progress and depopulation, Cypriot villages retain their graces even as they struggle to survive

Travel Facts

Arriving and departing

The Republic of Cyprus is the recognised government of Cyprus. Since 1974, however, almost 38 per cent of the northern part of the island has been under the military occupation of Turkey. This territory has been illegally declared the Turkish Republic of Northern Cyprus (TRNC), a declaration that has been condemned by the UN which, in its resolution 541/83, considers it legally invalid.

The TRNC is not recognised by any country except Turkey; this situation has practical implications for visitors. For the official UN position on the situation, see the statement reproduced on page 288.

Republic of Cyprus

Passports must be valid for three months beyond the date of arrival. Tourists from most European, North American, Middle Eastern, Pacific rim and many African and Asian countries may stay for up to three months without a visa. Nationals of other countries must apply for a visa. Travellers arriving may enter only through Larnaka and Pafos International Airports and the ports of Larnaka, Limassol and Pafos. Entry stamps from the Turkish Cypriot zone are considered illegal, and visitors bearing such stamps on their passports may find that they are refused admission into the Republic of Cyprus.

By air

Larnaka International Airport is the main airport for both scheduled and charter flights, while **Pafos International Airport** is mainly a charter airport. Airport tax is included in the ticket price.

Car rental, catering, foreign exchange and other passenger facilities are available at the airports, but not always on a 24-hour basis. Duty-free shops are located in the departure lounges. (Nicosia International Airport is closed and occupied by the United Nations Force in Cyprus, although it is possible that it may reopen.)

By sea

Passenger services connect Piraeus near Athens, the island of Rhodes, Haifa in Israel, Port Said in Egypt, Latakia in Syria and Jounieh in Lebanon with Limassol and Larnaka.

Turkish-occupied Cyprus

Passports are valid for a stay of three months. Prior visas are not required by any nationality; entry visas are issued on arrival. Immigration officers will not stamp passports, if so requested, to avoid difficulties for tourists planning subsequent visits to the Republic of Cyprus and Greece.

By air

The main airport is **Ercan**, with a second one at **Geçitkale**. Flights, including charter flights, to either are only possible via Turkey (usually Istanbul or Izmir).

By sea

Ferry services operate to the ports of Kyrenia (Girne) and Famagusta (Gazimağusa) from Mersin and Tasucu in Turkey.

Transfers

Airlines do not operate coach services to and from the airports, but many tour operators do so for their own passengers. Metered taxis, plentiful and reasonably priced, operate from the airports to all locations, but avoiding a long taxi journey may be an important factor in choosing Larnaka or Pafos as an entry point.

Unmetered taxis, but with fixed official tariffs, operate from both airports in the Turkish Cypriot zone.

Customs

Republic of Cyprus Visitors may import without payment of duty: 250g tobacco (or the equivalent in tobacco products, for example 200 cigarettes); 1 litre spirits; 2 litres wine; (no tobacco or alcohol allowance for under-17s); one bottle of perfume up to 600cl, and 250cl eau de toilette; articles of any other description (excluding jewellery) up to the value of CY£100.

The Republic of Cyprus has applied for membership of the European Union; travellers within the EU are no longer allowed to import duty-free goods. Importing agricultural products and propagating-stock without permission is prohibited.

Visitors can export up to CY£100 in Republic of Cyprus currency. There is no limit to the amount of currency that can be imported, but amounts above the equivalent of US$1,000 should be declared. Unspent foreign currency can be exported, including those amounts above the US$1,000 limit which have already been declared.

Turkish-occupied Cyprus Duty-free allowances are 500g tobacco (or the equivalent – for example, 400 cigarettes); 1 litre wine; 1 litre spirits; 100cl perfume. There is no limit on importing foreign currency, which can also be exported freely up to US$10,000, provided it has been declared at the time of arrival.

Travel insurance

Personal insurance should be taken out before leaving to cover medical, accident, loss and theft. Tour operators, travel agencies and banks, can arrange insurance for you.

253

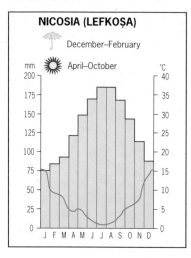

NICOSIA (LEFKOŞA)

December–February

April–October

Essential facts

Climate
The island has a long, very hot and dry summer, a short spring and autumn, and a usually mild, relatively wet winter, which can see snow in the Troodos Mountains. The average peak daytime temperature in July and August is 35°C and in January 15°C, although maximum summer temperatures inland can reach 40°C and minimum winter temperatures drop below 0°C in the mountains.

There is no rainfall, as a rule, between June and September, and by the end of the summer dust can be a problem. A pullover or other warm clothing is desirable for evenings in the mountains, even in summer; otherwise you will require little beyond a swimsuit and shorts and T-shirts. The best time to visit for temperate weather is from March to May and from about mid-September to mid-October. At the earlier time, there is fine weather and carpets of spring flowers and greenery. July and August together comprise the hottest, busiest and most expensive vacation period, but in compensation this time is also the liveliest and best for getting that holiday tan. Winter has its bonus points too, when skiing in the morning and swimming in the afternoon are possible; for denizens of the frozen north this is an ideal time for a warm-weather break.

National holidays
Republic of Cyprus
- **New Year's Day** 1 January
- **Epiphany** 6 January
- **Green Monday** variable (50 days before Greek Orthodox Easter)
- **Greek Independence Day** 25 March
- **Anniversary of Cyprus Liberation Struggle** 1 April
- **Good Friday** (Greek Orthodox Church) variable
- **Good Saturday** (Greek Orthodox Church) variable
- **Easter Sunday** (Greek Orthodox Church) variable
- **Easter Monday** (Greek Orthodox Church) variable
- **Labour Day** 1 May
- **Pentecost–Kataklysmos** (Festival of the Flood) variable
- **Assumption of Our Lady** 15 August

Thanks to 3,000 hours of sunshine, suntans are all but guaranteed

- **Cyprus Independence Day**
  1 October
- **'Ochi' Day (Greek National Day)** 28 October
- **Christmas Day** 25 December
- **Boxing Day** 26 December

Turkish-occupied Cyprus
- **New Year's Day** 1 January
- **Seker Bayrami** (Sugar Festival) variable (end of Ramadan); lasts three days
- **National Sovereignty and Children's Day** 23 April
- **Labour Day** 1 May
- **Youth and Sports Day** 19 May
- **Kurban Bayrami (Festival of the Sacrifice)** variable; lasts four days
- **Peace and Freedom Day** 20 July
- **Communal Resistance Day** 1 August
- **Victory Day** 30 August
- **Turkish National Day** 29 October
- **Prophet Muhammad's Birthday** variable
- **Independence Day (Turkish Republic of Northern Cyprus)** 15 November

Time
Cyprus time is on Eastern european Time: Greenwich Mean Time (GMT) plus two hours in winter and plus two hours in summer. For most of the year, Cyprus is one hour ahead of Western Europe, two hours ahead of the UK and Ireland, six hours ahead of US Eastern Standard Time and eight hours behind Australia (Sydney).

Money matters
Republic of Cyprus The unit of currency is the Cyprus pound (CY£). Notes are available in denominations of CY£20, CY£10, CY£5 and CY£1; coins in 50¢, 20¢, 10¢, 5¢, 2¢ and 1¢.

Turkish-occupied Cyprus The unit of currency is the Turkish lira (TL).

International credit and charge cards are widely accepted in the Republic of Cyprus, but less so in Turkish Cyprus, and almost never at petrol stations in either. Traveller's cheques can be exchanged for Cyprus pounds or Turkish lire, as appropriate, at banks, exchange bureaux and hotels,

and can be used to settle bills in hotels and restaurants, and in some shops.

Thomas Cook traveller's cheques are now available in CY£50 and CY£20 denominations. Eurocheques are accepted with a supporting Eurocheque card.

Automatic cashpoint machines are widely available and accept some foreign Eurocheque cards, credit cards and charge cards.

All 'hard' currencies are accepted at banks, hotel exchanges and so on in the Republic of Cyprus. In Turkish Cyprus only US dollars, British pounds and German marks have general acceptance.Many businesses will exchange these currencies at favourable rates.

Banking hours in the Republic of Cyprus are Monday to Friday 8–12:30,. Banks in the main resort areas and all towns provide an after-noon tourist service of 3:30–5, occasionally later than this. In Turkish Cyprus, banks open 8–noon in summer; 8–noon, 2–4 in winter.

255

Credit and charge cards are widely accepted in towns and resorts

Getting around

Finding your way
It is essential to obtain up-to-date maps (see page 268) as place-name spellings are currently changing to a new transliteration system. Be warned, however, for although your map may use Larnaka and Pafos, the signs you come across in the towns

Car-rental companies will supply you with a telephone number to dial in the event of a breakdown. Other situations in the Republic of Cyprus may be handled by the Cyprus Automobile Association tel: 02-313131 – 24 hours, or by phoning a vehicle recovery service (see the Yellow Pages business telephone directory).

There are good roads in most areas

themselves may still use the old spellings of Larnaca and Paphos.

Car rental
Republic of Cyprus Hired cars are called 'Z cars', for their distinctive red licence-plates with a 'Z' prefix. There are three categories of operation: the major international rental companies, with a reputation for reliability but usually at a higher price; national groups which offer the advantages of the majors but usually at a lower price; and local firms with very good rates but whose cars may be older or less well maintained. Jeeps are popular, but those with open tops put passengers at risk of severe sunburn, as well as being dusty in dry conditions. If collision-damage waiver insurance is not taken, renters may be liable for a large initial sum in the event of an accident, although this may be covered by their own travel insurance.

Turkish-occupied Cyprus Similar points to those raised above apply in Turkish-occupied Cyprus, except that the major international groups do not operate and car hire is cheaper. Most companies offer both left-hand- and right-hand-drive vehicles, but as driving is on the left it is safer to opt for right-hand drive.

Car-rental companies should provide a telephone number in the event of a breakdown.

Driving tips
National and international driving licences are valid in both north and south. Green Card insurance is not accepted, only car insurance issued by an authorised agent for Cyprus. Third-party cover is the legal minimum, but comprehensive cover may make more sense. Traffic moves on the left, and road-traffic signs are on the left. Distances and speed limits are posted in kilometres and kilometres per hour (km/h). Speed limits are 50km/h (30mph) in built-up areas, 80km/h (50mph) on main

roads and 100km/h (60mph) on motorways. Dipped headlights are mandatory from 30 minutes after sunset to 30 minutes before sunrise. The intense glare of the sun can require the use of sunglasses. Front seat-belt use is compulsory. Children under five cannot sit in the front passenger seat, and children aged from five to ten can only do so if a child's seat-belt is fitted.

Fuel stations are plentiful in towns and major resorts, but not outside them, particularly in the mountains and other remote areas, and in all cases are rarer in Turkish-occupied Cyprus. Leaded petrol and diesel are both widely available, unleaded petrol less so. Most stations are open Monday to Friday 6am–6pm and to 4pm on Saturdays; most close on Sunday; automatic vending is available in Nicosia and all seaside areas on a 24-hour basis, with payment by bank notes and, less widely, credit card.

Most aspects of driving are an improvement on the norm in Mediterranean countries. The major exception is local drivers overtaking recklessly on busy roads, even where corners and gradients hide oncoming vehicles. Farmers in pick-ups may force tourists' Z registration cars into the verge on roads not wide enough for two vehicles, though this is less evident in the Turkish-occupied areas of Cyprus.

The Republic of Cyprus has three excellent four-lane motorways (Nicosia–Pafos, Nicosia–Larnaka and Limassol–Larnaka), as well as many well-maintained two-lane roads. There are also some good mountain roads. On the roughest stretches, drivers need to be determined to reach their objective.

On many roads in Turkish-occupied Cyprus army transport may have priority.

Public transport
Buses Three kinds of bus service exist in both zones: urban, interurban and rural. Urban services in Nicosia, Limassol, Larnaka, Pafos, Kyrenia (Girne) and Famagusta (Gazimağusa) are adequate, if hardly luxurious. Interurban services are regular, fares are cheap and most buses run direct from town to town. Rural buses connect villages with the nearest town, generally with only one return service per day, leaving in the morning and returning in the evening. Many smaller villages have no bus service.

Public transport is adequate in the towns, less so in the countryside

257

Getting around

Taxis
Republic of Cyprus There are three types of taxi service: urban, rural and interurban.

Urban taxis are available 24 hours a day in towns and major resorts and from airports, and can be booked by telephone or hired from their rank or base. These taxis have meters, minimum and waiting charges, and charges for luggage weighing more than 12kg (which may be waived).

Rural taxis operate in country areas, are unmetered and can be hired from their base or by telephone; a charges chart is carried by the driver, although it may be wise to ask for an estimate of the fare.

Shared service taxis, which can be booked by telephone, are a direct and convenient alternative to the slow and roundabout bus service. They carry between four and seven main bus stops, and whose journey begins when they are full.

Cycling
Bicycles can be the best option for getting around in the resorts and even, with a little caution, in the towns. Bikes are easy to hire in most resorts, and offer a more tranquil way of getting close to Cyprus's nature than the mopeds or motorbikes which are also available.

Mountain-bikes can be hired for the kind of rugged trails which are common all over Cyprus, as well as in the actual mountains: the Troodos and Kyrenia (Beşparmak) ranges. Mopeds are the most popular, but high-powered dirt-bikes are also available for off-road expeditions.

On foot
Hitch-hiking is permitted in both north and south, except on motorways and motorway accesses.

Reasonably priced, taxis are a popular means of getting around

passengers on regular journeys between the four main towns, picking up and dropping off at the passenger's requested location, for a very low fixed charge.

Turkish-occupied Cyprus Similar conditions apply to those in the Republic of Cyprus, except that taxis are not metered. Instead, they have a list of official charges from which the fare can be established for long journeys. Dolmuş are minibuses which operate directly between towns, from the main

Some walking and hiking routes have been established in the Troodos and Kyrenia (Beşparmak) Mountains and in the Akamas Peninsula. For these and more individualistic expeditions, water and food should be taken along, while serious climbing and hill-walking requires proper equipment. Local tourist offices can often provide or suggest guided or independent walking itineraries in their localities. See also the various walking itineraries in this book.

Student and youth travel
Cyprus has not really developed the kind of low-cost infrastructure that

Organised excursions to the most popular sights are widely available

makes 'bumming around Europe' part of the rites of passage of many students, preferring to concentrate instead on package tourism. The shortage of accommodation at the low end of the price scale is being made up only slowly and without official encouragement. Nevertheless, there are some youth hostels, while the 'hotels without star' classification offers other possibilities.

There are a number of youth hostels catering for members of the International Youth Hostels Association. Non-members are also accepted. There are youth hostels at:

- **Nicosia** 5 Hadjidaki Street tel: 02-674808 or 670027.
- **Agia Napa** 23 Dionysios Solomou Street tel: 03 723113 or c/o 02-674808 or 670027.
- **Larnaka** 27 Nicolaou Rossou Street tel: 04 621188.
- **Pafos** 37 Eleftheriou Venizelou Avenue tel: 06-232588.
- **Troodos** Troodos–Kakopetria road, Troodos village tel: 05-422400. The hostel is open from April to October.

Further information is available from the **Cyprus Youth Hostel Association**, PO Box 21328, 1506 Nicosia, Republic of Cyprus

tel: 02-304860; fax: 02-442896. In addition, there is the **Stavros tis Psokas Rest House**, Pafos Forest tel: 06-722338 or 06 332144. Advance reservations are essential at this small guest-house near the moufflon reserve in the Pafos Forest.

Arranging excursions

Most tour operators arrange day-trips to archaeological, historical, religious and scenic sites. These include: monasteries and Byzantine churches in the Troodos Mountains; the Sanctuary of Aphrodite, the ruins of Salamis and Kourion; the wild and scenic Akamas and Karpas (Karpaz) peninsulas; crusader castles in the Kyrenia (Bešparmak) Mountains; and Nicosia within the Venetian walls. Tourist guides can be contacted via tourist information offices or, in the Republic of Cyprus, through the **Cyprus Tourist Guides Association**, PO Box 4942, Nicosia tel: 02-457755.

259

Facilities for young and independent travellers are slowly improving

In the Republic of Cyprus you need never go without your daily paper

Communications

Media
Republic of Cyprus There is a daily English newspaper, the *Cyprus Mail* and a weekly, the *Cyprus Weekly*. In addition, the *International Herald Tribune* is obtainable on the day of publication and many British and Irish newspapers are widely available are one day after publication, as are newspapers of most Western European countries.

Many hotels have satellite television, with stations including CNN International, BBC World Service Television and BSkyB. The Cyprus Broadcasting Corporation (CyBC), Logos, Antena, Pafos TV and Sigma stations feature movies and programmes from Britain, the USA and other English-language countries with their original soundtrack and Greek subtitles. CyBC2 has a 5-minute news summary in English every day at about 9pm. In addition, CyBC Radio's Channel 1 has a daily English news broadcast, while Channel 2 features occasional programmes in English and, from Monday to Saturday, June to September, the information programme *Welcome to Cyprus*. The

BBC World Service Radio and Voice of America can also be picked up. The British Forces Broadcasting Service (BFB) is on the air 24 hours a day, with a diet of music, magazine programmes and news aimed at the British Sovereign Bases' personnel and their families.

Turkish-occupied Cyprus There is a weekly English newspaper, *Cyprus Today*. *Kibris Monthly*, a soft-propaganda organ of the Public Information Office, includes much general information. International newspapers are rarely found. The Bayrak Radio and Television Service (BRTK) broadcasts occasional programmes in English.

Post offices
Republic of Cyprus Most post offices are open: September to June Monday to Wednesday and Friday 7.30am–1.30pm, Thursday 7.30am–1.30pm and 3–6pm; July and August Monday to Friday 7.30am–1.30pm. In addition, the District Post Office and Eleftheria Square Post Office in Nicosia, District Post Office and City Centre Post Office in Limassol, District Post Office in Larnaka and District Post Office in Pafos are Open: September to June Monday, Tuesday, Thursday and Friday 7.30am–1.30pm and 3–6pm, Wednesday 7.30am–1.30pm, Saturday 8.30–10.30am; July and August Monday, Tuesday, Thursday and Friday 7.30am–1.30pm and 4–7pm, Wednesday 7.30am–1.30pm, Saturday 8.30–10.30am.As well as selling stamps and delivering letters, post offices also provide airmail, express, registered, courier, package, poste restante and other services.

Turkish-occupied Cyprus Offices open May to October Monday 7.30am–2pm and 3.30–6pm, Tuesday to Friday 7.30am–2pm; November to April Monday to Friday 8am–1pm and 2–5pm. Post intended for this zone has to be addressed c/o Mersin 10, Turkey, not direct to Cyprus.

Telephone and fax
To telephone abroad from both north and south, dial 00 + country code +

area code (minus the initial 0) + subscriber number. Some country codes:

Australia 61
Canada 1
Eire 353
New Zealand 64
South Africa 27
UK 44
USA 1

Republic of Cyprus Public telephones accept 5¢, 10¢ and 20¢ coins, or CY£3, CY£5 and CY£10 telecards (available from post offices, souvenir shops and newsagents). Calls made from hotel rooms are expensive. The country code for the Republic of Cyprus is 357. Area codes are: Nicosia 02; Agia Napa/Protaras 03; Larnaka 04; Limassol/Platres 05; Pafos/Polis 06; mobile 09. If phoning from abroad, delete the initial 0. Fax machines are generally available.

Turkish-occupied Cyprus The same direct-dialling system as in the Republic of Cyprus operates from both coin-operated and telecard phones. Public telefax units are not widely available, but most hotels will allow guests the use of their fax. The country code for Turkish-occupied Cyprus is 90392. There are no area codes, only seven-digit subscriber numbers, though you can identify the location of a number from the first two digits – eg Nicosia 22; Kyrenia (Girne) 81; Famagusta (Gazimağusa) 36; Morfou (Güzelyurt) 71.

Language guide
The island's two languages are Greek and Turkish. English is widely spoken, and German is quite common in Turkish-occupied Cyprus, and increasingly so in the Republic of Cyprus.

261

SOME USEFUL WORDS AND PHRASES

ENGLISH	GREEK	TURKISH
good morning	kaliméra	günyadın
good afternoon	kalispéra	iyi akşamlar
good night	kaliníkta	iyi geçeler
goodbye	chérete	allaha ısmarladık
please	parakaló	lütfen
thank you	efcharistó	mersi/teşckkür ederim
yes	ne	evet
no	óchi	hayır
how much?	póso káni?	fiyati nedır?
where is...?	poo íne...?	nerede...?
how are you?	ti kánete/te kánis?	nasılsınız?
sorry/excuse me	signómi	ozür dilerim
one	éna	bir
two	dío	iki
three	tria	üç
four	téssera	dört
five	pénde	beş
six	éksi	altı
seven	eptá	yedi
eight	októ	sekiz
nine	ennía	dokuz
ten	deeka	on
Monday	Deftéra	Pazartesi
Tuesday	Trití	Salı
Wednesday	Tetárti	Çarşamba
Thursday	Pémpti	Perşembe
Friday	Paraskeví	Cuma
Saturday	Sávato	Cumartesi
Sunday	Kiriakí	Pazar

Emergencies

Crime and police
Crime is hardly a worry, as most Cypriots are much too civilised to take part in it. Some of one's fellow tourists can be less engaging, however. The usual precautions ought to be taken with regard to items left in open cars, handbags and valuables left lying around, particularly in busy tourist areas. Violent offences such as muggings are rare, although Cyprus is not completely immune to the imported hooligan syndrome. Offences and thefts should be reported to the police, if only for insurance purposes.

Most policemen in both south and north speak at least some English and are disposed to be tolerant of tourists on minor matters, although not to the extent of allowing them to take advantage of this. In Turkish-occupied Cyprus, the military police (ASIZ) are more in evidence than the civilian police, but in practice this makes little difference.

Visitors should note that it is a criminal offence to export antiquities, and possession of illegal narcotics will be treated seriously.

Embassies and consulates
Republic of Cyprus
Australian High Commission 2nd Floor, 4 Annis Komninis Street, Nicosia, tel: 02 473001
British High Commission Alexandrou Palli Street, Nicosia, tel: 02 473131/7
Canadian Consulate Room 403, Margarita House, 15 Themistocles Dervis Street, Nicosia, tel: 02 451630
US Embassy Metochion Avenue and Ploutarchou Street, Nicosia, tel: 02 476100

Turkish-occupied Cyprus With the exception of Turkey, Turkish-occupied Cyprus has no diplomatic representation, as the Turkish Republic of Northern Cyprus is not an internationally recognised state. However, the **British Council** 23 Mehmet Akif Avenue (tel: 227 4938) , **American Centre** 6 Saran Street (tel: 225 2440), and **Australian Representation Division** 20 Güner Türkmen Street (tel: 227 7332) in the

Turkish Cypriot sector of Nicosia fulfill some consular-type duties.

Emergency telephone numbers
Republic of Cyprus
Ambulance 199
Police 199
Fire service 199
Night pharmacies Larnaka: 1414; Limassol: 1415; Nicosia: 1412; Pafos: 1416; Paralimni (Agia Napa–Protaras): 1413.
General hospitals Larnaka: 04-330333; Limassol: 05 330777; Nicosia: 02 493600; Pafos: 06 240111; Paralimni (–Agia Napa–Protaras): 03-821211; Polis 06 321431

Turkish-occupied Cyprus
Ambulance 112
Police 155
Fire service 199
Night pharmacies Information is posted on pharmacy doors
General hospitals Nicosia 228 5441; Kyrenia (Girne) 815 2266; Famagusta (Gazimağusa) 366 2876; Morfou (Güzelyurt) 714 2125

Lost property
Items left at restaurants and cafés, and on buses and taxis have a high chance of being recovered, as most Cypriots are honest folk. When credit cards and cheques are lost, the issuing companies should be informed immediately. If the property has been stolen you should report it to the police, if only for insurance reasons.

Health
There are no mandatory vaccination requirements for either the south or the north. Health services and standards of hygiene range from adequate to excellent, although in remote areas health services are minimal and other standards may be rough and ready.

Blood which is intended for transfusions is AIDS-screened. Mosquitoes are common but are not malarial. Food and tap water are safe, but outside the mountains the taste of water is often poor; bottled mineral water is widely available.

Poisonous vipers can be encountered in spring and summer in rough country and in the mountains, and while the chance of this is very small and ought not to be exaggerated, a bite from one is potentially fatal. Caution, a hiking-stick and stout footwear are the best safeguards, while anti-venom serum from pharmacies can be self-administered. Anyone who has been bitten and has no serum should remain calm and reach medical assistance speedily with minimum exertion – advice which is designed to slow venom spreading through the bloodstream.

Less arcane emergencies are more common. Sunburn is liable to be the commonest complaint of all. Free emergency medical care is available at the casualty departments of state hospitals and clinics in both the south and north. Your own social insurance may cover other medical expenses; but you should have travel insurance to cover medical emergencies. All drugs are available at chemists without a prescription, and pharmacists can offer advice on treatment of simple ailments. (see 'Emergency Telephone Numbers', opposite, for telephone information numbers of out-of-hours chemists).

The local hospital at Pedoulas in the Troodos Mountains

Other information

Bed and breakfast accommodation

This is not one of Cyprus's strong selling points, particularly in the main resort areas. That said, there is a growing trend for local houses in villages in and around the Troodos Mountains and around Polis to offer accommodation as part of an effort to spread the monetary benefits of tourism around, without swamping villages with apartment blocks.

Camping

Republic of Cyprus Campsites are licensed by the Cyprus Tourism Organisation and there are only seven. Farmers and private landowners might grant permission to pitch a tent if asked, and there are isolated places along the coast and in the mountains where a modest campsite might be set up (but note that fires are forbidden in the forests and it is officially prohibited to camp outside registered sites).

Official campsites, with showers, toilets, shopping, restaurant and washing facilities, are at:

- **Forest Beach** On the beach 8km east of Larnaka centre (tel: 04-644514).
- **Agia Napa** West of the resort, near Nissi Beach tel: 03 721946.
- **Feggari Camping** Coral Bay, Pegeia, 11km north of Pafos tel: 06 621534.
- **Governor's Beach** Located 20km east of Limassol tel: 05 632300.
- **Geroskipou Zenon Gardens** Some 3km south of Pafos Harbour, near Geroskipou Beach tel: 06 242277.
- **Polis** Set amid eucalyptus on the beach 500m from the village centre tel: 06 321526. Open March to end October.
- **Troodos Mountains** Among pine forests 2km north of Troodos, off the road to Kakopetria tel: 05 421624. Open May to end October.

Turkish-occupied Cyprus As in the Republic of Cyprus, farmers and landowners may give camping permission if asked, and there are many out-of-the-way beaches and forest groves where it can't do much harm if campers are tidy and respectful of the environment (and light no fires in tinder-dry forests). A properly equipped site is:

- **Riviera Bungalows** On the sea, 5km west of Kyrenia (Girne) (tel: 822 2026).

There are a number of other small sites, without much in the way of facilities, at **Onur Camping** near Trikomo (Iskele), north of Famagusta (Gazimağusa) at **Nese Beach** south of Bogazi (Boğaz), and at **Aigialousa (Yenierenköy) Public Beach** and **Teresa Beach** near Aigialousa in the Karpas (Karpaz) Peninsula.

Self-catering accommodation

Apartments, studios, apartotels and villas are burgeoning, usually in the same locations as package-holiday hotels, but in some cases (villa developments, for example) in off-resort areas where isolation is part of the attraction. Again it is possible to book such accommodation after arrival, but the more usual method is to arrange it in advance as part of a holiday package.

Children

International and locally produced brands of baby foods, disposable nappies, creams and other items are available from pharmacies and supermarkets in both the north and south. There are few specifically child-oriented attractions, and some poorly protected historic and archaeological sites may be positively dangerous for children. Offsetting this, children are greatly valued by the Cypriots, and are made welcome in cafés and restaurants. Beaches and swimming pools offer endless diversions, so long as children are properly supervised and protected against sunburn. Almost all resort hotels provide baby-sitting services.

Visitors with disabilities

Services and access for disabled people are limited, but the situation is improving, especially with the implementation of new hotel regulations in the Republic of Cyprus. Some hotels, museums and public buildings have ramps for wheelchairs. Public transport is also a difficult proposition. A few parking spaces are reserved for disabled drivers at public places and at most parking areas. The Cyprus Tourism Organisation publishes a guide for disabled travellers. Some addresses for further information:
UK: Royal Association for Disability and Rehabilitation (RADAR), Unit 12, City Forum, 250 City Road, London EC1V 8AF, tel: 020-7250 3222.

US: Advancement of Travel for the Handicapped, 347 Fifth Avenue, Suite 610, New York, NY10016, tel: 212/447 7284; fax: 212 725 8253).

Opening times
Republic of Cyprus Shops are generally open as follows:
Summer Monday, Tuesday, Thursday and Friday 8am–1pm and 4pm–7pm ; Thursday and Saturday 8am–1pm.
Winter Monday, Tuesday, Wednesday and Friday 8am–1pm and 2:30pm–5:30pm; Thursday and Saturday 8am–1pm.

Turkish Cypriot zone Shop opening times can vary greatly, but bigger stores are generally open as follows:
Summer Monday to Saturday 8am–1pm and 4pm–7pm ; Saturday 7:30am–1pm.
Winter Monday to Saturday 9am–1pm and 2pm–6pm.

265

Apartments at Agia Napa

CONVERSION CHARTS

FROM	TO	MULTIPLY BY
Inches	Centimetres	2.54
Centimetres	Inches	0.3937
Feet	Metres	0.3048
Metres	Feet	3.2810
Yards	Metres	0.9144
Metres	Yards	1.0940
Miles	Kilometres	1.6090
Kilometres	Miles	0.6214
Acres	Hectares	0.4047
Hectares	Acres	2.4710
Gallons	Litres	4.5460
Litres	Gallons	0.2200
Ounces	Grams	28.35
Grams	Ounces	0.0353
Pounds	Grams	453.6
Grams	Pounds	0.0022
Pounds	Kilograms	0.4536
Kilograms	Pounds	2.205
Tons	Tonnes	1.0160
Tonnes	Tons	0.9842

MEN'S SUITS

UK	36	38	40	42	44	46	48
Rest of Europe	46	48	50	52	54	56	58
US	36	38	40	42	44	46	48

DRESS SIZES

UK	8	10	12	14	16	18
France	36	38	40	42	44	46
Italy	38	40	42	44	46	48
Rest of Europe	34	36	38	40	42	44
US	6	8	10	12	14	16

MEN'S SHIRTS

UK	14	14.5	15	15.5	16	16.5	17
Rest of Europe	36	37	38	39/40	41	42	43
US	14	14.5	15	15.5	16	16.5	17

MEN'S SHOES

UK	7	7.5	8.5	9.5	10.5	11
Rest of Europe	41	42	43	44	45	46
US	8	8.5	9.5	10.5	11.5	12

WOMEN'S SHOES

UK	4.5	5	5.5	6	6.5	7
Rest of Europe	38	38	39	39	40	41
US	6	6.5	7	7.5	8	8.5

Places of worship

Greek Orthodox churches can be found all over the Republic of Cyprus; even the tiniest hamlet will have one. They hold services on Saturday and Sunday, as well as on saints' days, and at other times are invariably locked. There are similarly large numbers of mosques in Turkish-occupied Cyprus, as well as a few in the Republic of Cyprus. Maronite and Armenian churches exist in various locations, as well as those dedicated to Roman Catholics, Anglicans, Baptists and other denominations in the main towns and resorts.

Sports and other activities

Cyprus is well endowed with outdoor sports possibilities: angling, both at sea and in reservoir lakes; cycling and mountain-biking; hiking and hill-walking; swimming; skiing; water-skiing; scuba-diving and snorkelling; shooting; tennis; golf; horse-riding; aerial sports, such as sky-diving and hang-gliding. In addition, there are activity holidays based on archaeology, architecture, arts and crafts, athletics, bird-watching, bridge, Byzantine art, motorsport (the Rothmans Cyprus Rally is held in September), cooking, the environment, fruit-picking, geology, philately, photography and wines. These are mostly practised in the Republic of Cyprus. Further information is available from

Flat out in the Troodos Mountains during the Rothmans Cyprus Rally

national tourism organisations and specialist tour operators.

Electricity

The electricity supply throughout Cyprus is 240 volts AC, 50 cycles, with 5-amp and 13-amp three-pin plugs. Adapters for connecting more than one low-current appliance are available from many hotels and are on sale in shops. Hotel rooms often have a 110-volt outlet for shavers.

Etiquette and local customs

Casual dress is acceptable in most non-business situations, whether for the theatre, dinner or visiting. Not all Cypriots, however, are delighted to see sweaty, all-but-naked bodies, straight off the beach, wandering into their shops and tavernas.

The sensitivities of Christian and Islamic religious institutions such as churches, mosques, monasteries and convents should be respected, with both men and women covering up properly and, in the case of mosques, removing their shoes. Worshippers should not be pestered with cameras.

Topless bathing at beaches and pools is usually acceptable, yet is much less common in Turkish-occupied Cyprus. Nude bathing is not acceptable in Cyprus, although at remote, unfrequented beaches such as those of the Akamas Peninsula, and private beaches in Turkish-occupied Cyprus you may be able to get away with it.

Girls, both Greek Cypriot and Turkish Cypriot, are far less sheltered than they used to be, particularly in the towns and bigger resorts, but family and religious safeguards – and sanctions – still exist and unwanted attentions can lead to trouble.

Photography

In what is surely one of the most photogenic islands in the Mediterranean, photography has become a security risk in many places. Military personnel and installations, including those of the UN and the British Sovereign Bases, are strictly off limits for photography, and this can also apply to innocent locations and family snapshots close by.

Museums may require a permit for photography. Flash photography is generally forbidden in historic churches, especially those with fragile icons and frescos, and visitors tempted to sneak a few are reminded that the flash causes damage to the works of art. Cameras, film, batteries and rapid processing are all widely available, although less so in Turkish-occupied Cyprus.

Tipping

Restaurants and hotels include a ten per cent service charge in the bill, and VAT at eight per cent is levied on all customers' bills, but a small extra amount for good service is still appreciated. Taxi-drivers, hairdressers and chambermaids are as fond of tips as anywhere, but they don't hustle for them. Tipping is rather less common in Turkish-occupied Cyprus, especially for taxi-drivers, but here, too, customs are changing.

Toilets

Public toilets are few and far between in Cyprus. There are, however, lots of bars, cafés and tavernas with toilets, but being polite and buying a drink before using the facilities, as one should, tends to diminish the effect of the exercise. Toilet paper is normally not flushed away but placed in the receptacle provided, a practice in-tended to keep the plumbing unblocked.

Women travellers

A low crime level, means there is little likelihood of women travelling alone being subject to assault in Cyprus. Nevertheless, the risk cannot be ruled out completely and it makes sense to adopt common-sense measures, such as not hitch-hiking alone.

There is no need to be over-concerned about dress in most circumstances, but women must respect religious Christian and Muslim sensitivities. Few, if any, women in Turkish-occupied Cyprus are veiled. In remote areas, social attitudes are conservative.

Tourist offices

Republic of Cyprus
The **Cyprus Tourism Organisation (CTO)** headquarters, for mail enquiries only, are at PO Box 24535, 19 Lemesou Avenue, 1390 Nicosia (tel: 02 337715; fax: 02 331644; email: cytour@cto.org.cy). Branches can be found at:

Agia Napa 12 Kryou Nerou Avenue, tel: 03 721796.

Larnaka Vasileos Pavlou Square, tel: 04 654322.

Larnaka Airport Passenger terminal, tel: 04 643000.

Limassol 15 Spyrou Araouzou Street, tel 05 362756; 22 Georgiou A' Street, Potamos tis Germasogeias (tel: 05 323211).

Limassol Harbour Passenger terminal, tel: 05 343868.

Nicosia 35 Aristokyrou Street, Laïki Geitonia, tel: 02 674264.

Pafos 3 Gladstonos Street, tel: 06 232841.

Pafos Airport Passenger terminal, tel: 06 422833.

Pano Platres Village square, tel: 05 421316.

Polis 2 Agiou Nikolaou Street (tel: 06 322468).

Overseas offices
UK Cyprus Tourist Office, 17 Hanover Street, London W1R 0AA, tel: 020-7569 8800; fax: 020-7499 4935).

US Cyprus Tourism Organisation, 13 East 40th Street, New York, NY 10016, tel: 212/683 5280; fax: 212 683 5282).

Turkish-occupied Cyprus
The address of the **Ministry of Tourism** is Lefkoşa, c/o Mersin 10, Turkey. Tourist information offices can be found at:

Ercan Airport Passenger terminal, tel: 231 4639.

Famagusta (Gazimağusa) Fevzi Cakmak Caddesi, tel: 366 2864.

Kyrenia (Girne) Kordon Boyu (yacht harbour), tel: 815 2145.

Nicosia Selcuklu Caddesi (tel: 228 9629).

Overseas offices
European Union TRNC Office, Tourism Section, 284 Avenue Louise, 1050 Brussels, Belgium, tel: 02 648 4870; fax: 02 648 7088).

UK TRNC Tourist Office, 29 Bedford Square, London WC1B 3EG (tel: 020-7631 1920; fax: 020-7631 1948).

US TRNC Tourist Office, 1667 K Street, Suite 690, Washington DC 20006 (tel: 202 887 6198; fax: 202 467 0685).

Maps and information
Republic of Cyprus The Cyprus Tourism Organisation (CTO) and its local tourist information offices provide free and paid-for maps and information. Bookshops, news-vendors and souvenir shops also sell maps, guide books and other information books. A good road map (such as the AA/Macmillan *Cyprus Traveller's Map*) is essential when travelling off the main highways.

Turkish-occupied Cyprus Offices at Nicosia, Kyrenia (Girne), Famagusta (Gazimağusa) and Ercan Airport dispense free maps and brochures, as well as more detailed, paid-for information.

Hotels & Restaurants

HOTELS

The Cyprus Tourism Organisation (CTO) publishes a list of officially registered and classified hotels. Local CTO offices also have lists for their areas. Hotels are rated from one star to five stars, with an additional 'hotels without star' category. Room and other rates are approved by the CTO for a fixed period, and must be displayed on notices in rooms. Overcharging is an offence. Off-season prices show considerable reductions over those of the high season.

Cyprus is mainly a tourist destination, although the towns and resorts have business- and conference-oriented establishments. The mainly package-tourism market means that most hotel rooms are block-booked. Independent travellers will find a dearth of family hotels and pensions of the kind that make staying a day or two then moving on an integral part of their vacation experience. Package-oriented hotels will not, however, turn such customers away if they have room.

In attempting to shift its tourist industry up-market, the CTO has limited growth in new hotel construction and favoured four- and five-star hotels. With no corresponding improvement in the tourism 'product', many hotels operate below their capacity, offering the possibility of negotiating favourable rates. The two major exceptions to this are in the Troodos Mountains and around the Akamas Peninsula, where hotels are subject to limits on size, and development is not encouraged.

The situation in the Turkish-Cypriot zone is marked by a lack of accommodation compared with the Republic of Cyprus, and fewer resort areas. Lower demand does not offset this. Most visitors are from Turkey, but arrivals from Europe show a slow but steady increase. Growth is impeded because the international community does not recognise the Turkish Republic of Northern Cyprus.

The following hotels have been divided into three price categories:
£££ = expensive
££ = moderate
£ = budget

NICOSIA

Greek Cypriot sector

Asty (£)
12 Prigkipou Karolou Street tel: 02-773030
This good hotel is surrounded by an area of Nicosia that is noted for its nightlife possibilities.

Averof (£)
19 Averof Street tel: 02-4773447
This smart little family-run hotel has the next best thing to its own swimming pool, being a five-minute walk from the outdoor Municipal Swimming Pool (and hence a long way from the town centre).

Carlton (£)
13 Zinas Kanther Street tel: 02-442001
Good-value hotel in a reasonably convenient location.

Classic (££)
94 Rigainis Street tel: 02-464006
Business-oriented hotel in a fully renovated old building near Pafos Gate. Rooms are modern, air-conditioned and comfortable, though without much in the way of extras, and with double-glazed windows that cut out noise from the busy street. There's a fitness centre, business centre and international restaurant.

City Hotel (£)
215 Lidras Street tel: 02-463113
This hotel is ideal for anyone who wants to be where the action is in Nicosia, and to not spend much money being there.

Cleopatra (££)
8 Florinis Street tel: 02-445254
Somewhat more expensive than higher-star-rated hotels, but with excellent facilities, including a swimming pool, fine restaurant, health centre and conference suite.

Crown (£)
13 Filellinon Street tel: 02-7733
Clean and friendly little hotel, but not ideally situated for the old town.

Denis (£)
19 Diagorou Street tel: 02-330315
Suburban idyll, or inconvenience, can be had in this good-value hotel that lies close to the city's lung of the Athalassa Forest Park.

Europa (££)
16 Alkaiou Street tel: 02-454537
This good-value hotel is situated near to busy Georgiou Griva Digeni Avenue, one of the city's principal traffic arteries.

Excelsior (££)
4 Fotiou Stavrou Pitta Street tel: 02-368585
A position not too far from the city walls is this establishment's principal claim.

Hilton (£££)
116 Archiepiskopou Makariou III Avenue tel: 02-377777
Nicosia's premier hotel, a modern and efficient five-star establishment, located between the city centre and the Larnaka–Limassol motorway. The hotel's swimming pool is a big plus in Nicosia's scorching summer; also has a well-equipped business centre.

Holiday Inn (££)
70 Rigainis Street tel: 02-665131
This high-quality hotel lies just inside the city walls near the Pafos Gate, and has a fine Japanese restaurant, the Bonzai, and a crêperie,, the Café Opera Crêperie, next door.

Ledra (££)
Georgiou Griva Digeni Avenue tel: 02-352086
A recently renovated, business-oriented hotel set amidst landscaped gardens (not to be confused with the city's historic Ledra Palace Hotel, now a UN base).

Philoxenia (£££)
Aglangias Avenue tel: 02-499700
Top-flight business traveller's hotel, next to the Cyprus International Conference Centre and Aglangias Municipal Park.

Regina Palace (£)
42 Rigainis Street; entrance off Fokionou Street tel: 02-463051
One of several good-value hotels within the Venetian Walls, close to Laïki Geitonia and the Lidras Street shopping area.
Venetian Walls (£)
38 Ouzounian Street tel: 02-450805
A small bed-and-breakfast hotel with reasonable facilities for the price. It occupies a good position adjacent to the walls, near the Pafos Gate.

Turkish Cypriot sector

Ender Hotel (£)
12 Şehit Ismail Dümenci Street tel: 227 8612
Simple, friendly and clean hotel located midway out of town from the city walls.
Sabri's Orient (£)
1 Bedrettin Demirel Avenue tel: 227 2161
Located on the edge of Nicosia on the Kyrenia (Girne) road, the hotel is run by Sabri Tahir of *Bitter Lemons* fame.
Saray (££)
Atatürk Square tel: 228 3115
Turkish Cypriot Nicosia's premier hotel, the Saray is a fairly uninspired-looking place, but it is a good hotel. Traditional Cypriot and standard European cuisine are available in the restaurant overlooking the square.
Selimiye Pansiyon (£)
27 Mahmut Paşa Street tel: 227 8586
An unpretentious place offering value for money for travellers on a tight budget.

THE SOUTHEAST

Agia Napa area

Adams Beach (££)
Nissi Avenue tel: 03-721 275
An international holiday hotel rated a shade below five stars, with its own pocket-handkerchief-sized beach and an enormous range of sports and leisure facilities, including (if you require it) bungee-jumping.
Alion Beach (£££)
Kryou Nerou Avenue tel: 03-722900
As with all top-class hotels in Agia Napa, the Alion Beach is devoted to beach holidays with an added touch of style.
Anesis (£)
7 Oktovriou 1 Street tel: 03-721104
Regular tourist hotel, midway between the resort centre and the harbour, with facilities to suit a higher-grade establishment.
Asterias Beach (££)
Makronisos tel: 03-721901
A well-regarded hotel on the beach west of Agia Napa in an area of sand dunes and greenery. The hotel's happy hours, barbecues and entertainment evenings sum up its fun-oriented approach.
Bella Napa Bay (££)
Kryou Nerou Avenue tel: 03-721601
A straightforward and unpretentious hotel, built on a hillside not far from the shore.

Christofinia (££)
112 Nissi Avenue tel: 03-721610
The Christofinia is part of a line of hotels commanding the approaches to Nissi Bay. It lacks an ideal waterfront position but gets close enough.
Chrysland (£)
82 Tefkros Anthias Street tel: 03-721311
In a quieter district than is the norm in Agia Napa, the Chrysland represents good value for money.
Cornelia (£)
23 Archiepiskopou Makariou III Avenue tel: 03-721406
This bed-and-breakfast hotel is in a good location.
Dome (££)
Makronisos tel: 03-721006
A remarkably big hotel even by Agia Napa's standards, with two extensive stretches of beach, the Dome is a beach-holiday hotel par excellence.
Florida (££)
Kryou Nerou Avenue tel: 03-721821
The Florida is a reasonably priced resort hotel, considering the range of facilities on offer, although there is a road to cross on the way to the beach and it is a fair walk to the resort centre.
Grecian Bay (£££)
Kryou Nerou Avenue tel: 03-721301
Top-flight hotel on its own sandy beach and boasting an unrivalled range of facilities, including those for conferences. This is the kind of place that some of its guests never find the need to leave.
Grecian Sands (££)
44 Kryou Nerou Avenue tel: 03-721616
Not far from its starrier sister hotel, the Grecian Bay, the Grecian Sands offers a slightly slimmer diet of holiday facilities, but equal proximity to the beach.
Kermia Beach (££)
75 Cape Gkreko (Kavo Gkreko) Avenue, Korakistres tel: 03-721401
A modern but quite charming bungalow complex on a marvellous strip of coast midway between Agia Napa and Cape Gkreko, with an isolated feeling far from typical of the Agia Napa area.
Leros (£)
Archiepiskopou Makariou III Avenue tel: 03-721126
A small and inexpensive hotel aimed at the budget traveller, of a kind that Agia Napa could really do with more of.
Marine Life (£)
95 Nissi Avenue tel: 03-721330
Moderately priced bed-and-breakfast hotel with the kind of seaside position usually occupied by bigger, more expensive hotels.
Napa Sol (£)
79 Nissi Avenue tel: 03-722044
Reasonable prices and personably small size make this hotel one of the more interesting places to stay at Nissi Beach for travellers who are particularly keen to avoid the big resort hotels.

Napia Star (££)
*12 Archiepiskopou Makariou III Avenue
tel: 03-721540*
Deep in the heart of Agia Napa, this is an excellent hotel built around its own swimming pool.

Nissi Beach (££)
Nissi Avenue tel: 03-721021
In the prime beach-resort area of Nissi Bay, west of Agia Napa, the Nissi Beach is a typically low-rise, middle-brow, high-density hotel located right on the sand.

Pavlonapa Beach (££)
72 Nissi Avenue tel: 03-722400
A smaller establishment than is the norm in this area, the Pavlonapa Beach lacks a few of the facilities that are available at its bigger sisters, but its superb location on the first fine bay out of Agia Napa to the west makes up for this.

Sancta Napa (££)
9 Oktovriou 1 Street tel: 03-721011
An ideal, moderately priced location for those who like to have the sea, the pool and the nightlife high-spots all within easy reach. If the bustle gets too intense, the harbour is equally close by for a fast getaway by cruise boat.

Larnaka area

Arion (£)
26 Galileo Street tel: 04-637200
Side-street hotel in the town centre, whose owner-manager takes good care of his guests.

Atalanti (£)
Umm Haram Street tel: 04-656800
A clean and simple bed-and-breakfast hotel in the old backstreets between the fishing harbour and Salt Lake.

Baronet (£)
*Archiepiskopou Makariou III Avenue
tel: 04-636111*
Popular with the new East European market for Cyprus, the Baronet is a simple bed and breakfast near the northern edge of Larnaka, well positioned for restaurants and the seafront.

Beau Rivage (££)
Larnaka–Dhekelia road, Pyla tel: 04-646600
The Beau Rivage is an excellent mid-range hotel, with scented gardens, its own wide stretch of beach and good facilities for children.

Cactus (£)
6–8 Shakespeare Street tel: 04-627400
A family-run in-town hotel that doesn't miss the beach, thanks to a simple but elegant style and a staff who are far from prickly. Also has a small swimming pool.

Eva (£)
*Larnaka–Dhekelia road, Oroklini
tel: 04-645100*
One of the cheaper hotels on the coast road, near the village of Oroklini, the Eva is a friendly family-run hotel.

Faros Village (££)
Perivolia tel: 04-422111
Located 14km south of Larnaka, near the lighthouse at Cape Kiti. This area is only slowly opening up to tourism. Its ruggedness makes up for the lack of facilities compared with the coast north of Larnaka. The Faros Village is one of this area's better properties.

Filanta (£)
*Corner of Archiepiskopou Makariou III Avenue
and Kolokotronis Street tel: 04-637444*
Not far from the harbour and on a busy main thoroughfare, the light and airy Filanta Hotel has a swimming pool at the back.

Flamingo Beach (££)
Piyale Paşa Street tel: 04-650621
A good seafront property in southern Larnaka, well placed for the Salt Lake though perhaps a little close to the airport.

Four Lanterns (££)
19–24 Athinon Avenue tel: 04-652011
An excellent bet for travellers who want to be in town and on the seafront – in this case the Foinikoudes Promenade – and in a recently renovated, characterful hotel which offers a high standard of service.

Golden Bay (£££)
Larnaka–Dhekeleia road, Pyla tel: 04-645444
Caters for its British guests with an English pub, and for golfers with a pitch-and-putt course. One of Cyprus's top-rated seaside hotels, the Golden Bay provides a high standard of service and facilities, including a Roman-style, colonnaded indoor pool.

Harry's Inn (£)
Thermopyles Street tel: 04-654453
A small, friendly typically Cypriot hotel. It has just nine rooms and 15 beds and does only bed and breakfast. Located a few minutes walk from the seafront, near the tourist information office. Hard to find better value for money.

Henipa (££)
*Grigori Afxentiou Avenue, Oroklini
tel: 04-646022*
In compensation for its off-beach location, the Henipa is a fair bit smaller and a little cheaper than many beach hotels.

Karpasiana Beach Sunotel (££)
Larnaka–Dhekelia road, Oroklini tel: 04-645001
The Karpasiana is a fairly typical hotel among the many along the shore north of Larnaka, but it does have a sheltered stretch of beach and good value to recommend it.

Larco (£)
Portou tel: 04-657006
Embedded in Larnaka's old Turkish quarter, this is a quite large and busy hotel, serving breakfast-only to guests.

Lenios Beach (££)
*Larnaka–Dhekelia road, Oroklini
tel: 04-646100*
An attractive smaller hotel on a fairly deserted stretch of sand just outside Larnaka, offering a quieter scene for swimming and sunbathing.

Les Palmiers (£)
12 Athinon Avenue tel: 04-627200
A well-managed hotel with a first-class seafront location and moderate prices. A welcome contrast with the big resort hotels.

Lordos Beach (££)
Larnaka–Dhekleia road tel: 04-647444
The Lordos Beach lies no more than a ten-minute drive north of Larnaka centre. Its balconies gaze sideways at the sea, but there is a patch of sand for getting a closer look.

Onisillos (£)
17 Onisillos Street tel: 04-651100
A Turkish-quarter location not far from Agios Lazaros Church and Larnaka Fort puts this otherwise unremarkable hotel into the good-value, well-positioned class.

Palm Beach (££)
Larnaka–Dhekelia road, Oroklini
tel: 04-644500
On the coast road a few kilometres north of Larnaka, the Palm Beach offers a high level of facilities for a slightly lower price than could be expected. On-site bungalows are available.

Pavion (£)
11 Faneromenis Street tel: 04-656688
A gem of a place for the committed budget traveller whose idea of a good time is to be right in the centre of the action.

Princess Beach Sunotel (££)
Larnaka–Dhekelia road, Oroklini
tel: 04-645500
Focused equally on bungalows in addition to its main hotel block, the Princess Beach is not quite in the royalty class but its beach is busy.

Rebioz (£)
98 Archiepiskopou Makariou III Avenue
tel: 04-635300
This area of the main road running northwards out of town is fine for nightlife and restaurants but lacking in charm.

Sun Hall (££)
6 Athinon Avenue tel: 04-650400
This big, blocky hotel lies across the road from a palm-tree-lined stretch of sand near Larnaka's marina. The town's main shopping and taverna centre is situated right next door.

Sveltos Beach (£)
Piyale Paşa Street tel: 04-657240
A block of apartments beside Mackenzie Beach at the southern end of Larnaka, offering in-town access to another kind of ambience from that of the coast road to the north.

Three Seas (£)
Perivolia tel: 04-422901
The Three Seas occupies a fine position beside the lighthouse at scenic Cape Kiton, 14km south of Larnaka, and its modest prices add to the attraction.

Vergi (£)
Larnaka–Dhekelia road, Pyla tel: 04-644666
A relatively quiet position off the highway recommends the Vergi to visitors who want to be near the beach but without the bustle of the seafront resort hotels.

Protaras area

Adelais Bay (££)
Green Bay tel: 03-832600
Set a little way back from the beach in a quieter area south of Protaras, the Adelais Bay offers a slight variation on the standard beach hotel, with some good nature walks nearby.

Anaïs Bay (££)
Pernera Harbour tel: 03-831351
A quite charming, smallish hotel by Protaras standards. It is family-run and has a hint of Cypriot, as opposed to international, flavour.

Cavo Maris Beach (££)
Green Bay tel: 03-832043
A good-value location in a fairly isolated spot, the Cavo Maris stays focused on delivering a quality beach holiday.

Golden Coast (££)
Pernera Harbour tel: 03-831366
Stylish hotel overlooking the fishing shelter on a stunning stretch of coast. The hotel's greenery-bedecked swimming pool adds to the exotic feel.

Grecian Park (£££)
Cape Greko (Kavo Gkreko)–Paralimni road
tel: 03-832000
A superbly equipped and located resort hotel, the Grecian Park's vast blue swimming pools compete with the translucent waters of the nearby sea.

Odessa (££)
Protaras tel: 03-831645
Set slightly back from the main road in Protaras, near Flamingo Beach, with the resort's bustling nightlife happening all around it.

San Antonio (£)
123 Grigori Afxentiou Street, Paralimni
tel: 03-821561
Set well back from the coast, at Paralimni village, the San Antonio offers local ambience and a focus away from the beach.

Silver Sands Beach (££)
Flamingo Beach tel: 03-831590
The Silver Sands Beach occupies the next stretch of sand along from the renowned Fig Tree Bay, and provides a little more in the way of peace and tranquillity.

Sunrise Beach (££)
Protaras tel: 03-831501
Part of the hotels complex around the northern corner from Fig Tree Bay, the top-class Sunrise Beach Hotel has an unsurpassed position on the beach.

Tsokkos Protaras (££)
Protaras tel: 03-831363
Right at the heart of the Protaras experience, which means beach holidays and nightlife.

THE SOUTHWEST

Limassol area

Acropole (£)
21 Malekidi Street tel: 05-362706
A dinky little place in a good central location near Limassol's seafront promenade. The room rates will suit the thinnest pocketbook.

Adonia Beach (££)
Amathus Avenue tel: 05-321111
A beach hotel that is moderately priced in relation to its facilities. Located 9km east of Limassol.

Alasia (££)
6 Haydari Street tel: 05-332000
For those who prefer an in-town to a seafront location, the Alasia is situated just off the inner ring road in Limassol. A heated outdoor swimming pool may compensate for the lack of beach and sea.

Hotels & Restaurants

Amathus Beach (£££)
Amathus Avenue tel: 05-321152
Near ancient Amathus, this top-flight hotel belongs to the Leading Hotels of the World organisation. Cypriot cookery demonstrations add a tasteful touch.

Apollonia Beach (£££)
Potamos Germasogeias tel: 05-323351
Right in the heart of Limassol's tourist district, the Apollonia answers to the description 'bustling'. A good place for children, as it has a small but sheltered stretch of sand.

Aquamarina (££)
139 Spyrou Araouzou Street tel: 05-374277
It is hard to beat this hotel's location opposite Limassol's palm-tree-lined seafront promenade.

Aquarius Beach (£)
11 Amathus Avenue tel: 05-322042
Hotel apartments offering bed and breakfast and with a seaside garden, 5km east of Limassol.

Arsinoe (££)
Amathus Avenue tel: 05-321444
Midway between the Potamos Germasogeias seafront and hotel-pressed ancient Amathus, located 6km east of Limassol, this is a medium-sized hotel at the mid-point of its price bracket.

Asteria Beach (££)
Potamos Germasogeias tel: 05-321177
Smack in the middle of the Potamos Germasogeias seafront hotel complex, the Asteria Beach is a long way from being tranquil but is well placed if you are looking for fun.

Astoria (£)
13a Malekidi Street tel: 05-362708
The Astoria is a fairly typical backstreet hotel whose principal advantages are price and a chance to get closer to the real Limassol.

Atlantica (££)
Potamos Germasogeias tel: 05-321141
A reasonably high-standard outfit despite its fairly intimidating size, the Atlantica at least puts its heart behind the package deals it mostly offers.

Avenida Beach (££)
Amathus Avenue tel: 05-321122
The Avenida Beach is smaller and more personable than the average beachfront hotel, thanks to its family ownership. Located beside the sea 11km east of Limassol.

Azur (££)
Potamos Germasogeias tel: 05-322667
Quite a stylish place lying just a few minutes away from the beach and with its own swimming pool. Easy access to the nightlife whirl.

Best Western Pavemar (££)
147 Oktovriou 28 Avenue tel: 05-587000
Rooftop swimming pool offers a superb view over Akrotiri Bay – or more accurately over the hotels that line Akrotiri Bay.

Caravel (£)
Proussis Street, Amathus tel: 05-321533
Situated only 200m from the beach, this little hotel 6km east of Limassol is on a very human scale.

Chez Nous Hotel (£)
2 Aktinou Street, Potamos Germasogeias tel: 05-323033
A fairly small hotel with the family touch, in a busy area surrounded by hotels that may look more impressive but do not necessarily deliver better service.

Churchill (££)
Oktovriou 28 Avenue, Agios Athanasios tel: 05-324444
Occupies a position towards the edge of Limassol, at a point where the town begins to give way to the ribbon development that stretches along the eastern shore.

Continental (£)
137 Spyrou Araouzou Avenue tel: 05-362530
Budget travellers often do best in terms of location and don't mind having fewer facilities considering the price differential. These factors, together with its popularity among Cypriot families, make the Continental a good bet.

Crusader Beach Sunotel (££)
Potamos Germasogeias tel: 05-321333
Richard the Lionheart may or may not have landed on this beach, but the hotel's guests certainly do.

Curium Palace (££)
2 Lordou Vyronou Street tel: 05-363121
A family-owned hotel which proudly displays an interesting collection of objets d'art and antique furnishings. Located back from the beach, it overlooks Limassol's Municipal Gardens with their tiny zoo and open-air theatre.

Eastland (£)
23a Drousioti Street tel: 05-377000
Bed-and-breakfast hotel of good standing in an area of quiet streets well back from the seafront promenade and ideally suited for budget travellers.

Elena Beach (££)
39 Amathus Avenue tel: 05-322855
Quite reasonable hotel, 8km east of Limassol, with its own access to the beach and all the other facilities that are expected of a package-tour establishment.

Elias Beach (££)
Amathus Avenue tel: 05-325000
Has its own horse-riding centre and a reasonable position on the beach 11km east of Limassol.

Episkopiana (££)
Episkopi village tel: 05-234233
A full refurbishment of this hotel should bring its facilities up close to the highest level in Cyprus and offer good value for money, while its location at Episkopi puts it in the heart of a scenic area.

Four Seasons (£££)
Amathus Avenue tel: 05-310222
As well as its first-class beach hotel and sporting facilities, the Four Seasons is a spa resort of a kind unique in Cyprus. Thalassotherapy is the name of this particular game, with sea-water hydromassage and sea-weed therapy treatments adding up to a 'body holiday'.

Golden Arches (££)
Amathus Avenue tel: 05-322433
One wonders how much of ancient Amathus lies under this resort hotel which abuts on the site 9km east of Limassol.

Hawaii Beach (£££)
Amathus Avenue tel: 05-311333
Situated 11km east of Limassol, adjacent to a boat marina, and featuring the full range of resort-hotel facilities, as is fairly standard on this stretch of coast.

Kanika Beach (££)
Oktovriou 28 Avenue tel: 05-356000
A slightly smaller cousin of the Kanika Pantheon, this one occupies a beachfront site not far from the Municipal Gardens.

Kanika Pantheon (££)
Kanika Centre, corner of Oktovriou 28 Avenue and I Metaxa Street tel: 05-591111
Located in a complex of shops, restaurants and hotels near the centre of Limassol and across the main road from the beach, the Kanika Pantheon makes a slight change in ambience from the standard beach hotel.

King Richard (££)
63 Amathus Avenue tel: 05-321330
Somewhat simpler than many hotels in this area 8km east of Limassol, it nevertheless offers a good standard of service and comfort

Le Meridien (£££)
Amathus Avenue tel: 05-634000
Part of the string of hotels running east along Akrotiri Bay outside Limassol, Le Meridien is 13km from the city. It has two fine restaurants serving French and international cuisine, and an enormous swimming pool. A little bridge reaches across the hotel's private bay.

Le Village (£)
242 Archiepiskopou Leontiou I Avenue tel: 05-368126
Bed and breakfast only at this friendly little place, well sited for exploring Limassol.

L'Onda (£££)
Potamos Germasogeias tel: 05-321821
A good deal smaller than the colossal hotels that dominate this area, L'Onda focuses on de luxe suites and offers a more personal service than is the norm hereabouts.

Marathon Beach (££)
Amathus Avenue tel: 05-320122
Part of a take-your-pick bunch of hotels on the busy seafront 6km east of Limassol.

Mediterranean Beach (££)
Amathus Avenue tel: 05-311777
This big and bustling resort hotel, on the beach 9km east of Limassol, offers four weeks for the price of three.

Metropole (£)
6 Ifigenia Street tel: 05-362686
Forget the stylish cosmopolitan name: it would be hard to find a place closer to the street scene than this modest little hotel.

Miramare (££)
Amerikanas Street, Potamos Germasogeias tel: 05-321662
Surrounded by gardens in a slightly secluded spot, this is otherwise a standardly equipped mid-market hotel.

Navarria (££)
Amathus Avenue tel: 05-320855
Located 6km east of Limassol, the Navarria's graceful blue complements that of the sea.

Old Bridge (£)
21 Kranou Street tel: 05-321200
Reasonably priced hotel well within reach of the sea and surrounded by the bright lights of Germasogeia.

Park Beach (££)
Georgios 'A' Street, Potamos Germasogeias tel: 05-321301
The park of the title refers to the hotel's pretty little garden, whose scents are at least as notable as the hotel itself.

Pefkos (£)
86 Misaouli and Kavazoglou Street tel: 05-377077
A chance to see what life is like on the other side of town, in this moderate hotel apartment block on the road out of Limassol to the west.

Poseidonia Beach (£££)
Amathus Avenue tel: 05-321000
Only 6km from Limassol, between Potamos Germasogeias and ancient Amathus, this is one of the closer out-of-town hotels. It has a heated swimming pool.

St Raphael (£££)
Amathus Avenue tel: 05-321100
Located close to the ruins of ancient Amathus some 12km east of Limassol: it has a Pleasure Harbour with water sports facilities.

Sunny Beach (£)
Oktovriou 28 Avenue tel: 05-591999
Its name just about says it all for this determinedly holiday-oriented hotel hard by the beach on the road out of town.

Sylva (£)
124 Griva Digeni Street tel: 05-321660
Surrounded by more touristy establishments, this is a good standard town hotel in an area where the street dog-legs towards the sea.

Trans (£)
Amathus Avenue tel: 05-322268
One of the more moderately priced places amidst the behemoths of Akrotiri Bay, 8km east of Limassol.

THE TROODOS MOUNTAINS

Agros

Rodon (££)
Agros village tel: 05-521201
Off the beaten track in the eastern Troodos, the Rodon is a big, modern, low-rise hotel that doesn't do much to enhance the village's character but makes a good base for exploring the rugged and sparsely populated Pitsilia district. There's a swimming pool and sauna and you have great mountain views from your window.

Kakopetria

Hekali (£)
22 Griva Digenis Street tel: 02-922501
Modest is the best description for this friendly hotel. Prices are modest too.

275

Hellas (££)
4 Mammantos Street tel: 02-922450
Mid-range and mid-sized, with 30 rooms, the Hellas provides a comfortable introduction to the mountain lifestyle.
Kifissia (£)
tel: 02-922421
With a scenic outlook over a plunging stream (more usually a dried-up stream-bed), the Kifissia's 37 rooms are often full.
Makris Sunotel (££)
48 Mammantos Street tel: 02-922419
A comfortable and nicely situated small hotel.

Pano Platres

Edelweiss (£)
53 Kalidonia Street tel: 05-421335
Quite a small hotel which brings a touch of Alpine charm to the Troodos.
Forest Park (£££)
tel: 05-421751
Situated in its own extensive grounds amidst the forest and with a heated swimming pool and tennis courts, this is the top-class resort hotel of the Troodos Mountains.
Lanterns (£)
tel: 05-420134
This is one of several fine, unpretentious hotels that make the Troodos Mountains a pleasant change from resort -based coast culture
New Helvetia (£)
6 Helvetia Street tel: 05-421348
A fine restaurant and a shaded location distinguish this renovated hotel near the edge of Pano Platres village.
Pendeli Hotel (£)
Archiepiskopou Makariou III Avenue
tel: 05-421736
Modern facilities include a swimming pool in what is one of the most comfortable hotels in the village.
Splendid (£)
tel: 05-421424
Simple but comfortable mid-sized hotel in the village where the action is in these mountains.

Pedoulas

Churchill Pinewood Valley (££)
Prodromos–Pedoulas road tel: 02-952211
Set among pine and cedar forests, this is one of the most attractive hotels in the mountains.
Christy's Palace (£)
Main street tel: 02-952655
Modern, bright, family-run hotel that combines straightforward home comforts with a friendly approach. It has a fair taverna and great views across the village to the surrounding hills.
Mountain Rose (£)
Main street tel: 02-952727
Pine furnishings in the rooms and public spaces add a distinctive touch to this hotel on the steep main street into the village. Though minimally equipped, the rooms are reasonably comfortable and the in-house taverna is adequate. The Mountain Rose scores through its character and friendly welcome.

Troodos village

Jubilee (£)
tel: 05-421647
Ideally placed for anyone looking to exploit the good hiking country in these parts.
Troodos (££)
tel: 05-421635
A fairly small but pleasantly sited, reasonably priced hotel which is comfortably cosy in winter as well as summer.

THE WEST

Pafos area

Agapinor (££)
26 Nikodimos Mylonas Street
tel: 06-233927
Recently fully renovated, the Agapinor is an efficiently run modern hotel with a mixed business and holiday clientele. It has a fine position in Ktima, near the market, the main shopping centre and the bus terminal.
Alexander the Great (££)
Poseidonos Avenue tel: 06-265000
Just off the southern end of the harbour, the 'Alex' doesn't have a perfect beach location but is well up to standard in all other respects.
Amalthia Beach (££)
Kisonerga tel: 06-247777
With coastal development rapidly extending north of Pafos, this resort hotel has claimed a rocky spot beside a tiny beach.
Annabelle (£££)
Poseidonos Avenue tel: 06-238333
Rocky groves around the swimming pool represent the Annabelle's effort to fit in with its environment – not easy for such a big, though generally attractive resort hotel.
Cynthiana Beach (££)
Kisonerga tel: 06-233900
Located near banana plantations on a headland with a small private beach near Kisonerga, 7km north of Pafos, the Cynthiana Beach combines relative isolation with full-service resort-hotel facilities.
Cypria Maris (££)
Poseidonos Avenue tel: 06-264111
Sheltered swimming off its own beach at Geroskipou and a swimming pool surrounded by greenery are distinguishing features of this well-established beach hotel.
Imperial Beach (£££)
Poseidonos Avenue tel: 06-245415
One of the many – perhaps too many – top-rated hotels in the Pafos area, offering much the same resort-hotel diet.
Kings (£)
38 Tafon ton Vasileon Avenue tel: 06-233497
Excellent-value accommodation at an adequate hotel near the Tombs of the Kings.
Laura Beach (£££)
Chlorakas tel: 06-244900
Extensive garden, indoor and outdoor pools, a special area for sea bathing, and sports facilities. All in a distinctive red, white and blue resort hotel, 5km north of Pafos.

Ledra Beach (££)
Theas Aphrodites Avenue tel: 06-264848
Just 2.5km south of Pafos harbour, this is an attractively built and well-served hotel on the beach at Geroskipou.

Leptos Coral Beach (£££)
Coral Bay tel: 06-621711
A fairly colossal resort hotel which all but dominates the wonderful sands at Coral Beach some 10km north of Pafos. Its five-star rating is merited in terms of facilities. Busy beach.

New Olympus (£)
12 Lordou Vyronos Street tel: 06-232020
One of the small and friendly gems of Pafos, the New Olympus still boasts a pool and a good location in town.

Paphiana Sunotel (££)
Konia tel: 06-260252
An inland hotel, just outside this village 4km east of Pafos, which is ideal for those who want to be a little closer to the country.

Paphian Bay (££)
Poseidonos Avenue tel: 06-264333
At the southernmost, Geroskipou side, of Pafos, this is basically a beach-holiday and watersports hotel.

Paphiessa (££)
2 Agios Filon Street tel: 06-245555
Its more than personal size sets off this fine hotel, and its prices are interesting too.

Paphos Beach (££)
Poseidonos Avenue tel: 06-233091
Well positioned at the eastern end of Pafos harbour, this is a first-class resort hotel for those who like to be in the thick of the action.

Park Mansion (£)
16 Pavlou Melas Street tel: 06-245645
Easily one of the classic hotels in Pafos, this is a fully restored Venetian mansion, overlooking the Municipal Gardens in central Pafos.

Pelican Inn (£)
102 Apostolou Pavlou Street tel: 00-232827
Diminutive guest-house beside the harbour offers a chance to get closer to Cyprus and the Cypriots. Has a fine associated restaurant.

Pioneer Beach (££)
Poseidonos Avenue tel: 06-246500
Typical of the Geroskipou area resort hotels, but with its own private beach.

Porto Paphos (££)
Poseidonos Avenue tel: 06-242333
A short distance only from Pafos harbour, and fairly typical of the mid-range resort hotels in Kato Pafos.

Pyramos (£)
4 Agias Anastasias Street tel: 06-235161
A small, family-run hotel with balustraded balconies above the arcaded bar.

Queen's Bay (££)
Kisonerga tel: 06-246600
On a fairly isolated and wild part of the coastline, at Kisonerga, 9km north of Pafos.

Roman (££)
Agios Lambrianos Street tel: 06-245411
Features a Byzantine castle look which distinguishes this downtown hotel from the many nearby resort establishments. Boasts a small rooftop tennis court.

Theofano (££)
Danaïs Street tel: 06-265700
On a more human scale for those visitors who cannot easily live with the colossal size that is more usual in Pafos.

Trianon (£)
99 Archiepiskopou Makariou III Avenue tel: 06-232193
A small and, for the low-budget independent traveller, good-value guest-house.

Venus Beach (£££)
Tafon ton Vasileon Avenue tel: 06-249200
This hotel has an unrivalled seafront location near the superb Hellenistic-era Tombs of the Kings.

Pissouri

Bunch of Grapes Inn (£)
Pissouri Village tel: 05-221275
A traditional taverna/hotel, with basic accommodation. Noted for its excellent Sunday lunch.

Columbia Beach (££)
Pissouri Beach tel: 05-221201
A high-standard hotel which dominates the as-yet hardly developed sands 5km south of Pissouri village.

Polis–Latsi area

Akamas (£)
14 Griva Digenis Street, Polis tel: 06-321330
With a good position in Polis village, this fine little hotel is close to whatever action there is in this peaceful part of Cyprus.

Aphrodite Beach (££)
Latsi–Baths of Aphrodite road tel: 06-321001
Continues what has become a firmly established, recent Cypriot tradition – building character-free hotels in places that are full of natural beauty. When its blocky, modern lines are fully discounted, this is still a small and friendly, family-run hotel, beside the beach and within easy reach of the Akamas Peninsula.

Droushia Heights (££)
Drouseia tel: 06 332351
A high-sited hotel at the inland village of Drouseia south of Polis. The location is ideal for exploring the nearby vineyard country and the more remote Akamas Peninsula.

Elia Latchi Holiday Village (££)
Latsi tel: 06-321011
Close to the sea and Latsi fishing harbour, this small complex of studios and apartments is at the heart of a largely undeveloped coastal area.

Marion (£)
Marion Street, Polis tel: 06-32159
Small and friendly hotel near Polis, a village where traditional Cypriot style has not yet been overwhelmed.

Souli (££)
Neo Chorio road tel: 06-321088
A simple, comfortable hotel that occupies a beautifully isolated location overlooking the sea. An ideal place for getting away from it all. Also has a seafront restaurant with an excellent fish menu.

277

Stavros tis Psokas

Stavros tis Psokas Rest House (£)
Pafos Forest tel: 06-722338 or 06-332144
With just seven rooms and a few suites with
shower and fireplace, this isolated wilderness
rest-house/hostel requires advance reserva-
tion.

THE NORTH

Bellapais (Beylerbeyi) area

Altinkaya (£)
Kazafani (Ozanköy) tel: 815 5001
This pretty little family-run establishment on the
Kyrenia–Bellapais (Girne–Beylerbeyi) road, consists of 12 bungalows grouped around a
swimming pool and incorporates a restaurant
that is popular with locals.

Ambelia Village (££)
*Bellapais–Kato Dhikomo (Beylerbeyi–Dikmen)
road tel: 815 2175*
A garden-screened apartment complex located
300m above sea level and above the village of
Bellapais.

Bellapais Gardens (££)
*Kyrenia–Bellapais (Girne–Beylerbeyi) road
tel: 815 6066*
Its swimming pool fed by a spring once used by
the ancient Romans, this small de luxe villa
complex nestles in an idyllic setting among
lemon groves, below the ruined Gothic abbey of
Bellapais.

Kyrenia (Girne) area

Atlantis (£)
3 Eftal Akça Street tel: 815 2505
Modern building angling just back from the old
harbour.

Bristol (£)
Hürriyet Avenue tel: 815 6570
An excellent-value hotel on Kyrenia's main
shopping street, with clean rooms and a good
Turkish restaurant.

British Hotel (£)
10 Eftal Akça Street tel: 815 2240
It would be hard to beat this location on the
harbourside at Kyrenia, overlooking the open-air
terraces and moored yachts.

Courtyard Inn (£)
Karakum tel: 815 3343
Small and inexpensive pension with a nice
restaurant situated a few kilometres east of
Kyrenia.

Dome (£££)
Kordonboyu tel: 815 2453
Modernisation has cost it brownie points with
genuine ex-colonials (it now has a casino and
disco) but this elegant hotel is still the place of
choice for holidaymakers in the know and in the
money.

Dorana (££)
Hürriyet Avenue tel: 815 3521
A relaxing, friendly family hotel not far from the
harbour, and with a position on the main shopping street which ought to be noisy but isn't.

Grand Rock (££)
Kordonboyu tel: 815 5709
Appropriately named, as its beach is mostly
rocks. A city-centre location and efficiently
modern approach compensate for this.

Kyrenia Oscar Club (££)
Karakum tel: 815 4801
Fairly standard holiday hotel, with pool and
other facilities, including beach. A courtesy bus
runs from the hotel to the nearby town centre.

Liman (££)
Kordonboyu tel: 815 2001
Liman is located in a bustling part of town
around the corner from the old harbour. The
hotel's café terrace across the road is shaded
by the entwined branches of Kyrenia's 'Loving
Trees'.

Socrates (£)
Hürriyet Avenue tel: 815 1291
A family hotel which boasts a leafy courtyard
café and a location on Kyrenia's main shopping
street close to the old harbour.

Yeni Anadol (£)
Hürriyet Avenue tel: 815 2319
A garden and playground make this a good
town-centre location for families with young
children.

Lapithos (Lapta) area

Celebrity Bungalows (£££)
*Kyrenia–Vavilas (Girne–Güzelyalı) road
tel: 821 8751*
Situated on the coast near the village, the hotel
has a private beach and a casino among its
full range of resort-hotel facilities.

Château Lambousa (£££)
*Off Kyrenia–Vavilas (Girne–Güzelyalı) road
tel: 821 8751*
With superbly atmospheric Turkish architecture,
in the style of a turreted castle, the Château is
a taste of old-fashioned class with a modern
touch. Its shaded balconies look out over palm-
fringed gardens to the sea.

Deniz Kızı (££)
*Karavas (Alsancak)
tel: 821 8710*
A family-run hotel noted for its plain but tasty
Turkish cooking. Overlooks a secluded sandy
bay near this village, at a spot where the sea
makes the hotel's outdoor pool almost superfluous.

Mare Monte (££)
*Karavas (Alsancak)
tel: 821 8310*
A vine-shaded open-air restaurant beside the
Mediterranean is one of the attractions of this
hotel. The Mare Monte also has its own beach,
tranquil setting and beautifully scented
gardens.

On The Waterfront (££)
*Kyrenia–Lapithos (Girne–Lapta) road
tel: 821 8922*
On the seafront at Lapithos, this small restaurant beside a swimming pool and bar is owned
by a Turkish Cypriot expatriate from London.
You can sample his fine Cypriot cuisine inside
or on a breezy outside terrace.

THE EAST

Bogazi (Boğaz) area

Bogaz (££)
Famagusta–Bogazi (Gazimağusa–Boğaz) road
tel: 371 2559
Situated on the coast road across from the fishing harbour and the shore, the Bogaz is a pleasantly quiet modern hotel. Guests have the use of the swimming pool and tennis courts at the nearby Hotel View (see below).

Cyprus Gardens Resort Village (££)
Famagusta–Bogazi (Gazimağusa–Boğaz) road
tel: 371 2552
The Cyprus Gardens consists of a complex of bungalows and small villas beside the sea, within a fine, scented garden. Pool and tennis courts are complemented by horse-riding facilities.

Giranel (£)
Famagusta–Bogazi (Gazimağusa–Boğaz) road
tel: 371 2455
Located about half-way between Bogazi and the Famagusta Bay resort complex north of Salamis, the Giranel is a simple but pleasant enough hotel near the sea.

Hotel View (££)
Off Famagusta–Bogazi (Gazimağusa–Boğaz)
road tel: 371 2651
The Hotel View occupies a superb location on a hill behind Bogazi, overlooking the sea. Beautiful gardens complement the hotel's stylish looks, and it also offers good sports facilities and a swimming pool.

Famagusta (Gazimağusa) area

Altun Tabya (£)
7 Kızılkule Yolu tel: 366 5363
A simple but clean and friendly small hotel inside the city walls. Evening meals are available on request in the Turkish restaurant.

Panorama (£)
Ilker Karter Avenue tel: 366 5880
Located just outside the old town, the Panorama is a family-run hotel with a friendly owner. The Turkish and European cooking is complemented by his enthusiasm for pizza.

Palm Beach (£££)
Havva Sentürk Avenue tel: 366 2000
A very stylish, flamingo-pink hotel with a pool and casino and a fine seafront location south of the walled city. Its outlook in another direction, however, is towards the adjacent barbed-wire barricades and dereliction of Famagusta's abandoned resort suburb of Varosha (Maraş).

Karpas (Karpaz) Peninsula

Blue Sea (£)
Rizokarpaso–Cape Apostolos Andreas (Dipkarpaz–Zafer Burnu) road tel: 372 2393.
A tiny hotel with a superb seaside setting southeast of Rizokarpaso. In the beautiful but hotel-poor Karpas, the Blue Sea is a jewel almost beyond price – yet costs very little.

Salamis area

Park (££)
Famagusta–Bogazi (Gazimağusa–Boğaz) road
tel: 378 8217
On its own beach right by the sea, this Bavarian-style country hotel has all the facilities to be expected in a modern resort hotel, yet combined in a fairly small and attractive package.

Salamis Bay Conti (£££)
Famagusta–Bogazi (Gazimağusa–Boğaz) road
tel: 378 8201
The principal resort hotel on the sandy stretch of Famagusta Bay some 10km north of Famagusta, the Salamis Bay is a large, well-equipped complex, with swimming pool, sauna and sports facilities. Local colour and charm are not to be expected, however.

Vazaro (££)
Famagusta–Bogazi (Gazimağusa–Boğaz) road
tel: 378 8212
Located next to the Salamis Bay Hotel, the Vazaro is a more individualistic kind of place, and although it lacks some facilities, the Salamis Bay's swimming pools and sports facilities are available for use by guests.

279

RESTAURANTS

Cyprus has a strong tradition of local cuisine combining Greek and Turkish elements with influences from Europe and the Levant. This is not evident in hotels which serve bland international fare, a disclaimer that may also apply to hotels with high star-ratings. The resorts offer a vast choice of outlets where the ingredients of Cypriot cuisine may be present yet where quality has been sacrificed in the interests of speed. There are, however, restaurants and tavernas, in all areas and price categories, where the authentic taste of Cyprus is preserved and served with commitment and style. The trick is to go where the Cypriots go.

The following restaurants are divided into three categories:
£££ = expensive
££ = moderate
£ = budget

NICOSIA

Greek Cypriot sector

Abu Faysal (££)
31 Klimentou Street
tel: 02-760353 or 367785
Excellent Lebanese restaurant whose well-considered presentation of a distinctive culinary tradition is augmented by an atmospheric garden terrace and old mansion-style interior.

Aegeon (£)
40 Ektoros Street tel: 02-433297
Traditional taverna near Famagusta Gate, where several such venues rub shoulders with modern style.

Archontiko (££)
27 Filokyprou Street tel: 02-450080
Meze and outdoor eating in good weather in a taverna which is more or less typical of those in the renovated Laïki Geitonia district.

Armenaki (£)
15 Sans Souci Street tel: 02-378383
Family-run Armenian restaurant with good taste and modest prices.

Axiothea (££)
8 Axiotheas Street tel: 02-430787
It seems incongruous to eat so well in such a relaxed ambience, with Green Line barricades as a backdrop, but this is traditional Nicosia at its best.

Bonzai (£££)
*Holiday Inn, 70 Rigainis Street
tel: 02-665131*
Stylish and authentic, this is the place to go for original Japanese food – sushi, sashimi and teppan yaki. There's a daily buffet lunch.

Chang's China (££)
1 Akropolis Street tel: 02-351350
Considering that foreign cuisine is thin on the ground in Nicosia, this is an adequate if not overly memorable taste of China.

Erenia (£)
*64a Archiepiskopou Kyprianou Avenue
tel: 02-422860*
A specialist in meze and Cypriot charm, this diminutive taverna is well worth the trip into suburban Strovolos from the city centre.

Konatzin (£)
10 Delfi Street tel: 02-776990
Vegetarian meze and meat-based dishes at a romantic converted house with garden.

Mattheos Georgiou (£)
6 Oktovriou 28 Square tel: 02-755846
A superior example of the working-class cafés near the Green Line. Simple traditional dishes at extremely low cost and friendly service.

Plaka Taverna (££)
*8 Stlianou Lena Street, Egkoni
tel: 02-352898*
Could be considered one of Nicosia's essential eating experiences, for its excellent *meze*. The service can be casual.

Scorpios (££)
1 Stassinou Street tel: 02-351850
A popular restaurant with Nicosians and some-what off the tourist track, combining international cuisine with local dishes.

Ten Lanterns (£)
5 Kefallinia Street tel: 02-421410
Unpretentious local restaurant which makes up in fine-tasting food for what it lacks in style.

Trattoria Romantica (££)
*13 Evagoras Pallikarides Street
tel: 02-377276*
Alfresco and indoor dining in a fine restaurant. Home-made pasta and pure Italian ambience.

Xefoto (££)
6 Aeschylou Street tel: 02-477840
Smarter and a shade more adventurous than is the norm for Laïki Geitonia, Xefoto has a stylish café on the ground floor, a darkly romantic din-ing room on the first floor and a terrace on the narrow, pedestrians-only street out front.

Turkish Cypriot sector

Anibal (££)
Near children's park tel: 227 4835
Meze and kebabs Turkish Cypriot style in a convivial restaurant close to the Green Line.

Saray Roof (££)
Atatürk Square tel: 228 3115
Turkish and European cuisine is served in the restaurant of Turkish Cypriot Nicosia's top-rated Saray Hotel, which overlooks the square.

THE SOUTHEAST

Agia Napa area

Georgis Flambé Restaurant (£)
9 Ippocratou Street tel: 03-721504
A hale and hearty kind of place, not untypical of Agia Napa, whose specialities are brandy-flamed dishes served outdoors in summer.

Le Bistro (£££)
11 Odyssea Elyti Street tel: 03-721838
The authentic and romantic backdrop of a 70-year-old building with courtyard and garden accompanies the international cooking in this highly regarded Agia Napa institution.

Potamos (£)
Potamos Creek
Excellent if rather plain fish restaurant in a scenic setting beside the blue-painted fishing boats at the harbour near Xylofagou.

Larnaka area

Aphrodite (££)
Larnaka–Dhekelia road tel: 04-644701
Good Cypriot food in an elegant restaurant.

Archontiko (££)
24 Athinon Avenue tel: 04-655905
The Archontiko serves Cypriot specialities in a picturesque old building beside the seafront Foinikoudes Promenade, with the associated Archontissa steak-house.

Dionyssos (££)
7b Agkyras Street tel: 04-653658
Seafront restaurant specialising in grills and steaks, near Larnaka Fort.

Manhattan (£)
*Larnaka–Dhekelia road, Dhekelia
tel: 04-644481*
Family restaurant on the coast-road strip.

Monte Carlo (££)
28 Piyale Paşa Street tel: 04-653815
Stylishly named and stylishly done seafront restaurant with a balcony overlooking the Mediterranean and a nice line in traditional Cypriot cuisine.

Pila Tavern (££)
*Frenaritis Complex, Larnaka–Dhekelia road
tel: 04-645990*
Specialising in fish, this simple seaside taverna is popular with Cypriot families and with tourists who appreciate hearty Cypriot cooking.

The Tudor Inn (££)
28a Lala Mustafa Street tel: 04-625608
Steaks are the house speciality and their supporting dishes are well produced.

Protaras area

Anemos Beach Restaurant (£)
Fig Tree Bay tel: 03-831488
Close to the ideal, and idyll, of the seaside taverna in a busy resort, where low cost combines with good food.

Blue Bay (£)
Protaras Harbour tel: 03-831048
In a place where few tourist tavernas have much to recommend them, other than low price, the Blue Bay has at least an enthusiastic proprietor and a reasonable setting.

Dherynia Gardens (££)
116 Eleftheria Street, Paralimni
tel: 4824522
A touch of French class and an international style helps to distinguish this restaurant from the more usual tourist fare served around this area.

THE SOUTHWEST

Lefkara

Lefkara Tourist Pavilion (£)
Pano Lefkara village square tel: 04-342211
In an area of little other than tourist-oriented tavernas, this is as good as any, and reasonably priced.

Limassol area

Calcutta (££)
Georgiou I Street, Anna Court, Potamos Germasogeias tel: 05-322511
This is not the best Indian restaurant in the world, yet it is not unreasonably priced, and anyway there is little choice in this category.

Fiesta (££)
Amathus Avenue, near turning for Agios Tychon tel: 05-322755
International cuisine.

Longmen (££)
60 Academy Street tel: 05-318844
Untypically modern exterior disguises a fine Chinese restaurant on the road out of Limassol.

Porta (££)
17 Genethliou Mitela Street tel: 05-360339
Good traditional Cypriot food served in the unlikely setting of a converted donkey stable in the old Turkish quarter, near the mosque.

Richard and Berengaria (£)
23 Eirinis Street tel: 05-363863
Ultra-cheap and modest little family-run bar suited to a snack-oriented break from sightseeing, across the road from Limassol Castle.

Scottis Steakhouse (££)
38 Souli Street tel: 05-335173
As its name implies, Scottis specialises in steaks, but very good ones, making this place popular with Cypriots and visitors alike.

Xydas (£££)
22 Anthemidos Street, Amathus
tel: 05-728336
First-class seafood restaurant serving fresh fish. A touch of class.

Zygi

Apovathra (££)
Village seafront tel: 04-332414
In this fishing village and seafood centre, where taverna quality is variable, Apovathra is a steady performer. Choose your own freshly caught fish and eat it by the sea.

THE TROODOS MOUNTAINS

Foini

Phini Taverna (££)
tel: 05-421828
Traditional Cypriot dishes, plus mountain-stream trout, steaks and the like at this delightful taverna in a lovely village.

Kakopetria

Maryland at the Mill (££)
tel: 02-922536
The outlook is reason enough for a visit to this restaurant in the Troodos foothills. The food, particularly the trout (from fish farms), is excellent, though the restaurant is rather touristy.

Pano Platres

Kaledonia (££)
Kaledonia Building tel: 05-421404
A no-frills but lip-smackingly good mountain taverna, specialising in *meze*.

Pendeli Hotel Restaurant (££)
tel: 05-421736
This hotel restaurant favours the international style of cuisine, with reasonably good quality.

Pedoulas

To Vrysi (££)
Village centre tel: 02-952240
Also known as 'Harry's Spring Water Restaurant' this place was founded in 1929. It still sells traditional food, a cut above the usual, in a homely, cluttered setting.

Troodos village

Civic Restaurant (£)
tel: 05-422102
Prettily situated small restaurant on a hillside just outside Troodos village, which makes an ideal place for an alfresco lunch.

THE WEST

Pafos area

Araouzos (£)
Main street, Kathikas (between Pafos and Polis) tel: 06-632076
Family taverna that serves simple, tasty village food – whatever mamma feels like cooking that day – In a rustic setting, with ingredients from local farms, accompanied by Kathikas' own excellent Vasilikon white wine.

281

Charlie's (££)
8c Dionysou Street tel: 06-235667
A taverna with local colour serving fish and grills at a modest price.
Chef's Tavern (££)
1 Akamantou Avenue, Pegeia tel: 06-621243
The square of this village uphill from Coral Bay has a cluster of good tavernas, most of them busy in summer. This one is usually quieter, although it is just downhill from the square and trained chef Andreas' meze and other traditional dishes are more finely prepared, and served in a garden terrace in summer.
Democritos (££)
1 Dionysou Street tel: 06-233371
Greek dance and other floorshows complement the menu in this very Cypriot taverna, which makes good use of its kleftiko clay oven.
Dover (£££)
Aspasia Court, Otellou Street tel: 06-248100
European-style seafood restaurant with a touch of class, that rings the changes on taste in its finely prepared Mediterranean fish dishes and also puts thought into presentation.
Les Etoiles (££)
1 Diagorou Street tel: 06-234083
Les Etoiles is a large taverna of steady quality, catering to both local and international taste, and to formal and informal style.
Mediterranean Taverna (££)
3 Agia Napa Street tel: 06-235684
Seafood specialities are the choice in this backstreet taverna in Kato Pafos.
Mother's (£)
Basilica Centre, Apostolou Pavlou Street
tel: 06-236474
A simple but relaxed and good-quality restaurant, for those who miss home cooking while on holiday.
Nostalgia (££)
8 Tafon ton Vasileion Road tel: 06-247464
Russian influence in Cyprus is growing. Here is a chance to taste its culinary impact on Pafos.
Pelican Inn (££)
102 Apostolou Pavlou Street tel: 06-246886
Its specialities are fish and other seafood dishes, including lobster, served in a congenial setting at the old harbour.
Phuket (£££)
Tafon ton Vasileon Avenue, Kato Pafos
tel: 06-236738
Original Chinese cooking, which has made a big impact on Pafos since the restaurant opened.
San Lorenzo (££)
Poseidonos Avenue tel: 06-248638
Regional Italian cuisine and piano music make a pleasant change from a too-steady diet of Greek cooking.
Seven Saint George's Tavern (££)
Pavlou Krineou Street (off Danaïs Avenue)
tel: 06-263176
Officially called 'Efta Aï Yiorkhides Taverna', but most visitors have difficulty pronouncing that, hence the English alternative. An old Cypriot dwelling with a big garden, converted to a distinctive, sophisticated meze house. There's a good vegetarian selection, as well as meat, and excellent home-produced house wine.

Pissouri

Bunch of Grapes Inn (£)
tel: 05-221275
A fully restored, century-old inn in the centre of the village, with a romantic courtyard restaurant.
Hani (£)
Limassol–Pafos road tel: 05-221211
A transport café with a difference: good taste and friendly service, which make it popular with Cypriots in the know.
Palio Limanaki (£)
Pissouri Beach tel: 05-221288
In an area where choice is limited, the Palio Limanaki at least benefits from a fine beachside position and simple, tasty Cypriot food.

Polis–Latsi area

Baths of Aphrodite (££)
Opposite Baths of Aphrodite trail entrance
tel: 06-321457
Simple clifftop taverna that does a good lunchtime salad and excellent fish, and is ideally placed for anyone emerging from a long, hot walk in the Akamas Peninsula.
Chix Chox (££)
Central Square, Polis tel: 06-321669
One of a cluster of reasonable-quality tavernas, many with street terraces, this one serves both Cypriot and international cuisine.
Paradise Place (££)
Coast road between Pomos and Pachyammos
tel: 06-342537
An agreeably ramshackle taverna that attracts locals as well as visitors with its delicately prepared, highly individualistic, Cypriot and world cuisine, including vegetarian dishes, with added improvisational touches. Watch the sunset to the strains of classical music and jazz.
Porto Latchi (££)
Seafront, Latsi tel: 06-321529
Housed in a 17th-century Cypriot dwelling, this taverna takes a stellar part in the Latsi specialism of high-quality seafood.
Yiangos and Peter (££)
Fishing harbour, Latsi tel: 06-321411
The harbour at Latsi has no shortage of good seafood tavernas which also serve meat-based dishes. This has a fine waterfront atmosphere and good cooking.

THE NORTH

Agios Epiktitos (Çatalköy)

Lemon Tree (££)
Kyrenia–Agios Epiktitos (Girne–Çatalköy) road
tel: 824 4045
A country house on the coast road near the turn-off for the Hazreti Ömer Mosque, serving first-class fresh seafood.
Zia's (££)
tel: 824 4027
A seafood restaurant on the southern fringe of the village, with a good reputation among local people.

Bellapais (Beylerbeyi)

Kybele (£££)
Grounds of Bellapais Abbey tel: 815 7531
Atmospheric bar, restaurant and wine house
with the ruined abbey as a back-drop.

Kyrenia (Girne) area

Çanlı Balik (££)
Kordonboyu tel: 815 2182
Good-quality seafood restaurant beside the
fishing boats in Kyrenia harbour.
Courtyard Inn (££)
Karakum tel: 815 5566
The Courtyard caters mainly to expatriate resi-
dents, chiefly British and German, as well as to
tourists from those countries. It is, however,
quite a pretty place and its cuisine is good.
Efendi's House (£)
6 Kamil Paşa road tel: 815 1149
A restaurant with a fine pedigree and a reputa-
tion for the quality and style of its food, and
the Turkish atmosphere is guaranteed.
Harbour Club (£££)
Kordonboyu tel: 815 2211
In the shadow of Kyrenia Castle, this is expen-
sive by Turkish Cypriot standards but its
top-flight seafood and French style dishes are
unsurpassed, while its setting and décor add
to the experience.
Hilarion Village (££)
*Trimithi–Karmi (Edremit–Karaman) road
tel: 822 2574*
A good country restaurant, which serves up
Sunday roasts and features fondue evenings.
Marabou (££)
Kordonboyu tel: 815 2292
Steaks are the tastily different touch the
Marabou adds to Kyrenia harbour's usual
seafood dishes.
Niyazi's (£)
Kordonboyu tel: 815 2160
Around the corner from Kyrenia harbour,
Niyazi's is a very reasonable traditional Turkish
Cypriot restaurant, which guarantees that
kebabs are a good buy.
Set (£)
Kordonboyu tel: 815 2336
Straightforward seafood restaurant beside the
yacht harbour.
Tepebaşi (££)
Nurettin Ersin Street tel: 815 2380
A somewhat out-of-the way place (on a side-
street off the junction of Sehitler Avenue,
Bedrettin Demirel Avenue and Kharamanlar
Avenue), but with a fine view over Kyrenia,
Tepebaşi is the locals' choice for a good
Turkish Cypriot meal. Superb atmosphere.

Lapithos (Lapta) area

Ali Paşa's (£)
*Kyrenia–Lapithos (Girne–Lapta) road
tel: 821 8942*
A large and rather ugly-looking seafront
taverna, but the good cooking and an enthusiastic proprietor more than make up for this.

Altinkaya (££)
*Kyrenia–Lapithos (Girne–Lapta) road
tel: 821 8341*
A popular, high-quality restaurant on the coast
near the Turkish Cypriot Peace and Freedom
Monument, and specialising in seafood.
Rita on the Rocks (££)
Karavas (Alsancak) tel: 821 8922
On the seafront at Lapithos, this small restau-
rant beside a swimming pool and bar, serves
Cypriot and international cuisine.

THE EAST

Famagusta (Gazimağusa) area

Agora (££)
17 Elmas Tabya Street tel: 366 5364
Kebabs and other well-prepared Turkish fare.
Cyprus House (££)
Polat Paşa Bulvari tel: 366 4845
Dine Turkish-style amidst relics of antiquity and
objets d'art in the garden of Famagusta's for-
mer British police station.
Koca Reis (££)
*On the beach besides the Salamis Bay Hotel
tel: 378 8229*
Specialising in fish, this restaurant boasts a
laid-back owner and an equally laid-back hen
which wanders among the tables, secure in the
knowledge that the fish dishes are so good
nobody will ask for chicken.
Palm Beach Hotel Restaurant (£££)
Havva Sentürk Avenue tel: 366 2000
Excellent international cuisine and good
Turkish specialities.

Karpas (Karpaz) Peninsula

Blue Sea (£)
*Rizokarpaso–Cape Apostolos Andreas
(Dipkarpaz Zafer Burnu) road*
A small seafood restaurant attached to an
excellent hotel. Superb seaside setting south-
east of the village of Rizokarpason (Dipkarpaz).

Salamis–Bogazi (Boğaz) area

Akdeniz (££)
*Famagusta–Bogazi (Gazimağusa–Boğaz) road
tel: 378 822*
Located a little north of the access road to the
Salamis Bay Hotel, this is a fairly typical
Turkish Cypriot restaurant, serving tasty food.
Carli's (££)
Fishing harbour, Bogazi tel: 371 2626
Seafood restaurant beside the harbour.
Eyva (££)
*Famagusta–Bogazi (Gazimağusa–Boğaz) road
tel: 378 8235*
Good-quality Turkish cuisine and atmosphere in
this restaurant situated on the coast road to
Salamis. Also features live entertainment.
Kocatepe (££)
Fishing harbour, Bogazi tel: 371 2620
Slightly more upmarket than is the norm in
Bogazi, Kocatepe, overlooking the harbour,
concentrates on seafood and does it very well.

Index

Index

287

Picture credits

The Automobile Association would like to thank the following photographers and libraries for their assistance in the preparation of this book.

HEADQUARTERS BRITISH FORCES CYPRUS (B Gamble) 106b British servicemen. **HULTON DEUTSCH COLLECTION** 39 President Makarios, 40/1 Cyprus riots, 40 EOKA soldiers, 41 Turkish armed forces, 51 Archbishop Makarios, 60, 61 Rauf Denktaş 197 British troops. **IMAGES COLOUR LIBARY** (front cover c). **J LAMBROU** 12b Atimas, 18/9, 19 Limassol Carnival, 72b Nicosia Theatre Festival, 138/9 Xionia, 138c, 139 Xionia skiers. **MANSELL COLLECTION** 23b Map, 25 Statue, 29 Evagoras of Cyprus, 34a Isaac of Cyprus & Coeur de Lion. **MARY EVANS PICTURE LIBRARY** 34b Richard I, 35b Geoffroi de Lusignan, 38a, 38b British soldiers. **NATURE PHOTOGRAPHERS LTD** 12a Loggerhead hatchlings (J Sutherland), 13 Fox cub (O Newman), 183 Southern festoon (P R Sterry). **PICTOR INTERNATIONAL, LONDON** (spine). **ROYAL GEOGRAPHICAL SOCIETY LIBRARY** 36b Map. **SUPERSTOCK LTD** (front cover a).

The remaining photographs are held in the Automobile Association's own photo library (**AA PHOTO LIBRARY**) and were taken by Alex Kouprianoff, with the exception of: back cover, 4a, 4b, 6/7, 7b, 20a, 31b, 32/3, 32, 43, 54, 56, 57a, 58b, 64, 69b, 71a, 73, 88, 91b, 94, 107, 112, 115a, 127a, 133a, 136a, 141, 146, 147, 154, 157b, 158, 161, 166/7, 168/9, 168, 169, 171a, 179a, 191, 196b, 201, 254, 258, 260a, 264/5, 266 which were taken by M Birkitt; pages 58a, 217a, 218, 225b, 238, 240b, taken by R Bulmar, 85b, taken by K Paterson, pages 3, 22b, 43b, 71b, 84, 96, 105, 113a, 119a, 119b, 125a, 132a, 148, 178, 181, 187b, 192a, 239b, 244c, 245,b, 260b, 263, taken by R Rainford and pages 21, 30a, 35a, 198, 199, 203, 209b, 219b, 220, 223a, 228/9, 242, 243, 249, taken by H Ulucam.

Contributors

Original designer: KAG Design
Original copy editor: Jennifer Speake
Revision copy editor: Grapevine Publishing Services   Revision verifier: George McDonald

Statement on the position of the United Nations

There have been a great many debates on Cyprus at the United Nations and a veritable blizzard of Security Council and General Assembly resolutions. In a nutshell, the UN aims to restore the legal, constitutional basis of the Republic of Cyprus, reaffirm the rights of both communities in the constitution, and end military occupation. Inevitably, one or other community objects to some aspect of this approach, and the Secretary General's mission of 'good offices' has always run into the sand due to this kind of opposition. Security Council resolution 541 of 18 November 1983, following the unilateral Turkish Cypriot foundation of the 'Turkish Republic of Northern Cyprus', is a key element of the UN position.

The Security Council,
Having heard the statement of the Foreign Minister of the Government of the Republic of Cyprus,
Concerned at the declaration by the Turkish Cypriot authorities issued on 15 November 1983 which purports to create an independent State in northern Cyprus,
Considering that this declaration is incompatible with the 1960 Treaty concerning the establishment of the Republic of Cyprus and the 1960 Treaty of Guarantee,
Considering, therefore, that the attempt to create a 'Turkish Republic of Northern Cyprus' is invalid, and will contribute to a worsening of the situation in Cyprus,
Reaffirming its resolutions 365 (1974) and 367 (1975),
Aware of the need for a solution of the Cyprus problem based on the mission of good offices undertaken by the Secretary General,
Affirming its continuing support for the United Nations Peacekeeping Force in Cyprus,
Taking note of the Secretary General's statement of 17 November 1983,
1 Deplores the declaration of the Turkish Cypriot authorities of the purported secession of part of the Republic of Cyprus;
2 Considers the declaration referred to above as legally invalid and calls for its withdrawal;
3 Calls for the urgent and effective implementation of its resolutions 365 (1974) and 367 (1975);
4 Requests the Secretary General to pursue his mission of good offices, in order to achieve the earliest possible progress towards a just and lasting settlement in Cyprus;
5 Calls upon the parties to cooperate fully with the Secretary General in his mission of good offices;
6 Calls upon all States to respect the sovereignty, independence, territorial integrity and non-alignment of the Republic of Cyprus;
7 Calls upon all States not to recognize any Cypriot State other than the Republic of Cyprus;
8 Calls upon all States and the two communities in Cyprus to refrain from any action which might exacerbate the situation;
9 Requests the Secretary General to keep the Security Council fully informed.